Children and the Law

B

Essential Readings in Developmental Psychology

Series Editors: Alan Slater and Darwin Muir
Queen's University, Kingston, Ontario and the University of Exeter

In this brand new series of nine books, Alan Slater and Darwin Muir, together with a team of expert editors, bring together selections of readings illustrating important methodological, empirical and theoretical issues in the area of developmental psychology. Volumes in the series and their editors are detailed below:

Infant Development	*Darwin Muir and Alan Slater*
Childhood Social Development	*Wendy Craig*
Childhood Cognitive Development	*Kang Lee*
Adolescent Development	*Gerald Adams*
The Nature/Nurture Debate	*Steven Ceci and Wendy Williams*
Teaching and Learning	*Charles Desforges and Richard Fox*
Language Development	*Michael Tomasello and Elizabeth Bates*
Children and the Law	*Ray Bull*

Each of the books is introduced by the volume editor with a rationale behind the chosen papers. Each reading is then introduced and contextualized within the individual subject debate as well as within the wider context of developmental psychology. A selection of further reading is also assigned, making each volume an ideal teaching resource for both classroom and individual study settings.

Children and the Law
The Essential Readings

Edited by Ray Bull

Copyright © Blackwell Publishers Ltd 2001
Editorial matter copyright © Ray Bull, Alan Slater and Darwin Muir 2001

First published 2001

2 4 6 8 10 9 7 5 3 1

Blackwell Publishers Ltd
108 Cowley Road
Oxford OX4 1JF
UK

Blackwell Publishers Inc.
350 Main Street
Malden, Massachusetts 02148
USA

British Library Cataloguing in Publication Data

A CIP catalogue record for this book is available from the British Library.

Library of Congress Cataloging-in-Publication Data

Children and the law: the essential readings/edited by Ray Bull.
p.   cm. – (Essential readings in developmental psychology)
Includes bibliographical references and index.
ISBN 0-631-22682-6 (alk. paper) – ISBN 0-631-22683-4 (pb. : alk. paper)
1. Child witnesses.   2. Children – Legal status, laws, etc.   3. Psychology, Forensic.
4. Interviewing in child abuse.   I. Bull, Ray.   II. Series.
K5483.C45 2001
347'.066'083 – dc21

2001018138

Typeset in 10½ on 13 pt Photina
by Best-set Typesetter Ltd., Hong Kong
Printed in Great Britain by MPG Books, Bodmin, Cornwall

This book is printed on acid-free paper

Contents

Acknowledgements

Bruck, M., Ceci, S., and Hembrooke, H. (1998). Reliability and credibility of young children's reports. *American Psychologist*, 53, 1998. Copyright © 1998 by the American Psychological Association. Reprinted with Permission.

Finkelhor, D. and Dzuiba-Leatherman, J. (1994). Victimization of children. *American Psychologist* 49, 1994. Copyright © 1994 by the American Psychological Association. Reprinted with permission.

Goodman, G., Tobey, A., Batterman-Faunce, J., Orcutt, H., Thomas, S., Shapiro, C., and Sachsenmaier, T. (1998). Face to face confrontation: Effects of closed-circuit technology and children's eyewitness testimony and jurors' decisions. *Law and Human Behavior* 22, 1998, reprinted by permission of Kluwer Academic/Plenum Publishers, New York.

Huffman, M. L., Warren, A., and Larson S. (1999). Discussing truth and lies in interviews with children: Whether, why and how? *Applied Developmental Science* 3, 1999.

Kendall-Tachett, K., Meyer-Williams, L., and Finkelhor D. (1993). Impact of sexual abuse in children: A review and synthesis of recent empirical studies. *Psychological Bulletin* 113, 1993. Copyright © 1993 by the American Psychological Association. Reprinted with permission.

Loeber, R., Farrington, D., Stouthamer-Loeber, M., Moffitt, T., and Caspi, A. (1998). The development of male offending: Key findings from the first decade of the Pittsburgh youth study. *Studies on Crime and Crime Prevention* 7, 1998.

Perry, N., McAuliff, B., Tam, P., Claycomb, L., Dostal, C., and Flannagan C. (1995). When lawyers question children: Is justice served? *Law and Human Behavior* 19, 1995, reprinted by permission of Kluwer Academic/Plenum Publishers, New York.

Quas, J., Goodman G., Bidrose, S., Pipe M. E., Craw, S., and Ablin D. (1999). Emotion and memory: Children's long term, remembering, forgetting and suggestibility. *Journal of Experimental Child Psychology* 72, 235–70, copyright © 1999 by Academic Press, reprinted by permission of the publisher. All rights of reproduction in any form reserved.

Siegal, M. and Peterson C. (1996). Breaking the mould: A fresh look at children's understanding of questions about lies and mistakes. *Developmental Psychology* 2, 1996. Copyright © 1996 by the American Psychological Association. Reprinted with permission.

Vizard, E., Monck, E. and Misch, P. (1995). Child and adolescent sex abuse perpetrators: A review of the research literature. *Journal of Child Psychology and Psychiatry* 36, 1995, © Association for Child Psychology and Psychiatry, published by Cambridge University Press.

Introduction

In many countries the increase in reported crime and a growing awareness of children's involvement as victims, witnesses, or perpetrators
have resulted in children being more involved with the law. This has
led to a greater emphasis within psychology and allied disciplines on
work to expand our knowledge of developmental issues relevant to legal
settings.

'Children and the Law' is now a topic, not only in undergraduate
psychology programmes, but also in professional training such as
that for law students, social workers and police officers. Even
people from the legal world (notorious for being too busy to acquire
new knowledge!) are taking the trouble to take relevant courses.
One such course is the M.Sc./Diploma in 'Child Forensic Studies:
Psychology and Law' that I run at the University of Portsmouth, UK,
and world-wide the number of specialized courses such as this is
growing.

In the past, children were often ignored by legal systems because of
the belief that anyone below the age of around 10 years was 'incompetent'. There was a belief that young children were not sufficiently
advanced developmentally to participate in legal proceedings, either as
witnesses, or as perpetrators, or as parties to divorce proceedings, and
so on. However, developmental research in the last twenty years or so
has clearly shown that young children are much more competent than
was believed.

Unfortunately, legal procedures will often not keep pace with new psychological knowledge about children's competence. This has often resulted in legal procedures designed with adults in mind being thrust upon children. Very recently, there has been a realization across the globe that equality of opportunity and human rights require that children be treated appropriately.

Children are, sadly, sometimes treated very inappropriately. I have been asked to provide an 'expert report' in several dozen legal cases involving children as (alleged) victims of, or witnesses to, adult wrongdoing. Since my expertise has to do with how best to conduct investigative interviews with children (Milne and Bull, 1999) or with adults (Memon and Bull, 1999), I am usually provided with a transcript, and often a video recording, of the interview(s) with the child(ren) in a criminal or civil case. Quite often what the children seem to be recounting in these interviews brings tears to my eyes, especially when what they are saying appears not to have been biased by poor interviewing.

As the years have gone by the quality of investigative interviews conducted by relevant professionals (for example, police officers, social workers) has largely improved. Nevertheless, sometimes children provide accounts which contain aspects that seem so improbable (for example in one case being hung from the ceiling in a small cage) that one wonders what really has happened to them! It is at times like these that I realize how much we still have to learn about children, and how important it is that psychologists persevere in their quest for relevant knowledge (often in the face of a lack of research funding, or the temptation to hide in the laboratory conducting easy research on students!).

Although psychology is a very deep and broad discipline encompassing all aspects of life, it does have essential, core features. Five core aspects involve social psychology, biological psychology, cognitive psychology, developmental psychology, and research methods. In most syllabi these are taught separately, often by different people who nevertheless criticize their students for a lack of awareness (for example in their course work or examination answers) of the other core areas. 'Children and the Law' offers a great opportunity for students to bring together knowledge from each core area. Obviously, developmental aspects are involved, but these interact with social (for example communicating, interviewing), cognitive (for example memory, language), and biological (for example stress, emotion) aspects. Furthermore, ingenious research methods are often required which demand good awareness of ethical principles.

'Children and the Law' thus offers, nay requires, a multi-faceted psychological approach, set in a multi-disciplinary context. Having read this book, students will be in no doubt about the importance of this topic. It is divided into five parts. The items in part I focus on the victimization of children and on the impact of crime, particularly sexual abuse, on children. In part II the items examine the reliability and credibility of young children's accounts (sometimes after long delays), how to assess the accuracy of such accounts, and children's ability to recognize strangers. Part III focuses on children's understanding of what a lie is and on the effects of this on interviews. Children's performance in the legal system is looked at in part IV, and part V has an emphasis on children as perpetrators of crimes. The book contains ten seminal papers plus summaries of another three extremely important papers: two of these summaries have been written especially for this book by members of the original research teams.

A crucial link between the various parts of this book is the notion that it may largely be victimized children who go on to commit crime, including child abuse. If we can learn more about child victimization, more about how to assist children to give full and truthful accounts, and more about how best to accommodate child witnesses/victims in our legal systems, then we may be in a better position to do justice for children.

References

Memon, A., & Bull, R. (1999). *Handbook of the psychology of interviewing.* Chichester: Wiley.

Milne, R., & Bull, R. (1999). *Investigative interviewing: Psychology and practice.* Chichester: Wiley.

Part 1

Child Victimization

ONE

Victimization of Children

Introduction

In many countries until the 1980s or 1990s most people believed that the victimization of children was a relatively rare phenomenon. Indeed, in some countries this may still be the case. However, in North America, Britain, Australia and other countries, newspapers, TV, radio and other aspects of the media have publicized the unpalatable fact that a sizeable proportion of children are victims of crime, maltreatment and neglect.

However, even though the media took the responsible step of making society aware of child victimization, this awareness was initially based on the particular cases reported by the media. What was needed was a well-informed overview of the extent of the problem.

In their seminal paper David Finkelhor and Jennifer Dziuba-Leatherman provide such an overview. Though you may find some of the data they provide distressing, for example that children are more often assaulted, raped or robbed than are adults, an awareness of the prevalence and typology of child victimization is essential. Also of crucial importance is information concerning the impact of victimization on children, especially being victimized by adults known to them, as is often the case, sadly, for young children.

We need to try to understand why the victimization of children is much more common than we would like to believe. Also required is a prioritized research agenda which sets out the most urgent questions and the feasibility of being able to answer them.

While much of developmental psychology, quite rightly, focuses on how children achieve positive things, we can no longer fail to ignore the negative outcomes of their victimization.

Suggested reading

Finkelhor, D. (1998). A comparison of the responses of preadolescents and ado-lescents in a national victimisation survey. *Journal of Interpersonal Violence*, 13, 362–82.

Victimization of Children

David Finkelhor and
Jennifer Dziuba-Leatherman

Although the issue of child victimization has elicited considerable attention from professionals and the public, the interest has largely been frag-
mented. Writers and advocates have tended to confine themselves to
certain specific topics, such as child abuse, child molestation, or stranger
abduction, and few have considered the larger whole (for exceptions, see
Best, 1990; Christoffel, 1990; McDermott, Stanley, & Zimmerman-
McKinney, 1982; Morgan & Zedner, 1992). Unfortunately, this frag-
mentation has inhibited the recognition and development of what
should be a very important field: the general victimology of childhood.
Such a general victimology would highlight more clearly the true vulnerability of children to victimization, the overlap and co-occurrence of
different types of victimization, and the common risk factors and effects.
It is our goal to assemble disparate statistics and knowledge about the
victimization and maltreatment of children in order to define such a
field. We will review findings on the incidence, risk factors, and effects
of child victimization and suggest integrative concepts.

Children are More Victimized than Adults

One reality, not widely recognized, is that children are more prone to victimization than adults are. For example, according to the 1990 National
Crime Survey (NCS; Bureau of Justice Statistics, 1991), the rates of

Table 1.1 Crime victimization rate per 1,000: adolescents versus adults

	Age in years	
Crime	12–19	20+
Assault[a]	58.45	17.85
Robbery[a]	11.53	4.73
Rape[a]	1.60	0.50
Homicide[b]	0.09[c]	0.10

Some figures shown in this table did not appear in original source but were derived from data presented therein.

[a] National Crime Survey, 1990 (Bureau of Justice Statistics, 1992).
[b] Uniform Crime Report, 1991 (Federal Bureau of Investigation, 1992).
[c] Rate is for ages 10–19.

assault, rape, and robbery against those aged 12–19 years are two to three times higher than for the adult population as a whole (table 1.1). Homicide is the only violent crime category for which teens are somewhat less vulnerable than adults.[1]

This disproportionate victimization of children is also confirmed in studies that gather information from adults on their lifetime experience with crime. For example, in the first national survey to ask adult women about their lifetime experiences of forcible rape, 61% of the rapes occurred before the age of 18 (Kilpatrick, 1992). This translates roughly into a fivefold higher rape risk for children.

The disproportionate victimization of children would be even more evident if the NCS and other studies were not so deficient in their counting of incidents of family violence (Garbarino, 1989), to which children are enormously more vulnerable than adults. For example, in the National Family Violence Survey (Straus, Gelles, & Steinmetz, 1980), adults reported that they inflicted almost twice as much severe violence (which includes beating up, kicking, hitting with a fist or object) against a child in their household than they did against their adult partner (table 1.2). When to family violence we add the frequent

Table 1.2 Family violence victimization rate per 1,000: children versus adults, 1985

Perpetrator–victim relationship	Any violence	Severe violence[a]
Spouse to spouse	158	58
Parent to child	620	107

Source: National Family Violence Resurvey, 1985 (Straus & Gelles, 1990).

[a] Includes kicking, biting, hitting with fist or object, beating up, using or threatening to use knife or gun.

occurrence of peer and sibling assaults against younger children – experiences that have virtually no equivalent among adults (Pagelow, 1989) – evidence strongly suggests that children are more victimized than adults are.

Statistics on Child Victimization

To illustrate the spectrum of child victimization, we have arrayed the national statistics gleaned from more than a dozen sources in table 1.3 in rough order of magnitude. (See appendix for list of sources.) We limited our notion of victimization to crimes, interpersonal violence (acts carried out with the intention or perceived intention of physically hurting another person, Gelles & Straus, 1979), child abuse, and certain related acts, such as abduction, that have been highlighted in the current wave of interest in child victimization. We included only forms of victimization for which there were scientifically defensible national estimates.

One of the interesting features of child victimology is that children suffer from certain types of violence that have been largely excluded from traditional criminologic concern. The first is assaults against young children by other children, including violent attacks by siblings. Prevailing ideology has tended to treat these as relatively inconsequential.[2] But from the point of view of the child, it is not clear, for example, why being beaten up by a peer would be any less traumatic or violative than it would be for an adult (Greenbaum, 1989).

Table 1.3 Rate and incidence of various childhood victimization

Type of violence/ age in years	Rate per 1,000	No. victimized	Year	Source	Report type[a]
Sibling assault					
3–17	800.0	50,400,000[b]	1975	NFVS-1	C
3–17	530.0	33,300,000[c]	1975	NFVS-1	C
Physical punishment					
0–17	498.6	31,401,329[d]	1985	NFVS-2	C
Theft					
11–17	497.0	—	1978	NYS	S
12–15	89.2	—	1990	NCS90	S
Assault					
11–17	310.6	—	1978	NYS	S
Grade 8	172.0	—	1988	NASHS	S
12–15	53.3	—	1990	NCS90	S
Vandalism					
11–17	257.6	—	1978	NYS	S
Robbery					
11–17	245.8	—	1978	NYS	S
Grade 8	160.9	—	1988	NASHS	S
12–15	13.6	—	1990	NCS90	S
Rape					
Grade 8	118.0	—	1988	NASHS	S
11–17	78.0	—[e]	1978	NYS78	S
12–15	1.8	—	1990	NCS90	S
Physical abuse					
0–17	23.5	1,480,007	1985	NFVS-2	C
0–17	10.5	673,500	1991	50-SS	A
0–17	4.9	311,500	1986	NIS-2	A
Neglect					
0–17	20.2	1,293,120	1991	50-SS	A
0–17	11.3	710,700[f]	1986	NIS-2	A
Sexual abuse					
0–17	6.3	404,100	1991	50-SS	A
0–17	2.1	133,600	1986	NIS-2	A
Family abduction					
0–17	5.6	354,100[g]	1988	NISMART	C
0–17	2.6	163,200[h]	1988	NISMART	C
Psychological maltreatment					
0–17	3.0	188,100	1986	NIS-2	A
0–17	2.5	161,640	1991	50-SS	A

Table 1.3 *Continued*

Type of violence/ age in years	Rate per 1,000	No. victimized	Year	Source	Report type[a]
Nonfamily abduction					
0–17	0.05–0.07	3200–4600[j]	1988	NISMART	A
0–17	0.003–0.005	200–300[j]	1988	NISMART	A
Homicide					
0–17	0.035	2,233	1991	UCR91	A
Abduction homicide					
0–17	0.001–0.002	43–147	1988	NISMART	A

Some figures shown did not appear in original source but were derived from data presented therein. Dash = Unable to compute for entire population (0–17). NFVS-1 = National Family Violence Survey, 1975 (Straus & Gelles, 1990); NFVS-2 = National Family Violence Resurvey, 1985 (Straus & Gelles, 1990); NYS = National Youth Survey (Lauritsen, Sampson, and Laub, 1991); NCS90 = National Crime Survey, 1990 (Bureau of Justice Statistics, 1992); NASHS = National Adolescent Student Health Survey (American School Health Association, 1985); NYS78 = National Youth Survey, 1978 (Ageton, 1983), 50-SS = Annual Fifty State Survey, 1990 (Daro & McCurdy, 1991); NIS-2 = National Study of the Incidence and Severity of Child Abuse and Neglect, 1988 (Sedlak, 1991); NISMART = National Incidence Study of Missing, Abducted, Runaway and Thrownaway Children, 1990 (Finkelhor, Hataling, & Sedlak, 1990); UCR91 = Uniform Crime Reports, 1991 (Federal Bureau of Investigation, 1992). Categories listed are not necessarily distinct and mutually exclusive. Under some victimization categories, estimates of several studies have been listed, sometimes showing widely divergent numbers. These differences stem from two factors in particular: the source of the report and the definition of the activity. Of the three main sources of reports – children themselves, caretakers knowledgeable about children's experiences, and agencies such as police and child protection services – children and caretakers are quite likely to provide many more accounts than are available from agencies alone. Estimates also diverge because some studies used more careful or restrictive definitions.

[a] Report type: A = agency; C = caretaker; S = self-report.
[b] Any violence.
[c] Severe violence.
[d] Excludes corporal punishment in schools.
[e] Girls only.
[f] Physical and emotional neglect.
[g] Broad scope.
[h] Policy focal.
[i] Legal definition.
[j] Stereotypical kidnapping.

An even more problematic type of noncriminalized violence toward children is spanking and other forms of corporal punishment. There are signs that a normative transformation is in progress regarding corporal punishment (Greven, 1990). A majority of states have banned it in schools, and several Scandinavian countries have outlawed its use even by parents. Some social scientists have begun to study it as a form of victimization with short- and long-term negative consequences (Daro & Gelles, 1991; Hyman, 1990; Straus, in press).

This is far from an exhaustive inventory of all the victimizations children could be said to suffer. For example, bullying and emotional abuse by peers have received some deserved attention (Olweus, 1978). Moreover, children have been plausibly described as victims when crimes are committed against other members of their household (Morgan & Zedner, 1992). Finally, there are many types of criminal victimizations, such as involvement in child prostitution, for which we could identify no reliable national statistics.

Typology of Child Victimizations

Examining the figures in table 1.3 and recognizing their methodological limitations, definitional imprecision, and variability, we nonetheless suggest that the types of child victimization reflected there should be broken into three broad categories according to their order of magnitude (figure 1.1). First, there are the pandemic victimization that occur to a majority of children in the course of growing up. At a minimum these include assault by siblings, physical punishment by parents, and theft, and probably also peer assault, vandalism, and robbery. Second, there are what might be called acute victimizations. These are less frequent – occurring to a minority, although perhaps a sizable minority, of children – but may be of generally greater severity. Among these we would include physical abuse, neglect, and family abduction. Finally, there are the extraordinary victimizations that occur to a very small number of children but that attract a great deal of attention. These include homicide, child abuse homicide, and nonfamily abduction.

Several observations follow from this typology. First, there has been much more public and professional attention paid to the extraordinary and acute victimizations than to the pandemic ones. For example,

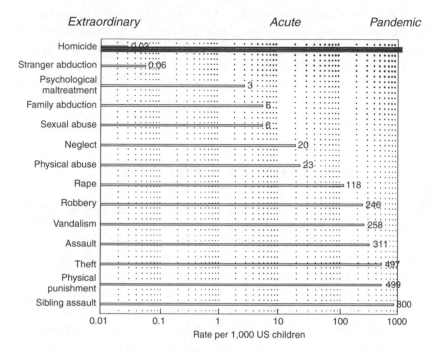

Figure 1.1   Typology of child victimization

sibling violence, the most frequent victimization, is conspicuous for how little it has been studied in proportion to how often it occurs. This neglect of pandemic victimizations needs to be rectified. For one thing, it fails to reflect the concerns of children themselves. In a recent survey of 2,000 children aged 10–16 years, three times as many were concerned about the likelihood of being beaten up by peers as were concerned about being sexually abused (Finkelhor & Dziuba-Leatherman, in press-b). The pandemic victimizations deserve greater attention, if only because of their alarming frequency and the influence they have on children's everyday existence.

Second, this typology can be useful in developing theory and methodology concerning child victimization. For example, different types of victimization may require different conceptual frameworks. Because they are nearly normative occurrences, the impact of pandemic victimizations may be very different from extraordinary ones, which children experience in relative isolation.

Finally, the typology helps illustrate the diversity and frequency of children's victimization. Although homicide and child abuse have been widely studied, they are notable for how inadequately they convey the variety and true extent of the other victimizations that children suffer. Almost all the figures in table 1.3 have been promoted in isolation at one time or another. Viewed together, they are just part of a total environment of various victimization dangers with which children live.

Why is the Victimization of Children So Common?

When the victimization of children is considered as a whole and its scope and variety more fully appreciated, it prompts a number of interesting and important theoretical questions. The first concerns why the victimization of children is so common. Obviously this is a complex question; a complete answer will undoubtedly require the explanation of elevated risks for different categories of children for different kinds of victimization. However, some generalizations may apply. Certainly the weakness and small physical stature of many children and their dependency status put them at greater risk. They cannot retaliate or deter victimization as effectively as can those with more strength and power. The social toleration of child victimization also plays a role. Society has an influential set of institutions, the police and criminal justice system, to enforce its relatively strong prohibitions against many kinds of crime, but much of the victimization of children is considered outside the purview of this system.

Another important generalization about why children are at high risk for victimization is that children have comparatively little choice over whom they associate with, less choice perhaps than any segment of the population besides prisoners. This can put them in more involuntary contact with high-risk offenders and thus at greater jeopardy for victimization. For example, when children live in families that mistreat them, they are not free or able to leave. When they live in dangerous neighborhoods, they cannot choose on their own to move. If they attend a school with many hostile and delinquent peers, they cannot simply change schools or quit. The absence of choice over people and environments affects children's vulnerability to both intimate victimization and street crime. Although some adults, like battered women and the poor, suffer similar limitations, many adults are able to seek divorce or change their residences in reaction to dangerous conditions. Adults also have more ready access to cars and sometimes have the option to live and work alone. Children are obliged to live with other people, to travel collectively, and to work in high density, heterogenous environments, which is what schools are. In short, children have difficulty gaining access to the structures and mechanisms in society that help segregate people from dangerous associates and environments.

Differential Character of Child Victimization

A second interesting theoretical question concerns how the victimization of children differs from the victimization of adults. Children, of course, suffer from all the victimizations that adults do (including economic crimes like extortion and fraud), but they also suffer from some that are particular to their status. The main status characteristic of childhood is its condition of dependency, which is a function, at least in part, of social and psychological immaturity. The violation of this dependency status results in forms of victimization, like physical neglect, that are not suffered by most adults (with the exception of those, like the elderly and sick, who also become dependent).

The dependency of children creates a spectrum of vulnerability for victimizations. Interestingly, the victimization categories that we have identified in table 1.3 can be arrayed on a continuum, according to the degree to which they involve violations of children's dependency status (figure 1.2). At one extreme is physical neglect, which has practically no meaning as a victimization except in the case of a person who is dependent and needs to be cared for by others. Similarly, family abduction is a dependency-specific victimization because it is the unlawful removal of a child from the person who is supposed to be caring for him or her. Psychological maltreatment happens to both adults and children, but the sensitive psychological vulnerability of children in their dependent relationship to their caretakers renders such parental behavior a major threat to normal child development (Claussen & Crittenden, 1991; Hart & Brassard, 1987). This is why society considers psychological maltreatment of children a form of victimization that warrants an institutional response.

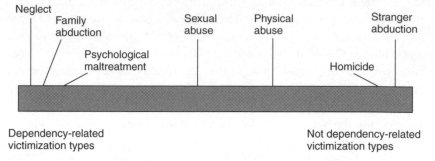

Figure 1.2   Dependency continuum for child victimization types

At the other end of the continuum are forms of victimization that are defined without reference to dependency and which exist in similar forms for both children and adults. Stranger abduction is prototypical in this instance because both children and adults are taken against their will and imprisoned for ransom or sexual purposes. Homicide is similar; the dependency status of the victim does little to define the victimization. In some cases, to be sure, children's deaths result from extreme and willful cases of neglect, but there are parallel instances of adult deaths resulting from extreme and willful negligence.

Finally, there are forms of child victimization that should be located along the midsection of the dependency continuum. Sexual abuse falls here, for example, because it encompasses at least two different situations, one dependency-related, one not. Some sexual abuse entails activities, ordinarily acceptable between adults, that are deemed victimizing in the case of children because of their immaturity and dependency. But other sexual abuse involves violence and coercion that would be victimizing even with a nondependent adult.

In the case of physical abuse, there is also some mixture. Although most of the violent acts in this category would be considered victimizing even between adults, some of them, like the shaken baby syndrome, develop almost exclusively in a caretaking relationship in which there is an enormous differential in size and physical control.

The dependency continuum is a useful concept in thinking about some of the unique features of children's victimizations. It is also helpful in generating hypotheses about the expected correlates of different types of victimization, such as variations according to age.

Developmental Victimology

Childhood is such an extremely heterogenous category – 4-year-olds and 17-year-olds having little in common – that it is inherently misleading to discuss child victimization in general without reference to age. We would expect the nature, quantity, and impact of victimization to vary across childhood with the different capabilities, activities, and environments that are characteristic of different stages of development. A good term for this might be *developmental victimology*. Unfortunately, we do not have good studies of the different types of victimization across all the ages of childhood with which to examine such changes.

There are two plausible propositions about age and child victimization that could be a starting place for developmental victimology. One is that victimizations stemming from the dependent status of children should be most common among the most dependent, hence the youngest, children. A corollary is that as children grow older, their victimization profile should more and more resemble that of adults.

One can examine such propositions in a crude way with the data that are available. In fact, it is apparent (table 1.4) that the types of victimization that are most concentrated in the under-12 age group are the dependency-related ones (see the dependency continuum in figure 1.2), particularly family abduction and physical neglect. Victimizations such as homicide and stranger abduction, which we grouped at the non-dependency end of the continuum, involve a greater percentage of teenagers. However, not everything falls neatly into place; sexual abuse seems anomalously concentrated among teenagers, too. We believe this to be an artifact of the National Incidence Study (NIS) data on sexual abuse (National Center on Child Abuse and Neglect, 1981), which was based only on reported cases and thus undercounted sexual abuse of young children.[3] When the incidence of sexual abuse is based on data from retrospective self-reports, 64% of victimizations occur before age 12 (Finkelhor, Hotaling, Lewis, & Smith, 1990), a pattern more consistent with the hypothesis and the place of sexual abuse on the dependency continuum.

For additional insights about development and victimization, one can look also at child homicide, the type of victimization to which a developmental analysis has been most extensively applied (Christoffel, 1990; Crittenden & Craig, 1990; Jason, 1983). Child homicide has a

Table 1.4 Victimization of younger children

Type of victimization	% of victims under 12 years of age	Source
Family abduction	81[a]	NISMART (R)
Physical neglect	70	NIS-2C
Psychological maltreatment	58[b]	NIS-2C, NSCANR
Physical abuse	56	NIS-2C
Sexual abuse	40	NIS-2C
Stranger abduction	27	NISMART (R)
Homicide	21[c]	UCR91

Some figures shown in this table did not appear in original source but were derived from data presented therein. NISMART (R) = National Incidence Study of Missing, Abducted, Runaway and Thrownaway Children, 1990 (Authors' reanalysis of published data; Finkelhor, Hotaling, & Sedlak, 1990); NIS-2C = National Study of the Incidence and Severity of Child Abuse and Neglect, 1988 (Powers, & Eckenrode, 1992); NSCANR = National Study on Child Abuse and Neglect Reporting, 1983 (American Association for Protecting Children, 1985); UCR91 = Uniform Crime Reports, 1991 (Federal Bureau of Investigation, 1992).

[a] Broad scope.
[b] Reflects midpoint of two divergent estimates.
[c] Age group for this category is under 10.

conspicuous bimodal frequency, with high rates for the very youngest and oldest children (figure 1.3). But the two peaks represent very different phenomena. The homicides of young children are primarily committed by parents, most often using their hands – so-called "personal weapons." In contrast, the homicides of older children are committed mostly by peers and acquaintances, most often with the use of firearms.

Although the analysts do not agree entirely on the number and age span of the specific developmental categories for child homicides, a number of propositions are clear. There is a distinct group of neonaticides, or children killed on the first day or within the first few weeks of life. Homicide at this age is generally considered to include many isolated mothers dealing with unwanted children. After the neonatal period, there follows a period in which homicides are still primarily committed by caretakers using personal weapons, but the motives and circumstances are thought to be somewhat different. These appear to be mostly cases of fatal child abuse that occur as a result of parents'

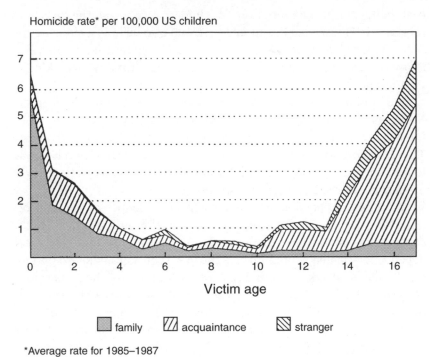

Figure 1.3 Relationship of child homicide victims to perpetrators

attempts to control child behavior (Christoffel, 1990; Crittenden & Craig, 1990). As children become of school age and older, the nature of child homicide becomes incrementally more like adult homicide. Killings by parents and caretakers decline, and those by peers and acquaintances rise. Firearms become the predominant method.

These trends clearly suggest that the types of homicide suffered by children are related to the nature of their dependency and to the level of their integration into the adult world. These trends provide a good case for the importance and utility of a developmental perspective on child victimizations and a model of how such an approach could be applied to other types of victimization.

Intrafamily Victimization

Unlike many adults, children do not live alone; most live in families. Thus, another plausible principle of developmental victimology is that more of the victimization of children occurs at the hands of relatives. We illustrated this in table 1.2 and also table 1.3, showing the sheer quantity of victimization by relatives apparent in the elevated figures on sibling assault (table 1.3), which outstrip any other kind of victimization.

The findings on homicide also suggest a developmental trend: Younger children have a greater proportion of their victimizations at the hands of intimates and correspondingly fewer at the hands of strangers. They live more sheltered lives, spend more time in the home and around family, and have less wealth and fewer valuable possessions that might make them attractive targets for strangers.

An additional possible principle is that the identity of perpetrators may vary according to the type of victimization and its place on the dependency continuum (figure 1.2). Victimizations that are more dependency-related should involve more perpetrators who are parents and family members. Accordingly, parents are 100% of the perpetrators of neglect and psychological maltreatment (Sedlak, 1991), the most dependency-related victimizations. However, they represent only 51% of the perpetrators of sexual abuse (Sedlak) and 28% of the perpetrators of homicide (Jason, Gilliand, & Taylor, 1983). This pattern occurs because the responsibilities created by children's dependency status fall primarily on parents and family members. They are the main individuals in a position to violate those responsibilities in a way that would create victimization. Thus, when a sick child fails to get available medical attention, it is the parents who are charged with neglecting the child, even if the neighbors also did nothing.

Gender and Victimization

Developmental victimology needs to take account of gender as well. On the basis of the conventional crime statistics available from the NCS and Uniform Crime Reports (UCR), boys would appear to suffer more homicide (2.3 : 1), more assault (1.7 : 1), and more robbery (2.0 : 1) than girls, whereas girls suffer vastly more rape (8.1 : 1). But this primarily pertains to the experience of adolescents and does not consider age and gender variations.

Because gender differentiation increases as children grow older, a developmental hypothesis might predict that the pattern of

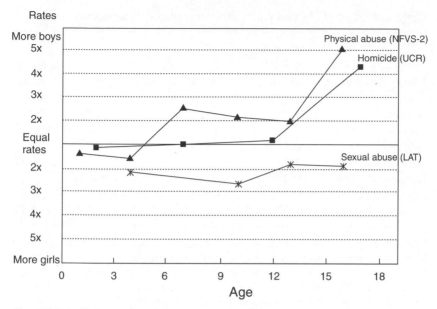

Rates

Note: NFVS-2 = National Family Violence Resurvey, 1985 (Straus & Gelles, 1990); UCR = UCR91, Uniform Crime Report (Federal Bureau of Investigation, 1992). LAT = Los Angeles Times Poll (Finkelhor, Hotaling, Lewis, & Smith, 1990).

Figure 1.4   Gender differences in victimization rates

victimization would be less gender-specific for younger children. That is, because younger boys and girls are more similar in their activities and physical characteristics, there might be less difference between sexes in the rate of victimization.

This pattern does indeed appear to be the case at least for homicide, the type of victimization for which we have the best data (figure 1.4). Rates of homicide are quite similar for younger boys and girls, even up to age 14, after which point the vulnerability of boys increases dramatically.

However, this increased differentiation with age is less apparent for other types of victimization. In contrast to homicide, for example, for sexual abuse we might expect that it would be girls who would become increasingly vulnerable as they age. However, the national data do not show this. They show girls at roughly twice the risk of boys throughout childhood, with no increase during adolescence.

Table 1.5   Rate of physical injury due to childhood victimization

Type of victimization	Rate of injury per 1,000 children	% of all victims sustaining injury	Source	Age in years
Assault	19.23	33	NCS90	12–19
Physical abuse	3.59	84	NIS-2	0–17
Robbery	2.71	24	NCS90	12–19
Physical neglect	1.39	52	NIS-2	0–17
Family abduction	0.22	04	NISMART	0–17
Sexual abuse	0.09	05	NIS-2	0–17
Stranger abduction	0.007–0.015	14–21	NISMART	0–17

Some figures shown in this table did not appear in original source but were derived from data presented therein. NCS90 = National Crime Survey, 1990 (Bureau of Justice Statistics, 1992); NIS-2 = National Study of the Incidence and Severity of Child Abuse and Neglect, 1988 (Sedlak, 1991); NISMART = National Incidence Study of Missing, Abducted, Runaway and Thrownaway Children, 1990 (Finkelhor, Hotaling, & Sedlak, 1990).

So it looks as though a developmental pattern in gender differentiation may apply to some forms of victimization but not others. This mixed picture in regard to gender and age merits more study. Some victimization types may have unique gender patterns reflecting their particular dynamics. However, we may also be suffering from inadequate data that are clouding the true situation.

Effects of Child Victimization

Homicide is currently one of the five leading causes of child mortality in the United States (Goetting, 1990). In addition to the more than 2,000 homicide deaths that occur each year (FBI, 1992), one needs to add a sizeable proportion of 1,200 child abuse and neglect fatalities, an estimated two-thirds of which are not often counted in the homicide statistics (Ewigman, Kivlahan, & Land, 1993). Victimization also results in a substantial toll of nonfatal injuries that are more difficult to count accurately. The NIS estimated that 317,700 children suffered serious or moderate physical injuries in one year (table 1.5) as a result of physical abuse or neglect or sexual abuse, that is, injuries for which observable symptoms, such as bruises, lasted at least 48 hours. From the NCS, one can estimate that approximately 523,300 12- to 19-year-olds sustained physical injury due to an assault in 1990, and approximately 132,900 received hospital care as a result of any kind of violent crime. A Massachusetts study suggested that each year 1 in every 42 teenage boys receives hospital treatment for an assault-related injury (Guyer, Lescohier, Gallagher, Hausman, & Azzara, 1989).

Children's level of development undoubtedly influences the nature and severity of injuries resulting from victimization, although few analyses have taken such a developmental approach. An obvious example is the greater vulnerability of small children to death and serious harm as a result of inflicted blows. Another obvious example is the higher likelihood of older children to contract sexual-abuse-related HIV infection, because older children suffer more penetrative abuse (Kerns & Ritter, 1991).

In addition to physical injury, there is a growing literature documenting that victimization has grave short- and long-term effects on children's mental health. For example, sexually victimized children appear to be at a nearly fourfold increased lifetime risk for any psychiatric disorder and at a threefold risk for substance abuse (Saunders, Villeponteaux, Lipovsky, Kilpatrick, & Veronen, 1992; Scott, 1992). Scott estimated that approximately 8% of all psychiatric cases within the population at large can be attributed to childhood sexual assault.

Although they do not involve such specific epidemiological assessment, other studies have also demonstrated increased rates of mental health morbidity for other types of childhood victimization, including physical abuse (Kolko, 1992), psychological maltreatment (Briere & Runtz, 1990), and physical punishment (Straus, in press).

In addition to general mental health impairments, a proposition that has been established across various types of victimization is that a history of such victimization increases the likelihood that someone will become a perpetrator of crime, violence, or abuse. Although this popular shibboleth has been criticized and qualified (Kaufman & Ziegler, 1987), evidence to support it comes from a wide variety of methodologies, such as longitudinal follow-ups (McCord, 1983; Widom, 1989a), studies of offender populations (Hanson & Slater, 1988), and surveys of the general population (Straus et al., 1980) and concerns a wide variety of perpetrations, including violent crime, property crime, child abuse, wife abuse, and sexual assaults (for review, see Widom, 1989b). An important qualification is that victims are not necessarily prone to repeat their own form of victimization. But the proposition that childhood victims are more likely to grow up to victimize others is firmly established.

Theory about post-traumatic stress disorder (PTSD) is being applied to, and may be a unifying concept for, understanding common psychological effects of a wide variety of child victimizations (Eth & Pynoos, 1985), including abuse in schools (Hyman, Zelikoff, & Clarke, 1988). Terr (1990) has made some effort to cast PTSD in a more developmental framework, but its application is mostly anecdotal.

Sexual abuse is the only area in which a developmental approach to the psychological impact of victimization has advanced on the basis of empirical studies (Kendall-Tackett, Williams, & Finkelhor, 1993). For example, in reaction to sexual abuse, symptoms of sexualization seem to appear more frequently among pre-school than among school-age girls, who seem more aware of appropriate and inappropriate sexual conduct (Friedrich et al., 1992). This is the direction the whole area of child victimization needs to take.

Research Needs

The research needs in this field of child victimization are vast and urgent, given the size of the problem and the seriousness of its impact, and they range from studies of risk factors to studies of treatment efficacy. In the limited space of this review, we mention only three important points.

First, if we are to take child victimization seriously, we need much better statistics to document and analyze its scope, nature, and trends. We need comprehensive, yearly, national and state figures on all officially reported crimes against children and forms of child abuse. These need to be supplemented by regular national studies (one is currently in progress; Finkelhor & Dziuba-Leatherman, in press-a) to assess the vast quantity of unreported victimization, including family violence and child-to-child and indirect victimizations. Currently, the NCS records crime victimizations only down to age 12. The UCR in the past has made no age information available about crimes, with the exception of homicide. Because the national data-collection system for child abuse fails to include all states and has severe methodological limitations, the information cannot be aggregated nationally or compared across states (National Center on Child Abuse and Neglect, 1992).

Second, we need theory and research that cuts across and integrates the various forms of child victimization. One example is the research illustrating how forms of victimization occur together (Claussen & Crittenden, 1991) or create vulnerability for one another (Russell, 1984). Another good example is the work on PTSD in children, which has been applied to the effects of various victimizations: sexual abuse, corporal punishment-related abuse in schools, stranger abduction, and the witnessing of homicide (Eth & Pynoos, 1985; Hyman et al., 1988; Terr, 1990). Similar cross-cutting research could be done on other subjects, such as what makes children vulnerable to victimization or how responses by family members buffer or exacerbate the impact of victimization. To be truly synthetic, this research needs to study the pandemic victimizations, not just the acute and the extraordinary, which have been the main foci in the past.

Finally, the field needs a more developmental perspective on child victimization. This would start with an understanding of the mix of victimization threats that face children of different ages. It would include the kinds of factors that place children at risk, including ecological factors, and the strategies for victimization avoidance that are appropriate at different stages of development. It would also differentiate how children, with all their individual differences, react and cope at different stages with the challenges posed by victimization. It is only through this more differentiated approach that we can understand how victimization leaves its mark on children's lives.

Notes

1 Unfortunately, this contrast is muddied by the fact that the NCS does not have rates on children under 12 years of age, and, although they are usually classified as young adults, 18- and 19-year-olds – a very high-risk group – are treated as children. Even if one reclassifies 18- and 19-year-olds as adults and assumes no victimizations at all for children younger than 12, the overall rate for children, based on NCS data, would still be higher than the overall rate for adults.

2 The following quote in a discussion of the meaning of the NCS statistics on adolescents is an example: "A student who is coerced into surrendering the

Twinkies in his or her lunchbox to a school bully is, by strict definition, a victim of robbery. These events, although unpleasant and perhaps frightening, are not as alarming as suggested by the labels 'assault' and 'robbery' " (Garofalo, Siegel, & Laub, 1987, p. 331). This is common stereotypy of peer victimizations, even though the kind of chronic bullying, terrorizing, and intimidation that characterizes the lives of many children in school and in their neighborhood has almost no equivalent for adults, except perhaps in the case of battered wives (Greenbaum, 1989). There is also a tendency to see violence among children, particularly young children, as fighting and not as victimization. It is important to point out that this is not a distinction made in any of the statistics regarding adult victimization. That is, an adult who is assaulted in a fight he or she may have "started" (according to some observers) will nonetheless be counted as a victim in the NCS.

3   The undercount stems from two problems: (a) Most sexual abuse reports, unlike other forms of child maltreatment, start from children's own disclosures, which are more difficult for younger children to make. (b) Much sexual abuse goes on for extended periods of time before being disclosed, and the age data in the NIS are based on age at the time of report, not age at onset.

References

Ageton, S. S. (1983). *Sexual assault among adolescents*. Lexington, MA: Lexington Books.

American Association for Protecting Children (1985). *Highlights of official child neglect and abuse reporting, 1983*. Denver, CO: American Humane Association.

American School Health Association (1985). *The national adolescent student health survey: A report on the health of America's youth*. Kent, OH: Author.

Best, J. (1990). *Threatened children: Rhetoric and concern about child-victims*. Chicago: University of Chicago Press.

Briere, J., & Runtz, M. (1990). Differential adult symptomatology associated with three types of child abuse histories. *Child Abuse and Neglect, 14*, 357–64.

Bureau of Justice Statistics (1991). *Teenage victims: A national crime survey report* (NCJ-128129). Washington, DC: US Department of Justice.

Bureau of Justice Statistics (1992). *Criminal victimization in the United States, 1990: A national crime victimization survey report* (NCJ-134126). Washington, DC: US Department of Justice.

Christoffel, K. K. (1990). Violent death and injury in U.S. children and adolescents. *American Journal of Diseases of Children, 144*, 697–706.

Claussen, A. I. E., & Crittenden, P. M. (1991). Physical and psychological maltreatment: Relations among types of maltreatment. *Child Abuse and Neglect, 15,* 5–18.

Crittenden, P. A., & Craig, S. E. (1990). Developmental trends in the nature of child nomicide. *Journal of Interpersonal Violence, 5,* 202–16.

Daro, D., & Gelles, R. (1991). *Public attitudes and behaviors with respect to child abuse prevention 1987–1991* (Working paper No. 840). Chicago: National Center on Child Abuse Prevention Research, National Committee for Prevention of Child Abuse.

Daro, D., & McCurdy, K. (1991). *Current trends in child abuse reporting and fatalities: The results of the 1990 annual fifty state survey* (Working paper No. 808). Chicago: National Center on Child Abuse Prevention Research, National Committee for Prevention of Child Abuse.

Eth, S., & Pynoos, R. S. (1985). *Post-traumatic stress disorder in children.* Washington, DC: American Psychiatric Press.

Ewigman, B., Kivlahan, C., & Land, G. (1993). The Missouri Child Fatality Study: Underreporting of maltreatment fatalities among children younger than five years of age: 1983 through 1996. *Pediatrics, 91,* 330–7.

Federal Bureau of Investigation (1992). *Crime in the United States, 1991: Uniform crime reports.* Washington, DC: US Department of Justice.

Finkelhor, D., & Dziuba-Leatherman, J. (in press-a). Children as victims of violence: A national survey. *Pediatrics.*

Finkelhor, D., & Dziuba-Leatherman, J. (in press-b). Victimization prevention programs: A national survey of children's exposure and reactions. *Child Abuse and Neglect.*

Finkelhor, D., Hotaling, G. T., Lewis, I. A., & Smith, C. (1990). Sexual abuse in a national survey of adult men and women: Prevalence, characteristics, and risk factors. *Child Abuse and Neglect, 14,* 19–28.

Finkelhor, D., Hotaling, G. T., & Sedlak, A. (1990). *Missing, abducted, runaway, and thrownaway children in America: First report.* Washington, DC: Juvenile Justice Clearinghouse.

Friedrich, W. N., Grambsch, P., Damon, L., Hewitt, S. K., Koverola, C., Wolfe, V., Lang, R. A., & Broughton, D. (1992). Child Sexual Behavior Inventory: Normative and clinical comparisons. *Psychological Assessment, 4,* 303–11.

Garbarino, J. (1989). The incidence and prevalence of child maltreatment. In L. Ohlin & M. Tonry (eds.), *Family violence* (pp. 219–61). Chicago: University of Chicago Press.

Garofalo, J., Siegel, L., & Laub, J. (1987). School-related victimizations among adolescents: An analysis of National Crime Survey narratives. *Journal of Quantitative Criminology, 3,* 321–38.

Gelles, R. J., & Straus, M. A. (1979). Determinants of violence in the family: Towards a theoretical integration. In W. R. Burr, R. Hill, F. I. Nye & I. L. Reiss (eds.), *Contemporary theories about the family* (vol. 1). New York: Free Press.

Goetting, A. (1990). Child victims of homicide: A portrait of their killers and the circumstances of their deaths. *Violence and Victims, 5*, 287–96.

Greenbaum, S. (1989). *School bullying and victimization* (NSSC resource paper). Malibu, CA: National School Safety Center.

Greven, P. (1990). *Spare the child: The religious roots of punishment and the psychological impact of physical abuse.* New York: Knopf.

Guyer, B., Lescohier, I., Gallagher, S. S., Hausman, A., & Azzara, C. V. (1989). Intentional injuries among children and adolescents in Massachusetts. *The New England Journal of Medicine, 321*, 1584–9.

Hanson, R. L., & Slater, S. (1988). Sexual victimization in the history of sexual abusers: A review. *Annals of Sex Research, 4*, 485–99.

Hart, S. N., & Brassard, M. R. (1987). A major threat to children's mental health: Psychological maltreatment. *American Psychologist, 42*, 160–5.

Hyman, I. A. (1990). *Reading, writing and the hickory stick: The appalling story of physical and psychological abuse in American schools.* Lexington, MA: Lexington Books.

Hyman, I. A., Zelikoff, W., & Clarke, J. (1988). Psychological and physical abuse in the schools: A paradigm for understanding post-traumatic stress disorder in children and youths. *Journal of Traumatic Stress, 1*, 243–67.

Jason, J. (1983). Child homicide spectrum. *American Journal of Diseases of Children, 137*, 578–81.

Jason, J., Gilliand, J. C., & Taylor, C. W. (1983). Homicide as a cause of pediatric mortality in the United States. *Pediatrics, 72*, 191–7.

Kaufman, J., & Ziegler, E. (1987). Do abused children become abusive parents? *American Journal of Orthophychiatry, 57*, 186–92.

Kendall-Tackett, K. A., Williams, L. M., & Finkelhor, D. (1993). Impact of sexual abuse on children: A review and synthesis of recent empirical studies. *Psychological Bulletin, 113*, 164–80.

Kerns, D. L., & Ritter, M. L. (1991, September). *Data analysis of the medical evaluation of 1,800 suspected child sexual abuse victims.* Paper presented at the Ninth National Conference on Child Abuse and Neglect. Denver, CO.

Kilpatrick, D. (1992). *Rape in America: A report to the nation.* Charleston, SC: Crime Victims Research Center.

Kolko, D. J. (1992). Characteristics of child victims of physical violence: Research findings and clinical implications. *Journal of Interpersonal Violence, 7*, 244–76.

Lauritsen, J. L., Sampson, R. J., & Laub, J. H. (1991). The link between offending and victimization among adolescents. *Criminology, 29*, 265–92.

McCord, J. (1983). A forty year perspective on effects of child abuse and neglect. *Child Abuse and Neglect, 7*, 265–70.

McDermott, M. J., Stanley, J. E., & Zimmerman-McKinney, M. A. (1982). The victimization of children and youths. *Victimology, 7*, 162–77.

Morgan, J., & Zedner, L. (1992). *Child victims: Crime, impact, and criminal justice.* Oxford, England: Clarendon Press.

National Center on Child Abuse and Neglect (1982). *Study findings. National Study of the Incidence and Severity of Child Abuse and Neglect* (OHDS Publication No. 81–30325). Washington, DC: Department of Health and Human Services.

National Center on Child Abuse and Neglect (1992). *National child abuse and neglect data system* (Working Paper No. 1): *1990 summary data component* (DHHS Publication No. ACF 92–30361). Washington, DC: Department of Health and Human Services.

Olweus, D. (1978). *Aggression in the schools: Bullies and whipping boys.* Washington, DC: Hemisphere.

Pagelow, M. D. (1989). The incidence and prevalence of criminal abuse of other family members. In L. Ohlin, & M. Tonry (eds.), *Family violence* (pp. 263–314). Chicago: University of Chicago Press.

Powers, J., & Eckenrode, J. (1992, March). *The epidemiology of adolescent maltreatment.* Paper presented at the Fourth Biennial Meeting of the Society for Research on Adolescence, Washington, DC.

Russell, D. (1984). *Sexual exploitation: Rape, child sexual abuse, and workplace harassment.* Beverly Hills, CA: Sage.

Saunders, B. E., Villeponteaux, L. A., Lipovsky, J. A., Kilpatrick, D. G., & Veronen, L. J. (1992). Child sexual assault as a risk factor for mental disorders among women: A community survey. *Journal of Interpersonal Violence, 7,* 189–204.

Scott, K. D. (1992). Childhood sexual abuse: Impact on a community's mental health status. *Child Abuse and Neglect, 16,* 285–95.

Sedlak, A. J. (1991). *Supplementary analyses of data on the national incidence of child abuse and neglect.* Rockville, MD: Westat.

Straus, M. A. (in press). Corporal punishment of children and depression and suicide in adulthood. In J. McCord (ed.), *Coercion and punishment in long-term perspective.* Cambridge, England: Cambridge University Press.

Straus, M. A., & Gelles, R. J. (1990). *Physical violence in American families: Risk factors and adaptations to violence in 8,145 families.* New Brunswick, NJ: Transaction.

Straus, M., Gelles, R., & Steinmetz, S. K. (1980). *Behind closed doors: Violence in the American family.* Garden City, NY: Anchor Press.

Terr, L. (1990). *Too scared to cry.* New York: Harper Collins.

Widom, C. S. (1989a). The cycle of violence. *Science, 244,* 160–6.

Widom, C. S (1989b). Does violence beget violence? A critical examination of the literature. *Psychological Bulletin, 106,* 3–28.

Appendix
Sources of data

Acronym	Survey
50-SS	Annual Fifty State Survey, 1990 (Daro & McCurdy, 1991).
LAECA	Los Angeles Epidemiologic Catchment Area data (Scott, 1992).
LAT	*Los Angeles Times* Poll (Finkelhor, Hotaling, Lewis, & Smith, 1990).
NASHS	National Adolescent Student Health Survey (American School Health Association, 1985).
NCS90	National Crime Survey, 1990 (Bureau of Justice Statistics, 1992).
NCSTEEN	National Crime Survey, 1979–1988 (as presented in Bureau of Justice Statistics, 1991).
NFVS-1	National Family Violence Survey, 1975 (Straus & Gelles, 1990).
NFVS-2	National Family Violence Resurvey, 1985 (Straus & Gelles, 1990).
NISMART	National Incidence Study of Missing, Abducted, Runaway and Thrownaway Children, 1990 (Finkelhor, Hotaling, & Sedlak, 1990).
NSCANR	National Study on Child Abuse and Neglect Reporting, 1983 (American Association for Protecting Children, 1985).
NIS-1	National Study of the Incidence and Severity of Child Abuse and Neglect, 1981 (National Center on Child Abuse and Neglect, 1981).
NIS-2	National Study of the Incidence and Severity of Child Abuse and Neglect, 1988 (Sedlak, 1991).
NIS-2C	National Study of the Incidence and Severity of Child Abuse and Neglect, 1988 (as presented in Powers & Eckenrode, 1992).
NYS	National Youth Survey (Lauritsen, Sampson, & Laub, 1991).
NYS78	National Youth Survey, 1978 (Ageton, 1983).
UCR91	Uniform Crime Reports, 1991 (Federal Bureau of Investigation, 1992).

TWO

The Impact of Sexual Abuse on Children

Introduction

One type of child victimization that can have profound, long-lasting negative outcomes for children is sexual abuse. Once society began to realize that children were subject to sexual abuse the need to determine its likely impact was recognized as being urgent. In particular, psychologists (and others) wanted to develop knowledge concerning how best to assist children to try to cope with the impact of sexual abuse, right through to adulthood where necessary.

In their review of the rather limited previous work, Kathleen Kendall-Tackett and her colleagues draw together many small-scale studies from a variety of disciplines, something that psychologists often fail to do. Many of the studies they review compared children thought to have been sexually abused with children believed not to have been abused, in order to arrive at a categorization of the wide range of symptoms reported in the literature. While such studies could be taken to provide information concerning the impact of sexual abuse, many of them made the mistake of comparing children in treatment with ordinary children not in treatment, instead of with children in treatment but not for sexual abuse. Even so, and perhaps surprisingly, children believed to have been sexually abused by no means show a similar pattern of symptoms, and a proportion manifest no apparent symptoms at all. However, the impact of sexual abuse is likely to vary with the nature of the abuse, who perpetrated it, and the age of the child. Also complicating the issue is the problem of reliably determining whether a child (a) has been sexually abused or (b) has not, in fact, been sexually abused. Children who have been abused may not always be willing to divulge this, and children who are thought to have been abused may not have been. Thus, determining the impact of sexual abuse is, at least in part, reliant on the reliability of children's accounts, which is the focus of part II of the book.

Suggested reading

Wyatt, G., & Powell, G. (1988). *Lasting effect of child sexual abuse*. Thousand Oaks, CA: Sage.

Impact of Sexual Abuse on Children: A Review and Synthesis of Recent Empirical Studies

Kathleen A. Kendall-Tackett,
Linda Meyer Williams, and David Finkelhor

Until recently, the literature on the impact of child sexual abuse consisted disproportionately of retrospective studies of adults. For example, the conclusions of a widely cited review (Browne & Finkelhor, 1986) were based on only 4 studies of children, compared with 23 studies of adults. Not surprisingly, most reviews combined studies of both groups, because research focused on children was rare.

Since 1985, however, there has been an explosion in the number of studies that have concentrated specifically on sexually abused children. Some studies have even focused on specific types of child victims, such as preschoolers, boys, or victims of ritualistic abuse. The studies of child victims have been distinct in several important ways from the research on adults. First, researchers studying children have often used different methodologies, many times relying on parents' or clinicians' reports rather than on children's self-reports. In addition, they have often evaluated specifically child-oriented symptoms, such as regressive behavior. These methodologies and the concentration on child-oriented symptoms make this research more relevant to intervention and treatment with children than the research on the effects of sexual abuse on adults, from which the implications for the treatment of children were difficult to extrapolate.

Research on children has allowed for a developmental perspective and included the first efforts at longitudinal studies of sexual abuse victims. This literature also has important relevance to other theory and research concerning how children process trauma, for example, how trauma expresses itself at various developmental stages, its role in the development of later psychopathology, and the mediating effects of important factors such as familial and community support. Therefore, research on the effect of sexual abuse on children is worthy of its own review.

We undertook such a review to (a) bring together literature from a broad spectrum of fields, including medicine, social work, psychology, and sociology; (b) highlight areas where there is agreement and disagreement in findings; (c) draw conclusions that may be useful for clinicians currently working with child victims and researchers studying this problem; and (d) suggest directions for future research and theory.

Domain

In the present review, we included studies of child victims of sexual abuse,[1] in which all subjects were 18 years of age or younger (see Appendix). In all of these studies, quantitative results of at least one of the following types were reported: a comparison of sexually abused children with nonabused children or norms (clinical and/or nonclinical) or the age of victims who manifested some symptom. Certain other studies that did not contain these types of data, yet included other relevant data on intervening variables or longitudinal findings, are not listed in the appendix but are referenced in the appropriate sections. The majority were published within the past 5 years. Because there has been so much research on this topic in the past few years, we also included some unpublished material (most of the manuscripts are currently under review), located through researchers who specialize in research in this area. Although we undoubtedly missed some articles, we are confident that we were able to locate most of them because of the network of researchers we contacted.

Excluded from the present review were nonquantitative or case studies. We also excluded studies in which all subjects manifested a certain behavior (such as teen prostitution or running away) but only some of them had been sexually abused. (In contrast, in the studies we included in the present review, all subjects had been abused.) Finally, we excluded studies that involved both adult and child victims (e.g., ages 15–45) and combined results from these two groups.

The studies used samples from several different sources, but primarily drew from sexual abuse evaluation or treatment programs. Some investigators recruited from specific subgroups of victims, such as day-care victims. Most investigators combined victims of intra- and extrafamilial abuse. The samples also included a wide variety of ages, covering the entire spectrum from preschool to adolescence. The sample sizes ranged from very small ($N = 8$) to large ($N = 369$), with the majority between 25 and 50 children. Approximately half (55%) the studies included comparison groups, and six had both nonabused clinical and nonabused nonclinical controls. This is a major improvement over studies conducted even 10 years ago. The studies used a variety of sources for assessment, including parent report, chart review, clinician report, and children's self-report.

In reviewing these studies, we first looked at the findings with regard to symptoms and then examined the intervening variables that affected these symptoms. We then paid particular attention to the longitudinal studies undertaken thus far. Finally, we drew conclusions for theory and future research.

Comparison of Abused and Nonabused Children

A wide range of symptoms have been examined in the studies in which sexually abused children have been compared with nonabused clinical or nonclinical children (or norms). Table 2.1 groups these symptoms together under major headings. As shown in column 1, by far the most commonly studied symptom was sexualized behavior, often considered the most characteristic symptom of sexual abuse. Sexualized behavior usually included such things as sexualized play with dolls, putting objects into anuses or vaginas, excessive or public masturbation, seductive behavior, requesting sexual stimulation from adults or other children, and age-inappropriate sexual knowledge (Beitchman, Zucker, Hood, daCosta, and Akman, 1991). Other symptoms that appeared in many studies included anxiety, depression, withdrawn behavior, somatic complaints, aggression, and school problems.

Table 2.1 Sexually abused (SA) versus non-sexually abused (NSA) children: nonclinical and clinical comparison groups

	Nonclinical		Clinical			
Symptom	Total no. studies	SA > NSA[a]/ no. studies	No. studies in which SA > NSA[a]	No. studies in which there was no difference	No. studies in which SA < NSA[b]	Total no. studies
Anxiety	14	5/8	1	2	0	3
Fear	6	5/5	1	0	2	3
Post-traumatic stress disorder						
Nightmares	3	1/1	1	—	—	1
General	5	1/1	1	0	0	1
Depression						
Depressed	17	10/11	1	2	2	5
Withdrawn	14	11/11	1	1	3	5
Suicidal	7	0/1	—	—	—	—
Poor self-esteem	11	3/6	—	—	—	7
Somatic complaints	16	9/11	1	3	3	7
Mental illness						
Neurotic	3	2/2	0	2	2	4
Other	12	6/7	0	4	2	6
Aggression						
Aggressive antisocial	15	10/11	0	1	6	7
Cruel	2	2/2	0	1	0	1
Delinquent	7	6/6	0	1	3	4

Sexualized behavior						
Inappropriate sexual behavior	23	8/8	6	2	0	8
Promiscuity	2	—	—	—	—	—
School/learning problems	13	5/6	0	1	2	3
Behavior problems						
Hyperactivity	9	5/7	0	1	4	5
Regression/immaturity	7	2/2	1	0	1	2
Illegal acts	4	—	—	—	—	—
Running away	6	1/1	—	—	—	—
General	5	2/2	—	—	—	—
Self-destructive behavior						
Substance abuse	5	—	—	—	—	—
Self-injurious behavior	4	1/1	—	—	—	—
Composite symptoms						
Internalizing	10	8/8	0	2	1	3
Externalizing	11	7/7	0	1	2	3

The numbers in column 2 do not necessarily add up to the number in column 1 because column 1 includes some studies in which only the percentage of children with symptoms was specified.

[a] SA > NSA = SA children were more symptomatic than NSA children.

[b] SA < NSA = SA children were less symptomatic than NSA children.

Column 2 shows the number of studies in which sexually abused children were more symptomatic than their nonabused counterparts. The denominator is the number of studies in which this comparison was made. For many symptoms, a difference was found in all of the studies in which such a comparison was made. These symptoms were fear, nightmares, general post-traumatic stress disorder (PTSD),[2] withdrawn behavior, neurotic mental illness, cruelty, delinquency, sexually inappropriate behavior, regressive behavior (including enuresis, encopresis, tantrums, and whining), running away, general behavior problems, self-injurious behavior, internalizing, and externalizing.[3] The symptom with the lowest percentage of studies in which a difference was found (besides suicidal behavior, for which a difference was found in only one study) was poor self-esteem (50%). This may be in part because poor self-esteem is so common and has so many possible causes. It may also be because this symptom was the one most frequently measured by child self-report, a method that may underestimate pathology (see 'Methodological Issues and Directions for Future Research'). Nonetheless, for almost every symptom examined, including self-esteem, in most studies sexually abused children were found to be more symptomatic than their nonabused counterparts.

The comparison between sexually abused children and other clinical, nonabused children (i.e., children in treatment) tells a possibly different story, however (columns 3–5). For many of the symptoms measured, sexually abused children were actually less symptomatic than these clinical children in the majority of the studies. Sexually abused children showed only two symptoms consistently more often than nonabused clinical children: PTSD (just one study) and sexualized behavior (six of eight studies). Thus, sexually abused children tended to appear less symptomatic than their nonabused clinical counterparts except in regard to sexualized behavior and PTSD. These results must be interpreted very cautiously, especially in the light of two features of the clinical comparison groups with which abused children were often compared. First, most clinical comparison groups of so-called nonabused children probably actually do contain children whose abuse simply has not been discovered. In this case, the comparison is not a true abused-versus-nonabused comparison. Second, clinical comparison groups generally contain many children who are referred primarily because of their symptomatic behavior. Naturally these children are likely to be more symptomatic than children referred not because

Table 2.2 Average effect sizes for seven symptoms of sexual abuse

Symptom	No. studies	Effect sizes		
		Range of η^2	Average η	Average η^2
Aggression	4	.37–.71	.66	.43
Anxiety	3	.01–.28	.39	.15
Depression	6	.06–.68	.59	.35
Externalizing	5	.08–.52	.57	.32
Internalizing	6	.11–.70	.62	.38
Sexualized behavior	5	1.9–.77	.66	.43
Withdrawal	6	.12–.68	.60	.36

of symptoms, but because of something done to them (i.e., abuse). Thus, the lower levels of symptoms in sexually abused children may say more about the clinical comparisons than about the sexually abused children themselves.

For a synthesis of findings such as in table 2.1, a comparison of effect sizes would ordinarily be preferable to the so-called simple box score approach we used. Unfortunately, most of the studies we reviewed did not present data in a form amenable to the calculation of effect sizes. We were, however, able to calculate effect sizes (table 2.2) for seven symptoms on which enough studies had provided adequate information for a comparison of abused and nonabused nonclinical children (all between-groups comparisons[4]). The symptoms were anxiety, sexualized behavior, depression, withdrawal, aggression, internalizing, and externalizing.

Table 2.2 shows that sexual abuse status alone accounted for a very large percentage of the variance for all seven symptoms, with the sexually abused children manifesting significantly more of all these symptoms. The highest effect sizes (etas) were for the acting-out behaviors, such as sexualized behaviors and aggression. Sexual abuse status accounted for 43% of the variance for these two behaviors and 32% of the variance for externalizing. Such a large effect size is less surprising for sexualized behavior than it is for more global symptoms such as aggression and externalizing, which could have a variety of underlying causes.

Sexual abuse status also accounted for a large percentage of the variance (35–38%) for the internalizing behaviors – internalizing, depression, and withdrawal. The smallest percentage of variance accounted for was for anxiety (15%) but even this is a large effect.

Overall, the results of effect size analysis support the conclusion drawn from table 1 that being sexually abused was strongly related to some symptoms specific to sexual abuse, such as sexualized behavior, as well as a range of more global symptoms such as depression, aggression, and withdrawal. Nonetheless, sexually abused children did not appear to be more symptomatic than were other clinical children, except in the case of PTSD and sexualized behavior.

Percentages of Victims with Symptoms

Many researchers simply reported whether sexually abused children were more symptomatic than nonabused children. Yet it is also important to know the actual percentage of victims with each symptom. Some symptoms may occur more often in sexually abused than nonabused children but occur so rarely that they are of little concern for the majority of children in treatment. The actual frequency of such symptoms in the population of abused children can be an important guide to clinicians in diagnosis and treatment. Furthermore, this information is helpful for clinicians and researchers who may want to anticipate the consequences of abuse or develop theory about the process of recovery from abuse. In table 2.3, we synthesize information about these frequencies.

The range of children with each symptom varied widely from study to study, which is not unusual given the heterogeneity of sources. Therefore, for each symptom we calculated a weighted average across all studies, dividing the total number of children with a symptom by the total number of children in all the studies reporting on that symptom.

Across all studies, the percentage of victims with a particular symptom was mostly between 20% and 30%. It is important to note that, with the exception of PTSD, no symptom was manifested by a majority of victims. However, there have been relatively few studies of PTSD, and half the children included in this calculation were victims of

Table 2.3 Percentage of sexually abused children with symptoms

Symptom	% with symptom	Range of %s	No. studies	N
Anxiety	28	14–68	8	688
Fear	33	13–45	5	477
Post-traumatic stress disorder				
Nightmares	31	18–68	5	605
General	53	20–77	4	151
Depression				
Depressed	28	19–52	6	753
Withdrawn	22	4–52	5	660
Suicidal	12	0–45	6	606
Poor self-esteem	35	4–76	5	483
Somatic complaints	14	0–60	6	540
Mental illness				
Neurotic	30	20–38	3	113
Other	6	0–19	3	533
Aggression				
Aggressive/antisocial	21	13–50	7	658
Delinquent	8	8	1	25
Sexualized behavior				
Inappropriate sexual behavior	28	7–90	13	1,353
Promiscuity	38	35–48	2	128
School/learning problems	18	4–32	9	652
Behavior problems				
Hyperactivity	17	4–28	2	133
Regression/immaturity	23	14–44	5	626
Illegal acts	11	8–27	4	570
Running away	15	2–63	6	641
General	37	28–62	2	66
Self-destructive behavior				
Substance abuse	11	2–46	5	786
Self-injurious behavior	15	1–71	3	524
Composite symptoms				
Internalizing	30	4–48	3	295
Externalizing	23	6–38	3	295

severe ritualistic abuse from Los Angles-area day-care cases (Kelly, in press-a), thus inflating the percentage. If we exempt these unusually severely abused children, the average percentage of victims with symptoms of PTSD was 32%, near the level of other frequently occurring symptoms such as poor self-esteem (35%), promiscuity (38%), and general behavior problems (37%). Because the Child Behavior Checklist (CBCL; Achenbach & Edelbrock, 1984) was used in a large number of studies, we also calculated the percentage of children in the clinical range (or with "elevated scores") for internalizing and externalizing symptomatology.

Overall, the percentage of victims with the various symptoms may seem low to those with a clinical perspective. Part of the problem with the analysis of these composite percentages was that many of the symptoms did not occur uniformly across all age groups. We therefore re-examined the weighted percentages presented in table 2.3, grouped by the age of the child at assessment. Percentages were calculated for preschool-age (approximately 0–6 years), school-age (approximately 7–12 years), adolescent (approximately 13–18 years), and mixed age (e.g., 3–17 years) groups. The ages reported in different studies varied and overlapped a bit from these guidelines but by and large fell within these ranges. From a developmental standpoint, we should emphasize that these were very crude cuts across large developmental periods. Furthermore, they represented age at the time of report, not at the onset or end of molestation. In addition, there was no control for the context in which the abuse occurred or the variables that mediated the effects of that abuse.

The results of this analysis (table 2.4) hint at possible developmental patterns. Differentiating the samples on the basis of major age groups appeared to yield more focused and consistent findings than when age groups were mixed.

For preschoolers, the most common symptoms were anxiety, nightmares, general PTSD, internalizing, externalizing, and inappropriate sexual behavior. For school-age children, the most common symptoms included fear, neurotic and general mental illness, aggression, nightmares, school problems, hyperactivity, and regressive behavior. For adolescents, the most common behaviors were depression; withdrawn, suicidal, or self-injurious behaviors; somatic complaints; illegal acts; running away; and substance abuse. Among the symptoms that appeared prominently for more than one age group were nightmares,

Table 2.4 Percentage of children with symptoms by age group

Symptom	% of subjects (No. studies/No. subjects)			
	Preschool	School	Adolescent	Mixed
Anxiety	61	23	8	18
	(3/149)	(2/66)	(1/3)	(4/470)
Fear	13	45	—	31
	(1/30)	(1/58)		(2/389)
Post-traumatic stress disorder				
Nightmares	55	47	0	19
	(3/183)	(1/17)	(1/3)	(2/402)
General	77	—	—	32
	(1/71)			(3/80)
Depression				
Depressed	33	31	46	18
	(3/149)	(2/66)	(3/129)	(2/409)
Withdrawn	10	36	45	15
	(1/30)	(1/58)	(2/126)	(3/446)
Suicidal	0	—	41	3
	(1/37)		(3/172)	(2/397)
Poor self-esteem	0	6	33	38
	(1/25)	(1/17)	(1/3)	(4/438)
Somatic complaints	13	—	34	12
	(2/54)		(1/44)	(2/442)
Mental illness				
Neurotic	20	38	24	—
	(1/30)	(1/58)	(1/25)	
Other	0	19	16	3
	(1/37)	(1/58)	(2/69)	(1/369)
Aggression				
Aggressive/antisocial	27	45	—	14
	(3/154)	(1/58)		(3/446)
Delinquent	—	—	8	—
			(1/25)	
Sexualized behavior				
Inappropriate sexual	35	6	0	24
behavior	(6/334)	(1/17)	(1/3)	(7/999)
Promiscuity	—	—	38	—
			(2/128)	

Table 2.4 *Continued*

	% of subjects (No. studies/No. subjects)			
Symptom	Preschool	School	Adolescent	Mixed
School/learning problems	19 (2/107)	31 (1/58)	23 (2/69)	17 (2/418)
Behavior problems				
Hyperactivity	9 (2/55)	23 (2/75)	0 (1/3)	—
Regression/immaturity	36 (4/159)	39 (2/75)	0 (1/3)	15 (2/389)
Illegal acts	—	—	27 (1/101)	8 (3/469)
Running away	—	—	45 (3/172)	4 (3/469)
General	62 (1/17)	—	—	28 (1/49)
Self-destructive behavior				
Substance abuse	—	—	53 (2/128)	2 (3/658)
Self-injurious behavior	—	—	71 (2/128)	1 (1/369)
Composite symptoms				
Internalizing	48 (1/69)	—	—	24 (2/226)
Externalizing	38 (1/69)	—	—	23 (2/226)

depression, withdrawn behavior, neurotic mental illness, aggression, and regressive behavior.

To date, the majority of data on the effects of sexual abuse on children have been collected cross-sectionally, with data obtained only once per child. Nevertheless, from this cross-sectional data it is possible to hypothesize some developmental trajectories of changes in symptomatology. The question remains, however, as to whether these changes in symptomatology occur within a given child at different stages or represent developmental changes in response to sexual abuse at the time of report.

Depression appeared to be a particularly robust symptom across age groups and was also one that appeared frequently in adults molested as children, as two recent reviews have indicated (Beitchman et al., 1992; McGrath, Keita, Strickland, & Russo, 1990). School and learning problems were also fairly prominent in all three age groups, especially school-age children and adolescents. This is a symptom that would not appear in adults but could be parallel to employment difficulties in adults, because both are structured environments to which the person must report every day and both require equivalent types of skills.

Behavior labeled as antisocial in preschool- and school-age children might be labeled as illegal in adolescents. Similarly, the results of our analysis and a recent review by Beitchman et al. (1991) indicate that sexualized behaviors may be prominent for preschool-age children, submerge during latency (or the school-age period), and re-emerge during adolescence as promiscuity, prostitution, or sexual aggression. These same symptoms might manifest themselves as sexual dysfunction or sex offending in adulthood, although this has yet to be demonstrated empirically.

The results presented in table 2.4 suggest that much symptomatology is developmentally specific and that generalizing across large age groups distorts the patterns. Fortunately, this is more a problem of data analysis and presentation of findings than it is of data collection, so future research should be able to address this issue.

Percentages of Asymptomatic Victims

In addition to the percentage of children with specific symptoms, another important statistic is the percentage of children with no symptoms. This figure has important clinical implications for the group of children in whom the impact of abuse may be muted or masked. Unfortunately, few investigators have reported on such asymptomatic children, perhaps out of concern that such figures might be misinterpreted or misused.

Nonetheless, when investigators have made such estimates, they have found a substantial, an perhaps to some surprising, proportion of the victims to be free of the symptoms being measured. For example,

Caffaro-Rouget, Lang, and vanSanten (1989) found that 49% were asymptomatic at their assessment during a pediatric examination. Mannarino and Cohen (1986) found that 31% were symptom free, and Tong, Oates, and McDowell (1987) found that 36% were within the normal range on the CBCL. Finally, Conte and Schuerman (1987b) indicated that 21% of their large sample appeared to have had no symptoms at all, even though their assessment included both very specific and broad items such as "fearful of abuse stimuli" and "emotional upset."

There are several possible explanations why so many children appeared to be asymptomatic. The first possibility is that the studies did not include measures of all appropriate symptoms or the researchers were not using sensitive enough instruments. In most individual studies, only a limited range of possible effects were examined. Thus some of the asymptomatic children may have been symptomatic on dimensions that were not being measured.

Another possibility is that asymptomatic children are those who have yet to manifest their symptoms. This could be either because the children are effective at suppressing symptoms or have not yet processed their experiences or because true traumatization occurs at subsequent developmental stages, when the children's victim status comes to have more meaning or consequences for them (Berliner, 1991). We would expect these children to manifest symptoms later on. In one study that supports this interpretation (Gomes-Schwartz, Horowitz, Cardarelli, & Sauzier, 1990), the asymptomatic children were the ones most likely to worsen by the time of the 18-month follow up: 30% of them developed symptoms. To date, no one has replicated this finding, however.

A final explanation is that perhaps asymptomatic children are truly less affected. Research indeed suggests there is a relationship between the seriousness and duration of the abuse and the amount of impact (see 'Intervening Variables' section, below). The asymptomatic children might be those with the least damaging abuse. They may also be the most resilient children, the ones with the most psychological, social, and treatment resources to cope with the abuse.

In fact, all three explanations may be simultaneously correct. Unfortunately, the issue of asymptomatic children has been peripheral until recently. Too few researchers have even mentioned the issue, and fewer still have looked at the correlates of being symptom free. Future studies need to address this issue more fully, not as a sidebar of unusual findings, but as a central topic in its own right.

Intervening Variables

In many studies (25 of the 46 we reviewed), researchers have tried to account for variations in the children's symptomatology by examining characteristics of the abuse experience. The results for variables with consistent findings are listed in table 2.5. Variables with contradictory or confusing results are discussed in this section.

Age at the time of assessment has been the most commonly considered intervening variable. The majority of studies indicated that children who were older at the time of assessment appeared to be more symptomatic than those who were younger. However, most of these studies did not control for the effect of duration (those who were older may have had longer molestations), identity of the perpetrator (intrafamilial perpetrators may have been able to continue the abuse for a longer time), or severity of the molestation (older victims may have experienced more severe sexual acts). In three studies, no significant differences related to age at time of assessment were found (Einbender & Friedrich, 1989; Friedrich, Urquiza, & Beilke, 1986; Kolko, Moser, & Weldy, 1988); in one study, younger children were more symptomatic (Wolfe, Gentile, & Wolfe, 1989); and in one study there was a curvilinear relationship between age and symptomatology, with the middle age range being more symptomatic (Gomes-Schwartz, Horowitz, & Sauzier, 1985). Although the data appear to indicate roughly that older children are more negatively affected, these results should be interpreted with caution because of the lack of control over other relevant variables.

Age of onset is another possible intervening variable. However, age of onset was related to symptoms in only one study, which showed that those with early age of onset were more likely to manifest symptoms of pathology (Zivney, Nash, & Hulsey, 1988). In two other studies no difference was found in level of pathology for early versus late age of onset. By and large, it appears that age of onset must be fit into a total conceptual model of molestation. Research is insufficient to permit any conclusions about whether early versus late age of onset is more likely to lead to greater symptomatology. Age of onset might be related more to other characteristics of the abuse (such as identity of the perpetrator) than to overall number and severity of symptoms. Although the relationship of age of onset to symptomatology in children is not clear

Table 2.5 Influence of intervening variables

| Variable | No. studies | | Direction of findings |
	With significant difference in impact	Total	
Age of child			
At assessment	7	10	Older children were more symptomatic in five studies.
At onset	1	3	Not clear.
Sex of child	5	8	Patterns of symptoms different for boys and girls.
Penetration/severity	6	10	Oral, anal, or vaginal penetration was related to increased symptoms.
Frequency	4	6	Higher frequency was related to increased symptoms.
Duration	5	7	Longer duration was related to increased symptoms.
Perpetrator	7	9	Symptoms were increased when perpetrator had close relationship with child.
No. perpetrators	1	3	Not clear.
Lack of maternal support	3	3	Lack of support was related to increased symptoms.
Force	5	6	Use of force was related to increased symptoms.
Time elapsed since last abusive incident	1	3	Not clear.
Child's attitudes and coping style	2	2	Negative outlook and coping style were related to increased symptoms.

at this time, in two recent studies an early age of onset was found to be related to amnesia among adult survivors (Briere & Conte, 1989) and late presentation for treatment (Kendall-Tackett, 1991).

With regard to sex of the subject, consistent differences in the reaction of boys and girls to molestation have been found in only a few studies. The scarcity of these findings is in sharp contrast to the popular belief that boys are likely to manifest externalizing symptoms and girls are more likely to exhibit internalizing symptoms. The absence of consistent gender differences is all the more interesting because girls are more likely to suffer intrafamilial abuse, which has been associated with more severe effects (Finkelhor, Hotaling, Lewis, & Smith, 1990). The lack of more systematic attention to gender differences may be due in part to the small number of male victims in most studies and the possibility that, because of bias in the identification of male victims, only the most symptomatic boys end up in clinical samples. It may also be due to the fact that comparison of boys and girls has produced too few interesting differences to motivate researchers to place it in center focus. Nevertheless, researchers should address the issue of sex of the victims in future reports.

Penetration (oral, anal, or vaginal) did influence the impact of sexual abuse in the majority of studies, but most researchers differed in their definitions of severity of abuse. To further add to the confusion, some of the investigators added together all the sexual acts that a victim experienced, and therefore their indices of severity included the severity as well as the number of sexual acts. Even with all these variations, it appeared that molestations that contained some form of penetration were more likely to produce symptoms than molestations that did not.

The identity of the perpetrator is another factor that has been related to the impact of abuse. The weight of the evidence indicated that a perpetrator who was close to the victim caused more serious effects than one who was less close. To date there does not appear to be a uniform coding scheme for closeness, however. For example, fathers and stepfathers are often coded in the same category. Researchers should try to determine a measure of emotional closeness or degree of caretaking responsibility rather than relying on the kinship label of the perpetrator–victim relationship.

On a similar note, the impact of the number of perpetrators is not clear. The number of perpetrators was positively correlated with number of symptoms in one study, negatively correlated with number of symptoms in another, and not correlated with symptoms in another. Future research should address this issue.

Time elapsed since the last abusive incident and assessment is a variable with intuitive appeal, but it has been examined in very few studies. Only 55% of the articles in the present review even mentioned time elapsed, and it varied from a few days to several years. In only three studies was the possible relationship between time elapsed and the impact of abuse examined. In one study (Friedrich et al., 1986), children became less symptomatic over time, whereas in two other studies (McLeer, Deblinger, Atkins, Foa, & Ralphe, 1988; Wolfe et al., 1989) it made no difference. It appears to be too early to decide whether time elapsed is correlated with the number of symptoms. Therefore, we should find out more about this variable before we assume that it makes no difference.

In summary, the findings of the various studies reviewed indicated that molestations that included a close perpetrator; a high frequency of sexual contact; a long duration; the use of force; and sexual acts that included oral, anal, or vaginal penetration lead to a greater number of symptoms for victims. Similarly, as all the studies that included these variables indicated, the lack of maternal support at the time of disclosure and a victim's negative outlook or coping style also led to increased symptoms. The influence of age at the time of assessment, age at onset, number of perpetrators, and time elapsed between the end of abuse and assessment is still somewhat unclear at the present time and should be examined in future studies on the impact of intervening variables.

It should be kept in mind when interpreting these findings that certain intervening variables are highly correlated. For example, intrafamilial abuse normally occurs over a longer time period and involves more serious sexual activity (i.e. penetration). These natural confounds make it difficult to fully analyze the independent effects of intervening variables. Very few studies have included more than one or two of these variables, and almost no one has statistically controlled for their effects.

Longitudinal Studies

Perhaps the most encouraging development in the field has been the appearance of longitudinal studies (Bentovim, vanElberg, &

Boston, 1988; Conte, 1991; Everson, Hunter, & Runyan, 1991; Friedrich & Reams, 1987; Gomes-Schwartz et al., 1990; Goodman et al., in press; Hewitt & Friedrich, 1991; Mannarino, Cohen, Smith, & Moore-Motily, 1991; Runyan, Everson, Edelson, Hunter, & Coulter, 1988; Valliere, Bybee, & Mowbray, 1988; Waterman, in press). Most of these studies have followed children for approximately 12–18 months, with a few ranging from 2 to 5 years (Bentovim et al., 1988; Waterman, in press). These studies allow a perspective on two important issues: (a) what is the course of symptomatology over time, and (b) what contributes to recovery?

The picture provided by the longitudinal studies is tentative, but some generalizations are possible. Overall, symptoms seemed to abate with time. The pattern of recovery was different for different symptoms, and some children actually appeared to worsen.

Abatement of symptoms

Abatement of symptoms has been demonstrated in at least seven longitudinal studies covering all age groups (Bentovim et al., 1988; Conte, 1991; Gomes-Schwartz et al., 1990; Goodman et al., in press; Hewitt & Friedrich, 1991; Mannarino et al., 1991; Runyan et al., 1988). For example, Gomes-Schwartz et al. (1990) noted substantial diminution of emotional distress in 55% of the victims (mixed age group) over 18 months. In Bentovim et al.'s (1988) study, social workers found improvement in the level of symptoms in 61% of the children. Hewitt and Friedrich (1991) noted that 65% of preschool-age children improved over a period of 1 year. About two thirds of even the ritualistically abused preschoolers, who were initially in the clinical range on the CBCL (Waterman, in press, had moved back into the normal range on follow-up).

Nonetheless, there was a sizable group – anywhere from 10% to 24% – of children who appeared to get worse (Bentovim et al., 1988 (10%); Gomes-Schwartz et al., 1990 (24%); Hewitt and Friedrich, 1991 (18%); Runyan et al., 1988 (14%). Some of these were children who had none of the symptoms measured at the time of initial assessment (Gomes-Schwartz et al., 1990).

Some investigators also noted a pattern in which symptoms tended · to abate. Gomes-Schwartz et al. (1990) found that signs of anxiety (e.g., sleep problems or fear of the offender) were most likely to disappear, whereas signs of aggressiveness (e.g., fighting with siblings) tended to persist or worsen. This was consistent with Mannarino et al.'s (1991) finding of a significant reduction over time in the internalizing but not the externalizing scales of the CBCL. Conversely, some symptoms may increase over time. For example, one symptom that may increase over time, at least for the under-12 group, is sexual preoccupations (Friedrich and Reams, 1987; Gomes-Schwartz et al., 1990). It is not entirely clear what this symptom abatement implies. Although some symptoms may be more transient than others, it does not necessarily mean that underlying trauma is resolved, but perhaps only that overt manifestations are more easily masked. Moreover, these changes may have less to do with abatement of trauma than developmental changes in symptomatology, with children at each age manifesting different types of symptoms.

There is a long list of correlates of improvement over time, but few of these findings have been demonstrated in more than one study. Age was not found to be strongly correlated with recovery in any study, although Goodman et al. (in press) found that 6–11-year-olds recovered most quickly in the very short term (3 months after the trial). Neither gender (Gomes-Schwartz et al., 1990; Goodman et al., in press, nor race and socioeconomic status (Gomes-Schwartz et al., 1990) have been factors in recovery. Children who were the most disturbed at the time of first assessment were found to make the most recovery (Gomes-Schwartz et al., 1990), but this may have been an artifact.

Family and treatment variables

A key variable in recovery was family support, demonstrated by several studies. Children who had maternal support recovered more quickly (Everson et al., 1991; Goodman et al., in press). Maternal support was demonstrated through believing the child and acting in a protective way toward the child. Waterman (in press) found that the least symptomatic children (5 years after disclosure) were those whose mothers were most supportive and whose families had less strain, enmeshment, and expressions of anger.

Interestingly, the effect of long-term therapy has not been extensively examined. In one study (Gomes-Schwartz et al., 1990), all clients received crisis intervention through the research project. The clients who showed the greatest amount of recovery (15% of subjects) were those who received therapy in the specialized program run by the research team. Those who received therapy in the community at large

(20% of subjects) did not appear to recover as well. The authors did not elaborate on the type of long-term therapy that clients received either through the researchers' program or in the community at large, however. In contrast, Goodman et al. (in press) found psychological counseling unrelated to improvement. But again, clients sought therapy in the outside community and there was no control for the type or quality of the therapy they received.

Court involvement

The impact of court involvement and testimony was also a focus of several of the longitudinal studies because of the intense public policy debate surrounding this issue. In one study (Goodman et al., in press), children involved in court proceedings were slower to recover over both a 7- and an 11-month period than children not involved in court. Recovery was particularly impeded among children who had to testify on multiple occasions, who were afraid of their perpetrators, and who testified in cases in which there was no other corroborating evidence. Whitcomb et al.'s (1991) findings echoed Goodman et al.'s Whitcomb et al. concluded that there were adverse effects for older children who had to undergo numerous, lengthy, or harshly contested courtroom testimony. The outcome of the trial (conviction or acquittal of the perpetrator), or the number of times that the child was interviewed did not relate to symptomatology (Goodman et al. in press).

Runyan et al. (1988) had more mixed findings with regard to the impact of court involvement. The children who had slower recovery in this study were those who were involved in a criminal case that was still not resolved 5 months after the initial evaluation. However, children whose cases had terminated more quickly with a conviction or plea bargain recovered just as quickly as children who had no court involvement at all. In fact, children who testified in juvenile court proceedings recovered more quickly. However, in a follow-up of adolescents from the same study, Everson et al. (1991) found that having to testify on multiple occasions caused negative effects, concurring with the findings of Goodman et al. (in press).

Although the longitudinal studies showed the risks involved in testimony, at least one cross-sectional study (Williams, 1991) confirmed that testimony in protected court settings can mitigate trauma. In this study of victims abused in day care, children who testified via closed-circuit television or videotaped testimony or in closed courtrooms suffered fewer symptoms of maladjustment than did children who testified in open court.

Overall, this small number of studies suggests that criminal court involvement posed risks to children's recovery, at least in the short run. But the risks were specifically associated with certain aspects of court involvement that can be modified or avoided. For example, negative impact can be lessened by resolving cases quickly, by preventing a child from having to testify on multiple occasions, and by not requiring a frightened child to face a defendant. Thus, although the research urges caution, it cannot be interpreted as a categorical argument against the prosecution of sexual abuse.

Revictimization

Follow-up studies lend an important perspective to the question of whether abuse victims are reabused in the year or two after disclosure. Most of the follow-up studies we reviewed showed the rate of reabuse to be between 6% and 19% (Bentovim et al., 1988 (16%); Daro, 1988 (19%); Gomes-Schwartz et al., 1990 (6%)), with follow-up ranging from 18 months to 5 years. Daro (1988) pointed out that the reabuse rate for sexually abused children in her study was still substantially lower than the reabuse rate for victims of neglect or emotional abuse.

Summary

In summary, in the first year or year and a half after disclosure, one half to two thirds of all children became less symptomatic, whereas 10–24% become more so. Six to nineteen percent experienced additional sexual abuse. Fears and somatic symptoms abated the most quickly; aggressiveness and sexual preoccupations were the most likely to remain or increase. Children's recovery was clearly assisted by a supportive family environment, and certain kinds of court experiences delayed recovery.

Discussion

The present review confirms the general impression that the impact of sexual abuse is serious and can manifest itself in a wide variety of symptomatic and pathological behaviors. There is virtually no general domain of symptomatology that has not been associated with a history of sexual abuse. Age and a variety of abuse-related factors can affect both the nature and the severity of symptoms. However, some sexually abused children may also appear to have no apparent symptoms. Indeed, approximately one third of sexually abused children in the studies we reviewed fell into this category. These findings have a number of important implications for theory development.

Core-symptom theories

The first and perhaps most important implication is the apparent lack of evidence for a conspicuous syndrome in children who have been sexually abused. The evidence against such a syndrome includes the variety of symptoms children manifest and the absence of one particular symptom in a large majority of children. Despite the lack of a single symptom that occurs in the majority of victims, both sexualized behavior and symptoms of PTSD occurred with relatively high frequency. These also appeared to be the only two symptoms more common in sexually abused children than in other clinical groups. Even though they do not occur in all victims, some theorists have forwarded PTSD and sexualized behaviors as the core manifestations of sexual abuse trauma (Corwin, 1989; Jampole and Weber, 1987; Wolfe et al., 1989), so the evidence pertaining to these two symptoms is worth reviewing more carefully.

The frequency of sexualized behavior in sexually abused children (including frequent and overt self-stimulation; inappropriate sexual overtures toward other children and adults; and compulsive talk, play, and fantasy with sexual content) is somewhat difficult to determine. Although it is the most regularly studied symptom, its occurrence varies enormously. Across six studies of preschoolers (the children most likely to manifest such symptoms) an average of 35% exhibited sexualized behavior. Friedrich et al. (1992), using an instrument specially designed to measure such behaviors, detected a somewhat higher percentage. But across all sexually abused children it may be only half of all victims. The lowest estimate (7%) was based on a very large study, including many well-functioning and older children (Conte and Schuerman, 1987b). Besides sample and methodological differences, other variations may well arise because the concept itself can be vague (sometimes it is called inappropriate sexual behavior, and other times it is called sexual acting out). Furthermore, some forms of sexualization may be quite minor and transitory (e.g., playing with anatomical dolls), whereas others may be deeply etched, even affecting a child's physiology. Putnam (1990; F. Putnam, personal communication, January 10, 1991) detected elevated hormone levels among some sexually abused girls and evidence that onset of puberty was advanced for these girls by as much as 1 year. Although such physiological changes could be the effect of sexualization or, alternatively, one of its sources, it suggests how profound and pervasive the impact of sexual abuse can be.

Although sexualization is relatively specific to sexual abuse (more so than symptoms such as depression), nonsexually abused children may also be sexualized. For example, Deblinger, McLeer, Atkins, Ralphe, and Foa (1989) found that 17% of physically (but not sexually) abused children exhibited sexually inappropriate behavior. Although sexualized behavior may be the most characteristic symptom of sexual abuse, and the one that best discriminates between abused and nonabused children, as many as half of victims may not be overtly sexualized, and this symptom does not occur only in sexually abused children. From a clinical point of view, this symptom may indicate sexual abuse but is not completely diagnostic because children can apparently appear to be sexualized for other reasons.

The evidence for PTSD as a central effect of sexual abuse is also its relative frequency (particularly in preschool- and school-age victims) and its higher incidence in sexual abuse victims than in other clinical groups. Although PTSD is relatively common in child sexual abuse victims, it is not a universal reaction. In the two most thorough clinical evaluations of PTSD (according to criteria in the revised third edition of the *Diagnostic and Statistical Manual of Mental Disorders*; American Psychiatric Association, 1987), 48% (McLeer et al., 1988) and 21% (Deblinger et al., 1989) of sexually abused children could be diagnosed as having PTSD. Although many other children have related symptoms, such as fears, nightmares, somatic complaints, autonomic arousal, and guilt feelings, it is not clear whether this is evidence for PTSD dynamics or other symptoms. More importantly, PTSD is not specific to sexual abuse in that many nonsexually abused children suffer from PTSD.

PTSD has served as a focal point for the analysis of sexual abuse trauma in part because it is a well-developed, generalized theory of traumatic processes. Finkelhor (1987), however, has raised some questions about how well the model of PTSD accounts for sexual abuse trauma. Theorists describe PTSD as resulting from experiences that are overwhelming, sudden, and dangerous (Figley, 1986; Pynoos & Eth, 1985). Much sexual abuse, however, lacks these components, especially abuse that occurs through manipulation of the child's affections and misrepresentation of social standards. Thus, although many children may suffer symptoms that are explained by the PTSD model, the theory and the empirical findings do not support PTSD symptomatology as universal to sexual abuse or as the most characteristic pattern.

There is at least one other core-symptom theory about the effect of sexual abuse, one that argues that the central damage is to children's self-image (Bagley & Young, 1989; Putnam, 1990). According to this view, it is the damaged self-image, not the sexual abuse per se, that leads to other difficulties. If this theory were true, disturbed self-esteem should be one of the most consistent, pervasive, and long-lasting effects of sexual abuse. Unfortunately, although many victims do have low self-esteem, researchers (e.g., Mannarino et al., 1991) have had considerable difficulty demonstrating this phenomenon. It is not certain whether poor self-esteem, which has been assessed primarily through self-reports, has been effectively measured. But the evidence to date does little to support the theory that self-esteem is the core element of sexual abuse traumatization.

Multifaceted models of traumatization

Overall, the absence of one dominant and consistent set of symptoms argues against these core-domain theories. Rather, these data suggest that the impact of sexual abuse is more complicated because it produces multifaceted effects. Several conceptual models are consistent with such a pattern. Finkelhor and Browne's (1985) model suggests that sexual abuse traumatizes children through four distinctive types of mechanisms, which account for the variety of outcomes. The four mechanisms have been termed (a) traumatic sexualization, (b) betrayal, (c) stigmatization, and (d) powerlessness. Traumatic sexualization includes a variety of processes such as the inappropriate conditioning of the child's sexual responsiveness and the socialization of the child into faulty beliefs and assumptions about sexual behavior. Betrayal includes the shattering of the child's confidence that trusted persons are interested in and capable of protecting him or her from harm.

Stigmatization covers all the mechanisms that undermine the child's positive self-image: the shame that is instilled, the ostracism the child suffers, and the negative stereotypes that are acquired from the culture and immediate environment. Finally, powerlessness comprises PTSD-type mechanisms (intense fear of death or injury from an uncontrollable event) as well as the repeated frustration of not being able to stop or escape from the noxious experience or elicit help from others. These mechanisms are present to varying degrees and in different forms in different abuse scenarios.

In addition, Finkelhor and Browne (1985) propose that certain symptoms are more closely related to certain dynamics. The sexualization symptoms have an obvious connection to the traumatic sexualization processes, self-esteem is connected to stigmatization, and fears and PTSD are connected to powerlessness. Little research has been carried out to confirm the model in part because of its complexity, the variety of different mechanisms posited, and the difficulty of clearly delineating and measuring them.

Other theorists have also adopted a multiple-dynamics approach to account for the seeming variety of sexual abuse symptoms. Briere (1992) has developed such a model whose dynamics include (a) negative self-evaluation, (b) chronic perception of danger or injustice, (c) powerlessness and preoccupation with control, (d) dissociative control over awareness, (e) impaired self-reference, and (f) reduction of painful internal states.

A different model posits sexual abuse as simply a generalized stressor. Although this model has not been specifically developed, it is another way to understand the impact of sexual abuse. In this model, the child is likely to develop problems in whatever area he or she may have had a prior vulnerability. This model predicts a high degree of similarity between the effects of sexual abuse and the effects of other childhood stressors such as parental divorce. There is some evidence to support this view, particularly our finding in the present review of similarity on some symptoms between sexually abused children and other clinical groups. On the other hand, sexually abused children do tend to exhibit some characteristics (e.g., sexualized behaviors) that are much more common among sexually abused children than they are among other clinical groups. These types of effects argue against sexual abuse as merely a generalized stressor.

A third model posits family dysfunction or a general maltreating environment, not the sexually abusive activities per se, as the root of the trauma in most sexually abused children (Clausen & Crittenden, 1991). This model is supported by apparent similarities in the range and types of problems manifested by all abused children. However, certain evidence from the studies included in the present review argues against such a conceptualization. First, the studies showed that nonabused siblings (i.e., children raised in the same dysfunctional families) displayed fewer symptoms than did their abused siblings (Lipovsky, Saunders, & Murphy, 1989). In addition, the review of the 25 studies in which the influence of intervening variables was examined (table 2.5) consistently showed strong relationships between specific characteristics of the sexual abuse and the symptomatology in the children (e.g., Newberger, Gremy, & Waternaux, 1990). All of this argues for traumatic processes inherent in the sexual abuse itself that are independent from a generalized family dysfunction or generalized maltreating environment.

This is not to say that prior vulnerabilities, a maltreating environment, and family dysfunction do not contribute to traumatization as well. Research such as Conte and Schuerman's (1987a, 1987b) demonstrates that both abuse-related factors and family dysfunction contribute to children's trauma. And Conte and Schuerman found that over time, the abuse-related factors were less influential than the continuing family processes, such as the amount of family support for the child. This suggests a grand model of sexual abuse trauma that includes effects that are both more and less specific to sexual abuse and that arise from the abusive acts in particular, which also interact with prior vulnerabilities of the child, the health or toxicity of the family environment, and the social response to the discovery of abuse.

Summary

The research to date points to an array of traumatizing factors in sexual abuse, with sexualization and PTSD as frequent, but not universal, processes. The traumatic impact of the abusive acts themselves (e.g., their frequency and severity) has been established, as well as the likely contribution of other familial and environmental conditions. The role of disturbance to self-esteem and of a child's prior dispositions or vulnerabilities has not been as well substantiated.

This theoretical discussion has implications for clinicians as well as researchers. The range of symptoms, the lack of a single predominant symptom pattern, and the absence of symptoms in so many victims clearly suggest that diagnosis is complex. Because the effects of abuse can manifest themselves in too many ways, symptoms cannot be easily used, without other evidence, to confirm the presence of sexual abuse. Yet the absence of symptoms certainly cannot be used to rule out sexual abuse. There are too many sexually abused children who are apparently asymptomatic. This finding is especially important for those conducting forensic evaluations.

It may be possible, as Corwin (1989) has argued, to find a combination of symptoms that is extremely diagnostic of sexual abuse, especially in certain subgroups of victims (e.g., preschool children with certain kinds of sexualized behavior and post-traumatic play), and research toward such a screening device may be warranted. But the evidence suggests that such a device would identify only a small percentage of victims and that one could conclude nothing at all from the absence of such symptom patterns.

Although conclusions such as these are useful, we also think this discussion highlights a glaring inadequacy in the literature: a nearly universal absence of theoretical underpinnings in the studies being conducted on this subject to date. Researchers evince a great deal of concern about the effects of sexual abuse but disappointingly little concern about why the effects occur. Few studies are undertaken to establish or confirm any theory or explanation about what causes children to be symptomatic. Rather, most researchers simply document and count the existence of symptoms and some of their obvious correlates. This accounts for one of the main reasons that, in spite of numerous studies since Browne and Finkelhor's (1986) review, there have been few theoretical advances.

Future studies need to turn to the development and confirmation of theory. Those who believe that different mechanisms result in different symptoms need to begin to search for such mechanisms. For example, if dissociation is theorized as an acquired strategy for escaping from unpleasant emotions, then researchers need to document the presence of the cognitive, affective, and physiological underpinnings to this mechanism and relate it to the trauma itself. By contrast, those who see sexual abuse as a generalized stressor need to conduct studies that relate the effects of sexual abuse to pre-existing vulnerabilities in coping. The dialogue about variables that mediate the effects of abuse needs to be expanded and ideas forwarded about how to study and test their existence. This process of improving research might be assisted when the sexual abuse researchers join forces with those who study related symptomatology in nonabused children. This has already happened in the work generated by the importation of PTSD theory into the field, and it is only by further developing this cross-fertilization that advances can continue.

Methodological Issues and Directions for Future Research

Although the studies we reviewed signal an enormous improvement in methodology, they highlight many major areas where current designs could be improved or refined. Some more specific suggestions for improvement are offered in this section.

Improvement in measures of impact

The literature on effects has relied extensively on parent-completed checklists of children's symptomatology, particularly the CBCL. However, two sets of findings have raised concern about the validity of these measures. One shows that mothers' judgments about their children's symptoms are highly related to their own level of distress and willingness to believe their children (Everson, Hunter, Runyan, Edelsohn, & Coulter 1989; Newberger et al., 1990). A second shows a poor association between parents' and children's own reports (Cohen & Mannarino, 1988; Kelly & Ben-Meir, in press).

It does seem plausible that parents might be biased reporters, especially in the context of a family problem like sexual abuse, where parents can experience strong feelings of guilt or ambivalence about a child's disclosure. But other findings suggest that parent reports are nonetheless relatively valid and, in the context of currently used instruments, probably better than their children's reports. For example, although depressed mothers reported more child symptoms than nondepressed mothers on the CBCL, the assessments still differentiated disturbed and nondisturbed children when depression was statistically controlled (Friedlander, Weiss, & Taylor, 1986). Moreover, mothers' ratings tended to be more similar to and correlated better with therapists' and teachers' ratings than with those of their children (Shapiro, Leifer, Martone, & Kassem, 1990; Tong et al., 1987). It appears from several studies (Cohen & Mannarino, 1988; Shapiro et al., 1990) that children's self-reports minimize problems like depression or low self-esteem that are noted by parents and therapists. Why this is so is not clear.

One clear implication from this is that researchers should not rely on children's self-reports alone. Ideally, assessments should be obtained from multiple sources, as Waterman, Kelly, McCord, and Oliveri (in press) recently did. In addition, research needs to be undertaken to improve the validity of parent reports and especially, if possible, children's self-assessments.

A second concern, raised in part by the issue of seemingly asymptomatic children, is whether the instruments currently being used are sensitive enough to measure consistently and accurately the trauma of sexual abuse. Several groups of researchers, recognizing particularly the limitations of the CBCL, have branched out in attempts to develop such sensitive measures. Friedrich et al. (1992) have greatly expanded CBCL symptom items in the domain of sexuality. Lanktree and Briere (1991, 1992) have adapted the Trauma Symptom Checklist, highly successful in differentiating sexually abused adults, for use with children. Wolfe et al. (1989) have developed scales to measure more sensitively PTSD-type symptomatology. Such efforts need to be continued and elaborated.

Greater differentiation by age and gender

Many researchers have studied subjects from very broad age ranges (e.g., 3–18 years) and grouped them together to discuss symptoms. Similarly, they have grouped boys and girls together. As shown in table 2.4, this grouping together of all ages can mask particular developmental patterns of the occurrence of some symptoms. At a minimum, future researchers should divide children into preschool, school, and adolescent age ranges when reporting the percentages of victims with symptoms. It would be better to provide even more detail on how age at assessment affects the manifestation of symptoms, by looking at smaller age ranges and typing this information into theory about children's social, emotional, and cognitive development during these difficult developmental periods. A parallel effort is needed with regard to gender.

Expanded analysis of intervening variables

The present review confirms that abuse-related variables are associated with outcome and thus should be regularly included in analyses. However, many other factors probably are influential as well, and more emphasis should be placed on understanding their role. These factors include children's intelligence, coping skills, prior adjustment, and cognitive interpretation of the abuse. It also includes children's family and social environment, as well as the actions taken by professionals in response to their disclosures. Another factor that needs to be regularly taken into account is time elapsed since the end of the abuse. In some samples, several years might have elapsed between the end of the abuse and the assessment of the child, and during this time symptoms may have abated.

Longitudinal research and developmental theory

A developmental perspective is one approach that may encourage more theory-driven research. Researchers using a developmental approach may also respond to some of the methodological issues raised here. Current research has tended to focus on assessments of trauma at a specific age or point in time (a snapshot approach), but it would also be helpful to know more about the course of symptomatology and recovery over time. For example, the symptomatology of a 15-year-old molested at age 4 may be different from that of a 15-year-old molested at age 14. Furthermore, symptoms may tend to recur at different developmental stages and asymptomatic children may later become symptomatic. Studies in which data are collected at more than one time point will encourage this developmental approach for studying sexual abuse and may answer many of our questions (see Baltes, 1987; Starr, MacLean, & Keating, 1991). Even in the absence of funding, any research on outcomes should at least pave the way for possible later follow-up by gaining permission to recontact subjects and by recording data that will facilitate such research in the future.

In addition to studying abuse at multiple time points, developmental research means incorporating the multiple dimensions of children's development. Changes occur in children's behaviors, thoughts, and emotions at every developmental stage. Research on the effects of sexual abuse on children tends to focus predominantly on behavioral and emotional symptoms while ignoring the effects of sexual abuse on cognitive and social development.

A number of research questions can be generated by examining sexual abuse within the multiple dimensions of children's development. For example, cognitive development could influence children's interpretations of sexual abuse and the symptoms they subsequently manifest. Specifically, as children mature, their thinking becomes less egocentric. This issue alone generates several possible research questions. For example, are young children more likely to see themselves as responsible for the abuse ("It happened because I was bad") than are less egocentric older children? Furthermore, are children who see themselves as responsible for the abuse more likely to engage in self-abusive or destructive behavior? How do internal attributions affect children's reactions to prosecution of the perpetrator? Are these attributions more likely to increase the children's sense of guilt when the perpetrator is punished?

Along these same lines, children's cognitive development can influence their emotional and social development and their interpretation of the perpetrators' actions. As thinking becomes decentered, children recognize that people can have both positive and negative traits and that they themselves can have both positive and negative feelings toward others. How does the gradual attainment of decentered thinking affect children's interpretations of the perpetrators' actions, their own behaviors, and the abuse itself? This is especially important to understand when the perpetrator is someone whom the child loves and trusts. Are children who can see conflicting traits in others more likely to report abuse because they see it as only one part of their relationship with the perpetrator ("I love him but I want the abuse to stop")?

These are but a few of the types of research questions that can be generated from examining abuse from a developmental and multidimensional perspective. Future researchers could make specific predictions based on developmental theory and clinical research on related topics (e.g., children's reactions to other types of childhood traumas). This type of framework would also allow researchers to incorporate information about intervening variables such as the timing and duration of the abuse and the identity of the perpetrator.

In summary, studies conducted with a developmental and multidimensional framework could readily incorporate the many intervening variables that modify the effects of abuse. In addition, such a framework offers a richer description of why children and adults manifest certain symptoms at each developmental stage and how people cope with psychic trauma. Developmental psychologists and child clinicians could collaborate to develop models of how children at each developmental stage might be affected by their abuse experience. Researchers studying child sexual abuse have looked in isolation at many of the factors related to the impact of abuse. Now it is time for us to combine them into more realistic models. Research of this type would provide helpful theoretical information about the mechanism and processing of psychological trauma in general. It would also provide guidelines on where clinicians can effectively intervene to aid children in their healing process.

Notes

1   Note that when we refer to victims, we mean victims who have come to public attention. The findings from the present review cannot be generalized to unreported victims, for whom impact may be substantially different. In a controversial study of unreported victims from The Netherlands, Sandfort (1982, 1984) claimed that certain (primarily adolescent) boys had relationships with adult pedophiles that they described in positive terms and appeared to have no negative effects. Because these boys were nominated for the research by the pedophiles themselves, who were involved in a pedophile advocacy group, it is difficult to know to what group of children such findings could be generalized.
2   In this article, we group post-traumatic stress disorder with symptoms even though we realize that it is a cluster of symptoms comprising a diagnostic category.
3   Internalizing and externalizing are composite symptoms found on the Child Behavior Checklist (Achenbach & Edelbrock, 1984). Internalizing is withdrawn behavior, depression, fearfulness, inhibition, and overcontrol. Externalizing includes aggression and antisocial and undercontrolled behavior.
4   The criteria for including a study in this review were as follows: the authors reported an exact t value or an F value from a univariate analysis of variance, they reported the degrees of freedom, and there was only one degree of freedom in the numerator. Eta allowed us to examine the effects of sexual abuse apart from sample size and therefore provided a standard coefficient by which to compare findings (Rosenthal, 1984). In addition, because eta

is comparable to a Pearson *r*, it provided an index of the strength of the relationship between sexual abuse status and manifestation of a symptom. Eta squared indicated how much of the variance was accounted for by the child's sexual abuse status. One needs to be cautious when interpreting results based on a small number of studies and widely ranging effect sizes. Unfortunately, very few investigators have reported results that are amenable to effect size calculations.

References

Achenbach, T. M., & Edelbrock, C. S. (1984). *Child behavior checklist.* Burlington VT: University of Vermont.

Adams-Tucker, C. (1982). Proximate effects of sexual abuse in childhood: A report on 28 children. *American Journal of Psychiatry, 139,* 1252–6.

American Psychiatric Association (1987). *Diagnostic and statistical manual of mental disorders* (3rd edn. rev.). Washington, DC: Author.

Bagley, C., & Young, L. (1989). Depression, self-esteem, and suicidal behavior as sequels of sexual abuse in childhood: Research and therapy. In M. Rothery & G. Cameron (eds.), *Child maltreatment: Expanding our concept of healing* (pp. 183–209). Hillsdale, NJ: Erlbaum.

Baltes, P. B. (1987). Theoretical propositions of live-span developmental psychology: On the dynamics between growth and decline. *Developmental Psychology, 23,* 611–26.

Basta, S. M., & Peterson, R. F. (1990). Perpetrator status and the personality characteristics of molested children. *Child Abuse and Neglect, 14,* 555–66.

Beitchman, J. H., Zucker, K. J., Hood, J. E., daCosta, G. A., & Akman, D. (1991). A review of the short-term effects of child sexual abuse. *Child Abuse and Neglect, 15,* 537–56.

Beitchman, J. H., Zucker, K. J., Hood, J. E., daCosta, G. A., Akman, D., & Cassavia, E. (1992). A review of the long-term effects of child sexual abuse. *Child Abuse and Neglect, 16,* 101–18.

Bentovim, A., vanElberg, A., & Boston, P. (1988). The results of treatment. In A. Bentovim, A. Elton, J. Hildebrand, M. Tranter, & E. Vizard (eds.), *Child sexual abuse within the family: Assessment and treatment* (pp. 252–68). London: Wright.

Berliner, L. (1991). The effects of sexual abuse on children. *Violence Update, 1,* 1–10.

Briere, J. (1992). *Child abuse trauma: Theory and treatment of the lasting effects.* Newbury Park, CA: Sage.

Briere, J., & Conte, J. (1989, August). *Amnesia in adults molested as children:*

Testing theories of repression. Paper presented at the 97th Annual Convention of the American Psychological Association, New Orleans, LA.

Browne, A., & Finkelhor, D. (1986). The impact of child sexual abuse: A review of the research. *Psychological Bulletin, 99,* 66–77.

Burgess, A., Hartman, C., McCausland, M., & Powers, P. (1984). Response patterns in children and adolescents exploited through sex rings and pornography. *American Journal of Psychiatry, 141,* 656–62.

Burns, N., Williams. L. M., & Finkelhor, D. (1988). Victim impact. In D. Finkelhor, L. M. Williams, & N. Burns (eds.), *Nursery crimes: Sexual abuse in daycare* (pp. 114–37). Newbury Park, CA: Sage.

Caffaro-Rouget, A., Lang, R. A., & vanSanten, V. (1989). The impact of child sexual abuse. *Annals of Sex Research, 2,* 29–47.

Clausen, A. H., & Crittenden, P. M. (1991). Physical and psychological maltreatment: Relations among types of maltreatment. *Child Abuse and Neglect, 15,* 5–18.

Cohen, J. A., & Mannarino, A. P. (1988). Psychological symptoms in sexually abused girls. *Child Abuse and Neglect, 12,* 571–7.

Conte, J. R. (1991). *Behavior of sexually abused children at intake/disclosure and 12 months later.* Unpublished manuscript.

Conte, J., & Schuerman, J. (1987a). Factors associated with an increased impact of child sexual abuse. *Child Abuse and Neglect, 11,* 201–11.

Conte, J., & Schuerman, J. (1987b). The effects of sexual abuse on children: A multidimensional view. *Journal of Interpersonal Violence, 2,* 380–90.

Corwin, D. L. (1989). Early diagnosis of child sexual abuse: Diminishing the lasting effects. In G. E. Wyatt & G. J. Powell (eds.), *Lasting effects of child sexual abuse* (pp. 251–70). Newbury Park, CA: Sage.

Daro, D. (1988). *Confronting child abuse: Research for effective program design.* New York: Free Press.

Deblinger, E., McLeer, S. V., Atkins, M. S., Ralphe, D., & Foa, E. (1989). Posttraumatic stress in sexually abused, physically abused, and nonabused children. *Child Abuse and Neglect, 13,* 403–8.

Einbender, A. J., & Friedrich, W. N. (1989). Psychological functioning and behavior of sexually abused girls. *Journal of Consulting and Clinical Psychology, 57,* 155–7.

Elwell, M. E., & Ephross, P. H. (1987). Initial reactions of sexually abused children. *Social Casework, 68,* 109–16.

Erickson, M. F. (1986, August). *Young sexually abused children: Socio-emotional development and family interaction.* Paper presented at the 94th Annual Convention of the American Psychological Association, Washington, DC.

Everson, M. D., Hunter, W. M., & Runyan, D. K. (1991, January). *Adolescent adjustment after incest: Who fares poorly?* Paper presented at the San Diego Conference on Responding to Child Maltreatment, San Diego, CA.

Everson, M. D., Hunter, W. M., Runyan, D. K., Edelsohn, G. A., & Coulter, M. L. (1989). Maternal support following disclosure of incest. *American Journal of Orthopsychiatry, 59,* 197–207.

Feltman, R. I. (1985). *A controlled correlational study of the psychological functioning of female paternal incest victims.* Unpublished doctoral dissertation.

Figley, C. R. (1986). *Trauma and its wake: Vol. II. Traumatic stress theory, research, and intervention.* New York: Brunner/Mazel.

Finkelhor, D. (1987). The trauma of child sexual abuse: Two models. *Journal of Interpersonal Violence, 2,* 348–66.

Finkelhor, D., & Browne, A. (1985). The traumatic impact of child sexual abuse: A conceptualization. *American Journal of Orthopsychiatry, 55,* 530–41.

Finkelhor, D., Hotaling, G., Lewis, I. A., & Smith, C. (1990). Sexual abuse in a national study of adult men and women: Prevalence, characteristics, and risk factors. *Child Abuse and Neglect, 14,* 19–28.

Friedlander, S., Weiss, D. S., & Taylor, J. (1986). Assessing the influence of maternal depression on the validity of the Child Behavior Checklist. *Journal of Abnormal Child Psychology, 14,* 123–33.

Friedrich, W., Beilke, R., & Urquiza, A. (1987). Children from sexually abusive families: A behavioral comparison. *Journal of Interpersonal Violence, 2,* 391–402.

Friedrich, W. N., Beilke, R. L., & Urquiza, A. J. (1988). Behavior problems in young sexually abused boys. *Journal of Interpersonal Violence, 3,* 21–8.

Friedrich, W. N., Grambasch, P., Damon, L., Hewitt, S. K., Koverola, C., Lang, R., & Wolfe, V. (1992). The Child Sexual Behavior Inventory: Normative and clinical comparisons. *Psychological Assessment, 4,* 303–11.

Friedrich, W. N., & Luecke, W. J. (1988). Young school-age sexually aggressive children. *Professional Psychology: Research and Practice, 19,* 155–64.

Friedrich, W. N., & Reams, R. A. (1987). Course of psychological symptoms in sexually abused young children. *Psychotherapy, 24,* 160–70.

Friedrich, W. N., Urquiza, A. J., & Beilke, R. L. (1986). Behavior problems in sexually abused young children. *Journal of Pediatric Psychology, 11,* 47–57.

Gale, J., Thompson, R. J., Moran, T., & Sack, W. H. (1988). Sexual abuse in young children: Its clinical presentation and characteristic patterns. *Child Abuse and Neglect, 12,* 163–70.

Gomes-Schwartz, B., Horowitz, J. M., Cardarelli, A. P., & Sauzier, M. (1990). The aftermath of child sexual abuse: 18 months later. In B. Gomes-Schwartz, J. M. Horowitz, & A. P. Cardarelli (eds.), *Child sexual abuse: The initial effects.* (pp. 132–52). Newbury Park, CA: Sage.

Gomes-Schwartz, B., Horowitz, J. M., & Sauzier, M. (1985). Severity of emotional distress among sexually abused preschool, school-age, and adolescent children. *Hospital and Community Psychiatry, 36*, 503–8.

Goodman, G. S., Taub, E. P., Jones, D. P. H., England, P., Port, L. K., Rudy, L., & Prado. L. (in press). Emotional effects of criminal court testimony on child sexual assault victims. *Monographs of the Society for Research in Child Development.* Chicago: University of Chicago.

Hewitt, S. K., & Friedrich, W. N. (1991, January). *Preschool children's responses to alleged sexual abuse at intake and one-year follow up.* Paper presented at the meeting of the American Professional Society on the Abuse of Children, San Diego, CA.

Jampole, L., & Weber, M. K. (1987). An assessment of the behavior of sexually abused and nonsexually abused children with anatomically correct dolls. *Child Abuse and Neglect, 11*, 187–92.

Kelley, S. J. (1989). Stress responses of children to sexual abuse and ritualistic abuse in day care centers. *Journal of Interpersonal Violence, 4*, 502–13.

Kelly, R. J. (in press-a). Overall level of distress. In J. Waterman, R. J. Kelly, J. McCord, & M. K. Oliveri (eds.), *Behind the playground walls: Sexual abuse in preschools.* New York: Guilford Press.

Kelly, R. J. (in press-b). Effects on sexuality. In J. Waterman, R. J. Kelly, J. McCord, & M. K. Oliveri (eds.), *Behind the playground walls: Sexual abuse in preschools.* New York: Guilford Press.

Kelly, R. J., & Ben-Meir, S. (in press). Emotional effects. In J. Waterman, R. J. Kelly, J. McCord, & M. K. Oliveri (eds.), *Behind the playground walls: Sexual abuse in preschools.* New York: Guilford Press.

Kendall-Tackett, K. A. (1991). Characteristics of abuse that influence when adults molested as children seek treatment. *Journal of Interpersonal Violence, 6*, 486–93.

Kolko, D. J., Moser, J. T., & Weldy, S. R. (1988). Behavioral/emotional indicators of sexual abuse in child psychiatric inpatients: A controlled comparison with physical abuse. *Child Abuse and Neglect, 12*, 529–41.

Lanktree, C., & Briere, J. (1991, January). *Early data on the Trauma Symptom Checklist for Children (TSC-C).* Paper presented at the meeting of the American Professional Society on the Abuse of Children, San Diego, CA.

Lanktree, C., & Briere, J. (1992, January). *Further data on the Trauma Symptom Checklist for Children (TSC-C): Reliability, validity, and sensitivity to treatment.* Paper presented at the San Diego Conference on Responding to Child Maltreatment, San Diego, CA.

Lindberg, F., & Distad, L. (1985). Survival responses to incest: Adolescents in crisis. *Child Abuse and Neglect, 9*, 521–6.

Lipovsky, J. A., Saunders, B. E., & Murphy, S. M. (1989). Depression, anxiety, and behavior problems among victims of father–child sexual assault and nonabused siblings. *Journal of Interpersonal Violence, 4,* 452–68.

Lusk, R. (in press). Cognitive and school-related effects. In J. Waterman, R. J. Kelly, J. McCord, & M. K. Oliveri (eds.), *Behind the playground walls: Sexual abuse in preschools.* New York: Guilford Press.

Mannarino, A. P., & Cohen, J. A. (1986). A clinical-demographic study of sexually abused children. *Child Abuse and Neglect, 10,* 17–23.

Mannarino, A. P., Cohen, J. A., & Gregor, M. (1989). Emotional and behavioral difficulties in sexually abused girls. *Journal of Interpersonal Violence, 4,* 437–51.

Mannarino, A. P., Cohen, J. A., Smith, J. A., & Moore-Motily, S. (1991). Six and twelve month follow-up of sexually abused girls. *Journal of Interpersonal Violence, 6,* 494–511.

McGrath, E., Keita, G. P., Strickland, B. R., & Russo, N. F. (1990). *Women and depression: Risk factors and treatment issues.* Washington, DC: American Psychological Association.

McLeer, S. V., Deblinger, E., Atkins, M. S., Foa, E. B., & Ralphe, D. L. (1988). Post-traumatic stress disorder in sexually abused children. *Journal of the American Academy of Child and Adolescent Psychiatry, 27,* 650–4.

Mian, M., Wehrspann, W., Klajner-Diamond, H., LeBaron, D., & Winder, C. (1986). Review of 125 children 6 years of age and under who were sexually abused. *Child Abuse and Neglect, 10,* 223–9.

Morrow, K. B., & Sorell, G. T. (1989). Factors affecting self-esteem, depression, and negative behaviors in sexually abused female adolescents. *Journal of Marriage and the Family, 51,* 677–86.

Newberger, C. M., Gremy, I., & Waternaux, C. (1990). *Mothers and children following sexual abuse disclosure: Connections, boundaries, and the expression of symptomatology.* Unpublished manuscript, Children's Hospital, Boston, MA.

Orr, D. P., & Downes, M. C. (1985). Self-concept of adolescent sexual abuse victims. *Journal of Youth and Adolescence, 14,* 401–10.

Putnam, F. W. (1990). Disturbances of "self" in victims of childhood sexual abuse. In R. Kluft (ed.), *Incest-related syndromes of adult psychopathology* (pp. 113–31). Washington, DC: American Psychiatric Press.

Pynoos, R. S., & Eth, S. (1985). Children traumatized by witnessing acts of personal violence: Homicide, rape, or suicide behavior. In S. Eth & R. S. Pynoos (eds.), *Post-traumatic stress disorder in children* (pp. 19–43). Washington, DC: American Psychiatric Press.

Rimsza, M. E., Berg, R. A., & Locke, C. (1988). Sexual abuse: Somatic and emotional reactions. *Child Abuse and Neglect, 12,* 201–8.

Rosenthal, R. (1984). *Meta-analytic procedures for social research.* Newbury Park, CA: Sage.

Runyan, D. K., Everson, M. D., Edelsohn, G. A., Hunter, W. M., & Coulter, M. L. (1988). Impact of legal intervention on sexually abused children. *Journal of Pediatrics, 113*, 647–53.

Sandfort, T. (1982). *The sexual aspects of pedophile relations.* Amsterdam: Pan/Spartacus.

Sandfort, T. (1984). Sex in pedophiliac relationships: An empirical investigation among a nonrepresentative group of boys. *Journal of Sex Research, 20,* 123–42.

Shapiro, J. P., Leifer, M., Martone, M. W., & Kassem, L. (1990). Multi-method assessment of depression in sexually abused girls. *Journal of Personality Assessment, 55,* 234–48.

Sirles, E. A., Smith, J. A., & Kusama, H. (1989). Psychiatric status of intrafamilial child sexual abuse victims. *Journal of the American Academy of Child and Adolescent Psychiatry, 28,* 225–9.

Starr, R. H., MacLean, D. J., & Keating, D. P. (1991). Life-span development outcomes of child maltreatment. In R. H. Starr & D. A. Wolfe (eds.), *The effects of child abuse and neglect: Issues and research* (pp. 1–32). New York: Guilford Press.

Tong, L., Oates, K., & McDowell, M. (1987). Personality development following sexual abuse. *Child Abuse and Neglect, 11,* 371–83.

Valliere, P. M., Bybee, D., & Mowbray, C. T. (1988, April). *Using the Achenbach Child Behavior Checklist in child sexual abuse research: Longitudinal and comparative analysis.* Paper presented at the National Symposium on Child Victimization, Anaheim, CA.

Waterman, J. (in press). Mediators of effects on children: What enhances optimal functioning and promotes healing? In J. Waterman, R. J. Kelly, J. McCord, & M. K. Oliveri (eds.), *Behind the playground walls: Sexual abuse in preschools.* New York: Guilford Press.

Waterman, J., Kelly, R. J., McCord, J., & Oliveri, M. K. (in press). *Behind the playground walls: Sexual abuse in preschools.* New York: Guilford Press.

Whitcomb, D., Runyan, D. K., DeVos, E., Hunter, W. M., Cross, T. P., Everson, M. D., Peeler, N. A., Porter, C. A., Toth, P. A., & Cropper, C. (1991). *Child victim as witness research and developmental program* (Final report to the Office of Juvenile Justice and Delinquency Prevention, Office of Justice Programs, US Department of Justice). Washington, DC: US Government Printing Office.

White, S., Halpin, B. M., Strom, G. A., & Santilli, G. (1988). Behavioral comparisons of young sexually abused, neglected, and nonreferred children. *Journal of Clinical Child Psychology, 17,* 53–61.

White, S., Strom, G. A., Santilli, G., & Halpin, B. (1986). Interviewing young sexual abuse victims with anatomically correct dolls. *Child Abuse and Neglect, 10,* 519–29.

Williams, L. (1991). *The impact of court testimony on young children: Use of protective strategies in day care cases.* Unpublished manuscript, Family Research Laboratory, University of New Hampshire.

Wolfe, V. V., Gentile, C., & Wolfe, D. A. (1989). The impact of sexual abuse on children: A PTSD formulation. *Behavior Therapy, 20,* 215–28.

Zivney, O. A., Nash, M. R., & Hulsey, T. L. (1988). Sexual abuse in early versus late childhood: Differing patterns of pathology as revealed on the Rorschach. *Psychotherapy, 25,* 99–106.

Appendix
Studies of the effects of sexual abuse on children

Author	Victims			Comparison children		
	Age	N	Source	Age	N	Source
Adams-Tucker (1982)	2–16	28	SAT I/E	—	—	—
Basta & Peterson (1990)	6–10	32	I/E	6–10	16	NA – community
Bentovim & Boston (1988); Bentovim, van Elberg, & Boston (1988)	2–16	411	SAT I/E	2–16	362	NA siblings
Burgess, Hartman, McCausland, & Powers (1984)	6–16	46	SAT E[a]	—	—	—
Burns, Williams, & Finkelhor (1988)	2–5	87	SAT/day care/E	—	—	—
Caffaro-Rouget, Lang, & van Santen (1989)	1–18	240	SAT I/E	2–18	113	NA – community
Cohen & Mannarino (1988)	6–12	24	SAT I/E	—	—	—
Conte & Schuerman (1987a, 1987b)	4–17	369	SAT I/E	4–17	318	NA – community
Deblinger, McLeer, Atkins, Ralphe, & Foa (1989)	3–13	29	Inpatient treatment I/E	3–13 3–13	29 29	Physically abused – inpatient treatment NA – inpatient treatment

Appendix Continued

Author	Victims			Comparison children		
	Age	N	Source	Age	N	Source
inbender & Friedrich (1989)	6–14	46	SAT I/E	6–14	46	NA – community
Elwell & Ephross (1987)	5–12	20	SAT I/E	—	—	—
Erickson (1986)	4–6	11	High-risk infant follow-up	4–6	67	NA – same group
Everson, Hunter, & Runyan (1991)	11–17	44	SAT I/E	—	—	—
Everson, Hunter, Runyan, Edelsohn, & Coulter (1989)	6–17	88	SAT I/E	—	—	—
Feltman (1985)	10–17	31	SAT I	10–17	24	NA – outpatient treatment
Friedrich, Beilke, & Urquiza (1987)	3–12	93	SAT I/E	3–12	64	NA – outpatient treatment
					78	NA – community
Friedrich, Beilke, & Urquiza (1988)	3–8	33	SAT I/E	—	—	—
Friedrich & Luecke (1988)	4–11	22	SAT I/E[b]	—	—	—
Friedrich & Reams (1987)	5–13	22	SAT I/E[c]	—	—	—
	3–7	8	SAT I/E	—	—	—

Study	Age	N	Measure/Abuse	Norms (Age)	N	Comparison group
Friedrich, Urquiza, & Beilke (1986)	3–12	85	SAT I/E	—	—	—
Gale, Thompson, Moran, & Sack (1988)	<7	37	SAT I/E	<7	35 13	NA – outpatient treatment Physically abused – outpatient treatment
Gomes-Schwartz, Horowitz, & Sauzier (1985); Gomes-Schwartz, Horowitz, Cardarelli, & Sauzier (1990)	4–18	113	SAT I/E	Clinical and nonclinical norms		
Jampole & Weber (1987)	3–8	10	SAT/NR	3–8	10	NA – community
Kelley (1989)	4–11	32 35	Day care Ritualistically abused in day care/E	4–11	67	NA – day care
Kelly (in press-a, in press-b); Kelly & Ben-Meir (in press); Lusk (in press)	4–14 15	69	Ritualistically abused in day care/SA/E	5–14	32	NA – day care
Kolko, Moser, & Weldy (1988)	5–14	7 22	SA/inpatient treatment/I/E SA and physically abused	5–14 5–14	44 30	NA – inpatient treatment Physically abused – inpatient treatment
Lindberg & Distad (1985)	12–18	27	Children's home/I	—	—	—
Lipovsky, Saunders, & Murphy (1989)	M = 12.2	100	SAT I	M = 12.3	100	NA siblings

Appendix Continued

Author	Victims			Comparison children		
	Age	N	Source	Age	N	Source
Mannarino & Cohen (1986)	3–16	45	SAT I/E	—	—	—
Mannarino, Cohen, & Gregor (1989)	6–12	94	SAT I/E	6–12	89	NA – outpatient treatment
					75	NA – community
McLeer, Deblinger, Atkins, Foa, & Ralphe (1988)	3–16	31	SAT I/E	—	—	—
Mian, Wehrspann, Klajner-Diamond, LeBaron, & Winder (1986)	<6	125	Chart review I/E	—	—	—
Morrow & Sorell (1989)	12–18	101	SAT I	—	—	—
Newberger, Gremy, & Waternaux (1990)	6–12	49	SAT I	—	—	—
Orr & Downes (1985)	9–15	20	SAT I/E	9–15	20	NA – emergency room pop
Rimsza, Berg, & Locke (1988)	2–17	72	SAT I/E/chart review	2–17	72	NA – clinic/chart review
Runyan, Everson, Edelsohn, Hunter, & Coulter (1988)	6–17	75	SAT I/E	—	—	—

Study	n	Type	Age	n	Age	Setting
Shapiro, Leifer, Martone, & Kassem (1990)	53	SAT I/E	5–16	70	3–16	NA – outpatient treatment
Sirles, Smith, & Kusama (1989)	207	SAT I/E	2–17	—	—	—
Tong, Oates, & McDowell (1987)	49	SAT I/E	3–16	49	3–16	NA – community
Valliere, Bybee, & Mowbray (1988)	34	Day care/E	4–13	136	5–11	NA – community Norms
White, Halpin, Strom, & Santilli (1988)	17	SAT/NR	2–6	23/18	2–6	NA – community/neglect
White, Strom, Santilli, & Halpin (1986)	25	SAT/NR	2–6	25	2–6	NA – community
Wolfe, Gentile, & Wolfe (1989)	71	SAT I/E	5–16	—	—	—
Zivney, Nash, & Hulsey (1988)	80	SAT I/E	3–16	70	3–16	NA – outpatient treatment

SAT = sexual abuse treatment or evaluation (outpatient unless indicated), I = intrafamilial abuse, E = extrafamilial abuse, NR = data not reported. SA = sexually abused, pop = population.

[a] Children in sex rings.
[b] Sexually aggressive victims.
[c] Nonsexually aggressive victims.

THREE

Child Maltreatment Rates

Introduction

The seminal 1995 paper by Claudia Coulton and her colleagues (see 'Suggested reading', below) reviews factors which may be associated with child maltreatment rates. In the summary of this article, especially written for this book, Beth Paterson notes that this pioneering study found that child maltreatment rates were significantly associated with aspects of impoverishment (such as poverty, unemployment, population loss) and of child-care burden (such as higher ratio of children to adults, lower proportion of elderly in the population). If we are to achieve a reduction in child maltreatment rates we will need to address such factors.

Suggested reading

Coulton, C., Korbin, J., Su, M., & Chaw, J. (1995). Community-level factors and child maltreatment rates. *Child Development*, 66, 1262–76 (summary).

Community-Level Factors and Child Maltreatment Rates

A Summary by Beth Paterson (University of Portsmouth) of a 1995 Article on Child Development

The article by Coulton, Korbin, Su, and Chaw (1995) presents a study designed to explore the influence of structural factors in the community that appear to be related to the varying rates of child maltreatment across communities.

The authors summarize the changes over the last two decades that have led to poor urban communities experiencing worsening conditions. Higher levels of unemployment and poverty as a result of industrial restructuring, racial segregation, and out-migration of two-parent and working families are highlighted as major factors to have contributed to the downward trend in these poorer communities. Over this same period of time reported rates of child maltreatment have risen dramatically. Although this rise in maltreatment is partially explained by increased public awareness and mandatory reporting laws, the authors remark that the concurrent rise in levels of poverty and levels of child maltreatment has increased interest in understanding the intricacies of this association.

The authors note that research on the ecology of child maltreatment has largely examined characteristics of individual maltreating families and has placed less emphasis on the significance of social and neighbourhood conditions that are common to these families. In contrast, a smaller branch of research has specifically highlighted factors of the community that appear to be related to increased levels of child maltreatment. This research has found that communities associated with high levels of child maltreatment are characterized by social impoverishment (Garbarino & Crouter, 1978; Garbarino & Sherman, 1980), lack of social coherence (Garbarino & Kostelny, 1992), low income, high rates of vacant housing (Zuravin, 1989), and high levels of unemployment (Steinberg, Castalano, & Dooley, 1981).

The authors of this article conducted a study designed to explicitly explore a number of these community-level factors and their relationships with rates of child maltreatment. The authors propose a framework for their study based on the theory of *Community Social Organization* (patterns and functions of formal and informal networks and institutions and organizations in a community). Research has shown high levels of community social organization to be associated with networks that are able to exert social control from within the community to promote prosocial behaviour and to successfully deter socially deviant behaviour (Sampson & Groves, 1989). Poverty, amongst other associated negative structural changes in economic status and family structure, has been shown to be related to lower levels of community social control and social organization (Bursik & Grasmick, 1993). The authors propose that for neighbourhoods where such negative structural changes have occurred the subsequent breakdown of levels in community social organization has led to increased levels of child maltreatment and other socially deviant behaviour (for example juvenile delinquency).

Methodology

The authors explore this concept with a cross-sectional study using (a) 177 urban census tracts in Cleveland, Ohio, with each census tract having an average of 2,000 residents, and (b) administrative agency data detailing reported child maltreatment rates for each census tract. In order to gauge the structural conditions associated with the level of community social organization of each census tract the authors chose a set of empirical indicators that characterized (i) economic status; (ii) population movement; (iii) age, gender and family structure of area; (iv) racial composition; and (v) geographical location (proximity of neighbourhood to other areas of poverty concentration). The authors further propose that the same structural conditions that influence the neglect and abuse of children would also influence other negative social conditions such as violent crime, drug trafficking, juvenile delinquency, and teen childbearing. They therefore collected administrative agency data detailing reported rates of these incidents to compare with child maltreatment rates and structural characteristics of each consensus tract.

The authors hypothesized that:

1   child maltreatment rates would be related to structural charac-
    teristics of neighbourhoods, these being i, ii, iii, iv, and v above;
2   these structural characteristics would also be related to higher
    levels of violent crime, drug trafficking, juvenile delinquency, and
    teen childbearing.

Results

The set of empirical indicators that characterized the structural conditions associated with the level of community social organization were intercorrelated to form a smaller number of factors. This principal components analysis resulted in three factors which explained 78% of the variance in child maltreatment rates. These three factors were:

1   *Impoverishment.* Indicators of this factor were high levels of:
    poverty, unemployment, vacant housing, population loss, female-
    headed households, and percentage black population.
2   *Child-care burden.* Indicators of this factor were higher ratio of
    children to adults and ratio of males to females, and lower per-
    centage of the elderly population.
3   *Instability.* Indicators of this factor were higher proportions of
    residents who: had moved to or from a different house within the
    last five years, lived in current home less than ten years, lived in
    current home less than one year.

In order to examine the effect of community structure on child maltreatment rates the above three factors, and the measure of geographic location (degree to which poor neighbourhoods are contiguous to other poor areas) were loaded into a regression coefficient model as independent variables, and child maltreatment rate was loaded into the model as the dependent variable. The regression coefficient found that the impoverishment factor had the greatest effect on child maltreatment rates. The child-care burden factor had a significant but weaker effect and the instability factor had the weakest effect of all. The geographical location of the tract relative to concentrated areas of poverty also affected maltreatment rates independent of the other three factors. In other words areas that were in close proximity to other high-poverty areas tended to have higher maltreatment rates. The deviant behaviours (violent crime, drug trafficking, juvenile delinquency, and teen child-bearing) as predicted were related to child maltreatment rates, as well as the impoverishment factor and the child-care burden factor.

Discussion and Conclusions

The authors conclude that variance in child maltreatment rates can be partially explained as a consequence of structural factors representing community social organization, as supported by previous research findings (Garbarino & Crouter, 1978; Garbarino & Kostelny, 1992). The structural factors that affected not only child maltreatment but also other socially deviant behaviours included: firstly, impoverishment (characterized by a concentration of single mothers living in abandoned areas high in poverty and unemployment); secondly, child-care burden (that is neighbourhoods with few adults available to supervise and provide care and developmental support for children); thirdly, instability (that is neighbourhoods characterized by households that move in or out of neighbourhoods frequently); and fourthly, geographical location (poor neighbourhoods in close proximity with other poor neighbourhoods). This study highlights further negative consequences of the rise in poverty in urban areas. The authors recommend that future research attempts to explore the processes by which these factors lead to high levels of child maltreatment among other socially deviant behaviour. In doing so it is hoped that such communities can be equipped to prevent rather than perpetuate such harmful behaviours.

References

Bursik, R. J., & Grasmick, H. G. (1993). *Neighbourhoods and crime*. New York: Lexington.

Coulton, C., Korbin, J., Su, M., & Chaw, J. (1995). Community-level factors and child maltreatment rates. *Child Development*, 66, 1262–76.

Garbarino, J., & Crouter, A. (1978). Defining the community context for parent–child relations: The correlates of child maltreatment. *Child Development*, 49, 604–16.

Garbarino, J., & Kostelny, K. (1992). Child maltreatment as a community problem. *Child Abuse & Neglect*, 16, 455–64.

Garbarino, J., & Sherman, D. (1980). High-risk neighbourhoods and high-risk families: The human ecology of child maltreatment. *Child Development*, 51, 188–98.

Sampson, R. J., & Groves, W. B. (1989). Community structure and crime: Testing social-disorganisation theory. *American Journal of Sociology*, 94, 775–802.

Steinberg, L., Castalano, R., & Dooley, D. (1981). Economic antecedents of child abuse and neglect. *Child Development*, 52, 975–85.

Zuravin, S. J. (1989). The ecology of child abuse and neglect: Review of the literature and presentation of data. *Violence and Victims*, 4, 101–20.

Part II

Reliability of Children's Accounts

FOUR

Reliability and Credibility of Children's Reports

Introduction

As noted in part I, assessing the impact of child victimization depends, in part, on being able reliably to determine whether a child has been victimized. This is also an issue in courts of law, especially criminal courts where defendants may well be sent to prison if the court decides that they have abused children.

Whether, in fact, a child has been victimized, and by whom, often depends on information provided from interviews with the child. In the not too distant past (for example the 1980s) investigative interviews with children conducted by police officers, social workers and therapists were by no means of an appropriate standard. Many demonstrated gross ignorance of the highly relevant knowledge available from developmental psychology concerning how to hold conversations with, and to ask questions of, children – especially young children.

In the 1990s a concerted effort was made by psychologists to assist interviewers to obtain reliable information from children who may have been victimized. One of the recent, greatest achievements of developmental psychology has been recommendations, based on high-quality research, of how to avoid suggestively questioning children. A culmination of such efforts has been the publication of relevant guidelines (see 'Suggested reading' below). In their paper Maggie Bruck, Stephen Ceci and Helene Hembrooke present an in-depth overview of relevant research.

Suggested reading

Milne, R., & Bull, R. (1999). *Investigative interviewing: Psychology and practice.* Chichester: Wiley.

Poole, D., & Lamb, M. (1998). *Investigative interviews of children: A guide for helping professionals.* Washington, DC: American Psychological Association.

Reliability and Credibility of Young Children's Reports: From Research to Policy and Practice

Maggie Bruck, Stephen J. Ceci, and
Helene Hembrooke

By the 1980s, there was an enormous change in society's sensitivity to and recognition of the problems of violence and abuse that were suffered by children. Spurred by an increased awareness of the pervasiveness of one crime, child sexual abuse, state after state revised its criminal procedures to enable prosecutors to deal more effectively with victims and defendants. This led to important changes in the legal system not only in the United States but also in other countries in the Western world (see Bottoms & Goodman, 1996; Davies, Lloyd-Bostock, McMurran, & Wilson, 1995). The most important of these changes was the relaxation of standards that had prevented many children from testifying in criminal and civil cases. Children for the first time were allowed to provide uncorroborated testimony in cases concerning sexual abuse – a crime that by its very nature often does not involve an eyewitness other than the perpetrator and the victim. A second major change involved the elimination of the competency requirement for child witnesses. There was also a raft of other legal changes and proposals that had far-reaching consequences for the structure of the legal system and in some cases for the constitutional safeguards of the defendants. In some cases, children are now permitted to give sworn and unsworn testimony behind screens that shield them from the defendant's gaze or by closed circuit TV (*Maryland v. Craig*, 1990). In some states, there has been a broadening of the receipt of children's hearsay statements (e.g., *Idaho v. Wright*, 1990; *White v. Illinois*, 1992; for a description of these cases and other changes, see Goodman et al., 1992; McGough, 1994).

Giving children their day in court has opened a Pandora's box of issues not only for the legal community but also for the mental health, social services, and social sciences communities. These issues have been magnified by the media's attention to a number of cases that either call into question the adequacy of existing safeguards for the protection of abused children (e.g., children, such as Lisa Steinberg, who were beaten to death by an abuser who was previously investigated for suspected abuse) or that call into question existing pretrial and trial procedures used to obtain and evaluate the testimony of young children (e.g., young children, such as those in Kern County, California, who made horrific allegations of sexual abuse after many hours and days of questioning by the police and social service workers; see Nathan & Snedeker, 1995). These two situations reflect two serious problems: underreporting of actual abuse and overreporting of abuse that has not occurred. To effectively deal with these two problems, we require a clear understanding of the strengths and weaknesses of children's memory and children's ability to report experienced events. The present article, while addressing both types of problems, focuses on the weaknesses of young children's reporting and memory. Of specific interest is the accuracy of children's reports and the degree to which they can be positively or negatively influenced by suggestive interviewing techniques. After reviewing the literature in this area, we discuss some of the unique strengths and weaknesses of children's recollections and conclude with the challenge this literature poses for social scientists and policymakers to develop protocols and procedures to maximize children's accuracy with the minimum abridgment of defendants' rights.

Child Sexual Abuse

The scope of the problem

Until very recently, there has been an annual increase in the number of reported and substantiated cases of sexual abuse. The increase in these estimates of abuse in part reflects society's growing sensitivity and hence recognition of existing problems that was prominently marked by the Mondale Act (1974), which mandated the reporting of suspected physical and sexual abuse involving children. The American Humane Association (1988) estimated a 2,000% increase in reports of sexual abuse between 1976 and 1986. In a more recent survey, it was conservatively estimated that between 1986 and 1993 there was an 83% increase in the number of sexually abused children (Sedlak & Broadhurst, 1996). However, for the first time in several decades this trend may now be reversing. In 1994, there were 141,628 substantiated reports of sexual abuse of children under the age of 18; in 1995, this figure was reduced to 126,095 (US Department of Health and Human Services, National Center on Child Abuse and Neglect, 1996, 1997). Similar reductions in the rates of substantiated reports of sexual abuse were recently reported by Wang and Daro (1996). Despite these decreases, an enormous number of children are still sexually abused.

An important issue regarding these figures is the degree to which they represent underreporting or overreporting.[1] On the one hand, it is argued that incidence estimates are very conservative because these include only reported cases; there are many cases of abuse that are never reported. For example, Kalichman (1993) estimated that only 40% of maltreatment cases are reported. The concerns about overreporting focus on the number of substantiated cases that are incorrectly classified. Some of these cases may be the result of false allegations, whereas others may be simply the result of false suspicions. Estimates of false-positive cases range from 5% to 35% (see Ceci & Bruck, 1995; Poole & Lindsay, in press). At times, some of these misclassified cases are detected and resolved. However, at other times, these may end up in the courtroom where children make false accusations about abuse perpetrated by their teachers, babysitters, or parents.

Concerns about underreporting and overreporting of child sexual abuse have been the impetus for a wave of research on children's autobiographical memory, children's suggestibility, and adults' judgments regarding the credibility of child witnesses. Some have argued that the surge of interest in the suggestibility and reliability of children's reports represents a step backward to the views of the earlier part of this century, when the prevailing wisdom was that children were dangerously vulnerable to coaching and suggestions and thus should not be admitted as courtroom witnesses (see Ceci & Bruck, 1993). However, the intent or impact of the new wave of research described below was not to discredit sexual abuse allegations made by children, but merely to set up a context in which the allegations could be realistically evaluated.

From a scientific point of view, this recent research has led to a greater understanding of the strengths and weaknesses of children's cognitive and social development. It has led us away from the strong positions that (a) children are hypersuggestible sponges, incapable of accurately remembering and reporting events, or (b) children have the same cognitive structures and mechanisms as adults and are as resistant to suggestions and as able to remember and report events as adults. On the applied side, this newer research is beginning to have some impact on the legal system in terms of the decisions that are made by trial and appellate courts (e.g., *State v. Michaels*, 1994; *United States v. Rouse*, 1996).

Diagnosing child sexual abuse

Although children testify in a range of criminal and civil cases, the research on children's suggestibility has had its largest impact in cases involving allegations of sexual abuse. This is primarily because of the lack of scientifically validated criteria for the diagnosis of sexual abuse. Specifically, in most cases there are no medical findings considered to be sufficiently diagnostic to substantiate abuse (see Bays & Chadwick, 1993). Usually there is no medical evidence, either because of lengthy delays in reporting or, as is often the case, because there is no penetration (e.g., fondling, exhibitionism, or oral copulation are the most common crimes). In the statistically rare case where genital or anal abnormalities are found, similar abnormalities can sometimes be found among nonabused children (Berenson, Heger, & Andrews, 1991). And if the problems associated with lack of hard medical evidence were not bad enough, there does not appear to be a single psychological profile that is diagnostic of child sexual abuse (Kendall-Tackett, Williams, & Finkelhor, 1993). Although there are a number of symptoms associated with validated cases of abuse, it turns out that either these symptoms are common childhood problems (e.g., regressive toileting, acting out, night tremors) or these symptoms are behavioral problems that are commonly found in other childhood psychopathologies. Consequently, to diagnose child sexual abuse, one must rely on the verbal report of the child witness.

In evaluating the child's testimony, it has become clear that it is of primary importance to understand the evolution of the child's reports.

The following pattern, one that is found in many cases involving child sexual abuse, has raised the most concerns. Here the child is initially silent: she does not make any unsolicited or spontaneous statements about abusive acts. Rather, the allegations emerge once an adult has a suspicion that something has occurred and starts to question the child. At first, the child denies the event happened, but with repeated questioning, interviewing, or therapy, the child may eventually make a disclosure. Sometimes after the disclosure is made, the child may recant, only to later restate the original allegation. There are two different interpretations of this pattern.

The first interpretation is that the progression from silence to denial to disclosure to recanting to restatement is common and perhaps even diagnostic of sexual abuse. Some professionals claim that children have a great deal of difficulty disclosing and may later recant because they are afraid or ashamed or even believe themselves to be culpable (for a review, see Bradley & Wood, 1996). Although there are some formal models of the disclosure process (e.g., Summit's 1983 child sexual abuse accommodation syndrome includes a series of stages: secrecy, helplessness, entrapment, disclosure, and retraction), it is important to point out that these models were not derived from scientific studies but from clinical intuitions. Nonetheless, there are a few studies that support the view that when directly asked about abuse, it is common for sexually abused children to not readily or consistently disclose their abuse. The most frequently cited of these studies was conducted by Sorensen and Snow (1991), who examined 116 cases from a sample of 630 children who had received therapy for sexual abuse. For the majority of the children, the disclosures were accidental, and at some point 75% of the children had denied that abuse had occurred. Even after making a disclosure, 22% of the children recanted their previous disclosures. In another study, Gonzalez, Waterman, Kelly, McCord and Oliveri (1993) found that 27% of 63 children in therapy recanted disclosure of daycare sexual and ritualistic abuse.

Unfortunately, there are a number of methodological features that mar the interpretation of such data. Of primary concern is the possibility that a number of the children in these studies may not have been sexually abused and that their disclosures were the result of the interviewing and therapeutic process (see Ceci & Bruck, 1995). This is particularly salient in the Gonzalez et al. (1993) study, which examined the disclosure patterns of the McMartin preschool child witnesses; claims of ritualistic abuse by the McMartin children were never substantiated, and they appear not to have been accepted as credible by jurors.[2]

There are other studies that provide a different perspective on the process of disclosure. For example, Jones and McGraw (1987) found only an 8% recantation rate among 309 validated sexual abuse cases seen at a child protection agency. In the most recent study of the patterns of disclosure among sexually abused children, Bradley and Wood (1996) found that among 234 validated cases, 5% of the children denied the abuse, and only 3% recanted their earlier reports of abuse. Clearly, although a small percentage of youngsters do appear to disclose their abuse reluctantly, with a smaller percentage subsequently recanting their disclosures, the overwhelming majority of children appear to maintain their claims and never deny them to officials once they are questioned.[3]

Despite the frail empirical evidence for the prevalence of the disclosure process among sexually abused children, it may well live on as a stubborn urban legend among frontline workers. For example, we recently surveyed the opinions and beliefs of 26 highly trained child protection workers. These investigators not only stated that recantation was part of the normal process of disclosure, but they also indicated that the research strongly supported their belief. This could translate into the following belief among child protective service workers: Abused children must be pursued or they will never disclose their abuse, and one should not readily accept their denials or recantations because truly abused children usually show these very behaviors (Conerly, 1986; MacFarland & Krebs, 1986).

There is a second interpretation of a disclosure pattern that begins with silence, then progresses to denial, and eventuates in disclosure (and sometimes ends in recantation): for some children, the disclosures may reflect the use of suggestive interviewing techniques. Which, in some situations, may elicit false reports. To discuss this hypothesis, we first focus on the concept of *suggestive interviewing techniques*.

Suggestive Interviews

Before the 1980s, most studies of suggestibility involved asking children a misleading question (i.e., a question that contains a false supposition) about some experienced or observed event (e.g., a story, a school demonstration). A consistent finding of this literature was that younger children were more suggestible than older children (for a review, see Ceci & Bruck, 1993). However, for the following reasons, this literature was of little value in assessing issues of reliability or suggestibility of children who make allegations of sexual abuse or other potentially distressing events. First, the age of the children studied was problematic. There was but one study in the first 80 years of this century that included preschool children (Lipmann & Wendriner, 1906) – the very age group that is the cause of most concern for modern-day courts. That is, a disproportionate number of sexually abused children are preschoolers, and a disproportionate number of court cases involve preschool witnesses (see Ceci & Bruck, 1995). Second, the children in these studies were questioned about neutral events that had little personal salience. For example, Lipmann and Wendriner (1906) found that preschoolers were progressively susceptible as the strength of misleading questions was increased. Thus, when 4- to 6-year-olds were asked about a nonexistent cabinet, only 6% falsely assented to the question, "Is there a cabinet in the room?"; when asked, "Isn't there a cabinet in the room?" the false assent rate rose to 25%. Finally, false answers reached a maximum of 56% when children were asked. "Is the door open in the cabinet in the room?" A related point that is illustrated by the previous example is that the questioning of the children in the experimental settings seemed to bear little if any similarity to the conditions under which children are questioned in actual cases.

In actual investigations, because children are rarely questioned under such neutral conditions about relatively benign events, it became clear to social scientists that there would have to be major revisions to existing paradigms and concepts to provide pertinent information to the court about whether or not a child's testimony could be the product of the interviewing methods. There have been three important changes in the direction of this research. First, preschool children were included in many of these newer studies. Second, studies increasingly were designed to examine children's suggestibility about events that were personally salient, that involved bodily touching, or that involved insinuations of sexual abuse. Third, the concept of suggestive techniques was expanded from the traditional view of asking misleading questions or planting misinformation to using a larger range of interviewing devices that will be discussed below. A recurring theme of these newer studies is the attempt to question children about the main actions that occurred during the experienced event rather than only about the peripheral details, such as the color of an actor's shoes. The ultimate challenge has been to ask questions in an ethically permissible manner about whether or not sexual actions occurred during these events.

With great ingenuity, a number of researchers have met this challenge. For example, Saywitz, Goodman, Nicholas, and Moan (1991) questioned 5- to 7-year-old girls about the details of a medical examination that for some children included a genital examination. The children were asked open-ended, direct, and misleading questions about touching and were also asked to demonstrate what happened to them by using anatomically detailed dolls. In a series of studies, Ornstein and his colleagues (Ornstein, Baker-Ward, Myers, Principe, & Gordon, 1995) asked 3- to 7-year-old children about their annual pediatric visits. These studies assessed the rate at which memories fade over different periods of delay as well as the degree to which children falsely include non-occurring events as part of their reports.

Thus, results of the Saywitz et al. (1991) and Ornstein et al. (1995) studies provide data as to how accurately children report salient events, which may include bodily contact, when they are questioned immediately following the events or after up to a three-month delay. These data also reflect how accurately children respond to open-ended and both direct questions and misleading questions when they are questioned by a neutral, unbiased interviewer. Under these conditions, the children were fairly but not entirely accurate about a number of salient events that involved bodily touching. The results also show a typical pattern, found across many studies, in which children provide more information in response to specific compared with open-ended questions. For example, in the Saywitz et al. study, few children mentioned the genital examination in response to the question, "Tell me everything that happened," but many did provide the required information in response to more specific questions. However, although children generally provide more information to specific question, it is generally the case that overall, accuracy rates are higher for responses to open-ended question. Furthermore, accuracy of responses to specific and misleading questions increases as a function of age (with preschoolers being the least accurate) and as a function of the delay between the interview and the actual event. Some data indicate that when accuracy drops off, it is not merely the case that children forget and therefore make errors of *omission* (i.e., failing to recall an actual event), but they also make errors of *commission* (falsely claiming to have experienced a nonevent). In Ornstein et al.'s study, children, especially the younger children, reported events that never happened. These reported nonevents included not only acts that could conceivably occur in a doctor's office but also acts that would not occur in the doctor's office and that would have connotations of abuse, at least to some adults (e.g., "Did the doctor lick your knee?" "Did the nurse sit on top of you?").

Although these data are important for understanding how specific types of questions may alter children's patterns of reporting, recall, and forgetting, they may have limited value for assessing the accuracy of children's statements when these are obtained under more suggestive situations that occur in some criminal investigations. In contrast to a number of child witnesses who are caught up in actual investigations, the children in these research studies were not repeatedly interviewed about alleged abusive events; identical questions were not repeated within and across interviews; nor were there threats or inducements to have the participants reply in a certain way. The interviewers in these studies were supportive and neutral, in contrast to what can happen when anxious parents, therapists, and legal officials, often repeatedly and over lengthy intervals, question child witnesses. Because these important elements are missing from research studies such as those cited above, it makes it difficult to generalize to forensic situations. It is this concern that has motivated another group of modern researchers to look more closely at the structure of conversations and interviews[4] between children and adults and to examine the effects of various interviewing practices on the accuracy of children's reports. As we show below, the development of this approach has been particularly important in understanding the putative pattern of disclosure that begins with secrecy and denial and that eventuates in allegations. In the next section, we discuss some suggestive elements of interviews that take place between adults and children.

Interviewer Bias and Suggestive Interviewing Techniques

A major dimension along which interviewers can be characterized is that of *interviewer bias*. Interviewer bias characterizes those interviewers who hold a priori beliefs about the occurrence or nonoccurrence of certain events and, as a result, mold the interview to elicit statements from the interviewee that are consistent with these prior beliefs. One of the hallmarks of interviewer bias is the single-minded attempt to gather only confirmatory evidence and to avoid all avenues that may produce negative or inconsistent evidence. Thus, while gathering evidence to support their hypotheses, interviewers may fail to gather any evidence that could potentially disconfirm their hypotheses. Biased interviewers do not ask questions that might provide alternate explanations for the allegations (e.g., "Did your mommy and daddy tell you that this happened, or did you see it happen?"). Nor do biased interviewers ask the child about events that are inconsistent with their hypotheses (e.g., "Who else beside your teacher touched your private parts? Did your mommy touch them, too?"). And biased interviewers do not challenge the authenticity of the child's report when it is consistent with their hypotheses (e.g., "It's important to tell me only what you saw, not what someone may have told you," or "Did that really happen"?). When children provide inconsistent or bizarre evidence, it is either ignored or else interpreted within the framework of the biased interviewer's initial hypothesis. In short, interviewer bias can be found whenever interviewers think they know the answers before the child divulges them and whenever interviewers view their task as one of "getting the goods" on the defendant.

Interviewer bias influences the entire architecture of interviews, and it is revealed through a number of different component features that are suggestive. For example, to obtain confirmation of their suspicions, biased interviewers may not ask children open-ended questions such as "What happened?" but may quickly resort to a barrage of very specific questions, many of which are repeated, and many of which are leading in the sense that the question stem presupposes the desired answer. When interviewers do not obtain information that is consistent with their suspicions, they may repeatedly interview children until they do obtain such information, sometimes subtly reinforcing responses consistent with their beliefs. Thus, child witnesses are often interviewed over a prolonged period of time, and they are reinterviewed on many occasions about the same set of suspected events (for a review, see Ceci, Bruck, & Rosenthal, 1995).

Stereotype inducement is another strategy that is sometimes found in biased interviews with children. Interviewers using this strategy give the children information about some characteristic of the suspected perpetrator. For example, children may be told that a person who is suspected of some crime "is bad" or "does bad things." For example, in one case, a preschooler told her interviewer that she was glad that the defendant was in jail because he was bad. When asked why she thought that he was bad, the child replied, "My mom told me."

Interviewer bias is also reflected in the atmosphere of the interview. Sometimes, interviewers provide much encouragement during the interview to put children at ease and to provide a highly supportive environment. Such encouraging statements can, however, quickly lose their impartial tone if an interviewer *selectively* reinforces children's responses by positively acknowledging statements (e.g., through the use of vigorous head nodding, smiling, and statements such as "Wow, that's great?") that are consistent with the interviewer's beliefs or hypotheses or by ignoring other statements that do not support the interviewer's beliefs. Some interviewers who feel an urgency and responsibility to obtain the desired disclosure may even use threats and bribes. For example, in some cases, children have been told that they will be reunited with their parents if they just tell the investigators how they were abused by their parents. To obtain full compliance from the children, interviewers often try to engage the children by co-opting their cooperation by telling them that they are helpers in an important legal investigation (in one case, children were given plastic police badges and taken on a visit to the police station) and sometimes by telling the children that their friends have helped or already told and that they should also tell. The following blatant example is taken from the Kelly Michaels case (for other examples, see Ceci & Bruck, 1995):

> Interviewer: Do you know that I've been talking to a lot of your buddies? I've been talking to Kit and I've been talking to Mart and . . . we've been talking about some stuff that's not so nice that's been happening at school with Kelly. . . . You can help us with giving some information on your friends that were hurt, okay?

Interview bias is also reflected in the use of some techniques that are specific to interviews between professionals and children. One of these involves the use of anatomically detailed dolls in investigations of sexual abuse. It is thought that these props facilitate reports of sexual abuse for children with limited language skills, for children who feel shame and embarrassment, and for children with poor memories of the abusive incident. In some cases, when interviewers suspected abuse before the children had made any allegations, they gave children anatomically detailed dolls and asked them to show how they had been sexually abused.

Another professional technique involves *guided imagery* or *memory work*. Interviewers sometimes ask children to first try to remember or pretend if a certain event occurred and then to create a mental picture of the event and to think about its details. In some cases, interviewers asked children to pretend about events that were consistent with the interviewers' beliefs but that had not been reported by the child witnesses.

This description of the architecture of interviews is based on our analysis of transcripts that have been made available to us by judges, attorneys, parents, and medical and mental health professionals who have concerns about the conduct of an interview and its potential impact on the reliability of a child's reports. As such, our description may not be representative of many or even most of the interviews carried out with children in forensic or therapeutic situations: undoubt-edly, there are many interviews that do not contain any of the features in our description. However, there is some recent evidence to indicate that a number of interviewers do in fact use some of the techniques described (Bull & Cherryman, 1995; Hulse, 1994; Lamb et al., 1996; Warren, Woodall, Hunt, & Perry, 1996; Yuille, Marxsen, & Menard, 1993). In these studies, interviewers mainly relied on specific or leading questions; several times during the interviews, they introduced infor-mation that the children had not volunteered, and they frequently repeated that new information in the course of a single interview.

Having qualified the basis of our descriptions, it is also important to state that the research in this area extends beyond a mere cataloging of the elements of potential bias. The next step, the empirical step, is to assess how these various biased components, in isolation as well as in combination, influence the accuracy of children's reports. This frame-work for describing and examining the components of interview bias greatly expands the meaning of the term *suggestive*. In the first 80 years of this century, most of the research on suggestibility focused on the effects of asking a single misleading question or of providing erroneous postevent information on the subsequent accuracy of reports. Now, the study of suggestive techniques includes strategies of repeated inter-viewing, repeated questioning within interviews, the use of threats and rewards, and other techniques that are intended to put the child at ease and to facilitate disclosure. Suggestive interviews now are conceived of as a complex comingling of motives, threats, and inducements, which may appear in the form of misleading questions, but not always.

A number of recent studies have examined the influence of a number of the biased techniques just described (for a review, see Ceci & Bruck, 1995). In these studies, children typically participated in some event and then were interviewed by using one or more of the alleged suggestive interviewing techniques listed above. The results of these newer studies show that the suggestive interviewing techniques just described can compromise the accuracy of children's reports. When used in combination, such techniques can be especially detrimental to the accuracy of young children's reports. In some of these studies, children fabricated whole events that never occurred; at times they were led to confuse suggestions with actual events to the point that they later insisted that the suggested events actually occurred. Importantly, these suggestive techniques do not merely influence recall of peripheral, unimportant details, but they lead to false claims about a wide range of events, many of which are personally meaningful, such as bodily touching that could be interpreted by adult interviewers as sexual in nature. And because children make false claims about unpleasant events, these newer studies are not open to the older criticism that children are only suggestible about unimportant, neutral details (Melton, 1992; Melton & Thompson, 1987).

For example, studies examined 3-year-old (Bruck, Ceci, Francoeur, & Renick, 1995) and 4-year-old (Bruck, Ceci, & Francoeur, 1995) children's memories of a just-completed medical examination in which half of the children received a genital examination and half did not. After the examination, the children were given an anatomically detailed doll and were asked to show on the doll how the doctor had touched them. In addition, they were provided with props (e.g., a spoon, a stethoscope) and asked to show how the doctor had used these. The wording of some of the questions was misleading for the children who had not received a genital examination, although these same questions could be considered to be correctly leading for children who *had* received a genital examination (e.g., "Show me on the doll how the doctor touched your penis").

The results for the 3- and 4-year-old children were almost identical. A significant proportion of children showed inaccurate touching.

Specifically, a substantial number of children who had a genital examination failed to show accurate touching when touching had in fact occurred. Some of these errors were omission errors (the children did not show any touching), but for the girls most of the errors involved showing overtouching (they inserted fingers into the genitalia or anus when this had not occurred). At the same time, a significant proportion of children who had not had a genital examination showed genital touching on the doll when it had *not* happened, a form of commission error. In the latter situation, had the child been touched in the manner that was demonstrated, it might have been quite painful. That is, a number of children (especially the girls) inaccurately showed the pediatrician inserting his finger or props into their genitalia or buttocks.

It seems that there are similar concerns about the use of anatomically detailed dolls with children as old as 6 years of age. Steward and Steward (1996) interviewed children (aged 3 to 6 years) three times after a pediatric clinic visit. With each interview, children's false reports of anal touching increased; by the final interview, which took place six months after the initial visit, more than one-third of the children made such errors of commission (see also Rawls, 1996, for errors of commission by children interviewed using a diagram of body parts).

Other studies reveal how the combination of certain suggestive interviewing techniques can produce false reports not only about touching but also about emotions. For example, in one study 6-year-olds were suggestively and repeatedly interviewed about some salient characteristics of a medical examination that had occurred approximately 12 months previously (Bruck, Ceci, Francoeur, & Barr, 1995). During this medical examination, the children had received an inoculation that for many was stressful and that for most was painful during the next few days. As a result of our repeated use of misinformation a year after the procedure, a number of children eventually came to report that our female research assistant rather than their male pediatrician had actually given them their inoculation and an oral vaccine. The results of this study highlight some other deleterious effects of repeating misinformation across interviews: Not only did some children directly incorporate the misinformation into their subsequent reports, but they also made other inaccurate claims that were not suggested (e.g., falsely reporting that the female research assistant had checked their ears and nose). These statements are inferences that are consistent with the erroneous suggestion that the female research assistant had administered the shot:

therefore she must have been the doctor, and therefore she carried out other procedures commonly performed by doctors. Finally, compared with control children who were not given any suggestions about how much the shot hurt or how much they cried, the misinformed children routinely underestimated their level of pain and crying as a result of erroneous suggestions about how brave and courageous they had been. Thus, young children may use suggestions in highly productive ways to reconstruct and at times distort reality about unpleasant bodily events.

These medical setting studies do not reveal whether it is easier to influence children's reports for unpleasant than for pleasant events. Data from two other studies do address this concern, however. In the first study (Ceci, Loftus, Leichtman, & Bruck, 1994), parents of preschool children told researchers about four true events involving their preschool children: a pleasant event (e.g., a birthday party), an unpleasant event (e.g., death of a pet), and two neutral events (e.g., wearing a blue sweater to school). The parents also verified that a list of four false events, devised by the research team, had never occurred to their children. There was a false pleasant event (taking a ride in a hot-air balloon), a false unpleasant event (falling off a bike and getting stitches) and two neutral events (waiting for a bus and watching a friend waiting for a bus). Preschool participants were asked to create images (using visualization techniques) about these real and fictional events and to tell researchers if they actually experienced the imaged events. The children were asked to do this once per week for 11 consecutive weeks. Assents to images of true events were at ceiling, indicating highly accurate memory of actual experiences. With time, however, children increasingly assented to fictional events, but their rates of assent for the pleasant event (a ride in a hot-air balloon) were much higher than those for the unpleasant event (a bicycle accident). These results indicate that it may be easier to influence children's reports for pleasant than for unpleasant events but that the latter is not impossible – in fact, it occurred with some frequency.

In a recently completed study (Bruck, Ceci, & Hembrooke, 1997), we compared children's assents to true and false events that were scripted to have positive or negative outcomes. Preschool children were asked to tell us about two true events and about two false events. Each child participated in one of the true events that was staged at their school. This involved the child helping a visitor in the school who had tripped and hurt her ankle. This event was labeled as *true-positive* because the child helped the visitor and was rewarded with verbal praise. The second true event varied across all the children: It involved an actual recent incident for which the child had been punished by the teacher or the parent. This event was labeled as *true-negative*. The *false-positive* event involved helping a lady find her monkey, which had become lost in the park. The *false-negative* event involved witnessing a man steal food from the day care. Unlike the other events, the false-negative event is a criminal act, and thus there are potentially serious implications of assenting to such scenarios.

Children were interviewed on five different occasions about the four events. In the first interview, the children were asked if the event had happened and, if so, to provide as many details as possible about its occurrence. The next three interviews included a combination of suggestive interviewing techniques that have been shown to increase children's assents to false events. These techniques included the use of peer pressure ("Megan and Shonda were there and they told me you were there, too"), visualization techniques ("Try to think' about what might have happened"), repeating (mis)information, and providing selective reinforcement. The same interviewer questioned the children for the first four interviews. In the fifth interview, a new interviewer questioned each child about each event in a nonsuggestive manner.

Across the five interviews, all children consistently assented to the true-positive event. However, children were at first reluctant to talk about the true-negative (punishment) event; many of the children denied that the punishment had occurred. With repeated suggestive interviews, the children agreed that the punishment had occurred. Similar patterns of disclosure occurred for the false events; that is, children initially denied the false events, but with repeated suggestive interviews they began to assent to these events. By the third interview, most children had assented to all true and false events. This pattern continued to the end of the experiment.

To summarize, a variety of interviewing techniques can result in young children making false allegations about a wide range of events. Sometimes these false reports involve their own bodies, and sometimes these reports involve false accusations about nonexistent crimes. Some commentators frequently object to these conclusions by claiming that the interviewing conditions used in the suggestibility studies are rarely used by professionals. We have already presented some evidence to dispute this claim. But even if we are wrong, and only a small number of professionals use these techniques, the lesson from scientific studies still stands: It is dangerous to use a number of these techniques. But there is another dimension of interviewing that we have not covered, namely, the use of suggestive techniques by nonprofessionals, such as parents. In a series of studies. Poole and Lindsay (1996, in press) have shown that mild suggestive techniques that are repeated by parents in the context of reading a book to their children can result in substantial memory distortion among children 3 to 8 years of age. Thus, our discussion of the negative impact of suggestive interviewing techniques is not limited to interactions between children and professionals.

The results of our newest study (Bruck et al., 1997) from the monkey and thief scenarios present a more complex picture of children's disclosures and also present a dilemma to professional interviewers. Specifically, the results illustrate the beneficial as well as the harmful consequences of using suggestive techniques to elicit reports from young children. For children who may not want to talk about unpleasant but true events, the use of repeated interviews with suggestive components did prompt them to correctly assent to previously denied events. However, the use of these very same techniques prompted children to assent to events that never occurred. These results provide support for the hypothesis that patterns of disclosure that begin with secrecy and denial and that eventuate in disclosure may reflect the use of suggesting interviewing techniques regardless of whether the reported event did or did not occur. At the end of this article, we discuss how policymakers may find effective ways to balance the risk that interviewers will fail to identify cases of genuine abuse against the risk of pursuing and creating false allegations.

The Credibility of Young Children's Reports

The ability of children to provide accurate reports is often discussed in terms of the credibility of their account or the reliability of their memories. These two terms are not the same, and one does not necessarily imply the other. The term *reliability* simply refers to the accuracy of the report. *Credibility*, on the other hand, refers to the believability that one assigns to a witness's testimony. A judgment about credibility is a subjective reality – it is an individual decision that is not necessarily based on the reliability or consistency of a child's recall but rather on its apparent plausibility. In fact, as we argue below, credibility and reliability can be orthogonal dimensions: Reports that are highly reliable (and accurate) may be judged as not very credible, and conversely, inaccurate reports are sometimes judged as highly credible.

Thus, returning to the research we have reviewed, it could be argued that although the accuracy of children's reports may be negatively influenced by a number of suggestive influences, this does not necessarily mean that they will appear credible to others. An intriguing question is whether a juror, a child development researcher, a child therapist, an experienced social worker, or a judge can differentiate children whose reports are accurate from those whose reports are a product of suggestive interviews. The existing evidence suggests that trained professionals cannot reliably tell the difference between these two kinds of children when the children have been subjected to repeated suggestive interviewing techniques that have been conducted over long periods.

One type of evidence for the above claim is provided by the Sam Stone study (see Leichtman & Ceci, 1995, for details). Here, young children between the ages of 3 and 6 were interviewed under a number of different suggestive conditions about a stranger named Sam Stone. The experimenter told some children that Sam Stone was a friend and that he was very clumsy. Over the next few weeks, these children were told numerous stories of Sam Stone's clumsiness. (This technique is called *stereotype induction*.) All children in the experiment eventually did meet Sam Stone: He made one visit to their classroom and was introduced to them during story time. The next day, the teacher showed all the children a soiled teddy bear and a ripped book (Sam had not defiled either of these objects). Every two weeks for the next few months some of the children were provided with repeated misinformation about Sam's visit (they were asked misleading question, e.g., "When Sam Stone tore the book, did he do it on purpose or was he being silly?"). Finally, at the end of 12 weeks all children were questioned by a new interviewer about what actually happened during Sam Stone's visit.

There were several important findings. First, children who had been repeatedly interviewed with the combination of stereotype induction and repeated misleading questions made the most false reports about what happened when Sam Stone visited the classroom. Second, there were significant age differences: Compared with 5 and 6-year-old children, 3 and 4-year-old children were more likely to make false claims about Sam vandalizing the bear and the book, to claim that they saw Sam do these things, and to maintain these claims when challenged by the interviewer.

Third, some children went beyond simple assents to Sam's misdeeds. These children provided false perceptual details as well as nonverbal gestures to embellish their false stories. For example, children used their hands to show how Sam had purportedly thrown a book up in the air; children reported seeing Sam in the playground, on his way to the store to buy chocolate ice cream, or in the bathroom soaking the teddy bear in water before smearing it with a crayon.

Finally, and most important to the issue of credibility, when experts (who included mental health professionals, research psychologists, judges, social workers, and prosecutors) were shown videotapes of children in the Sam Stone study and asked to judge the children's credibility, they were very inaccurate. They judged children whose reports were a product of suggestive interviewing as highly credible and believable, whereas those whose reports were more accurate were often judged to be less believable and credible (see Ceci, Crotteau-Huffman, Smith, & Loftus, 1994; Ceci, Loftus, et al., 1994, for similar results, and see Finlayson & Koocher, 1991; Horner, Guyer, & Kalter, 1993a, 1993b, for variability on professionals' judgments about children suspected of being abused).

Perhaps professionals have difficulty distinguishing accurate from inaccurate reports under conditions of repeated suggestions because many of the children have come to believe what they are telling adults. (We have referred to this state as *false belief* to distinguish it from acts of lying.) Children are not aware that their reports are factually false, and therefore there are no signs of duping, tricking, or rusing. They appear to be motivated to tell the truth; their reports seem quite consistent, embellished, and cohesive. When children believe what they are saying, it can be very difficult to detect errors.

In our recent work (Bruck et al., 1997), we have gone further in our search for potential markers of accurate and inaccurate reports. We hypothesized that perhaps on closer inspection, there may be linguistic markers that differentiate between true and false narratives that are the result of suggestive interviews. For example, we hypothesized that more subtle aspects of children's narratives, such as the total amount of information provided by the children, the number of spontaneous unprompted statements, the cohesiveness of the narrative, or the degree of elaboration, may differentiate true from false narratives. In addition, we examined the evolution of children's narratives to determine if true and false narratives became more similar with repeated interviewing. We also examined the consistency as well as the inconsistency of children's reports across repeated retellings. We reasoned that children may be more likely to repeat the same details and less likely to contradict themselves when repeating true rather than false narratives.

Our selection of linguistic markers was motivated by several areas of research. First, a number of studies have indicated that when children's reports are spontaneous or in response to open-ended questions (e.g., "Tell me what happened"), their reports are more accurate than those prompted by specific questions. (This finding has been consistently reported since the beginning of this century. For an early study, see Stern, 1910, as reported in Ceci and Bruck, 1995. For a recent study, see Peterson and Bell, 1996). Thus, we predicted that the narratives of the true events would contain more spontaneous statements than the narratives of the false events. Second, we selected several measures of narrative coherence (e.g., dialogue, complex temporal markers, elaborations) because these are characteristics of good narratives and more specifically of children's autobiographical narratives (Fivush, Haden, & Adam, 1995). We anticipated that measures of narrative coherence may occur less frequently in children's false narratives. Third, we examined consistency and inconsistency across interviews, because consistency of a child's report is often one of the most important criteria used by professionals in evaluating the reliability of children's allegations of abuse (Conte, Sorenson, Fogarty, & Rosa, 1991), and inconsistency in young children's reports lowers their credibility in the eyes of mock-jurors (Leippe, Romanczyk, & Manion, 1991).

To examine the distinguishability of true and false reports, we used the narratives that children produced in the monkey – thief study described above. The narratives that we examined were those in which the children fully assented to having participated in or witnessed the false or true event. Except for the true-positive event, the children provided few if any details at the first interview. However, by the second interview, there were no significant differences in the amount of information (i.e., the total number of details) that the children provided for the two false events and for the true-positive event. This pattern continued into the final interview. Most of the details were provided spontaneously, and by the second interview, the number of spontaneous utterances was similar for the false and true-positive events. In these analyses and others reported below, the children provided the fewest utterances for the true-negative (punishment) event. There are two possible explanations. First, the children may have provided minimal information because they were uncomfortable and ashamed. Second, the punishment events were less complex (e.g., the child was put in time-out for talking) than the other events, and thus there were fewer actual details to relate.

One of the motivations for repeating interviews, especially with young children, is to provide them with an opportunity to remember important details that they had not originally reported in the first interview. We found that repeated interviewing resulted in reports of new details (called reminiscences), but more reminiscences were produced for false than for true events. It is in fact possible that high rates of reminiscing may signify unreliable reporting, and this may be especially so when the reminiscences are produced after some lengthy delay. For example, Salmon and Pipe (1997) exposed children to a quasi-medical examination and then interviewed them soon after and one year later. They found that children's reminiscences of an event that had been experienced a year previously were largely inaccurate. More research on this important topic is needed before we can confidently state what types and rates of reminiscences are symptomatic of false accounts.

Our examination of the markers of narrative coherence (e.g., simple temporal markers, complex temporal markers, dialogue) and of elaboration (adjectives, adverbs) revealed similar results. After the first interview, there were rarely any between-event differences on these measures – for example, children used dialogue as frequently in true stories as in false stories. When there were differences, the false stories were more coherent than the true stories. Specifically, with time, narratives became more elaborate (the children used more emotional terms, and they included more adjectives and adverbs), but this held mainly for the false stories so that at the third interview, false narratives contained more elaborate details than did true narratives.

Next, we examined the consistency as well as the inconsistency of the children's stories. Consistency refers to the child's mentioning the same detail in more than one interview. Consistency did differentiate true from false stories, with true stories containing more consistent details. The inconsistency analysis did not produce the same results. Inconsistency was defined as the children reporting "A" in one interview but

"NOT-A" in another interview. For example, in one interview the child might say that he was with his parents, whereas in a later interview, he might say that he was by himself. The rates of inconsistency were generally low. Importantly, the proportions of inconsistent details were similar across true and false events.

Finally, we examined the number of inaccurate details provided in the true-positive narratives. We did not include minor incorrect details (such as the errors about the appearance of the confederate) but only inaccurate details that would be of major significance in the interpretation of the event. For example, after the first interview some children included the following types of inaccurate details in their narratives: "I called 9-1-1," "She fell many times," and "A man came and helped her." We found that with repeated interviewing, children included more inaccurate details in their narratives. Although the overall number of inaccurate details was relatively small compared with the number of accurate details, these would have a major consequence had they really happened.

The results of this study indicate that it is the first narrative that was elicited by nonsuggestive techniques that allowed the clearest differentiation between true and false stories. This is because children mainly denied the false stories, which as a result contained few details during the first narrative. However, with repeated interviews the false stories quickly came to resemble the true stories in terms of the number of details mentioned, the spontaneity of the utterances, the number of new details, inconsistency across narratives, the elaborativeness of the details, and the cohesiveness of the narrative. It is only consistency across tellings that differentiates true from false narratives. A word of caution on this observation is in order, however: It seems likely that consistency across narratives could become a less potent predictor if children are repeatedly interviewed. In addition, when false stories are told as a result of repeated suggestive interviewing, they take on additional qualities that make them seem more believable than true narratives. Specifically, after a number of interviews, false narratives contained more descriptive material than did true narratives.

Finally, the present results indicate that fine-grained analyses of false narratives produce similar patterns of results for unpleasant (negative) events as for pleasant (positive) events. Although some might argue that we obtained high rates of assents to false-negative events because the child was not a participant, it is not clear that our most recent data support this hypothesis. Although it was only suggested to the children that they might have seen a theft, many of those who did assent falsely created narratives in which they were participants. Children reported chasing the thief, being chased by the thief, hitting the thief, and similar types of actions. Therefore, it appears that if children are interviewed with a combination of suggestive techniques, many will assent to and create complex narratives of false-negative events.

Summary of Suggestibility Studies and Directions for New Research

Although we have concentrated on the conditions that can compromise reliable reporting, it is also important to acknowledge that under certain circumstances children are capable of providing accurate, detailed, and useful information. For example, in many of our own studies, children in the control group conditions (who were questioned in nonsuggestive interviews) often recalled events flawlessly (e.g., Bruck, Ceci, & Francoeur, 1995; Ceci, Loftus, et al., 1994; Leichtman & Ceci, 1995). This indicates that the absence of suggestive techniques allows even very young preschoolers to provide highly accurate reports, although they may be sparse in the number of details. Also, the results of a number of studies of children's autobiographical recall or memory for events indicate that children's recall is at times highly accurate and at times quite detailed about a large range of events (Baker-Ward, Gordon, Ornstein, Larus, & Clubb, 1993; Parker, Bahrick, Lundy, Fivush, & Levitt, in press; Peterson & Bell, 1996). What characterizes these studies is the neutral tone of the interviewer, the limited use of misleading questions (for the most part, if suggestions are used, they are limited to a single occasion), and the absence of the induction of any motive or bias for the child to make a false report.

An important implication of studies that emphasize the strength of children's memories is that they highlight the conditions under which children should be interviewed if one wishes to obtain reliable reports. Again, when children are interviewed by unbiased, neutral interviewers, when the number of interviews as well as the number of leading questions are kept to a minimum, and when there is an absence of threats, bribes, and peer pressure, then children's reports are at considerably less risk for taint. These are the conditions we must strive for when eliciting information from young children.

We also have not placed much emphasis on age differences in children's suggestibility. Many of the studies that we have reviewed in this article are not developmental in nature, in that only one age group, preschoolers, was included. However, there are other studies that do involve age group comparisons, and these overwhelmingly show that preschoolers are the most suggestible group. This conclusion is based on a previous literature review (Ceci & Bruck, 1993) that reported that in approximately 88% of the studies (14 out of 16) that involved comparisons of preschoolers to older children or to adults, preschool children were the most suggestible group. Since that publication, new studies on children's suggestibility are being published on a regular basis; these newer data continue the trend reported in 1993, with approximately four out of five studies demonstrating significant age differences in suggestibility.

Despite these strong age differences, it is nonetheless important to point out that it is premature and possibly even wrong to assume that only preschool children are suggestible or that there should be no concern about the reliability of older children's testimony if they are subjected to suggestive interviews. There are two prongs to this argument. First, developmental studies may underestimate the suggestibility of older children. That is, when preschoolers are included in the same study as older children, the task is usually designed to be suitable for the preschool children. As a result, the task often may be too easy for older participants, thus creating ceiling effects. It is difficult to create experimental situations that have the same meaning, interest, and difficulty for all age groups.

The second prong to the argument that older children are suggestible is that there is ample evidence that children do not reach adult levels of resistance to erroneous suggestions prior to early adolescence. There are some studies (see reviews by Ceci & Bruck, 1993, 1995) that include older children, and in these studies, the impact of suggestive interviewing techniques is frequently marked. For example, in some studies, 8-year-old, 9-year-old, and even 10-year-old children are significantly more suggestible than adults (Ackil & Zaragoza, 1995; Warren & Lane, 1995). Although it could be claimed that these studies have less relevance for the courtroom because they assessed children's memories of neutral events that did not involve participation, similar findings have been reported when children were suggestively interviewed about events in which they themselves participated. For example, when asked to recall the details of an event that occurred four years previously, children between the ages of 7 and 10 years were influenced by the atmosphere of accusation created by the experimenters, and they inaccurately reported events (Goodman, Wilson, Hazan, & Reed, 1989). In another study, a significant proportion of 8-year-olds reported that something "yuckie" was placed in their mouths when these nonevents were incorporated into stories that parents read to their children (Poole & Lindsay, 1996).

Even adults' recollections are impaired by suggestive interviewing techniques, albeit in reduced magnitude compared with the impairment obtained for very young children. For example, Loftus and Pickrell (1995) implanted false memories of being lost in a shopping mall in 25% of their participants. In other studies, Hyman and his colleagues implanted false childhood memories of spilling a punch bowl at a wedding for 38% of adult participants (Hyman & Pentland, 1996) or of being hospitalized for an ear infection in 20% of adult participants (Hyman, Husband, & Billings, 1995). Malinoski and Lynn (1995, 1996) showed that one can easily age-regress normal college students to remember events from before the first year of life. Interestingly, the success of memory implantations in adult participants seems to hinge on many of the same factors that we found to be suggestive in our interviews with children. For example, repetition of the misinformation, visual imagery induction, and the status of the suggester (interviewer) are important factors.

On the basis of this brief review, we conclude that there are solid reasons to assume that preschoolers are not the only age group that can be influenced by suggestive interviewing techniques. Thus, it is also important to extend the research to develop newer paradigms for middle childhood and even adolescence to examine the magnitude, boundary conditions, and factors (as discussed below) involved in the suggestibility of individuals of these age groups, which have been as neglected today as the preschool age group was during the first half of this century.

It should not be surprising that children can be influenced to give inaccurate reports – a finding that many seem to find depressing, negative, and disconcerting. Although some have tried to dilute this finding by referring to the strengths of children's memory and reporting, it is equally true that there are pronounced developmental differences that contribute to reporting, beliefs, and memory. There are developmental differences in the degree to which children accurately encode, store, and retrieve memories (Brainerd & Ornstein, 1991). There are developmental differences in forgetting, retention, and relearning curves (Brainerd, Reyna, Howe, & Kingma, 1990). Young children are especially prone to making source misattributions (Ackil & Zaragoza, 1995; Parker, 1995; Poole & Lindsay, 1996). Each of these factors is thought to contribute to suggestibility.

In the noncognitive domain, there are also developmental differences in social compliance and in the willingness to please an authority figure and to provide information when asked for it. Generally, young children believe adults and accept their statements as credible (Ackerman, 1983; Sonnenschein & Whitehurst, 1980). Thus, young children are more suggestible when interviewed by an adult than by a peer (Ceci, Ross, & Toglia, 1987), and they are more likely to be swayed when interviewed by an adult of high prestige or authority (Tobey & Goodman, 1992).

Although such frameworks for understanding developmental differences in suggestibility abound, there has been little research to provide empirical support for many of the hypothesized relationships. This is not to say that there has been no research. For example, some researchers have attempted to determine the relative importance of social versus cognitive factors in accounting for suggestibility effects (e.g., Ceci et al., 1987; Zaragoza, Dahlgren, & Muench, 1992). The results of these studies are inconsistent, and the issue as to the ascendance of one factor over the other remains unresolved. As we have argued in previous work (Ceci & Bruck, 1993), it seems that for now we can conclude that although social factors (e.g., desire to please powerful authority figures) are quite important, they do not appear to fully account for all suggestibility effects, and they probably interact with cognitive factors (strength of the memory trace, knowledge representations) to boost suggestibility in certain circumstances. For example, when an authority source is perceived as more powerful, children may pay greater attention to the erroneous message, thus allowing more of it to seep into their subsequent recollection. Conversely, it is possible that the degree to which social factors play a role has a cognitive basis; when memory traces are weak or nonexistent, children may be more compliant and willing to accept suggestions because there is no competing memory trace to challenge the suggestion.

We expect that in the next decade, researchers will devote much effort to developing and testing theoretical models of the mechanisms underlying suggestibility. By virtue of the phenomenon itself, the ensuing models, by necessity, will be complex and multidimensional, involving not only a host of cognitive factors (trace strength, the nature of the mnemonic representation, strategy use) and social factors (interviewer status, pressures to comply) but also biological factors (physiological reactivity). Moreover, we anticipate that the best models will also account for individual differences in suggestibility. As such, they may include personality factors (e.g., compliance, field independence, self-esteem), task factors (e.g., whether the test is retrieval intensive, number of exposures), and even demographic factors.

Policy Implications

The major implication that we see from this field of research can be simply summarized in five words: "training, training, and more training." Although the results that we report in this article have been replicated in a number of different laboratories and although they are accepted by many social scientists, interestingly, these data have not filtered down to the very communities that might most profit from them – those professionals who interview, assess, and treat children. It is surprising how little training frontline professionals receive in terms of interviewing children. When they are given guidelines, these rarely include any advice about how to be cautious and how to avoid contamination. Thus, it is not sufficient that professionals be provided with training; the training programs themselves must contain the most up-to-date and relevant materials. In the past five years, we have talked to dozens of groups of professionals involved in interviewing children, such as child protective service workers, law enforcement officials, and therapists. It is always surprising after each of these presentations to be told by experienced, highly placed professionals that this is the first time they have ever heard about this type of research.

To illustrate, in the summer of 1996, 26 child protection workers from around the world came to Cornell University for a two-week training conference. The majority of the participants had received a master's degree or better, and more than half were in positions of training, program development, or supervision, or were senior caseworkers. All but one of these individuals had five or more years of experience in the field. Before the training program, participants' practices and knowledge regarding the interviewing of children and of child development were assessed by means of a questionnaire.

Although these individuals reported an average of 75 hours of training in interviewing techniques, child development issues, or both, almost one-third reported no knowledge of the scientific literature related to interviewing or to child development. Of the remaining individuals who claimed to possess some knowledge of the scientific literature, the proportion of questions that they answered correctly was generally very low. For example, most participants agreed with the statement "Interviewers who believe that abuse has occurred should reinterview children who initially deny the abuse." Only 8 individuals reported knowing the research in this area, and their responses were relevant only 25% of the time. The results for questions concerning the use of selective reinforcement were much better; 90% of participants stated that the following statement was problematic: "In an interview it is important to be supportive of a child suspected of abuse by providing such statements as 'Don't be afraid to tell me what she did to you,' 'It's O.K. to tell, you will feel better once you have told me.'" However, only 10 individuals reported knowing the scientific evidence on this issue. Similarly, more than 50% of the participants had no knowledge of the scientific literature on developmental changes in suggestibility and on the use of anatomical dolls, but even when participants did state knowledge of the scientific literature, only 60% of these accurately stated that younger children are most suggestible and that children's play with anatomical dolls is not diagnostic of sexual abuse. Finally, for statements regarding the boundary conditions for suggestibility (e.g., preschoolers are more suggestible than older children for central details and for peripheral details), although more individuals claimed to possess scientific knowledge in this more than any other area, again the accuracy rate was very low, just over 30%.

Making the research available to practitioners is only a very first step. Even when the research is made available, long-existent beliefs and biases continue to influence not only what individuals objectively state that they know but also what they practice. It is very difficult to translate research into effective training programs, and such programs have a history of falling short (Doris, Mazur, & Thomas, 1995). The existing data indicate that good interviewing skills cannot be taught effectively in a short period of time (e.g., a 10-day session), and often interviewers fall back on old, ineffectual (and potentially dangerous), albeit more comfortable, habits after a period of time (Memon, Bull, & Smith, 1995). Presumably, much more time is needed for rehearsal with feedback of the trained skills – a luxury not readily afforded by most investigative agencies. Regardless of the difficulty of meeting these objectives, until professionals become familiar with this field of research and until they institute effective training programs, then we should expect to face a steady stream of cases that hinge on the reliability of the child's testimony and on the competence of the child's interviewers.

The second major policy implication of the research on the reliability of children's statements is the need to develop scientifically validated interviews. The ideal interviews will have to meet a number of criteria. First, they need to incorporate techniques that have been shown to be beneficial in eliciting complete and accurate testimony from children. For example, Saywitz and Snyder (1996) have developed a procedure to expand children's spontaneous reports by teaching them a narrative elaboration procedure. Sternberg et al. (1996) developed a rapport-building procedure that eventuated in children providing more spontaneous information. Carter, Bottoms, and Levine (1996) have delineated some components of a supportive interviewing technique that result in children's increased resistance to misinformation. At the same time, the ideal interview should not contain techniques that have been found to have harmful consequences (e.g., the use of anatomically detailed dolls, the use of props, the use of guided imagery). Many of these potentially detrimental techniques have been described in this article.

Next, the ideal interview must integrate or select these various techniques into a logical manner and age-appropriate format. That is, although a number of different studies point to the beneficial effects of certain types of procedures, one must be sure that each of these procedures continues to be effective when combined with other procedures. Furthermore, according to some methodologists, the ideal protocol should also contain the minimal number of techniques and phases that are necessary to elicit the required information. This criterion is sometimes referred to as *incremental validity* (see Wolfner, Faust & Dawes, 1993, for the application of this reasoning to interviews of child witnesses). Thus, in its development phase, the protocol would have to be tested to ensure that the inclusion of each element within the interview significantly enhances the amount of information obtained. If, when compared with some other element, an element does not increase information or actually results in less information, then that element should not be included as part of the protocol. Although it may seem harmless to allow such elements to remain, to do so would not facilitate the protocol's practical application. Sometimes it is very important that an interview be completed as expeditiously as possible, which means that a scientifically validated protocol should contain exactly the best combination of pieces, no more or less. This procedure is critical not only to ensure construct validity but also because of the exigencies that often accompany child interviews.

At present, there are a number of different interview protocols at various stages of development and validation (see Poole & Lamb, in press, for a full description). These include the Cognitive Interview (Fisher & Geiselman, 1992), the Step-Wise Interview (Yuille, Hunter, Joffe, & Zaparniuk, 1993), the Structured Interview (Memon, Cronin, Eaves, & Bull, 1993), and the National Institute of Child Health and Human Development protocol (Lamb, Sternberg, Esplin, Hershkowitz & Orbach, 1997). Each of these has been developed on scientific premises and is being tested in a variety of settings. One expects that these protocols will result in more systematic and improved interviews with young children.

Conclusions

At the beginning of this article, we discussed the reliability of young children's reports by focusing on some problems in the accurate diagnosis of child sexual abuse. Of particular concern is the pattern of disclosure in which the child initially denies but then later reports abuse. Although some professionals state that this is a common pattern among sexually abused child victims, the research reviewed in this article provides an alternative hypothesis that should be considered on a case-by-case basis: professionals should be alerted to the possible contaminating effects of suggestive interviewing techniques. We maintain that our discussion is not specific to child sexual abuse but applies also to other situations in which the child witness replies with denials to initial questions and only makes a serious allegation with suggestive questioning.

Although we have shown that to some degree young children's false allegations that emerge as a result of suggestive interviewing practices reflect cognitive and social factors characteristic of young children, it is

also the case that factors external to the children – those that charac-
terize suggestive interviews – probably have a predominant influence on
the emergence of children's false allegations. Thus, we do not view the
young child as an incompetent witness. Rather, if questioned under the
appropriate circumstances, the young witness may provide the court
with forensically important evidence. Because we view external rather
than internal psychological factors as most predictive of producing
false allegations, we urge the development of appropriate interviewing
schedules and training programs for professional interviewers.

Notes

1   Elsewhere, it has been surmised that the number of unreported cases is far
    greater than the number of falsely reported once (Ceci & Bruck, 1995),
    although this is speculation.
2   In general, claims of ritualistic abuse (e.g., animal or human sacrifices,
    cannabilism, witchcraft) that have been made by a number of child wit-
    nesses (for details, see Ceci & Bruck, 1995; Nathan & Snedeker, 1995) are
    viewed skeptically by the scientific community. To date, there is an over-
    whelming lack of evidence from two national surveys (Bottoms, Shaver, &
    Goodman, 1996; La Fontaine, 1994) for these claims.
3   It is beyond the scope of this article to explain discrepancies among studies
    on disclosure patterns or to postulate the factors that make some children
    reticent to disclose, such as the investigative setting, the supportiveness of
    the caretaker, and the absence of disclosure previous to the investigative
    interviews (see Sternberg et al., 1996).
4   Although interviews may be highly structured, they need not be. An inter-
    view, at minimum, is a verbal interaction between at least two people in
    which one of the participants (the interviewer) has the goal of obtaining
    specific information from one of the participants (the interviewee). As such,
    interviews are a particular type of conversation that can be carried out
    by a wide variety of professionals and nonprofessionals, such as child
    protection workers, police officers, mental health professionals, attorneys,
    parents, or teachers.

References

Ackerman, B. (1983). Speaker bias in children's evaluation of the external
    consistency of statements. *Journal of Experimental Child Psychology, 35*,
    111–27.

Ackil, J. K., & Zaragoza, M. S. (1995). Developmental differences in eyewitness suggestibility and memory for source. *Journal of Experimental Child Psychology*, *60*, 57–83.

American Humane Association. (1988). *Highlights of official child neglect and abuse reporting, 1986*. Denver, CO: Author.

Baker-Ward, L., Gordon, B., Ornstein, P. A., Larus, D., & Clubb, P. (1993). Young children's long-term retention of a pediatric examination. *Child Development*, *64*, 1519–33.

Bays, J., & Chadwick, C. (1993). Medical diagnosis of the sexually abused child. *Child Abuse & Neglect*, *17*, 91–110.

Berenson, A., Heger, A., & Andrews, S. (1991). Appearance of the hymen in newborns. *Pediatrics*, *87*, 458–65.

Bottoms, B., & Goodman, G. (eds.). (1996). *International perspectives on child abuse and children's testimony*. Thousand Oaks, CA: Sage.

Bottoms, B., Shaver, P., & Goodman, G. (1996). An analysis of ritualistic and religion-related child abuse allegations. *Law & Human Behavior*, *20*, 1–34.

Bradley, A., & Wood, J. (1996). How do children tell? The disclosure process in child sexual abuse. *Child Abuse & Neglect*, *20*, 881–91.

Brainerd, C. J., & Ornstein, P. A. (1991). Children's memory for witnessed events: The developmental backdrop. In J. L. Doris (ed.), *The suggestibility of children's recollections* (pp. 10–20). Washington, DC: American Psychological Association.

Brainerd, C., Reyna, V. F., Howe, M. L., & Kingma, J. (1990). The development of forgetting and reminiscence. *Monographs of the Society for Research in Child Development*, *55*(3–4, Serial No. 222), 1–93.

Bruck, M., Ceci, S. J., & Francoeur, E. (1995, March). *Anatomically detailed dolls do not facilitate preschoolers' reports of touching*. Paper presented at the annual meeting of the Society for Research in Child Development, Indianapolis, IN.

Bruck, M., Ceci, S. J., Francoeur, E., & Barr, R. J. (1995). "I hardly cried when I got my shot!": Influencing children's reports about a visit to their pediatrician. *Child Development*, *66*, 193–208.

Bruck, M., Ceci, S. J., Francoeur, E., & Renick, A. (1995). Anatomically detailed dolls do not facilitate preschoolers' reports of a pediatric examination involving genital touching. *Journal of Experimental Psychology: Applied*, *1*, 95–109.

Bruck, M., Ceci, S. J., & Hembrooke, H. (1997). Children's reports of pleasant and unpleasant events. In D. Read and S. Lindsay (eds.), *Recollections of trauma: Scientific research and clinical practice* (pp. 199–219). New York: Plenum Press.

Bull, R., & Cherryman, J. (1995). *Helping to identify skills gaps in specialist investigative interviewing: Enhancement of professional skills*. UK: Home Office Police Department.

Carter, C. A., Bottoms, B. L., & Levine, M. (1996). Linguistic and socioemotional influences on the accuracy of children's reports. *Law & Human Behavior, 20,* 335–58.

Ceci, S. J., & Bruck, M. (1993). The suggestibility of the child witness: A historical review and synthesis. *Psychological Bulletin, 113,* 403–39.

Ceci, S. J., & Bruck, M. (1995). *Jeopardy in the courtroom: A scientific analysis of children's testimony.* Washington, DC: American Psychological Association.

Ceci, S. J., Bruck, M., & Rosenthal, R. (1995). Children's allegations of sexual abuse: Forensic and scientific issues: A reply to commentators. *Psychology, Public Policy, and Law, 1,* 494–520.

Ceci, S. J., Crotteau-Huffman, M., Smith, E., & Loftus, E. W. (1994). Repeatedly thinking about non-events. *Consciousness & Cognition, 3,* 388–407.

Ceci, S. J., Loftus, E. W., Leichtman, M., & Bruck, M. (1994). The role of source misattributions in the creation of false beliefs among preschoolers. *International Journal of Clinical and Experimental Hypnosis, 62,* 304–20.

Ceci, S. J., Ross, D., & Toglia, M. (1987). Age differences in suggestibility: Psycholegal implications. *Journal of Experimental Psychology: General, 117,* 38–49.

Conerly, S. (1986). Assessment of suspected child abuse. In K. MacFarlane, J. Waterman, S. Conerly, L. Damon, M. Durfee, & S. Long (eds.), *Sexual abuse of young children: Evaluation and treatment* (pp. 30–51). New York: Guilford Press.

Conte, J. R., Sorenson, E., Fogarty, L., & Rosa, J. D. (1991). Evaluating children's reports of sexual abuse: Results from a survey of professionals. *American Journal of Orthopsychiatry, 78,* 428–37.

Davies, G., Lloyd-Bostock, S., McMurran, M., & Wilson, C. (eds.) (1995). *Psychology, law, and criminal justice: International developments in research and practice.* Berlin, Germany: Walter de Gruyter.

Doris, J., Mazur, R., & Thomas, M. (1995). Training in child protective services: A commentary on the amicus brief of Bruck and Ceci (1993/1995). *Psychology, Public Policy, and Law, 1,* 479–93.

Finlayson, L. M., & Koocher, G. P. (1991). Professional judgment and child abuse reporting in sexual abuse cases. *Professional Psychology: Research and Practice, 22,* 464–72.

Fisher, R. P., & Geiselman, R. E. (1992). *Memory-enhancing techniques for investigative interviewing: The cognitive interview.* Springfield, IL: Charles C Thomas.

Fivush, R., Haden, C., & Adam, S. (1995). Structure and coherence of preschoolers' personal narratives over time: Implications for childhood amnesia. *Journal of Experimental Child Psychology, 60,* 32–56.

Gonzalez, L., Waterman, J., Kelly, R., McCord, J., & Oliveri, M. (1993). Children's patterns of disclosures and recantations of sexual and ritualistic abuse allegations in psychotherapy. *Child Abuse & Neglect, 17,* 281–9.

Goodman, G. S., Taub, E. P., Jones, D. P., England, P., Port, L., Rudy, L.,

& Prado, L. (1992). Testifying in criminal court. *Monographs of the Society for Research in Child Development, 57*(5, Serial No. 229), 1–142.

Goodman, G. S., Wilson, M. E., Hazan, C., & Reed, R. S. (1989, April). *Children's testimony nearly four years after an event.* Paper presented at the annual meeting of the Eastern Psychological Association, Boston, MA.

Horner, T. M., Guyer, M. J., & Kalter, N. M. (1993a). The biases of child sexual abuse experts: Believing is seeing. *Bulletin of the American Academy of Psychiatry and Law, 21,* 281–92.

Horner, T. M., Guyer, M. J., & Kalter, N. M. (1993b). Clinical expertise and the assessment of child sexual abuse. *Journal of the American Academy of Child and Adolescent Psychiatry, 32,* 925–31.

Hulse, D. A. (1994). *Linguistic complexity in child abuse interviews.* Unpublished master's thesis, University of Tennessee at Chattanooga.

Hyman, I., Husband, T., & Billings, F. (1995). False memories of childhood experiences. *Applied Cognitive Psychology, 9,* 181–97.

Hyman, I., & Pentland, J. (1996). The role of mental imagery in the creation of false childhood memories. *Journal of Memory & Language, 35,* 101–17.

Idaho v. Wright, 497 U.S. 805 (1990).

Jones, D., & McGraw, J. M. (1987). Reliable and fictitious accounts of sexual abuse in children. *Journal of Interpersonal Violence, 2,* 27–45.

Kalichman, S. C. (1993). *Mandated reporting of suspected child abuse: Ethics, law, and policy.* Washington, DC: American Psychological Association.

Kendall-Tackett, K. A., Williams, L. M., & Finkelhor, D. (1993). Impact of sexual abuse on children: A review and synthesis of recent empirical studies. *Psychological Bulletin, 113,* 164–80.

La Fontaine, J. S. (1994). *The extent and nature of organised and ritual abuse. Research findings.* Department of Health. London: HMSO.

Lamb, M. E., Hershkowitz, I., Sternberg, K. J., Esplin, P. W., Hovav, M., Manor, T., & Yudilevitch, L. (1996). Effects of investigative utterance types on Israeli children's responses. *International Journal of Behavioral Development, 19,* 627–37.

Lamb, M. E., Sternberg, K. J., Esplin, P. W., Hershkowitz, I., & Orbach, Y. (1997). Assessing the credibility of children's allegations of sexual abuse: A survey of recent research. *Learning & Individual Differences, 9,* 175–94.

Leichtman, M. D., & Ceci, S. J. (1995). The effects of stereotypes and suggestions on preschoolers' reports. *Developmental Psychology, 31,* 568–78.

Leippe, M., Romanczyk, A., & Manion, A. P. (1991). Eyewitness memory for a touching experience: Accuracy and communication style differences between child and adult witnesses. *Journal of Applied Psychology, 76,* 367–79.

Lipmann, O., & Wendriner, E. (1906). Aussageexperimente im Kindergarten. *Beitr zur Psycologie der Aussage*(Stern), *2,* S418–23.

Loftus, E. F., & Pickrell, J. (1995). The formation of false memories. *Psychiatric Annals, 25,* 720–5.

MacFarlane, K., & Krebs, S. (1986). Techniques for interviewing and evidence gathering. In K. MacFarlane, J. Waterman, S. Conerly, L. Damon, M. Durfee, & S. Long (eds.), *Sexual abuse of young children: Evaluation and treatment* (pp. 67–100). New York: Guilford Press.

Malinoski, P., & Lynn, S. J. (1995, August). *The pliability of early memory reports.* Paper presented at the 103rd Annual Convention of the American Psychological Association. New York, NY.

Malinoski, P., & Lynn, S. J. (1996, November). *The temporal stability of early memory reports.* Paper presented at the annual convention of the Society for Clinical and Experimental Hypnosis. Tampa, FL.

Maryland v. Craig, 110 S. Ct. 3157 (1990).

McGough, L. (1994). *Fragile voices: The child witness in American courts.* New Haven, CT: Yale University Press.

Melton, G. (1992). Children as partners for justice: Next steps for developmentalists. *Monographs of the Society for Research in Child Development, 57*(5, Serial No. 229), 153–9.

Melton, G., & Thompson, R. (1987). Getting out of a rut: Detours to less traveled paths in child-witness research. In S. J. Ceci, M. P. Toglia, & D. F. Ross (eds.), *Children's eyewitness memory* (pp. 209–29). New York: Springer-Verlag.

Memon, A., Bull, R., & Smith, M. (1995). Improving the quality of the police interview: Can training in the use of cognitive techniques help? *Policy and Society, 5,* 53–68.

Memon, A., Cronin, O., Eaves, R., & Bull, R. (1993). The cognitive interview and child witnesses. *Issues in Criminological & Legal Psychology, 20,* 3–9.

Nathan, D., & Snedeker, M. (1995). *Satan's silence: Ritual abuse and the making of a modern American witch hunt.* New York: Basic Books.

Ornstein, P. A., Baker-Ward, L., Myers, J., Principe, G. F., & Gordon, B. N. (1995). Young children's long-term retention of medical experiences: Implications for testimony. In F. E. Weinert & W. Schneider (eds.), *Memory performance and competencies: Issues in growth and development* (pp. 349–71). Hillsdale, NJ: Erlbaum.

Parker, J. (1995). Age differences in source monitoring of performed and imagined actions on immediate and delayed tests. *Journal of Experimental Child Psychology, 60,* 84–101.

Parker, J., Bahrick, L., Lundy, B., Fivush, R., & Levitt, M. (in press). Effects of stress on children's memory for a natural disaster. In C. P. Thompson, D. J. Herrmann, J. D. Read, D. Bruce, D. G. Payne, & M. P. Toglia (eds.), *Eyewitness memory: Theoretical and applied perspectives.* Mahwah, NJ: Erlbaum.

Peterson, C., & Bell, M. (1996). Children's memory for traumatic injury. *Child Development, 67,* 3045–70.

Poole, D. A., & Lamb, M. E. (in press). *Investigative interviews of children: A guide for helping professionals.* Washington, DC: American Psychological Association.

Poole, D. A., & Lindsay, D. S. (1996, June). *Effects of parental suggestions, interviewing techniques, and age on young children's event reports.* Paper presented at the NATO Advanced Study Institute, Recollections of trauma: Scientific research and clinical practice, Port de Bourgenay, France.

Poole, D. A., & Lindsay, D. S. (in press). Assessing the accuracy of young children's reports: Lessons from the investigation of child sexual abuse. *Journal of Applied and Preventive Psychology.*

Rawls, J. (1996). How question form and body-parts diagrams can affect the content of young children's disclosures. Paper presented at the NATO Advanced Study Institute, Recollections of trauma: Scientific research and clinical practice, Port de Bourgenay, France.

Salmon, K., & Pipe, M. E. (1997). Providing props to facilitate young children's event recall: The impact of a one year delay. *Journal of Experimental Child Psychology, 65,* 261–92.

Saywitz, K., Goodman, G., Nicholas, G., & Moan, S. (1991). Children's memory of a physical examination involving genital touch: Implications for reports of child sexual abuse. *Journal of Consulting and Clinical Psychology, 59,* 682–91.

Saywitz, K. J., & Snyder, L. (1996). Narrative elaboration: Test of a new procedure for interviewing children. *Journal of Consulting and Clinical Psychology, 64,* 1347–57.

Sedlak, A., & Broadhurst, D. (1996). *Executive summary of the Third National Incidence Study of Child Abuse and Neglect.* Washington, DC: US Department of Health and Human Services.

Sonnenschein, S., & Whitehurst, G. (1980). The development of communication: When a bad model makes a good teacher. *Journal of Experimental Child Psychology, 3,* 371–90.

Sorensen, T., & Snow, B. (1991). How children tell: The process of disclosure of child sexual abuse. *Child Welfare, 70,* 3–15.

State v. Michaels, 136 N.J. 299, 642 A.2d 1372 (N.J., 1994).

Sternberg, K. J., Lamb, M. E., Hershkowitz, I., Yudilevitch, L., Orback, Y., Esplin, P., & Horav, M. (1996). Effects of introductory style on children's abilities to describe experiences of sexual abuse. *International Journal of Behavioral Development, 19,* 627–37.

Steward, M. S., & Steward, D. S., with Farquahar, L., Myers, J. E. B., Reinart, M., Welker, J., Joye, N., Driskll, J., & Morgan, J. (1996). Interviewing young children about body touch and handling. *Monographs of the Society for Research in Child Development, 61*(4–5, Serial No. 248).

Summit, R. (1983). The child sexual abuse accommodation syndrome. *Child Abuse & Neglect, 7,* 177–93.

Tobey, A., & Goodman, G. S. (1992). Children's eyewitness memory: Effects of participation and forensic context. *Child Abuse & Neglect, 16,* 779–96.

United States v. Rouse, F.3d 360 (8th Cir. 1996).

US Department of Health and Human Services, National Center on Child Abuse and Neglect. (1996). *Child maltreatment 1994: Reports from the states to the National Center on Child Abuse and Neglect.* Washington, DC: U.S. Government Printing Office.

US Department of Health and Human Services, National Center on Child Abuse and Neglect. (1997). *Child maltreatment 1995: Reports from the states to the National Center on Child Abuse and Neglect.* Washington, DC: U.S. Government Printing Office.

Wang, C. T., & Daro, D. (1996). *Current trends in child abuse reporting and fatalities: The results of the 1996 Annual Fifty State Survey.* Chicago: National Committee to Prevent Child Abuse.

Warren, A. R., & Lane, P. (1995). The effects of timing and type of questioning on eyewitness accuracy and suggestibility. In M. Zargoza (ed.), *Memory and testimony in the child witness* (pp. 44–60). Thousand Oaks, CA: Sage.

Warren, A. R., Woodall, C. E., Hunt, J. S., & Perry, N. W. (1996). "It sounds good in theory, but . . .": Do investigative interviewers follow guidelines based on memory research? *Child Maltreatment, 1,* 231–45.

White v. Illinois, 502 U.S., 112 S. Ct. 736 (1992).

Wolfner, G., Faust, D., & Dawes, R. (1993). The use of anatomical dolls in sexual abuse evaluations: The state of the science. *Applied and Preventative Psychology, 2,* 1–11.

Yuille, J. C., Hunter, R., Joffe, R., & Zaparniuk, J. (1993). Interviewing children in sexual abuse cases. In G. S. Goodman & B. Bottoms (eds.), *Child victims, child witnesses* (pp. 95–116). New York: Guilford Press.

Yuille, J., Marxsen, D., & Menard, K. (1993). *Interviewing and assessing children in sexual abuse investigations: A field study.* Unpublished report for the Ministry of Social Services. Victoria, British Columbia, Canada.

Zaragoza, M., Dahlgren, D., & Muench, J. (1992). The role of memory impairment in children's suggestibility. In M. L. Howe, C. J. Brainerd, & V. F. Reyna (eds.), *Development of long-term retention* (pp. 184–216). New York: Springer-Verlag.

FIVE

Children's Long-Term Remembering

Introduction

In a number of settings, but especially those relating to being the alleged victim of, or witness to, a crime, children are required to remember events from, what is for them, long ago. Recently, I was asked by an official inquiry to write a review of the literature on the ability of young children (aged 4 to 6 years) validly to recall events from years ago (when aged 2 to 4 years). The inquiry team wished to be able to come to a view as to whether young children could, indeed, produce correct accounts of past abuse.

Though few research studies have properly addressed this question, probably owing to the effort and cost involved, the paper by Jodi Quas and colleagues is an example of what can be achieved. In a study of outstanding quality they overcame the ethical problem of researchers purposely putting children through a negative experience. They also noted, unlike much research on children's memory, that even children of the same age may differ in important ways regarding their cognitive processing, their social compliance to inappropriate interviewing, and in the effects of stress and negative events upon them.

It is extremely important that when telling their story victimized children are believed. However, it is also very important that innocent people are not jailed for child abuse, especially since jail for those found guilty of child abuse is a very dangerous place.

Suggested reading

Ceci, S., & Bruck, M. (1995). *Jeopardy in the courtroom: A scientific analysis of children's testimony*. Washington, DC: American Psychological Association.

Emotion and Memory: Children's Long-Term Remembering, Forgetting, and Suggestibility

Jodi A. Quas, Gail S. Goodman,
Sue Bidrose, Margaret-Ellen Pipe,
Susan Craw, and Deborah S. Ablin

That emotions play a role in influencing the memorability of personal experiences has been recognized since, if not before, the early writings of Freud (Freud, 1915/1957, 1938; see also Christianson, 1992; Rapaport, 1942). According to Freud, experiences occurring prior to the age of approximately 6 years are "covered in a veil of amnesia." These memories, he believed, are repressed because of their emotional nature, specifically their underlying sexual and aggressive nature (1915/1957), and typically remain inaccessible to conscious recall into the adult years. Since Freud called attention to this phenomenon, a considerable amount of research has been devoted to the study of adults' earliest childhood memories. This research has resulted in a number of revisions to Freud's original ideas, including reduction in the age of the childhood-amnesia "barrier" to 2 or 3 years (Kihlstrom & Harackiewicz, 1982; Usher & Neisser, 1993) and the introduction of numerous other theoretical accounts explaining the inaccessibility of early memories (see Howe & Courage, 1993; 1997; Pillemer & White, 1989, for reviews).

Less well documented, however, is the role of trauma, or negative emotion more generally, in the selective forgetting of early childhood events as predicted by Freud's theory. The reasons for this dearth are largely methodological: in general, it has been difficult to examine empirically the accuracy of children's and adults' memories for highly stressful or traumatic events, including those of particular relevance to Freudian theory (e.g., events involving genital touch). Most of what is known about the recall of experiences with a strong emotional component has been based on studies of adults' retrospective accounts of their early experiences and on case studies or anecdotal reports of children's memory for traumatic events (Hewitt, 1994; Terr, 1988; Waldfogel, 1948). Recently, however, the study of children's memory for stressful medical procedures has opened the door to empirical investigations of emotion and memory in childhood (Bugental, Blue, Cortez, Fleck, & Rodriguez, 1992; Goodman, Hirschman, Hepps, & Rudy, 1991; Goodman, Quas, Batterman-Faunce, Riddlesberger, & Kuhn, 1994; Merritt, Ornstein, & Spicker, 1994; Peterson & Bell, 1996; Steward & Steward, 1997). What remains unknown, however, is how children's memories of emotional events are retained over long durations (but see Peterson & Parsons, 1996). Understanding children's remembering and forgetting of stressful events, including those involving genital contact, over long delays may provide theoretical insight into memory for traumatic experiences, for instance, into whether special memory mechanisms are involved.

Knowledge about children's long-term memory for stressful events can also provide valuable information about children's eyewitness capabilities. In eyewitness situations, children are most often questioned about events that happened to them personally (Goodman, Quas, Bulkley, & Shapiro, in press), and the questioning can occur months or even years after the alleged events occurred (Gray, 1993). Past research on children's memory and eyewitness testimony has identified a number of factors that can influence infants' and children's mnemonic capabilities, such as linguistic capabilities (e.g., Bauer & Wewerka, 1995; Fivush, Haden, & Adam, 1995), memory trace strength (e.g., Pezdek & Roe, 1995), source-monitoring capabilities (e.g., Ackil & Zaragoza, 1995; Parker, 1995), and interviewer biases and retrieval strategies (e.g., Goodman, Sharma, Considine, & Golden, 1995; Leichtman & Ceci, 1995; Liwag & Stein, 1995; see Newcombe's 1995 special issues of the *Journal of Experimental Child Psychology*). Most of these studies have not, however, examined how social and emotional factors influence children's long-term memory, particularly memory of a salient, stressful experience.

In the present study, we examined children's long-term memory for a documented medical procedure, voiding cystourethrogram fluoroscopy (VCUG), that involves painful and stressful genital contact. Our main objectives were to: (1) identify how age and delay influence children's long-term memory and investigate whether typical childhood amnesia effects would emerge; (2) examine how stress relates to children's memory following long delays; and (3) determine whether individual-difference factors predict children's long-term memory and suggestibility. We first review background literature relating to each of these objectives.

Childhood amnesia in adults and children

Although research on adults' earliest memories suggests that most adults fail to recall events unless they were at least 3 or 4 years of age when the events occurred (Dudycha & Dudycha, 1941; Sheingold & Tenney, 1982; Winograd & Killenger, 1983; however, see Usher & Neisser, 1993), research on children's early memories reveals a different pattern: Children often can remember events they experienced in early childhood (Fivush et al., 1995; Hamond & Fivush, 1991; Howard, Osborne, & Baker-Ward, 1997). Children who are almost 3 years old show implicit memory for experiences in infancy (Myers, Clifton, & Clarkson, 1987), and 2-year-olds show explicit memory for events experienced 6 months previously (Fivush, Gray, & Fromhoff, 1987). Once a long enough delay has ensued, however, children can no longer recall formerly accessible memories (Fivush et al., 1987; Goodman et al., 1991; Pillemer, 1992; Pillemer, Picariello, & Pruett, 1994). It is therefore important to assess how well young children can remember the same event, especially a stressful event involving salient body contact, over time spans ranging from a few months to many years.

Emotion and children's memory

Research on adults' early childhood memories suggests that emotion may have a facilitative effect on long-term retention (e.g., Howes, Siegel, & Brown, 1993; Kihlstrom & Harackiewicz, 1982; Usher & Neisser, 1993). Similarly, in studies of children's memory for stressful events, some researchers have observed a positive relation between stress and children's memory (e.g., Goodman et al., 1991). However, other researchers have uncovered negative (e.g., Bruck, Ceci, Francoeur, & Barr, 1995; Merritt et al., 1994) or no significant relations (Eisen, Goodman, Qin, & Davis, 1998; Howe, Courage, & Peterson, 1995; Peterson & Bell, 1996) between stress and memory in children. Two recent studies of children's memory for VCUG, the same medical procedure examined in the present research, have also revealed inconsistent findings. Goodman and colleagues observed children undergo a VCUG and tested their memory between 1 and 3 weeks later (Goodman et al., 1994; Goodman, Quas, Batterman-Faunce, Riddlesberger, & Kuhn, 1997). Although preliminary analyses indicated that distress was positively related to children's errors in response to direct questions about the procedure, when parents' attachment styles were also considered, the negative relations between stress and memory were no longer significant (see below). Merritt et al. (1994) assessed children's memory for VCUG immediately after the procedure and again 6 weeks later. Relations between stress and memory depended upon how stress was measured and when children's VCUG memory was tested. For example, medical staff's ratings of children's distress were negatively associated with children's memory initially but not after the delay, whereas parents' ratings of children's distress were unrelated to children's memory. Because the delays in Goodman et al.'s and Merritt et al.'s studies were fairly short (i.e., up to 6 weeks) and because studies of adults' earliest memories suggest that emotion may facilitate long-term memory, it was important to examine how stress related to children's long-term memory for VCUG.

Sources of individual differences

Recently researchers have attempted to identify sources of individual differences in children's memory of personal experiences (Howard et al., 1997; Ornstein, Principe, Hudson, Gordon, & Merritt, 1997; Stein & Boyce, 1995; Thompson, Clarke-Stewart, & Lepore, 1997). Three such sources are of potential importance to the present study: children's preparation, parent–child discussion, and parents' attachment.

Pre-VCUG preparation. Preparation for stressful medical procedures is known to affect children's emotional reactions (Clafin & Barbarin, 1991; Steward, 1993). Goodman et al. (1997) reported that how much information parents provided their children about what would happen during the VCUG before it occurred affected children's VCUG knowledge, which, in turn, influenced the amount of correct information they reported in the memory interview (see Ornstein et al., 1997, for similar results). It was therefore important to include a measure of children's pre-VCUG preparation in the present study.

Parent–child discussion. Discussion of an experience can also influence subsequent event memory (Goodman et al., 1994; Hamond & Fivush, 1991; Tessler & Nelson, 1994). Baker-Ward, Burgwyn, Ornstein, and Gordon (1995) found that children who asked more questions during a medical procedure later evinced better memory of it than children who asked fewer questions. Similarly, Goodman et al. (1994) found that children whose mothers discussed the VCUG with them after it occurred made fewer errors to direct questions than children whose mothers had not discussed the procedure with them. Although correlational in nature, these studies suggest that parent–child communication influences the content and accuracy of children's recollections.

Parental attachment. In the context of children's memory for emotional events, parent–child communication may be important, in part, because it reflects another variable, namely attachment. Adult attachment theory (Hazan & Shaver, 1987; Main, Kaplan, & Cassidy, 1985) suggests that secure parents are more willing than insecure parents to discuss with their children experiences that involve negative emotions, provide more coherent narrative structures when discussing those experiences, confer greater comfort and sympathy, and help modulate their children's affect (see Bretherton, 1993; Favez, 1997; Goodman et al., 1997). These interaction patterns may then lead to decreased distress and suggestibility about stressful events for children of secure parents, but the opposite pattern (i.e., greater distress and suggestibility) for children of insecure parents. Consistent with these predictions, Goodman et al. (1997) found that secure compared to insecure mothers were more likely to have talked to their child after the VCUG, to have explained it, to have asked questions, to have physically comforted their child, and to have attended to rather than ignored their child's emotional reactions. Further, parental attachment mediated relations between children's distress and memory performance. Children of avoidant parents displayed heightened stress initially, and children of anxious–ambivalent parents were particularly upset when their parents were required by doctors to leave the room midway through the procedure. During the memory interview, children of avoidant parents were particularly likely to err and to be suggestible. Therefore, in Goodman et al.'s study, parental attachment was related to parent–child discussion of the experience, parent comforting behavior, children's stress, and children's memory performance. These findings, while largely predictable from attachment theory, bear replication.

Children's False Event Memory

Of considerable recent interest has been children's suggestibility about never-experienced ("false") events. When young children are told that fictitious events occurred and asked to imagine what happened, a minority (e.g., one-third) will affirm they experienced one or more false events, with 3- to 4-year-olds being more prone to false reports than 5- to 6-year-olds (e.g., Ceci, Loftus, Leichtman, & Bruck, 1994; Leichtman & Ceci, 1995; Shyamalan, Lamb, & Sheldrick, 1995).

However, some researchers and clinicians contend that children can be more easily misled about trivial or positive experiences than about negative ones, especially negative events related to abusive activities (Alpert et al., 1996; Pezdek, Hodge, & Finger, 1997; Rudy & Goodman, 1991; Saywitz, Goodman, Nicholas, & Moan, 1991). In support of this perspective, Ceci, Loftus, et al. (1994) observed that children's false assent rates were higher for positive and neutral experiences (e.g., going on a hot-air balloon ride or waiting for a bus) than for negative experiences (e.g., falling off a tricycle and getting stitches). There remain, however, relatively few studies of children's false memory for negative nonexperienced events. Furthermore, it is unknown if children who assent to false events are more suggestible about experienced events as well, as one would expect if general suggestibility were involved.

The present study

In the present study, we examined children's long-term memory for VCUG, a test that many children find frightening, distressing, and also embarrassing. The doctor-ordered procedure involves the child lying on a table and being catheterized through the urethra. The child's bladder is filled with a contrast medium, and then the child is instructed to void.

X-rays are taken throughout the VCUG. The exact date of the VCUG and core components of the procedure (which is highly standardized) were known from medical records. Thus, we were able to examine the effects of both age at VCUG and delay since VCUG on children's memory accuracy and suggestibility. In addition, to evaluate relations among stress, individual differences, and memory, we collected information from parents about their romantic attachment style; how they prepared their child for the VCUG; their child's emotional reactions before, during, and after the VCUG; and how often they talked with their child about the procedure after it occurred.

We also questioned children about a false but salient and potentially painful event, namely a fictions medical test involving nose surgery. To ensure no child had experienced the nose test, it was modeled after a procedure not currently employed in modern medicine. The procedure was plausible, however, given that it was conducted by Sigmund Freud and Wilhelm Fliess in the late 1800s. The scientists (improperly) attempted to cure various medical problems that they felt were associated with past masturbation in Ms Emma Eckstein by surgically removing a bone from her nose (Masson, 1984). The woman almost died after the surgery, which left her with a deformed face and large cavity in her nasal region. Given that the surgical procedure is no longer in use and given that parents in our study confirmed that their children had not experienced similar surgery, we could be confident that any reports about nose surgery made by children would be false.

Based on previous research, a number of predictions were advanced. First, consistent with research indicating that the offset of infantile amnesia falls between 3 and 4 years (e.g., Pillemer et al., 1994; Sheingold & Tenney, 1982), we expected children who were 4 years of age or older at the time of VCUG to be more likely to remember the test than children who were younger than 4 years at the time of VCUG. Second, delay between the VCUG and memory test was predicted to be negatively related to children's memory accuracy, as is typically found in studies concerning relations between delay and memory, including memory for stressful events (e.g., Goodman et al., 1991). Third, children who were more rather than less prepared for the VCUG were expected to be less distressed during the medical test (Clafin & Barbarin, 1991) and evidence better memory for it (Goodman et al., 1997; Ornstein et al., 1997). Fourth, increased parent–child communication about the VCUG was predicted to have a positive effect on children's memory, as has been observed in other recent investigations (e.g., Hamond & Fivush, 1991). Fifth, consistent with results of Goodman et al. (1997), insecure parental attachment was expected to be related to inaccuracies in children's VCUG memory. Sixth, we predicted that children's age would be negatively related to creation of false memory (e.g., Ceci, Loftus, et al., 1994) and that suggestibility about the true event would be positively related to suggestibility about the false event. Finally, given inconsistencies across stress and memory studies, we did not develop specific a priori predictions about the effects of stress on children's memory, although interrelations among stress, memory, and parental attachment were examined.

Method

Participants

Participants included 43 children, aged 41 months (3 years 5 months) to 163 months (13 years 7 months) at the time of the memory interview ($M = 94$ months, $SD = 28.16$ months). All had undergone at least one VCUG between the ages of 2 and 7 years, and none had participated in previous studies of VCUG memory. A majority of children had only experienced one VCUG ($n = 30$), although 13 had experienced between two and four VCUGs ($M = 1.44$ VCUGs, $SD = .80$ VCUGs). Delay between children's most recent (i.e., target) VCUG and the memory test ranged from 8 to 69 months ($M = 38$ months, $SD = 15.93$ months). Twenty-two participants (7 male and 15 female, $M = 53$ months of age) were identified through hospital records in a medium-sized city in the United States, and 21 (6 male and 15 female, $M = 59$ months of age) were identified through hospital records in a similar-sized city in New Zealand. The majority of participants in both samples were middle class, and 35 were of European descent, 3 were of Latino descent, 2 were of Asian descent, and 3 were of other descent. In both countries, the medical files listed more children who had undergone the VCUG procedure, but many families were unable to be traced. Of those contacted, 83% of the US and 84% of the New Zealand parents agreed to participate. All families were paid for their participation.

Two age groups were created based on age at the time of VCUG. Children who were younger than 48 months when they underwent their most recent VCUG were categorized as young ($n = 17$, $M = 35.71$ months), and children who were 48 months or older when they experienced their most recent VCUG were categorized as old ($n = 26$, $M = 69.23$ months). Two delay groups were also created. Delays of less than 36 months were categorized as short ($n = 20$, $M = 23.95$ months), and delays of 36 months or longer were categorized as long ($n = 23$, $M = 51.13$ months).

Questionnaires

Demographic Questionnaire. This questionnaire, completed by parents, contained general questions about children's personal and family background, such as parents' education, family income, children's ethnicity, and children's health history.

Relationship Questionnaire (Bartholomew & Horowitz, 1991). This questionnaire measured romantic relationship style. On scales of 1 (not at all like me) to 7 (very much like me), respondents rated their similarity to each of four romantic attachment styles: secure, fearful avoidant, preoccupied, and dismissing avoidant. The measure has demonstrated reliability and correlates well with other measures of romantic attachment (Griffin & Bartholomew, 1994).

Emotional Reaction Questionnaire. This questionnaire, developed for the present study, tapped parents' judgments of their child's upset and fear immediately before, during, and immediately after the child's target VCUG. Ratings range from 1 (not upset/afraid) to 5 (very upset/afraid).

Parent–Child Communication Questionnaire (Goodman et al., 1994, 1997). This questionnaire concerned how parents prepared their child for the VCUG before it occurred and how often parents talked with their child about the VCUG afterward. Pre-VCUG preparation was scored on a 4-point scale: 1 = parent told child nothing about VCUG, 2 = parent told child that he/she would have a medical test, 3 = parent told child about core features of VCUG, and 4 = parent told child details about VCUG. The other questions asked how often mothers and fathers talked to their child about the VCUG immediately to 1 week after and from 1 week after to present, and were scored as 0 (never), 1 (infrequently), 2 (occasionally), or 3 (frequently).

Memory interview. The memory interview was divided into four sections: free recall, anatomically detailed doll and props demonstration, direct questions, and false-event questions. The free-recall and anatomical doll and props sections consisted of vague, general prompts asking the child to describe what happened when the child had "a test where they put a tube in [the child]." Follow-up prompts were asked if a child did not provide any correct information about the VCUG in response to the first prompt (i.e., "It was a long, thin tube and they put it inside you. Tell [and show] me about that test." "It was the time you got the treat/toy [via parental report] because you did so well at that test. Tell [and show] me about that test"). Note that the location of the tube's placement (i.e., in the genital area) was not mentioned in either the free recall or doll and props sections. For the anatomical doll and props questions, the child was handed the tube and doll and instructed to "show" and tell what happened. The props consisted of medical props, about half of which were items used during the VCUG (e.g., model of the X-ray table, catheter) and about half of which were items not used during the VCUG (e.g., stethoscope, reflex hammer), although some of the latter were relevant to the false event (e.g., fake scissors).

The third section consisted of direct questions (24 specific and 18 misleading) about what happened during the VCUG. The section began with a description of the symptom experienced by the child that led to the VCUG (e.g., if the child had frequent incontinence problems prior to experiencing the VCUG, the researcher said, "I need to know about the time you had that test with the tube because you had problems going to the bathroom"). Specific and misleading questions were counterbalanced such that, within each type, some correct answers were "yes" (e.g., "Did they put the tube in your [child's word for genitals]?" "The doctor didn't have a nurse or assistant in the room with him, did he?" when in fact there had been an assistant present), other correct answers were "no" (e.g., "Did you have to hold on to a pillow during that test?" "The walls in the room where you had that medical test were red, isn't that right?" when in fact the walls were not red), and still other correct answers were open-ended responses (e.g., "Who took you to the hospital to have that medical test?" "What color was the rug on the floor in the room where you got that test?" when in fact there had not been a rug). The direct questions concluded with a brief description of the VCUG and the question "Have you ever had this test?"

The fourth section of the interview concerned the false medical test that none of the children had experienced. The questions were designed to parallel as closely as possible those asked in the VCUG free-recall and anatomical doll and props sections, and the description of the VCUG at the end of the direct question section. The first prompt was "I want to ask you about another test that you had a while ago at the hospital. It was a medical test you had because you had problems with your nose. Tell me everything you remember about that test." For the doll and props false test questions, the child was told to use the scissors and medical items to show and tell what happened. As in the earlier sections, follow-up prompts were asked if a child did not describe any test in response to the first prompt (i.e., "Tell me about the test you had because you sneezed all the time. The test when the doctor put something up your nose." "Tell me about the test that made your nose bleed a little"). The section concluded with a brief description of the nose test, in which the doctor was said to have cut some bone out of the child's nose to stop the child from sneezing, followed by the question, "Have you ever had this test?" The description matched that used to describe the VCUG in length and in number and types of actions.

Procedure

A researcher contacted parents by phone and explained that we were conducting a study of children's perceptions of previous medical experiences. Although parents were informed that we would interview their child about prior medical experiences, parents were not explicitly told on the phone of our interest in VCUG or memory.[1] Interviews were typically scheduled at parents' homes, although 18% of the US parents elected to be seen at the university. All parents and children were interviewed individually.

Parent interview. A female researcher began by privately explaining to parents that we wanted to question their child about the VCUG. The researcher showed parents the questionnaires that would be administered as well as the anatomical doll and medical props, and then obtained parents' written consent to participate. No parent refused.

Next the parent was asked to complete the Demographic Questionnaire, Relationship Questionnaire, Emotional Reaction Questionnaire,
and Parent–Child Communication Questionnaire. Additionally, to verify
some of the child's answers, the parent was asked a few questions about
the child's target VCUG experience (e.g., who took the child to get
the test). The parent was also asked whether the child ever had any
procedure similar to the false medical test.

Child interview. After parental consent was obtained, a second female
researcher began the child interview. The researcher first explained that
she wanted to ask the child some questions about "doctor stuff," the
child could skip any question he or she did not want to answer, and the
child could stop at any time. The child's assent to be interviewed was
secured.

The memory interview was administered as follows:[2] First, the
researcher read the free-recall questions. Second, the researcher showed
the child the anatomical doll, and they undressed it together. The
researcher pointed out that the doll was special because it had parts
like the child. Next the researcher brought out the medical props one
at a time, alternating between VCUG and non-VCUG items. To ensure
the child was comfortable with and could use the doll and medical
props, the child was first asked to demonstrate what happens when
the child gets a shot and gets his or her throat checked. All children
performed these actions satisfactorily. Then the researcher handed the
child the tube and doll and asked the anatomical doll and prop VCUG
questions. Third, the researcher asked the child the direct questions
about the VCUG. Finally, the researcher questioned the child about the
false medical event. Prior to asking the anatomical doll and prop questions regarding the false event, the researcher handed the child the
doll and scissors. The interview was videotaped and later transcribed
verbatim.

Debriefing. After the interview, children were debriefed. This included
correcting misperceptions and, when applicable, explaining that it is
difficult to remember things that happened long ago. Children were
also either congratulated for resisting questions about the false event or
informed that the researcher made an error because they never had
the nose test. Finally, parents and children were thanked and parents
were paid.

Results

Coding

To score children's responses, we relied on medical records, knowledge of standard VCUG practice, and parental report. For each dependent measure, reliability of coding was established by two independent researchers on at least 23% of the children's responses with proportion of agreement at or above .89. Discrepancies were resolved through discussion. One or both researchers then scored all of the children's data.

Free recall and anatomical doll and props. The free-recall and anatomical doll and prop sections of the interview were transcribed and coded for correct and incorrect units of information about agents, actions, recipients, body parts, and objects. Verbal and demonstration units were transcribed and scored so that they were directly comparable. Thus, a child who said "a tube went in my peepee" received the same number of correct units (4: "tube" = agent, "went in" = action, "child" = recipient, "peepee" = body part) as a child who said nothing but demonstrated a tube being inserted into the doll's genital area. Inaccurate descriptions of the VCUG, information not related to the VCUG, and descriptions of other medical tests experienced by the child were all coded as incorrect. Thus, the statement "They got a big needle and sticked the tube in my belly button" received 5 incorrect units: agent (they), action (sticked), recipient (child), body part (belly button), and object (tube with needle). Correct and incorrect units were summed separately for the free-recall and anatomical doll and props sections.

Direct questions. Responses to the direct questions were scored as one of the following: correct, commission error, omission error, do-not-know, or unscorable. For example, to the specific question "Where did they put the tube when they put it inside you?", the response "in my privates" was scored as correct, "in my arm" was scored as a commission error, and "nowhere" was scored as an omission error. Unscorable responses composed 3% of children's answers to specific questions and 2% of their answers to misleading questions and are not considered further. Proportions were created by summing each type of response and dividing by the number of questions asked. Separate proportions were computed for specific and misleading questions.[3]

Overall VCUG access scores. After reading each child's responses to the entire interview, a researcher judged whether the child ever accessed memory of the VCUG. Each child's interview was rated as either 0 (no VCUG memory), 1 (possible vague memory of VCUG), or 2 (definite VCUG memory).

False medical event scores. Three scores were derived from children's responses to the false-event questions. First, a dichotomous variable was created to indicate whether (1) or not (0) the child ever falsely assented to the nose procedure. Second, a 4-point scale was created to score the extent of children's false reports across the entire false medical event section: 0 = child never made a false report about the nose test; 1 = child falsely assented that the nose test happened but did not provide any narrative details; 2 = child provided false narrative details, but the details were reproductions of information provided by the interviewer (e.g., when asked to show and tell what happened when the doctor put the tiny scissors up the child's nose, one child repeated the described action on the anatomical doll); 3 = child provided unique information about the false event (e.g., one boy said he forgot what happened when the doctor put the tube up his nose because he was asleep during that part of the test). Third, children's responses to the full description of the false event were scored as correct (denied it occurred), incorrect (assented it occurred), do-not-know, or unscorable.

Preliminary analyses

Correlations were computed to examine interrelations among gender, sample location (United States, New Zealand), age at time of VCUG, age at time of interview, delay between VCUG and memory interview, and number of VCUGs experienced. Age at interview was strongly related to age at VCUG and delay, $rs(43) = .73$, $ps \le .001$. Children who were younger at the time of interview were younger when they experienced the VCUG and were questioned following shorter delays. The particularly high correlation between age at VCUG and age at interview ($r = .85$) precluded examining both variables simultaneously or unconfounding fully their separate effects. With regard to the high correlation between delay and age at interview, see below. No other correlations were significant; rs (43) ranged from $-.23$ to $.23$.

Correlations of children's gender, sample location, and number of VCUGs with measures of children's VCUG memory were also calculated. Delay and age at VCUG were partialled. Children's gender was unrelated to their VCUG memory: $rs(39)$ ranged from $-.25$ to $.21$. Number of VCUGs was positively related to the amount of correct information about the VCUG provided in free recall, $r(39) = .40$, $p < .05$. Significant correlations emerged for sample location with the following variables: do-not-know responses to specific and misleading questions, $rs(39) \geq .38$, and correct responses to misleading questions, $r(39) = -.46$, $ps \leq .01$. Compared to US children, New Zealand children were more likely to say "I do not know" to specific and misleading questions and less likely to answer misleading questions accurately. Number of VCUGs experienced and sample location were then covaried or partialled from relevant analyses.

Effects of age at VCUG and delay

Our first two hypotheses were that children who were 4 years or older when they underwent their most recent VCUG would remember the procedure better than children who were younger than 4 years and that children questioned following shorter delays would evince better memory than children questioned following longer delays. To test these predictions, we conducted 2 (age at VCUG: young vs old) × 2 (delay: short vs long) analyses of variance (ANOVAs) with the memory variables entered as separate dependent measures. We conducted similar age × delay analyses of covariance (ANCOVAs) with number of VCUGs as the covariate because of its significant positive relation to children's memory (i.e., free recall correct). Significant ANOVA results are reported below when they were confirmed by the ANCOVAs. In addition, because a number of children who were younger at the time of the interview were necessarily in the short-delay group (e.g., children who were 4 years or younger at interview could only have had the VCUG up to a maximum of 2 years prior), we conducted one-way delay ANCOVAs with age at *interview* and number of VCUGs entered as covariates.[4] Finally, we examined effects of age at VCUG and delay for only those children who remembered the procedure. All significant effects are reported.

Analyses including all children. Children's free-recall and anatomical doll and props correct and incorrect units were entered into separate 2 (age at VCUG) × 2 (delay) ANOVAs.[5] Significant main effects of age (table 5.1) and delay, $F(1, 39) = 7.32$, $p = .01$, emerged for correct units children provided with the doll and props. As predicted, children 4 years or older at VCUG provided a greater amount of correct information with the doll and props than children younger than 4 years, and children interviewed following delays shorter than 3 years, $M = 2.50$ ($SD = 3.03$), provided more correct information than children interviewed following delays of 3 years or longer, $M = .96$ ($SD = 2.50$). The delay effect remained significant when the one-way delay ANCOVA was conducted with age at interview and number of VCUGs as covariates, $F(1, 39) = 12.58$, $p = .001$.

For specific questions, significant main effects of age emerged for proportion correct responses and commission errors (table 5.1), although the former became nonsignificant when number of VCUGs was covaried, $F(1, 38) = 3.76$, $p = .06$. Children who were younger when they experienced the VCUG made more commission errors to specific questions than children who were older at the time of VCUG. The main effect of delay was significant for proportion of commission errors and do-not-know responses, $Fs(1, 39) \geq 6.08$, $ps < .05$: Children questioned following shorter delays made more commission errors, $M = .20$ ($SD = .13$), and fewer do-not-know responses, $M = .13$ ($SD = .13$), than children questioned following longer delays, $Ms = .07$ ($SD = .07$) and .28 ($SD = .23$), respectively. However, the delay effects were no longer significant when age at interview and number of VCUGs were covaried in the one-way delay ANCO-VAs, $Fs(1, 39) \leq 1.52$.

When responses to misleading questions were analyzed, a significant main effect of age emerged for commission errors, indicating that younger children made more commission errors to misleading questions than older children (table 5.1). Main effects of delay were significant for commission errors, omission errors, and do-not-know responses, $Fs(1, 39) \geq 8.43$, $ps < .01$, indicating that children questioned following shorter delays made significantly more commission and omission errors and fewer do-not-know responses than children questioned following longer delays. Once again, these significant delay effects were no longer evident when age at time of interview and number of VCUGs were covaried, $Fs(1, 39) \leq 3.65$.

The main effect of age was significant when children's VCUG access score ($0 = $ no VCUG memory, $n = 13$; $1 = $ may have vague VCUG memory, $n = 4$; $2 = $ definite VCUG memory, $n = 26$) was entered into a 2 (age at VCUG) × 2 (delay) ANOVA. As expected, children 4 years or older at

Table 5.1 Children's mean memory performance by age at time of VCUG and delay with significant main effects of age at VCUG indicated (standard deviation in parentheses)

	Young			Old				
	Short (n = 10)	Long (n = 7)	Mean (n = 17)	Short (n = 10)	Long (n = 16)	Mean (n = 26)	F(1, 39)	p
Free recall (units)								
Total correct	1.90 (3.14)	.43 (1.13)	1.29 (2.57)	3.90 (4.15)	7.44 (9.70)	6.08 (8.10)	4.63	<.05
Total incorrect	2.30 (3.68)	1.00 (1.73)	1.76 (3.03)	4.00 (4.34)	2.13 (2.63)	2.85 (3.44)	1.87	
Anatomical doll and props (units)								
Total correct[b]	.60 (1.26)	.00 (.00)	.35 (1.00)	4.40 (3.13)	1.38 (2.91)	2.54 (3.30)	11.32	<.01[a]
Total incorrect	3.90 (3.31)	1.00 (1.73)	2.71 (3.08)	1.00 (2.83)	.94 (2.05)	.96 (2.32)	3.44	<.10
Specific questions (proportions)								
Correct responses	.40 (.13)	.56 (.13)	.46 (.15)	.67 (.16)	.57 (.22)	.61 (.20)	6.65	=.01
Commission errors	.27 (.12)	.10 (.06)	.20 (.13)	.13 (.10)	.05 (.08)	.08 (.09)	10.65	<.01[a]
Omission errors	.12 (.08)	.08 (.07)	.11 (.08)	.07 (.05)	.05 (.08)	.06 (.07)	3.52	<.10
Don't know responses	.14 (.13)	.22 (.17)	.18 (.15)	.12 (.13)	.31 (.25)	.23 (.23)	.23	
Misleading questions (proportions)								
Correct responses	.17 (.10)	.37 (.13)	.25 (.15)	.37 (.23)	.37 (.25)	.37 (.24)	2.47	
Commission errors	.53 (.11)	.27 (.17)	.42 (.18)	.33 (.20)	.12 (.08)	.20 (.17)	16.53	<.001[a]
Omission errors	.13 (.07)	.06 (.06)	.10 (.07)	.09 (.05)	.04 (.06)	.06 (.06)	2.64	
Don't know responses	.14 (.13)	.28 (.18)	.20 (.16)	.20 (.26)	.48 (.26)	.37 (.29)	3.09	<.10
VCUG access score	.50 (.85)	1.00 (.82)	.71 (.85)	1.80 (.63)	1.63 (.80)	1.69 (.74)	15.09	<.001[a]

Children classified as young were less than 4 years at VCUG, and children classified as old were 4 years or older. Short delays correspond to delays of less than 3 years between the VCUG and memory test, and long delays correspond to 3 years or more between the VCUG and memory test.

[a] These age effects remained significant when number of VCUGs was entered as a covariate into 2 (age) × 2 (delay) ANCOVAs.

[b] One-way age at VCUG and one-way delay ANOVAs, conducted because of a floor effect for children in the young, long delay group, confirmed significant main effects of age at VCUG and delay.

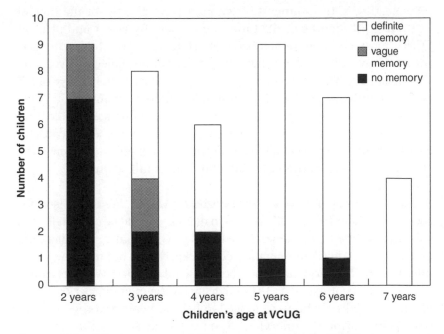

Figure 5.1 Whether or not children remembered the VCUG at any point during the interview as a function of their age in years at the time of VCUG

VCUG were more likely to evidence some memory of the VCUG compared to children less than 4 years at VCUG (table 1).

Childhood amnesia. By examining the data qualitatively, our study permitted exploration of an age cut-off for childhood amnesia. Based on retrospective childhood amnesia studies, one would expect that children who experienced a VCUG before the age of 3 or 4 years would not have any memory for it. As can be seen in figure 5.1, none of the nine children who were 2 years old when they experienced the VCUG provided clear memory of the test during the interview. For these children, the delay between VCUG and memory interview ranged from 9 to 63 months. The two 2-year-olds who provided vague evidence that may have been indicative of VCUG memory were 29 and 35 months when they experienced the VCUG and 55 and 90 months, respectively, when interviewed. Children who were age 3 when they underwent the VCUG performed much better, with four of the eight children clearly remembering it, the youngest of whom was 37 months at the time of VCUG and 59 months at the time of interview. By age 5 and older at VCUG, most children remembered it. However, one child who was 66 months at VCUG and another who was 83 months failed to reveal any VCUG memory. These two children were interviewed after delays of 57 and 45 months, respectively. Interestingly, children's memory of VCUG was never scored as "vague" if the VCUG occurred after age 3, indicating that VCUGs experienced after that age were either remembered relatively clearly or not accessible at all. Alternatively, it is possible that a few older children remembered the VCUG but chose not to talk about it.

Analyses including children who remembered the VCUG. We were also concerned with whether age differences in memory would be evident for the subset of children who remembered the VCUG. Would age predict only whether or not children remembered the experience, but not how much information children who remembered it could report? We thus examined the effects of age at VCUG and delay on the memory performance of the 26 children who were judged to have remembered the VCUG at some point during the interview (2 in the young, short-delay group; 2 in the young, long-delay group; 9 in the old, short-delay group; and 13 in the old, long-delay group). The reduced *n* precluded conducting ANOVAs. We instead computed correlations between children's age at VCUG and the memory variables with delay and number of VCUGs partialled, and between delay and the memory variables first with age at VCUG and number of VCUGs partialled and then with age at interview and number of VCUGs partialled.

With regard to age at VCUG, only one significant correlation was evident: Increases in the amount of correct information children provided with the anatomical doll corresponded to increases in their age at the time of their most recent VCUG, $r(22) = .46$, $p < .05$. However, the lack of age differences in children's performance needs to be interpreted with caution because of the small number of children included in the analyses. There were still substantial differences across age at VCUG for some (e.g., free-recall units correct: children younger than 4 years at VCUG, $M = 3.25$, $SD = 3.95$, $n = 4$; children 4 years or older at VCUG, $M = 7.00$, $SD = 8.47$, $n = 22$) though not all (e.g., proportion correct to specific questions: children younger than 4 years at VCUG, $M = .65$, $SD = .18$; children older than 4 years at VCUG, $M = .65$, $SD = .17$) memory measures.

When children's age at VCUG and number of VCUGs were partialled, delay was negatively related to correct units with the anatomical doll and props and to commission errors to misleading questions, $rs \leq -.41$, $ps < .05$, and positively related to do-not-know responses to specific and misleading questions, $rs(22) \geq .40$, $ps \leq .05$. However, when age at interview was substituted for age at VCUG, only the correlation between delay and anatomical doll and props correct units remained significant, $r(22) = -.55$, $p < .01$, such that, among children who remembered the VCUG, longer delays were associated with decreases in the amount of correct information children provided.

Summary. Results of analyses including all children confirmed our prediction regarding age differences in children's memory: Older children at time of VCUG were more likely than younger children to reveal memory of the VCUG procedure. Older children also provided more units of correct information with the doll and props and made fewer commission errors to specific and misleading questions. However, when memory in children who remembered the VCUG was examined separately, age at VCUG was no longer a robust predictor of memory performance. Younger and older children differed significantly only in the amount of correct information they provided with the anatomical doll and medical props: age at VCUG therefore predicted whether or not children remembered the VCUG and how much information they provided when minimally prompted, but not the accuracy of their answers to direct questions.

With respect to the influence of delay, our prediction was partially supported. As expected, compared to children interviewed after delays of 3 years or more, children interviewed after delays of less than 3 years provided a greater amount of correct information with the anatomical doll and props. This pattern was evident when all children were considered as well as when only those children who clearly remembered the VCUG were considered. However, in contrast to our expectations, longer delays were not associated with greater inaccuracies in children's memory or with heightened suggestibility.

Effects of stress

Prior research has been contradictory concerning effects of stress on memory. We were therefore especially interested in how stress would relate to children's long-term memory for VCUG. Mean stress ratings are presented in table 5.2. First, to identify potentially confounding variables, we correlated children's age at VCUG, number of VCUGs, and children's gender with their VCUG distress. Age at VCUG was inversely related to children's level of fear during and upset after the VCUG, $rs(37) \leq -.33$ $ps < .05$. Additionally, correlations with age partialled indicated that female children expressed more upset during the VCUG than male children, $r(35) = .42$, $p = .01$. Number of VCUGs was unrelated to children's stress; rs ranged from .24 to $-.30$.

Next, to examine relations between stress and children's memory, we created plot charts of the stress and memory variables. No nonlinear (e.g., inverted U-shaped) trends were evident. We then correlated, with age partialled, parents reports of children's stress (i.e., fear and upset ratings before, during, and after the VCUG) and children's VCUG memory. Similar to conflicting findings in the literature, our results were somewhat mixed. Increases in children's fear during and upset after the VCUG were associated with decreases in amount of correct information provided in free recall. When children's gender was partialled along with age at VCUG, increased fear after the VCUG was also associated with fewer correct units in free recall ($rs \leq -.32$, $ps \subseteq .05$, dfs ranged from 29 to 34). Greater upset and fear after the VCUG were associated with decreases in the amount of correct information provided with the anatomical doll and props, $rs = -.34$ and $-.43$, $ps < .05$, $dfs = 34$ and 30, although the relation between upset and correct information decreased slightly when age and gender were partialled, $r = -.30$, $p < .10$. These findings indicate that children's stress during and after the VCUG was negatively related to how much correct information they provided when minimally prompted.

Observed relations between stress and memory were somewhat different when children's responses to direct questions were considered. Greater upset prior to the VCUG was related to increases in children's correct and decreases in their do-not-know responses to misleading questions, $rs(34) = .37$ and $-.39$, respectively, and greater fear during the VCUG was associated with decreases in children's omission errors to misleading questions, $r(34) = -.36$, all $ps < .05$. Increased upset before the VCUG was also negatively related to proportion do-not-know responses to specific questions, $r(34) = -.32$, $p = .05$, although this correlation decreased to nonsignificant levels, $r = -.31$, $p < .10$, when age and gender were partialled. Thus, children who were more distressed

Table 5.2 Children's mean upset and afraid scores before, during, and after VCUG for each age and delay group (standard deviations in parentheses)

	Young			Old		
	Short (n = 7–8)	Long (n = 6–7)	Mean (n = 13–15)	Short (n = 8–9)	Long (n = 12–14)	Mean (n = 20–23)
Before						
Upset	2.38 (1.69)	2.14 (1.22)	2.27 (1.44)	3.00 (1.60)	2.71 (1.07)	2.82 (1.26)
Afraid	2.50 (1.51)	2.29 (1.50)	2.40 (1.45)	3.38 (1.41)	2.85 (1.14)	3.05 (1.24)
During						
Upset	4.00 (1.07)	4.43 (.79)	4.20 (.94)	3.89 (1.54)	4.14 (1.03)	4.04 (1.22)
Afraid	4.13 (1.13)	4.29 (.76)	4.20 (.94)	3.22 (1.92)	4.00 (1.29)	3.68 (1.59)
After						
Upset	3.13 (1.46)	3.29 (1.50)	3.20 (1.42)	1.89 (.93)	2.77 (1.74)	2.41 (1.50)
Afraid	3.00 (1.15)	2.67 (1.37)	2.85 (1.21)	1.50 (.76)	2.50 (1.68)	2.10 (1.45)

Upset and afraid ratings are based on 5-point Likert scales ranging from 1 (not upset/afraid) to 5 (very upset/afraid). Children classified as young were less than 4 years at VCUG. Children classified as old were 4 years or older. Short delays corresponded to less than 3 years between the VCUG and interview. Long delays corresponded to 3 years or more.

before and during the VCUG were less suggestible. Overall, the results indicate that the type of memory questions (e.g., free recall vs misleading questions) and the point of measurement of children's emotional reactions (e.g., before, during, or after a stressful event) may have different implications for their memory of, or at least willingness to talk about, a negative experience.

Sources of individual differences

To test our third prediction, that children who had been more prepared for the VCUG would be less stressed and display better memory than children who had been less prepared, we correlated parents' reports of child preparation for the VCUG with children's stress ratings and memory performance. Age at VCUG was partialled because of its significant positive relation to pre-VCUG preparation, $r(40) = .35$. Consistent with previous research (e.g., Clafin & Barbarin, 1991) and the first portion of our prediction, children who were more prepared for the VCUG were less upset and afraid both during and after the VCUG, $rs \leq -.33$, $df = 28 - 33$, $ps \leq .05$. However, correlations between parents' preparation and children's memory failed to support the second portion of our prediction; $rs(37)$ ranged from $-.20$ to $.28$.

Our fourth hypothesis was that increased parent–child discussion after the VCUG would be positively related to children's long-term memory. We correlated parents' reports of how frequently they and their children talked about the VCUG with the memory variables. With age at VCUG partialled, only one significant relation was observed: mother–child conversations immediately to 1 week after the VCUG were inversely related to children's commission errors to specific questions, $r(37) = -.41$, $p < .05$. This correlation remained significant when both age at VCUG and pre-VCUG preparation were partialled, $r(34) = -.42$, $p = .01$.

Our fifth hypothesis was that insecure parental attachment would be related to inaccuracies in children's memory for VCUG. We were also interested in the relations of parents' romantic attachment to children's VCUG distress, parents' pre-VCUG preparation of their children, and parent–child post-VCUG communication. One significant correlation emerged between parents' ratings of their similarity to the four attachment styles (secure, fearful avoidant, preoccupied, and dismissing avoidant) and children's levels of fear and upset (age at VCUG was partialled). Children who were more upset before the VCUG had parents who rated themselves higher on the fearful avoidant attachment scale, $r(33) = .52$, $p < .01$. No significant correlations emerged between parents' attachment style ratings and how much they prepared their children for the VCUG or talked with their children about it afterward; rs ranged from $-.23$ to $.24$; dfs ranged from 35 to 37.

Finally, we computed correlations between parents' ratings on the four attachment style scales and children's memory with age at VCUG partialled (table 5.3). We also conducted similar correlations with both age at VCUG and location (United States vs New Zealand) partialled because more New Zealand compared to US parents rated themselves high on the dismissing avoidant attachment scale. These latter results are reported when they differ from results of correlations partialling age at VCUG.[6]

Only parents' similarity to the two types of avoidant attachment styles (fearful and dismissing) was significantly related to children's memory performance. Higher scores on the fearful avoidant scale were associated with decreases in incorrect units children provided with the anatomical doll and props, increases in children's omission errors to specific questions, and decreases in children's do-not-know responses to misleading questions (although the latter correlation became non-significant when location was partialled, $r = -.30$, $p < .10$). A different pattern emerged between children's memory and parents' dismissing avoidant attachment scores: higher scores on this scale were associated with children making more commission errors to specific and misleading questions and providing fewer do-not-know responses to specific questions. These correlations became stronger when location was also partialled: commission errors to specific questions, $r = .43$; don't know responses to specific questions, $r = -.51$; and commission errors to misleading questions, $r = .47$; all $ps < .01$. Furthermore, when location was partialled, the following correlations with scores on the dismissing avoidant scale became significant: total correct units with anatomical doll and props, $r = .32$, $p < .05$; do-not-know responses to misleading questions, $r = -.42$, $p < .01$.

Because of the significant relation between fearful avoidance in parents and children's pre-VCUG upset ($r = .52$), we again conducted correlation between stress and children's memory with parents' fearful avoidance ratings partialled followed by correlations between parental attachment and children's memory with children's upset before the

Table 5.3 Correlations between parents' romantic attachment styles and children's memory, with children's age at VCUG partialled ($dfs = 38$)

	Secure	Fearful avoidant	Preoccupied	Dismissing avoidant
Free recall (units)				
Total correct	−.09	−.16	.03	.18
Total incorrect	−.12	.25	−.20	.02
Anatomical doll and props (units)				
Total correct	.03	−.01	−.05	.28[a]
Total incorrect	.14	−.37*	.13	.14
Specific questions (proportions)				
Correct responses	−.13	.11	−.04	.16
Commission errors	−.22	.25	−.17	.40**
Omission errors	.01	.32*	−.15	−.10
Don't know responses	.17	−.30	.17	−.33*
Misleading questions (proportions)				
Correct responses	.07	.30	−.04	−.09
Commission errors	−.18	.13	−.03	.41**
Omission errors	−.06	.08	−.27	−.01
Don't know responses	.06	−.33*	.14	−.21[a]
VCUG access score	−.20	.23	−.09	.19

Parents' rated their similarity to each of the four romantic attachment styles on scales of 1 (not at all like me) to 7 (very similar to me).

[a] These correlations became significant when age at VCUG and location were partialled, $ps < .05$.

*$p < .05$.

**$p < .01$.

VCUG partialled. Age was partialled as well. None of the significant relations between children's upset before the VCUG and their direct question responses and between fearful avoidance attachment in parents and children's direct question responses remained significant; rs ranged from −.27 to .27. In some cases, the lack of a significant relation after partialling seemed to result from a drop in statistical power. In other cases, the results suggested that the high correlation between parental fearful avoidant attachment and stress before the VCUG made it difficult to untangle their effects on children's responses to direct, especially misleading, questions.

In summary, as predicted, children with more insecure parents made a greater number of errors when recounting the VCUG than children with less insecure parents. Children of parents who rated themselves high on the fearful avoidant attachment scale were more upset prior to the start of the VCUG and, during the memory interview, were more likely to omit information, resulting in less incorrect information with the anatomical doll and props and more omission errors in response to specific questions. Children of parents who scored themselves high on the dismissing avoidant attachment scale were particularly suggestible about the VCUG, although these children also provided more units of correct information with the doll and props.

False event

Three children were not interviewed about the false event (parents refused in two cases, and the child did not complete the interview in the third case). Of the 40 children questioned, 17 made some type of false affirmation that the nose test had occurred, despite parents privately indicating that their children had not experienced a similar medical test. One of these children simply made a false assent to the nose test, 3 replicated information provided by the interviewer, and the remaining 12 gave some new information about the false medical event.

To investigate the relation between children's age and false reports, children were divided into three age-at-interview groups: 3–5-year-olds ($n = 11$, $M = 59.27$ months), 6–8-year-olds ($n = 17$, $M = 94.76$ months), and 9–14 years ($n = 12$, $M = 126.33$ months). Two one-way age-at-interview ANOVAs were conducted, one with whether or not children made a false report as the dependent measure and one with extent of false report as the dependent measure. Note that because the false event never occurred, there was no corresponding age at event or delay since event, nor were children's ages at VCUG or delay since VCUG relevant. Results, presented in table 5.4, revealed that the 3–5-year-olds scored significantly higher on both false-report measures than the 6–8 and 9–14-year-olds. The differences between the 6–8 and 9–14-year-olds were also significant. Thus, not surprisingly, children's

Table 5.4   Children's false reports of the nose procedure according to their age at the time of the interview (standard deviations in parentheses)

	Age group				
	3- to 5-year-olds (n = 11)	6- to 8-year-olds (n = 17)	9- to 14-year-olds (n = 12)	F(2, 37)	p
Whether or not child made false report[a]	.73[a] (.48)	.47[b] (.51)	.08[a] (.29)	6.16	<.01
Extent of child's false report[b]	2.18[a] (1.40)	1.18[b] (1.38)	.17[a] (.58)	8.02	=.001

A different subscript indicates significant differences based on planned comparisons, all $rs(1, 37) > 4.95$.

[a] Whether or not a child made false report was scored as 0 (child never makes false report) or 1 (child makes a false report at some point during the interview).
[b] Extent-of-false-report scores ranged from 0 (child makes no false report) to 3 (child provides unique, elaborate details).

age predicted their willingness to assent to the nonexperienced event and the extent of their false reports.

We also investigated relations of children's false reports to other experimental and performance characteristics by correlating whether or not children made a false report and the extent of their false reports with the VCUG memory variables; children's medical history, including number of VCUGs experienced; and parents' scores on the four romantic attachment scales. Age at interview was partialled. Whether or not children made a false report and the extent of their false elaborations were positively related to proportion correct responses to specific questions about the VCUG, $rs(37) \geq .31$, $ps \leq .05$, and negatively related to proportion of do-not-know responses to misleading questions, $rs(37) \leq -31$, $ps \leq .05$. The correlation between whether or not children made a false report and their proportion of do-not-know responses to specific questions closely approached significance, $r(37) = -.30$, $p = .06$.

Thus, children who answered the direct questions about the VCUG rather than saying "I don't know" tended to provide more false information when questioned about the nose test.

Only one significant correlation emerged when the false-report measures were correlated with parents' similarity to the four attachment styles and children's previous medical experiences (i.e., number of VCUGs, number of prior illnesses). With age at interview partialled, number of VCUGs was positively related to whether or not children made a false report, $r(37) = .40, p = .01$.

As a final point regarding children's false reports of the medical test, when read the full description and asked whether they ever experienced the nose test, only 5 children inaccurately reported that they had in fact received the nose test. An additional 11 responded "I don't know," and the remaining 24 children correctly answered "no" that they never underwent the procedure. Thus, children's false reports tended to occur in free recall after being provided with limited information about the procedure or with anatomical doll and props after being given the doll and scissors and being told to demonstrate what happened. Interestingly, 4 of the 5 children who incorrectly assented to the full description and 8 of the 11 children who responded with "I don't know" were from New Zealand. Thus, as was evident in preliminary analyses, cultural difference may well exist in children's resistance to false suggestions.

Discussion

The goal of this study was to investigate effects of age, delay, emotion, and individual-difference factors on children's long-term memory for a stressful medical procedure. The results provide new insight into theoretical issues regarding childhood memory and infantile amnesia. They also provide useful information for applied issues concerning child eyewitness capabilities.

Childhood amnesia

Consistent with previous research (e.g., Pillemer et al., 1994; Terr, 1988), children's age when they experienced the most recent VCUG emerged as a powerful predictor of whether or not they remembered the procedure. A qualitative examination of our data revealed that most children who were 2 years old when they experienced the VCUG provided no clear evidence of remembering it, although a few seemed to have a vague VCUG memory. In contrast, most children who were 3 years old at the time of the experience showed either clear memory of the stressful medical test or at least a possibly vague memory of it. Interestingly, if the event was experienced at age 4 years or older, most children remembered the experience, with vague memories no longer evident. In short, between 3 and 4 years of age appeared to be a crucial turning point for the accessibility of early VCUG memories.

When the performance of children who remembered the VCUG was examined, most significant age effects disappeared. The only difference was that younger children provided fewer units of correct information with the anatomical doll and props than did older children. Once again, given that the sample *n* decreased considerably, we may have lacked sufficient statistical power to detect significant relations between age at event and memory. Further research is needed to explore whether, for children who reveal memory of early experiences, children who were young at the time of the event remember such experiences as well as do children who were older.

Our findings are similar to those of two lines of research: studies that demonstrate a general cut-off age before which older children and adults do not remember early experiences (e.g., Pillemer et al., 1994; Sheingold & Tenney, 1982; Winograd & Killenger, 1983) and studies that indicate a few children can remember, even after lengthy delays, events experienced when they were mere toddlers (Hewitt, 1994; Myers, Perris, & Speaker, 1994; Terr, 1988). In one of the few investigations of children's memory for traumatic experiences, Terr (1988) found that most children who were younger than 36 months at the time of the trauma failed to reveal verbal memory of their experience, although a few provided "spot" or "scanty" verbal reports. Similarly, we found that a few children who were as young as 2 or 3 years of age at the time of the VCUG revealed some memory of it. For example, in free recall, one 5-year-old girl who was barely 3 (i.e., 37 months) when she experienced the VCUG said. "They put a catheter in there and um, I didn't want it and my dad holded me and I didn't want it just cuz I was afraid. . . . My mom. I was real brave. And my brother went there too to put his tubes in his car . . . and what happened is I didn't want it cuz I was real scared and I wasn't brave but I was. And there was toys there and a pretend flying airplane." Although much of the child's report could not be verified as correct (e.g., whether the child was brave), other parts of it indeed revealed her intact VCUG memory. These results, considered in conjunction with other findings, suggest that stressful and traumatic memories tend to be governed by similar, general age-related mechanisms that dictate whether early childhood experiences will be remembered in the long term. Proposal of a special memory mechanism for stressful events that alters the standard childhood-amnesia age effect does not seem warranted based on our data.

In contrast, we found only limited support for our second prediction, that increased delay would be associated with decreased accuracy of children's memory. Shorter delays (i.e., delays of less than 3 years) were associated with improved memory performance with the anatomical doll and props, but longer delays (i.e., 3 to almost 6 years) were not associated with greater inaccuracies in reporting or suggestibility. Although delay is typically associated with decreasing accuracy (e.g., Goodman et al., 1991; Pillemer et al., 1994; Poole & White, 1993), most studies of children's memory and suggestibility have not included delays up to 6 years. We may speculate that once a long enough delay has ensued, children's memory traces become so weak that many children realize they simply do not remember what happened and stop trying to provide answers to questions. Further investigation is needed to determine the conditions under which lengthy delays lead to beneficial versus deleterious effects on children's memory accuracy and suggestibility (see also Crotteau-Huffman, Crossman, & Ceci, 1996).

Stress, memory, and sources of individual differences

As expected, our results revealed considerable variability in how well children remembered the VCUG. We attempted to identify sources of this variability by examining how children's stress, parent–child discussion, and parental attachment related to children's memory.

Stress and memory. In the present study, stress did not have unidirectional facilitative or deleterious effects on children's memory. Rather, increased stress was associated with less detailed reports during the free-recall and anatomical doll and prop portions of the memory interview, but also with greater accuracy in response to misleading questions.

There are several possible explanations of our findings (cf. Bugental et al., 1992; Goodman et al., 1991). Concerning free recall and prop re-enactment, one explanation is that stress leads to increased forgetting or "repressing" of the event. Perhaps the free-recall and the anatomical doll and prop questions were not specific enough to cue the more stressed children to remember the VCUG. Then, children who were more distressed during the VCUG needed a greater amount of assistance (such as that provided by direct questions) in accessing the VCUG memory than did the less distressed children. An alternative, and we believe more plausible, explanation is that children's distress affected their willingness to talk about the VCUG. Thus, when asked the general questions about the "test with the tube," compared to less upset children, more upset children provided less information not because they failed to remember the VCUG, but because they did not want to talk about it.A 9-year-old girl's answers to the memory questions typify this type of avoidance. According to parental report, this child had been extremely upset and afraid before, during, and after the VCUG (i.e., she received scores of 5, the highest possible, for all stress measures). In free recall, when asked to describe the test with the tube, the child said, "A lot of things happened." When the interviewer asked, "Well, can you tell me them?" the child said she did not want to answer that question. Similarly, when asked to demonstrate with the anatomical doll and props, the child explained that she remembered the test, but she did not want to demonstrate what happened. However, one of the first specific questions was, "Where did they put the tube when they put it inside you?" Despite the child not providing any VCUG information until this point, the child responded correctly, stating that they put the tube in her "private." It is possible that a lack of willingness to talk about distressing events (including ones involving genital contact) leads to selective forgetting of them by the time adulthood is reached. It may also be that, in former studies, what appeared to be adverse effects of stress on children's memory can be accounted for, at least in part, by effects of stress on children's willingness to talk about upsetting events.

Concerning the decreased suggestibility of more distressed children, it is possible that these children were particularly motivated to counter false suggestions, given that emotional experiences may have greater personal significance. Alternatively, if greater stress actually led to stronger memories, the children may have been better able to detect false suggestions, even though they were less willing to talk about the event directly.

Importantly, distress at different times during the VCUG also had different implications for children's memory performance. Although children in Goodman et al.'s (1994, 1997) and Merritt et al.'s (1994) studies who were more upset during the VCUG evidenced somewhat more limited memory, in neither of these two studies was children's level of stress measured before the procedure began or after it ended. Because some stressful events, like the VCUG, can be anticipated, are relatively long in duration, and leave the child shaken subsequently, it may be useful to examine how stress before, during, and after an event affects children's memory. In addition, we propose that future researchers should investigate how stress at different time points interacts with other variables to affect children's long-term memory and suggestibility. For example, more needs to be known about how stress interacts with individual-difference variables to lead to enhanced memory, inhibited memory, or reticence to reveal memory.

Sources of individual differences. Recently, researchers have become interested in individual differences in children's memory capabilities (Goodman et al., 1994, 1997; Reese & Fivush, 1993; Tessler & Nelson, 1994). We chose to focus on two related issues – parent–child communication and attachment – because they have been found to influence children's memory for VCUG (Goodman et al., 1994, 1997) as well as memory for other emotional (Belsky, Spritz, & Crnic, 1996) and nonemotional (Main, 1991; Reese, Haden, & Fivush, 1993) events. We failed to find support for our prediction regarding relations between pre-VCUG preparation and children's memory, and only one correlation was supportive of the our prediction that post-VCUG communication would be significantly related to improved memory. How often mothers reportedly talked to their child up to 1 week after the VCUG was related to fewer commission errors to specific questions. This result parallels those obtained by Goodman et al. (1994), who found that mother–child discussion about the VCUG was associated with fewer commission and omission errors to direct questions.

We were surprised not to find stronger relations between memory and how parents prepared their children for the VCUG or how frequently parents talked to their children after the VCUG. Our retrospective methods of assessing children's preparation and parent–child communication, in which parents had to think back years in some cases, may be responsible for the lack of findings. In other studies, assessments of communication patterns have been made during (e.g., Reese et al., 1993) or shortly after (e.g., Goodman et al., 1994) a particular experience, which may result in greater accuracy of parental report. Another possibility is that type of parent–child communication, such as elaborative versus pragmatic talk (e.g., Reese et al., 1993), rather than frequency of communication primarily affects children's memory (see also Goodman et al., 1994). Thus, parent–child communication may need to be measured qualitatively rather than quantitatively to uncover reliable long-term effects on children's memory.

Our fifth hypothesis concerned relations of parents' attachment styles to children's long-term VCUG memory. As expected, parental insecurity was predictive of inaccuracies in children's responses to direct questions. Children whose parents tended toward a fearful avoidant attachment style made more omission errors to specific questions and somewhat fewer do-not-know responses to misleading questions than children whose parents tended less toward the fearful avoidant attachment style. On the other hand, children of parents characterized by a more rather than less dismissing avoidant attachment style showed heightened suggestibility (i.e., made more commission errors to specific and misleading questions). These results are similar to those obtained by Goodman et al. (1997; see also Goodman & Quas, 1996), who observed that children of avoidant parents made a greater proportion of commission and omission errors to misleading questions than did children of nonavoidant parents.

One explanation for our attachment and memory findings stems from research and theory concerning the intergenerational transmission of attachment, which posits that children's attachment styles are similar to those of their parents (Bowlby, 1969; Main, 1991; Main et al., 1985; van IJzendoorn, 1995). Adults who perceive themselves as displaying a fearful avoidant attachment style tend to be subassertive and introverted (Bartholomew, 1990; Bartholomew & Horowitz, 1991). To the extent that their children are similar to them, the children may also be generally shy, inhibiting their reports about an embarrassing or sensitive topic during an interview with a stranger. They might thus leave out information, resulting in a greater number of omission errors, and be inhibited in playing freely with toys, resulting in fewer incorrect anatomical doll and prop re-enactments.

Adult attachment research further indicates that adults who see themselves most similar to the dismissing avoidant attachment style tend to be cold, minimize subjective awareness of distress, and be overly self-assured (Bartholomew, 1990; Bartholomew & Horowitz, 1991). Moreover, adults classified as dismissing avoidant on the Adult Attachment Interview (George et al., 1985) are open to discussing their early childhood experiences, although their reports are often contradictory, illogical, and incoherent. Insofar as these styles are also evident in their children, such children may be overly confident and want to appear to be correct, which may make them prone to suggestions and commission errors. Moreover, they may have difficulty remembering the event coherently and instead provide contradictory and hence inaccurate responses. Consistent with these possibilities, in our study, children of parents who reported being more rather than less similar to a dismissing avoidant style made the greatest number of commission errors to direct questions and were thus particularly suggestible.

A second plausible explanation for our findings is that parents' romantic attachment, or more generally, parents' relationship quality, affects how they interact with their children (Feldman, Wentzell, Weinberger, & Munson, 1990; Rholes, Simpson, & Blakely, 1995), which in turn affects how children interpret, respond to, and remember stressful situations. Rholes et al. (1995) found that mothers who scored high on an index of avoidant romantic attachment were less supportive when interacting with their children in a teaching setting than were mothers who scored high on an index of secure attachment. Rholes et al. suggest that avoidant mothers engage in a "detached" interaction style with their children. A detached interaction style is particularly evident in avoidant adults when they encounter stressful situations (e.g., Fraley & Shaver, in press; Simpson, Rholes, & Nelligan, 1992), and mothers who evince a dismissing attachment style are often either nonresponsive or misattuned to their infants' bids for comfort (Haft & Slade, 1989). Finally, research also demonstrates that parents' interaction patterns (e.g., supportiveness after stressful experiences) can affect the accuracy and completeness of children's memory (e.g., Goodman et al., 1997; Reese et al., 1993). Combined, these findings suggest that parents' attachment styles may influence children's memory for stressful events.

These explanations remain speculative. Unfortunately, only a few studies have examined relations between children's attachment security and memory (Belsky et al., 1996; Farrar, Fasig, & Welch-Ross, 1997; Farrar, Welch-Ross, Caldwell, & Haight, 1995; Kirsch & Cassidy, 1997). Results of these studies are relevant to ours in that less securely attached children have greater difficulty than more securely attached children forming narrative reports and remembering early childhood experiences (Main, 1991).

Children's false-event memory

Children's false reports of a medical procedure that they never experienced were also assessed. Consistent with findings of recent research (e.g., Bruck, Hembrooke, & Ceci, 1997; Ceci, Huffman, Smith, & Loftus, 1994; Leichtman & Ceci, 1995), almost three-fourths of the 3- to 5-year-olds and half of the 6- to 8-year-olds in the present study assented to the false event at some point, thereby indicating that they experienced nose surgery. Children's responses ranged from merely assenting that the medical procedure occurred to producing spontaneous, unique details about the procedure. An 8-year-old boy's comments illustrate one of the more extreme false narratives. When asked to describe the time the child had a test in which the doctor put something up into the child's nose, the boy said, "Well, I remember he put it up my nose and he would just put something in the tubes and out of the tubes." Next, when given the scissors and instructed to demonstrate with the doll and tell what happened when he had the medical test because he sneezed all the time, this boy responded, "Like, I don't remember all the things about it. I just like remember they would just put those strings up my nose; then it hooked on to that thing again. In that little thing again that has the weird colored water in it." However, when provided with a detailed description of the false event and asked whether or not they experienced it, most children, including the 8-year-old boy just mentioned, correctly responded "no." Our results confirm that the type of questions asked can affect children's willingness to assent that fictitious negative events occurred. Importantly, and in contrast to frequent assumptions about suggestive questions, the most detailed (and in that sense most suggestive) questions in the present study led to better performance than the more general, less detailed questions.

Does children's susceptibility to "false memory" predict suggestibility about an experienced event? In our study, compared to children who made no or less elaborate false reports, children who made more elaborate false reports provided fewer do-not-know responses to specific and misleading questions. It thus appears that children who do not admit that they lack an answer to direct questions are particularly prone to "false memory" effects, at least when the false event concerns a personal experience that is in some ways similar to the true event (e.g., medical procedures).

We also attempted to identify sources of variability in children's false reports. Although parents' attachment styles and children's general medical history, at least in terms of number of illnesses, were unrelated to their false reports, number of VCUGs experienced was significantly related to whether or not children, at any point, falsely assented to the nose test. Children who have undergone many invasive medical procedures, including routine VCUGs and associated surgeries, may be especially willing to agree that they experienced yet another medical test. Such children may not fully understand the stressful procedures experienced and thus combine in memory (via scriptlike mental processes) more mundane and traumatic medical experiences. They may also be more traumatized generally and thus more emotionally needy and suggestible.

Our results lend themselves to new directions for empirical research on false memory. First, it would be of interest to examine in greater detail the relations between children's susceptibility to false memory and their reporting of experienced events, and to determine how cultural differences mediate such relations. Second, it would also be useful to understand if certain types of stressful experiences affect children's false-report rates. Third, in our study, we always interviewed children about the VCUG and then about the nose procedure. Although we know of no available evidence to suggest that the order of questioning may have affected children's suggestibility, such a possibility may be worthy of investigation.

Caveats

The present investigation provides new insight into factors affecting children's long-term memory for a salient, stressful experience and into children's false memory for a medical procedure. However, qualifications about our results also need mentioning. First, children's ages at the time of the interview were unavoidably related to their ages at time of event (i.e., children who were older at the time of VCUG were older at the time of the interview). Because of our interest in whether or not typical infantile-amnesia effects would be observed for a stressful medical procedure, we chose to focus our investigation on children's age at the time of the VCUG and delay since the procedure. However, it is possible that children's age when they were interviewed contributed to the observed age and delay effects (e.g., by affecting children's suggestibility). Additional research is needed with considerably larger samples to examine more precisely how age at event, delay, and age at interview may interact to affect long-term memory and suggestibility.

Second, with regard to our investigation of sources of individual differences in children's memory and suggestibility, we acknowledge that our results are correlational. Also, some findings may have emerged due to chance, given the necessity of conducting numerous analyses. Even so, many of the observed patterns were predicted based on prior research and theory, thus supporting the validity of our findings. In addition, we questioned parents retrospectively about their child's VCUG experience, including how distressed their child was and how often they talked with their child about it. Because long-term memory is subject to forgetting and distortion in adults as well as children, caution in interpreting results based on parental report is warranted.

Third, we offer several caveats concerning the attachment and memory findings. As yet, there is no definitive empirical evidence linking parents' romantic attachment to children's attachment, although romantic attachment has been linked to adults' interaction patterns with their children (e.g., Rholes et al., 1995; Rholes, Simpson, Blakely, Lanigan, & Allen, 1997). Also, we only measured one parent's, typically the mother's, attachment, but parents can vary considerably in their attachment styles. Finally, differences in children's or parents' temperament rather than parental attachment may explain our results. Merritt et al. (1994) found that differences in children's temperament accounted for variability both in children's distress during a VCUG and in their memory for it 6 weeks afterward. Future research is needed to examine links among parents' and children's attachment and temperament, children's reactions to stressful experiences, and children's memory and suggestibility. However, some of these variables (e.g., temperament and attachment, stress and attachment) may be so intertwined that it will be difficult to decipher their independent effects. In any case, it is of interest that we have now found significant relations between parental attachment and children's memory for VCUG in two separate studies.

Conclusions

The goal of this research was to examine children's long-term memory for a stressful event that involved invasive genital contact. Our results indicate that age at the time of an event may be a useful heuristic as to whether children will remember negative childhood experiences, and that, at least for the type of stressful event we studied, special memory mechanisms, such as Freudian repression, do not appear to be involved. The only finding suggestive of a special mechanism concerned a negative relation between stress and free-recall units of correct information: Children who had been more distressed during the VCUG provided less detail when asked general questions about what happened that did children who had been less distressed. Importantly, however, it is possible that distress decreased the children's willingness to talk about their VCUG experience and that no special memory mechanisms were involved. Delay between the event and test also affected children's memory, although longer delays did not correspond to greater inaccuracies. Stress at the time of an event decreased the quantity of information children provided when minimally prompted, but it also positively influenced their ability to answer misleading questions. Children's interactions with their parents and parents' romantic attachment styles revealed sources of individual differences related to children's memory capabilities. Children of parents whose romantic attachment was more similar to a dismissing avoidant style were particularly susceptible to suggestion. Children of parents whose romantic attachment was more like the fearful avoidant style were prone to omit information, but not to heightened suggestibility. And finally, when children were questioned about a medical test that never actually took place and given some information about it, a sizeable minority of young children falsely assented that the test occurred, although their assent rates dropped considerably after the false event was described in detail. Overall, our results attest to the importance of age, emotion, and individual-differences factors as determinants of children's long-term memory, forgetting, and suggestibility.

Notes

1   Parents who asked what we would be discussing with their child were given vague sample questions (e.g., what the child thinks happens when getting certain medical procedures, such as a shot). Parents were told that they could tell their child we wanted to talk about medical "stuff."

2   A few children mentioned early in the interview that they had undergone more than one VCUG. When this occurred, the interviewer asked the children to tell about the most recent VCUG. Although it is possible that children who experienced more than one VCUG were answering our questions based on a generic or script VCUG memory, the children often provided specific detail in free recall that was unique to their last VCUG experience (e.g., one child commented that whereas she was strapped down during her earlier VCUGs, she was not restrained in that way during her last VCUG because now she was "a big girl"). Additionally, the interviewer often provided cues specific to one particular VCUG experience, for example, by asking children to describe the test that took place at a certain hospital (a few children had VCUGs at different hospitals) or reminding children what toy they received after their most recent VCUG.

3   Aresine transformations were computed and substituted for proportions in analyses of the memory variables. The results did not change. Thus, proportions are reported in the text.

4   Note that although delay and age at interview were highly correlated, delay and age at VCUG were not, $r = .24$, n.s. Thus we do not report one-way delay ANCOVAs with age at VCUG covaried. Nor do we describe one-way age at VCUG ANCOVAs with delay covaried. In addition, correlations between both age at VCUG and delay with the memory variables, partialling possible confounding effects, were computed. Results of all these analyses confirmed ANCOVA findings reported in the text.

5   For the significant ANOVA main effects, all effect size estimates $f \geq .27$ (Cohen, 1988). The overall sample means (standard deviations in parentheses) are as follows: anatomical doll and props units correct, $M = 1.67$ (2.83); proportion commission errors to specific questions, $M = .13$ (.12); proportion commission errors to misleading questions, $M = .29$ (.21); and VCUG access, $M = 1.30$ (.91).

6   When location and age at VCUG were both partialled from the following correlations, the statistical significance of the relations did not change from those reported in the main text: attachment and children's distress measures, attachment and parental preparation measures, and attachment and parent–child communication measures.

References

Ackil, J. K., & Zaragoza, M. S. (1995). Developmental differences in eyewitness suggestibility and memory for source. *Journal of Experimental Child Psychology*, **60**, 57–83.

Alpert, J. L., Brown, L. S., Ceci, C. J., Curtois, C. A., Loftus, E. F., & Ornstein, P. A. (1996). *Final report working group of Investigation of Memories of Childhood Abuse*. Washington, DC: American Psychological Association.

Bachevalier, J. (1992). Cortical versus limbic immaturity: Relationship to infantile amnesia. In M. R. Gunnar & C. A. Nelson (eds.), *Minnesota Symposia on Child Psychology: Vol. 24. Developmental behavioral neuroscience* (pp. 129–53). Hillsdale, NJ: Erlbaum.

Baker-Ward, I., Burgwyn, E., Ornstein, P. A., & Gordon, B. (1995, April). Children's reports of a minor medical emergency procedure. In G. Goodman & L. Baker-Ward (Chairs), *Children's memory for emotional and traumatic events*. Symposium conducted at the Society for Research in Child Development, Indianapolis, IN.

Bartholomew, K. (1990). Avoidance of intimacy: An attachment perspective. *Journal of Social and Personal Relationship*, **7**, 147–78.

Bartholomew, K., & Horowitz, L. M. (1991). Attachment styles among young adults: A test of a four-category model. *Journal of Personality and Social Psychology*, **61**, 226–44.

Bauer, P. J., & Wewerka, S. S. (1995). One- to two-year-olds' recall of events: The more expressed, the more impressed. *Journal of Experimental Child Psychology*, **59**, 475–96.

Belsky, J., Spritz, B., & Crnie, K. (1996). Infant attachment security and affective–cognitive information processing at age 3. *Psychological Science*, **7**, 111–15.

Bowlby, J. (1969). *Attachment and loss: Vol. 1. Attachment*. New York: Basic Books.

Bretherton, I. (1993). From dialogue to internal working models: The co-construction of self in relationships. In C. A. Nelson (ed.), *Minnesota Symposia on Child Psychology: Vol. 26. Memory and affect in development* (pp. 237–63). Hillsdale, NJ: Erlbaum.

Bruck, M., Ceci, S. J., Francoeur, E., & Barr, R. (1995). I hardly cried when I got my shot! Influencing children's memories about a visit to their pediatrician. *Child Development*, **66**, 193–208.

Bruck, M., Hembrooke, H., & Ceci, S. J. (1997). Children's reports of pleasant and unpleasant events. In D. Read & S. Lindsay (eds.), *Recollections of trauma: Scientific research and clinical practice* (pp. 199–219). New York: Plenum.

Bugental, D. B., Blue, J., Cortez, V., Fleck, K., & Rodriguez, A. (1992). The influence of witnessed affect on information processing in children. *Child Development*, **63**, 774–86.

Ceci, C. J., Huffman, M. L., Smith, E., & Loftus, E. F. (1994). Repeatedly thinking about a non-event: Source misattributions among preschoolers. *Consciousness and Cognition*, **3**, 388–407.

Ceci, S. J., Loftus, E. F., Leichtman, M. D., & Bruck, M. (1994). The possible role of source misattributions in the creation of false belies among preschoolers. *International Journal of Clinical and Experimental Hypnosis*, **XLII**, 304–20.

Christianson, S. A. (1992). Emotional stress and eyewitness memory: A critical review. *Psychological Bulletin*, **112**, 284–309.

Clatin, C. J., & Barbarin, O. A. (1991). Does "telling" less protect more? Relationships among age, information disclosure, and what children with cancer see and feel. *Journal of Pediatric Psychology*, **16**, 169–91.

Cohen, J. (1988). *Statistical power analysis for the behavioral sciences*. Hillsdale, NJ: Erlbaum.

Crotteau-Huffman, M. L., Crossman, A., & Ceci, S. J. (1996, March). *An investigation of the long-term effects of source misattribution error: "Are false memories permanent?"* Poster presented at the American Psychology–Law Society biennial conference. Hilton Head, SC.

Dudycha, G. J., & Dudycha, M. M. (1941). Childhood memories: A review of the literature. *Psychological Bulletin*, **38**, 668–82.

Eisen, M. L., Goodman, G. S., Qin, J., & Davis, S. L. (1998). Memory and suggestibility in maltreated children: New research relevant to evaluating allegations of abuse. In S. Lynn (ed.), *Truth in memory* (pp. 163–89). New York: Guilford.

Farrar, M. J., Fasig, L. G., & Welch-Ross, M. (1997). Attachment and emotion in autobiographical memory development. *Journal of Experimental Child Psychology*, **67**, 389–408.

Farrar, J., Welch-Ross, M. K., Caldwell, L. G., & Haight, S. (1995, April). *Attachment self concept, and autobiographical memory development*. Poster presented at the Biennial Meeting of the Society for Research in Child Development, Indianapolis, IN.

Favez, N. (1997, April). *Patterns of maternal emotion regulation and the narratives of an affective event by preschoolers*. Poster presented at the Biennial Meeting of the Society for Research in Child Development, Washington DC.

Feldman, S. S., Wentzell, K. R., Weinberger, D. A., & Munson, J. A. (1990). Marital satisfaction of preadolescent boys and its relationship to family and child functioning. *Journal of Family Psychology*, **4**, 213–34.

Fivush, R., Gray, J. T., & Fromhoff, F. A. (1987). Two-year-olds talk about the past. *Cognitive Development*, **2**, 393–410.

Fivush, R., Haden, C., & Adam, S. (1995). Structure and coherence of preschoolers' personal narratives over time: Implications for childhood amnesia. *Journal of Experimental Child Psychology*, **60**, 32–56.

Fraley, R. C., & Shaver, P. R. (in press). Airport separations: A naturalistic study of adult attachment dynamics in separating couples. *Journal of Personality and Social Psychology*.

Freud, S. (1957). Repression. (C. M. Baines & J. Strachey, trans.). In J. Strachey (ed.), *The standard edition of the complete psychological works o Sigmund Freud*. London: Hogarth (original work published 1915).

Freud, S. (1938). Psychopathology of everyday life. In A. A. Brill (ed.), *The writings of Sigmund Freud*. New York: Modern Library.

George, C., Kaplan, N., & Main, M. (1985). *The Berkeley Adult Attachment Interview*. Unpublished protocol, University of California, Berkeley.

Goodman, G. S., Hirschman, J. E., Hepps, D., & Rudy, L. (1991). Children's memory for stressful events. *Merrill-Palmer Quarterly*, **37**, 109–58.

Goodman, G. S., & Quas, J. A. (1996). Trauma and memory: Individual differences in children's recounting of a stressful experience. In N. L. Stein, C. Brainerd, P. A. Ornstein, & B. Tversky (eds.), *Memory for everyday and emotional events* (pp. 267–94). Hillsdale, NJ: Erlbaum.

Goodman, G. S., Quas, J. A., Batterman-Faunce, J. M., Riddlesberger, M. M., & Kuhn, J. (1994). Predictors of accurate and inaccurate memories of traumatic events experienced in childhood. *Consciousness and Cognition*, **3**, 269–94.

Goodman, G. S., Quas, J. A., Batterman-Faunce, J. M., Riddlesberger, M. M., & Kuhn, G. (1997). Children's reactions to and memory for a stressful event: Influences of age, anatomical dolls, knowledge, and parental attachment. *Applied Developmental Science*, **1**, 54–75.

Goodman, G. S., Quas, J. A., Bulkley, J., & Shapiro, C. (in press). Innovations for child witnesses: A national survey. *Law, Psychology, and Public Policy*.

Goodman, G. S., Sharma, A., Thomas, S. A., & Considine, M. G. (1995). Mother knows best: Effects of relationship status and interviewer bias on children's memory. *Journal of Experimental Child Psychology*, **60**, 195–228.

Gray, E. (1993). *Unequal justice: The prosecution of child sexual abuse*. New York: Free Press.

Griffin, D. W., & Bartholomew, K. (1994). The metaphysics of measurement: The case of adult attachment. In K. Bartholomew & D. Perlman (eds.), *Advances in personal relationships: Vol. 5. Attachment processes in adulthood* (pp. 17–52). London: Jessica Kingsley.

Haft, W. L., & Slade, A. (1989). Affect attunement and maternal attachment: A pilot study. *Infant Mental Health Journal*, **10**, 157–72.

Hamond, N. R., & Fivush, R. (1991). Memories of Mickey Mouse: Young children recount their trip to Disneyworld. *Cognitive Development*, **6**, 433–48.

Hazan, C., & Shaver, P. R. (1987). Romantic love conceptualized as an attachment process. *Journal of Personality and Social Psychology*, **52**, 511–24.

Hewitt, S. K. (1994). Preverbal sexual abuse: What two children report in later years. *Child Abuse and Neglect*, **18**, 821–6.

Howard, A. N., Osborne, H. L., & Baker-Ward, L. (1997, April). *Childhood cancer survivors' memory of their treatment after long delays.* Poster presented at the Biennial Meeting of the Society for Research in Child Development, Washington, DC.

Howe, M. L., & Courage, M. L. (1993). On resolving the enigma of infantile amnesia. *Psychological Bulletin,* **113**, 305–26.

Howe, M. L., & Courage, M. L. (1997). The emergence and early development of autobiographical memory. *Psychological Review,* **104**, 499–523.

Howe, M. L., Courage, M. L., & Peterson, C. (1955). Intrusions in preschoolers' recall of traumatic childhood events. *Psychonomic Bulletin & Review,* **2**, 130–4.

Howes, M., Siegel, M., & Brown, F. (1993). Early childhood memories: Accuracy and affect. *Cognition,* **47**, 95–119.

Kihlstrom, J. F., & Harackiewicz, J. M. (1982). The earliest recollection: A new survey. *Journal of Personality,* **50**, 134–48.

Kirsch, S. J., & Cassidy, J. (1997). Preschoolers' attention to and memory for attachment-relevant information. *Child Development,* **68**, 1143–53.

Leichtman, M. D., & Ceci, S. J. (1995). The effects of stereotypes and suggestions on preschoolers' reports. *Developmental Psychology,* **31**, 568–78.

Liwag, M. D., & Stein, N. L. (1995). Children's memory for emotional events. The importance of emotion-related retrieval cues. *Journal of Experimental Child Psychology,* **60**, 2–31.

Main, M. (1991). Metacognitive knowledge, metacognitive monitoring, and singular (coherent) vs. multiple (incoherent) models of attachment. In C. M. Parkes, J. Stevenson-Hinde, & P. Marris (eds.), *Attachment across the life cycle* (pp. 127–59). London: Tavistock/Routledge.

Main, M., Kaplan, N., & Cassidy, J. (1985). Security in infancy, childhood and adulthood: A move to the theory of representation. In I. Bretherton & E. Waters (eds.), Growing points of attachment theory and research. *Monographs of the Society for Research in Child Development,* **50** (1–2, Serial No. 209), 66–104.

Masson, J. M. (1984). *The assault on truth: Freud's suppression of the seduction theory.* New York: Farrar, Straus, & Giroux.

Merritt, K. A., Ornstein, P. A., & Spicker, B. (1994). Children's memory for a salient medical procedure: Implications for testimony. *Pediatrics,* **94**, 17–23.

Myers, N. A., Clifton, R. K., & Clarkson, M. G. (1987). When they were very young: Almost-threes remember two years ago. *Infant Behavior and Development,* **10**, 123–32.

Myers, N. A., Perris, E. E., & Speaker, C. J. (1994). Three-year-olds remember a novel event from 20 months: Evidence for long-term memory in children? In R. Fivush (ed.), *Long-term retention of infant memories* (pp. 383–416). Hillsdale, NJ: Erlbaum.

Nelson, K. (1993). Events, narratives, memory: What develops? In C. A. Nelson (ed.), *Minnesota Symposium on Child Psychology: Vol. 36. Memory and affect in development* (pp. 1–24). Hillsdale, NJ: Erlbaum.

Ornstein, P. A., Principe, G. F., Hudson, A. E., Gordon, B., & Merritt, K. A. (1997, April). Procedural information and stress as mediators of children's long-term recall. In J. A. Quas & G. S. Goodman (Chairs), *Individual differences in children's memory and suggestibility: New research findings and directions.* Symposium conducted at the Biennial Meeting of the Society for Research in Child Development, Washington, DC.

Parker, J. F. (1995). Age differences in source monitoring of performed and imagined actions on immediate and delayed tests. *Journal of Experimental Child Psychology, **60**, 84–101.

Peterson, C., & Bell, M. (1996). Children's memory for traumatic injury. *Child Development, **67**, 3045–70.

Peterson, C., & Parsons, T. (1996, August). *Children's long-term memory for traumatic injury.* Paper presented at the XIVth Biennial ISSBD Conference, Quebec City, Canada.

Pezdek, K., Hodge, D., & Finger, K. (1997, April). *Planting false childhood memories for familiar versus unfamiliar events.* Paper presented at the Biennial Meeting of the Society for Research in Child Development, Washington, DC.

Pezdek, K., & Roe, C. (1995). The effect of memory trace strength on suggestibility. *Journal of Experimental Child Psychology, **60**, 116–28.

Pillemer, D. B. (1992). Preschool children's memories of personal circumstances: The fire alarm study. In E. Winograd & U. Neisser (eds.), *Affect and accuracy in recall: Studies of 'flashbulb' memories* (pp. 121–37). New York: Cambridge Univ. Press.

Pillemer, D. B., Picariello, M. L., & Pruett, J. C. (1994). Very long-term memories of a salient preschool event. *Applied Cognitive Psychology, **8**, 95–106.

Pillemer, D. B., & White, S. H. (1989). Childhood events recalled by children and adults. In H. W. Reese (ed.), *Advances in child development and behavior* (Vol. 21, pp. 297–340). Orlando, FL: Academic Press.

Poole, D., & White, L. T. (1993). Two years later: Effect of question repetition and retention interval on the eyewitness testimony of children and adults. *Developmental Psychology, **29**, 844–53.

Rapaport, D. (1942). *Emotions and memory.* Menninger Clinic Monograph Series, No. 2. New York: Wiley.

Reese, E., & Fivush, R. (1993). Parental styles of talking about the past. *Developmental Psychology, **29**, 596–606.

Reese, E., Haden, C. A., & Fivush, R. (1993). Mother–child conversations about the past: Relationships of style and memory over time. *Cognitive Development, **8**, 403–30.

Rholes, W. S., Simpson, J. A., & Blakely, B. S. (1995). Adult attachment styles and mothers' relationships with their young children. *Personal Relationship*, **2**, 35–54.

Rholes, W. S., Simpson, J. A., Blakely, B. S., Lanigan, L., & Allen, E. A. (1997). Adult attachment styles, the desire to have children, and working models of parenthood. *Journal of Personality*, **65**, 357–85.

Rudy, L., & Goodman, G. S. (1991). Effects of participation on children's reports: Implications for children's testimony. *Developmental Psychology*, **27**, 527–38.

Saywitz, K., Goodman, G. S., Nicholas, E., & Moan, S. (1991). Children's memories of physical examinations involving genital touch: Implications for reports of child sexual abuse. *Journal of Consulting and Clinical Psychology*, **59**, 682–91.

Shaver, P. R., & Hazan, C. (1993). Adult romantic attachment: Theory and evidence. In D. Perlman & W. H. Jones (eds.), *Advances in personal relationship* (Vol. 4, pp. 29–70). London: Jessica Kingsley.

Sheingold, K., & Tenney, Y. J. (1982). Memory for a salient childhood event. In U. Neisser (ed.), *Memory observed* (pp. 201–12). San Francisco: Freeman.

Shyamalan, B., Lamb, S., & Sheldrick, R. (1995, August). *The effects of repeated questioning on preschoolers' reports*. Poster presented at the American Psychological Association annual convention, New York, NY.

Simpson, J., Rholes, W. S., & Nelligan, J. S. (1992). Support-seeking and support-giving within couple members in an anxiety-provoking situation: The role of attachment styles. *Journal of Personality and Social Psychology*, **62**, 434–46.

Stein, N., & Boyce, T. (1995, April). The role of physiological reactivity in attending to, remembering, and responding to an emotional event. In G. Goodman & L. Baker-Ward (Chairs), *Children's memory for emotional and traumatic events*. Symposium conducted the Society for Research in Child Development Meetings, Indianapolis, IN.

Steward, M. S. (1993). Understanding children's memories of medical procedures: "He didn't touch me and it didn't hurt!" In C. A. Nelson (ed.), *Minnesota Symposia on Child Psychology: Vol. 26. Memory and affect in development* (pp. 171–225). Hillsdale, NJ: Erlbaum.

Steward, M. S., & Steward, S. (1997). Interviewing young children about body touch and handling. *Monographs of the Society for Research in Child Development*, **61** (Serial No. 248).

Terr, L. C. (1988). What happens to early memories of trauma? A study of twenty children under age five at the time of documented traumatic events. *Journal of the American Academy of Child and Adolescent Psychiatry*, **27**, 96–104.

Tessler, M., & Nelson, K. (1994). Making memories: The influence of joint encoding on later recall by young children. *Consciousness and Cognition*, **3**, 307–26.

Thompson, W. C., Clarke-Stewart, A., & Lepore, S. J. (1997). What did the janitor do? Suggestive interviewing and the accuracy of children's accounts. *Law and Human Behavior*, **21**, 405–26.

Tulving, E. (1972). Episodic and semantic memory. In E. Tulving & W. Donaldson (eds.), *Organization of memory* (pp. 381–403). New York: Academic Press.

Usher, J. A., & Neisser U. (1993). Childhood amnesia and the beginnings of memory for four early life events. *Journal of Experimental Psychology: General*, **122**, 155–65.

van IJzendoorn, M. H. (1995). Adult attachment representations, parental responsiveness, and infant attachment: A meta-analysis on the predictive validity of the Adult Attachment Interview. *Psychological Bulletin*, **117**, 387–403.

Waldfogel, S. (1948). The frequency and affective character of childhood amnesia. *Psychological Monographs*, **62**, 4–291.

Winograd, E., & Killenger, W. A. (1983). Relating age at encoding in early childhood to adult recall: Development of Flashbulb memories. *Journal of Experimental Psychology: General*, **112**, 413–22.

SIX

Children's Reports of Abuse

Introduction

In this summary of their very extensive 1998 paper Debra Poole and Stephen Lindsay overview many important issues regarding the assessment of children's reports of sexual abuse. They stress that there does not exist a scientifically validated procedure for reliably identifying children who have been sexually abused. They offer suggestions for how to design studies to reduce current misunderstandings about the features of accurate/inaccurate reports.

Suggested reading

Poole, D., & Lindsay, D. S. (1998). Assessing the accuracy of young children's reports: Lessons from the investigation of child sexual abuse. *Applied and Preventative Psychology, 7,* 1–26.

Assessing the Accuracy of Young Children's Reports

A Summary by Debra Poole
(Central Michigan University) and
D. Stephen Lindsay (University of Victoria)
of their 1998 Overview on Applied and
Preventative Psychology

During the past decade, the topic of child sexual abuse became a marquee issue for debates about the gap between science and social policy (Poole & Lindsay, 1998). Procedures for identifying abused children garnered supporters and critics from an interdisciplinary audience that included child advocates, memory researchers, social psychologists, decision scientists, and legal, medical, and mental health professionals. In the midst of sometimes bitter debate, one recurring conclusion cut across areas of specialization and political agendas: there is no scientifically validated procedure for reliably identifying children who have been sexually abused (Goodman, Emery, & Haugaard, 1998; Guyer, 1995).

This article summarizes central issues regarding the assessment of children's reports of sexual abuse. The first section briefly discusses why there is an urgent need to educate practitioners about potential sources of inaccuracy in children's event reports. The second section describes two approaches to assessing accuracy – the indicator and the assessments approaches – highlighting limitations in the existing database for both. The concluding section offers suggestions for designing and reporting studies that would help remedy misunderstandings about the characteristics of accurate and inaccurate reports.

Rethinking Validity Assessment: New Challenges to Old Assumptions

The authors review four factors that have generated concern about how professionals assess children's abuse status. Data indicate that a non-trivial percentage of abuse suspicions are ill founded (Ceci & Bruck, 1995), that several mechanisms can lead children to make inaccurate event reports (Bruck, Hembrooke, & Ceci, 1999), that practitioners vary widely in their decisions about whether abuse occurred in individual cases (particularly if evidence includes indicators that are only moderately or weakly correlated with abuse; e.g., Horner, Guyer, & Kalter, 1993), and that many practitioners base decisions (at least partially) on information that has been dismissed by the courts as scientifically unfounded. This state of affairs has shifted the direction of research on child sexual abuse and children's event reports from a focus on description to a comparative approach that explores ways of distinguishing between accurate and inaccurate reports.

Assessing the Accuracy of Young Children's Reports

Berliner and Conte (1993) identified two approaches to improving the validity of professionals' judgements of children's abuse status: the indicator approach, which seeks evidence that distinguishes between true and false reports, and the standards approach, which seeks to minimize contamination of children's reports by establishing best-practice standards for interviewing children. Following Berliner and Conte's organizational framework, we reviewed two directions of research relevant to assessing the accuracy of children's reports: studies of indicators of child sexual abuse and studies that have identified practices that affect the likelihood of reporting errors (i.e., the assessments approach).

Regarding indicators of abuse, we described results from studies of the discriminative value of behavioural indicators, the content and characteristics of children's reports, projective techniques, and family context. We concluded there is no scientifically validated procedure for combining indicators of abuse that can substitute for a child's verbal report of abuse. We also reviewed data on practices that affect the amount and accuracy of information children report under varying conditions, and used a Bayesian approach to explain why the costs and benefits of leading questions depend in part on the base rate of abuse among the children being interviewed.

Conclusions and Recommendations

We concluded with four recommendations for improving the interface between research and practice:

1   Assessing the accuracy of reports requires comparative information. Neither descriptions of abused children nor descriptions of the spontaneous true narratives of children who have witnessed events shed light on how to distinguish between true and false reports. Unfortunately, descriptive data that are assembled for other purposes are frequently transformed, as in the game of 'telephone', through a chain of secondary articles and workshops into ill-founded conclusions about bases for assessing abuse status. Researchers need to take special care to flag inappropriate uses of their findings, and practitioners need to scrutinize carefully the bases for claims offered in secondary sources.

2   The characteristics of true and false reports probably vary depending on children's assessment histories. Sexual abuse assessments involve judgements at many points in time, from initial suspicions or disclosures of abuse through subsequent investigations. Throughout this process, children's behaviours and the characteristics of their reports may evolve as a function of their experiences. In the best of all possible worlds, studies would select comparison groups that represent parallel points along this process. When this is impossible, investigators should alert readers to possible limitations of their results.

3   Developmental discontinuities are probably the rule rather than the exception. There are reasons to expect that the characteristics that distinguish between accurate and inaccurate reports will vary across development. Because qualifications about age ranges are easily lost when findings are cited in secondary sources, reviewers should be especially sensitive to the need to preserve information about age when they summarize results from other investigators.

4   It is an empirical question whether decision accuracy is improved by combining multiple indicators. It is common for articles on sexual abuse assessment to state that evaluators should tackle the uncertainty

issue by taking multiple factors into account, including the consistency of a child's report of abuse, the family context, and the presence of sexual behaviour that is indicative of abuse. However, none of these factors has proved to be strongly diagnostic of accuracy in isolation, and there are no data showing that these indicators in combination do a better job of distinguishing between true and false reports. A goal for future research is to evaluate multivariate models of decision-making.

References

Berliner, L., & Conte, J. R. (1993). Sexual abuse evaluations: Conceptual and empirical obstacles. *Child Abuse & Neglect*, 17, 111–25.

Bruck, M., Hembrooke, H., & Ceci, S. (1999). Children's reports of pleasant and unpleasant events. In J. D. Read & D. S. Lindsay (eds.), *Recollections of trauma: Scientific research and clinical practice*. New York: Plenum.

Ceci, S. J., & Bruck, M. (1995). *Jeopardy in the courtroom: A scientific analysis of children's testimony*. Washington, DC: American Psychological Association.

Goodman, G. S., Emery, R. E., & Haugaard, J. J. (1998). Developmental psychology and law: The cases of divorce, child maltreatment, foster care, and adoption. In W. Damon (series ed.), I. E. Sigel, & K. A. Renninger (vol. eds.), *Handbook of child psychology: Vol. 4. Child psychology in practice* (5th edn, 775–874). New York: Wiley.

Guyer, M. J. (1995). An overview of sexual abuse issues in child custody cases. *Michigan Family Law Journal*, 15–18.

Horner, T. M., Guyer, M. J., & Kalter, N. M. (1993). Clinical expertise and the assessment of child sexual abuse. *Journal of the American Academy of Child and Adolescent Psychiatry*, 32, 925–31.

Poole, D., & Lindsay, D. S. (1998). Assessing the accuracy of young children's reports: Lessons from the investigation of child sexual abuse. *Applied and Preventative Psychology*, 7, 1–26.

SEVEN

Child Eyewitness Accuracy

Introduction

In this summary of their 1998 overview paper Joanna Pozzulo and Rod Lindsay compare child and adult eyewitness identification accuracy. They note that when a lineup/identification parade does contain a face seen before, children (save for pre-schoolers) are as good as adults at choosing the correct face. However, if the face seen before is not, in fact, in the lineup then children less frequently make the correct response of 'not present'. The authors offer a number of explanations for this effect, several of which may be used to help improve children's performance.

Suggested reading

Pozzulo, J. D., & Lindsay, R. C. L. (1998). Identification accuracy of children versus adults: A meta-analysis. *Law and Human Behavior*, 22, 549–70 (summary).

Eyewitness Identification Accuracy of Children

A Summary by Joanna D. Pozzulo (Carleton University, Canada) and Rod Lindsay (Queen's University, Canada) of their 1998 Meta-Analysis on *Law and Human Behavior*

Historically, the legal system has viewed children as inferior to adult eyewitnesses (Ceci & Bruck, 1993, 1995; Whipple, 1912). Ceci and Bruck (1993) reported age differences in suggestibility but also that children are capable of recalling forensically relevant information. The accuracy and reliability of children's identification has received less attention.

Pozzulo and Lindsay (1998) performed a meta-analysis to determine whether children and adults produce similar eyewitness identification accuracy rates. Eyewitness studies containing 51 hypothesis tests of 1,066 child and 1,020 adult eyewitnesses were compiled. Three of the hypothesis tests explored the impact of simultaneous versus sequential lineups. An additional 16 hypothesis tests with 1,147 children examined whether children with versus without eyewitness training were more accurate. Studies were included that compared performance on eyewitness identification tasks of adults to preschoolers (4-year-olds), young children (5–6-year-olds), older children (9–10-year-olds), or adolescents.

Preschoolers were significantly less likely than adults to make a correct identification (.47, versus .67, $p < .01$). No other age group made significantly fewer correct identifications than adults (.71 versus .54; .47 versus .48; .66 versus .57, for young children, older children, and adolescents versus adults respectively). When the target is present in the lineup, only preschool-age children produce identification accuracy rates inferior to adults.

When presented with a target-absent lineup, children were consistently less likely than adults to correctly reject a lineup (.39 versus .98; .57 versus .65; .41 versus .70; .48 versus .74, for preschoolers, young children, older children, and adolescents versus adults respectively). Only the difference for young children (5–6-year-olds) was non-significant. Correct identification rates may be determined by memory processes, while correct rejection rates may be influenced by social factors as well (Pozzulo & Lindsay, 1999; Wells & Luus, 1990).

Low rates of correct rejection are a serious problem reducing the credibility of children's identification evidence. Sequential lineups increase correct rejection rates for adult witnesses (Lindsay & Wells, 1985). A similar impact on the identification decisions of children would be desirable. Using traditional (simultaneous) lineups, children (9–10-year-olds) were significantly less likely than adults to make correct rejections (.46 versus .62). When sequential lineups were employed, correct rejection rates increased for adults (.86), but decreased for children (.21). Sequential lineups do not resolve the problem of low correct rejection rates by children.

Training produces small and non-significant increases in correct rejections and thus is not an effective means for increasing correct rejections with children (.41 versus .35 for older children with versus without training).

We speculated on explanations for differential identification performance between children and adults across target-present and absent lineups.

Demand

Compared to adults, children may comply more with the demands of authority figures. A target-present lineup may elicit a correct response because the child sees the target and makes an identification. A target-absent lineup may elicit an incorrect response because the child thinks she must choose. The perceived pressure to pick someone may be lower for adults, or adults may be better able to resist such pressure, and thus are less likely to make a false identification.

Memory Trace

Developmental differences in attending to or encoding may exist such that memory trace strength for faces increases with age (Diamond & Carey, 1977; Nelson & Kosslyn, 1976). The target in a target-present lineup is the source of the memory. This match between the memory and target often leads to a correct identification even if the memory trace is weak. Presented with a target-absent lineup, a weaker memory trace may allow a lower criterion for a 'match'; thus an innocent lineup member is identified.

Processing Strategy

Adult facial recognition studies provide evidence of higher correct identification rates when a holistic or configural processing strategy is used to encode the face rather than featural processing (Wells & Hryciw, 1984). Children may use featural representations (Diamond & Carey, 1977). With a target-present lineup, a featural strategy may lead to correct identification. For example, a lineup member with a hairstyle similar to the witness' memory of the criminal may be the guilty party. With a target-absent lineup, a holistic strategy is necessary for accuracy. Even if there is a lineup member with a hairstyle similar to the witness' memory, he/she is not the guilty party and other information must be employed to reach a correct decision.

Future Research

From a theoretical perspective, we need to delineate the processes engaged in by children and adults when making an identification. From an applied perspective, we need to modify current identification procedures to increase identification accuracy with children of all ages with a particular focus on increasing correct rejections.

References

Ceci, S. J., & Bruck, M. (1993). Suggestibility of the child witness: A historical review and synthesis. *Psychological Bulletin*, 113, 403–39.

Ceci, S. J., & Bruck, M. (1995). *Jeopardy in the courtroom*. Washington, DC: American Psychological Association.

Diamond, R., & Carey, S. (1977). Developmental changes in the representation of faces. *Journal of Experimental Child Psychology*, 23, 1–22.

Lindsay, R. C. L., & Wells, G. L. (1985). Improving eyewitness identifications from lineups: Simultaneous versus sequential lineup presentations. *Journal of Applied Psychology*, 70, 556–64.

Nelson, K. E., & Kosslyn, S. M. (1976). Recognition of previously labelled and unlabelled pictures by 5-year-olds and adults. *Journal of Experimental Child Psychology*, 13, 133–49.

Pozzulo, J. D., & Lindsay, R. C. L. (1998). Identification accuracy of children versus adults: A meta-analysis. *Law and Human Behavior*, 22, 549–70.

Pozzulo, J. D., & Lindsay, R. C. L. (1999). Eliminating the innocent: Enhancing the accuracy and credibility of child witnesses. *Journal of Applied Psychology*, 84, 167–76.

Wells, G. L., & Hryciw, B. (1984). Memory for faces: Encoding and retrieval operations. *Memory and Cognition*, 12, 338–44.

Wells, G. L., & Luus, C. A. E. (1990). Police lineups as experiments: Social methodology as a framework for properly-conducted lineups. *Personality and Social Psychology Bulletin*, 16, 106–17.

Whipple, G. M. (1912). Psychology of testimony and report. *Psychological Bulletin*, 9, 264–9.

Truth and Lies

EIGHT

Children's Understanding About Lies

Introduction

Crucial to children's interaction with the law and legal proceedings is their understanding about lies. In a number of countries (for example England) young children (under 7 years) were precluded until fairly recently from giving evidence in criminal trials. One of the reasons for this was the legal world's belief that young children had little understanding of what lies are, and consequently may not tell the truth. Those of us who have worked hard to enhance children's contribution to law should not presume that the legal world is totally ignorant of developmental psychology! Indeed, the work of one of the world's best-known developmentalists, Jean Piaget, is a main reason why the law has assumed that young children have little understanding of what lies are.

Piaget, *The moral judgement of the child* (Penguin, 1932), investigated Swiss children's understanding of lying by telling them pairs of stories. Here are two of them:

> [1] A little boy [or a little girl] goes for a walk in the street and meets a big dog who frightens him/her very much. So then he/she goes home and tells his/her mother he/she has seen a dog that was as big as a cow.

> [2] A child comes home from school and tells his/her mother that the teacher had given him/her good marks, but it was not true; the teacher had given him/her no marks at all, either good or bad. Then his/her mother was very pleased and rewarded him/her.

When asked which of the two had told a lie, and was the naughtiest, children under about 7 years would typically say that the first child was the naughtiest and should be punished, because 'it could never happen' (seeing a dog as big as a cow), whereas the second child was less naughty because it *could* have been true! These findings have often been interpreted as meaning that young children do not understand what lies are, but a careful reading of Piaget's work clearly indicates that they understand that the second child is telling a lie.

Piaget made a major contribution to developmental psychology several decades ago, but in his studies of lies and false belief he is often misunderstood, and his technique of asking children to compare pairs of stories often underestimates their real understanding. More recent research has rectified many of these mistakes and misunderstandings, and it has demonstrated that young children are more likely to be able to make a competent contribution to legal proceedings than was previously believed. If the form of questioning is appropriate to them, and if the topic is of relevance, then according to those work of Michael Siegal and Candida Peterson, young children may well have an adequate appreciation of what lies are.

Suggested reading

Bussey, K. (1992). Lying and truthfulness: Children's definitions, standards, and evaluative reactions. *Child Development*, 63, 129–37. (This article is available in Blackwell's *Childhood Cognitive Development: The Essential Readings*, edited by Kang Lee (2000).)

Bussey, K., & Grimbeek, E. (2000). Children's conception of lying and truth-telling: Implications for child witnesses. *Legal and Criminological Psychology*, 5, 187–99.

Breaking the Mold: A Fresh Look at Children's Understanding of Questions About Lies and Mistakes

Michael Siegal and Candida C. Peterson

According to Piaget (1932/1977), young children have little or no understanding of the nature of lies as deceptive statements intended to mislead others. They label all false statements as lies and do not distinguish between a deliberately false statement and a genuine mistake made by a speaker who believes that he or she has spoken truthfully.

Later studies have re-examined Piaget's position by investigating variables such as the speaker's intent to speak truthfully or falsely, the beliefs of the listener, the material consequences of a lie, and the extent of its departure from objective truth (e.g., Strichartz & Burton, 1990; Wimmer, Gruber, & Perner, 1984, 1985). Although the results have challenged at least some elements of Piaget's original position, to date there has been little evidence to contradict the notion that young children's conception of lying is marked by what Wimmer et al. termed *lexical realism* in that they regard all false statements – including guesses and unintentional mistakes – as lies. The purpose of this article is to re-examine the effects of the form and the domain of questioning on the ability of young children to distinguish mistakes from lies.

Conversational Implications of Questions

Philosophers of language such as Grice (1975) have pointed out that adult conversation is characterized by rules or maxims that direct speakers to "say no more or no less than is required (which can be termed the *Maxim of Quantity*). Try to say the truth and avoid falsehood (*Maxim of Quality*). Be relevant and informative (*Maxim of Relation* or *Relevance*). Avoid ambiguity and obscurity (*Maxim of Manner*)" (p. 45). In communication between adults, it is usually mutually understood that the rules may be broken to communicate implications in conversation. Adults know that speakers may be uninformative and state the obvious for purposes of irony or that they may speak more or less than is required out of politeness or scientific curiosity. But children who are inexperienced in conversation may not share the purpose underlying such departures from conversational rules and may be unfamiliar with the referents of certain words and forms of language. Their early conversational habits are in tune with the speech input of caregivers who, for the most part, have not set aside conversational rules. In many societies, when caregivers speak to young children, they generally shorten their utterances and do not say more or less than is necessary to sustain conversation; they are clear, relevant, and informative in referring to objects and events in the here and now, and they are keen to correct truth value in the child's speech rather than errors of syntax (Brown & Hanlon, 1970; De Villiers & De Villiers, 1978, pp. 192–8; Ferguson, 1977). Therefore, when young children's answers require an understanding of the implications of conversations, they may respond incorrectly, not because they do not know the answer, but because the conversational worlds of adults and children diverge.

Because explanations in science require answers that are often irrelevant to the pragmatic, localized concerns of the layperson (Hart & Honoré, 1985), this clash of conversational worlds is particularly likely to arise in specialized, experimental settings. In these settings, to probe the depth and certainty of children's understanding, experimenters may inadvertently set aside conversational rules and pose questions to which the answer seems obvious or repeat a question when an answer has already been given. Unlike adults who are experienced in conversation and can recognize the implications that flow from different forms of questioning, young children are liable to misinterpret an experimenter's purpose or use of language in these situations.

For example, children's knowledge of false beliefs may be viewed as a prerequisite for understanding the intentionally deceptive basis of lying (Leekam, 1992). A scientific concern in research is to determine whether children can predict in what way a character's false beliefs will lead to an undesired outcome (Wellman & Bartsch, 1988). But if children as laypersons do not recognize that the scientific purpose of the task is to determine whether children can detect that others' thoughts may be initially mistaken, they may not understand that the experimenter's question "Where will a person (with the false belief) look for the object?" in fact implies "Where will the person look first?" Instead, the purpose may appear to be something more familiar and straightforward to their local concerns: to test whether they can predict a child's behavior in achieving a goal. In this sense, the message in the question is liable to depart from the quantity rule by saying less than is required and be interpreted as "Where will the person have to look for her kitten in order to find it?" Thus even 3-year-olds often respond correctly when they are explicitly asked to predict the initial behavior of a story character with a false belief in a manner that avoids the need to follow the conversational implications of an experimenter's questioning (Siegal & Beattie, 1991; see also Leslie, 1994). Sullivan and Winner (1993) have also shown that 3-year-olds have the ability to understand the nature of false beliefs in a naturalistic context in which another person's mistaken belief about reality is made salient. As is documented elsewhere (Siegal, 1991a, 1991b, in press; Siegal & Peterson, 1994) in an analysis that builds on earlier observations of the importance of child's interpretation of language and contexts (Donaldson, 1978), the pragmatics of well-intentioned questioning techniques can at least in some cases obscure children's authentic knowledge.

Conversation and Lexical Realism in Children's Answers to Questions About Lying

Conversational and contextual factors can also influence children's responses on false belief tasks designed to test lexical realism. In apparently failing to distinguish between lies and mistakes, their answers may reflect their own local concerns rather than the scientific purpose of an experimenter's questions. For example, Piaget (1932/1977, pp. 134–8) asked children to guess the age of certain adults. Following an incorrect answer, the children were then told to say whether this was a lie or not. They responded that this was a lie, even though some had protested that they had not produced a false statement on purpose. With regard to

Piaget's age-guessing situation, an inaccurate guess of a person's age may possibly be termed a lie because children might have been led to believe that the estimator should have known better and that the more inaccurate the guess, the more unskillful or deceitful it is. Children may import their own relevance to the interviewer's question and evaluate the skill of the guess rather than the beliefs and intentions of the person who answers incorrectly.

Similarly, in a series of six experiments designed to investigate the notion of lexical realism, Wimmer et al. (1984) found that even children as young as 4 years often rewarded a protagonist who had unintentionally made a false statement on the basis of what he or she thought to be true. Paradoxically, many of the same children still answered the question of whether or not the speaker had lied by saying that he had. Wimmer et al. (1985) carried out a follow-up study designed to examine the effects produced by the order in which the children were asked questions. The gave 4- and 5-year-olds stories in which a protagonist with a false belief was said to have the intention of truthfully communicating information about the location of an object to a listener. Half the children who recognized that the character held a false belief were first asked a lexical question, "Did (name of speaker) lie to (name or listener) or did he/she not lie to her/him?", followed by a moral reward question, "What would you give to (name of speaker), a gold star because he was nice to (name of listener) or a black point because he/she was nasty to her/him?" For the other half, the moral reward question was presented before the lexical one. Out of 29 children who first said in reply to the lexical question that the protagonist had lied, only 3 switched to evaluating his or her moral behavior positively; however, 22 out of 34 switched from having first evaluated an actor's moral behavior positively to saying in reply to the lexical question that the actor had lied.

Wimmer et al. (1985) maintained that children's lexical realism is so strong that it "overrides" their mature moral judgments on the basis of the unintended nature of a protagonist's false statement. Another possibility is that the children may not have shared the relevance of the situations and questions because they had not been provided with contexts based on making mistakes. Contrary to the quantity rule to say no less than is required, the children were not even given the opportunity in the test questions of choosing the alternative that the character could have made a mistake. To young children who are conversationally inexperienced, it may not be apparent that to choose the lexical alternative "not lie" for a false statement implies that a protagonist could have made a mistake.

As Ekman (1985, p. 25) has pointed out, the *Oxford English Dictionary* states, "In modern use, the word (lie) is normally a violent expression of moral reprobation, which in polite conversation tends to be avoided." Children whose answers reflect their own local concerns might after all reason, Why would an adult go to the trouble to raise the question of lying in a hypothetical protagonist's behavior unless the implication was to use this information in answering the test questions? Particularly in a setting in which the purpose and relevance of the questioning is not readily apparent, they may infer that an adult would not ask about lying unless he or she thought that lying had taken place. The implication that a lie has taken place may be so powerful that it undermines the viability of a mistake as the implicit alternative that is left unstated in the lexical question. An example of this form of implication in adult conversation is provided by Grice (1975): "Suppose that A and B are talking about a mutual friend, C, who is now working in a bank. A asks B how C is getting on in his job, and B replies, 'Oh quite well, I think; he likes his colleagues, and he hasn't been to prison yet'" (p. 43). The implication is that this unconventional or abnormal information, "C hasn't been to prison yet," should be used by A in considering the behavior of C. In this sense, it is similar to the implication of introducing the suggestion of lying in questions about a protagonist's behavior. Before mention was made of lying, the children in Wimmer et al.'s (1985) study were likely to evaluate protagonists in terms of their truthful intentions. However, after lying was mentioned, they were likely to reply that a protagonist had lied.

Conversational factors may have influenced the results of Strichartz and Burton's (1990) research albeit somewhat differently than in Wimmer et al.'s (1985) research, which used a different methodology. In this study, adults and children aged 3 to 11 years were given eight stories that represented combinations of three variables that followed the criteria proposed by Coleman and Kay (1981) for explaining the usage of the verb *lie*: whether or not a speaker's statement matches the facts, whether or not the speaker intends to deceive, and whether or not the speaker believes a statement is true. Success was dependent on comparing simultaneously factuality with mental states about intentions and beliefs. For example, one story opened with a puppet character called Lee knocking over a cup. Then another character, his brother Chris, stated that he himself had knocked over the cup (even though he had not realized that Lee had actually done so). When their mother asked who was the culprit, Chris first privately exclaimed, "Oh no! I don't want Mom to know." He told his mother, "I spilled it." Finally, he stated that he had not meant to say that.

This story was aimed to represent an intentionally deceptive, factually incorrect statement. To follow the details, children not only had to make sense of verbal statements that were at odds both with the character's actions and expressed intentions, but they also had to decide how to interpret vacillations in the characters' descriptions of their mental states without rationales provided in the stories. For preschoolers who are used to receiving messages about present events, the sheer volume of Chris's changing ideas about whether to tell the truth is liable to be perceived as a departure from the quantity rule to say no more than what is required. Furthermore, the children in the Strichartz and Burton (1990) study were required to answer a triple-barrelled test question. Depending on the counterbalancing condition, they were asked, "When Chris said 'I spilled it', was Chris telling the truth, something else, or a lie?" Even if they could keep in mind three possibilities in reference to a single, selected phrase in the story, children who do not recognize that the purpose of the stories is to determine their knowledge about truth, lies, and mistakes may view the situation in terms of their own local concerns. They may regard the purpose as simply to determine whether a child's statement was correct and interpret the test question as simply, "Was Chris right?" In such a murky conversational environment, it is not surprising that the 4- and 5-year-olds disregarded beliefs and intentions in judging whether a statement was a lie and that many 3-year-olds were not even able to make systematic use of factuality in their answers.

Consistent with this view, Bussey (1992) presented children as young as 4 years with stories about characters who committed misdeeds and then either lied or told the truth about their actions. She found that 4-year-olds distinguished lies from truthful confessions at a level that was above chance, though they were less accurate and less confident of their judgments than were 7-year-olds, who scored almost perfectly. Though not directly addressing the issue of lexical realism, Bussey's results suggest that young children can comprehend stories about deception when motives and behaviors are straightforward and described in simple terms. Therefore previous research indicating that lexical realism is present in children's conceptions of lies and mistakes is liable to have involved departures from conversational rules in contexts in which children might not have shared the purpose and relevance of the questioning.

Focus of Present Investigation: Questioning in the Domain of Food and Contamination

In our investigation, we sought to examine both conversational and domain-specific processes in children's understanding of lies and mistakes. One aim was to re-examine the extent to which young children distinguish mistakes from lies when they were asked questions in the form "Was it a lie or a mistake?" rather than "Did he (or she) lie?" or "Did he (or she) lie or not lie?" By providing *mistake* as an alternative to *lie*, we sought to enable children to indicate that a statement was false but not necessarily morally reprehensible. The purpose was to counter the strong moral connotation of the term *lie* that can be interpreted to imply that an interviewer suspects that lying has occurred.

A second aim was to examine the effect of the domain of questioning on children's responses. As Rozin (1990) pointed out, the problem of identifying foods that are safe to eat is important to survival. It requires an adaptive specialization in intelligence and must be solved early in development. Rozin has defined sensory-affective (taste, smell, and appearance), ideational (culturally appropriate or symbolic), and anticipatory (beneficial or dangerous) criteria for classifying a food as edible or inedible. In solving problems in the domain of food and contamination that are highly relevant to their own concerns (in line with the Gricean maxim of relation), children are constrained to acquire a knowledge of these classification criteria and are apt to recognize that the purpose of questions is to determine their ability to detect edible substances and to reject those that are inedible. Thus their understanding that the purpose of the questioning is to determine the basis for how a substance could be wrongly regarded as edible would be facilitated.

Because it has been shown that 3-year-olds can identify a substance that appears good to eat but is in reality contaminated (Au, Sidle, & Rollins, 1993; Kalish, in press; Siegal & Share, 1990), the situations given to the children in our studies involved food that contained concealed contaminants. We assumed that children are familiar with this domain of knowledge that is highly relevant to their own concerns (in line with the conversational rule, "Be relevant"). In this specific domain, our hypothesis was that they would be unlikely to display evidence of lexical realism and that they would be likely to recognize whether a false statement was a lie or a mistake.

The children in our studies attended child-care centers, kindergartens, and preschools located in middle-class areas of Brisbane, Australia. All children had written parental consent for their participation. No child participated in more than one experiment.

Experiment 1

Method

Participants

These were 110 children divided into three age groups of 37 three-year-olds (mean age = 3 years 8 months; range = 3 years 0 months; to 3 years 11 months), 45 four-year-olds (mean age = 4 years 4 months; range = 4 years 0 months to 4 years 11 months), and 28 five-year-olds (mean age = 5 years 4 months; range = 5 years 0 months to 5 years 9 months).

Procedure

An experimenter showed each child individually a slice of moldy bread and pointed to two teddy bears, one who was an onlooker and the other who had his back turned away. The experimenter said, "Here's a slice of moldy bread. Is it OK or not OK to eat?" (All the children said that it was not OK, demonstrating that they understood the context of questions about food avoidance.) "Let's put some vegemite" (an Australian breakfast spread) "over the mold so we can't see it." She then asked the child two questions in one of four formats: For example: (a) "This bear didn't see the mold on the bread. He told a friend" (at this point, the experimenter produced a stuffed animal toy) "that it was OK to eat. Did the bear lie or make a mistake?" and (b) "This bear did see the mold on

Table 8.1 Number of children in each age group correctly identifying bears' lies and mistakes in Experiment 1

Age group	n	Onlooker bear as lying		Bear with back turned as making a mistake	
		No.	%	No.	%
3 years	37	25	67.6	22	59.5
4 years	45	33	73.3	31	68.9
5 years	28	22	78.6	20	71.4

the bread. He told a friend" (at this point, the experimenter produced another stuffed animal toy) "that it was OK to eat. Did the bear make a mistake or lie?" The orders of the questions and the alternatives (mistake or lie) were alternated across the children in three other formats.

Results and discussion

The numbers of correct responses for children in the three age groups are shown in table 8.1. A clear majority in each group correctly responded that the onlooker bear had lied and that the bear who had had his back turned made a mistake. Correct response scores out of a total of two for the children in each group were analyzed in a one-way analysis of variance (ANOVA). Although performance increased with age, the difference among the groups was not significant, $F(2, 107) = 1.047$.

Of the 37 children in the 3-year-old group, 15 were correct on both questions, 17 were correct on one question, and 5 children were correct on neither. Comparable figures for the 45 4-year-olds were 24, 16, and 5, respectively and, for the 28 5-year-olds, 16, 10, and 2. The chance probability that the children could be correct by chance was 50% on each question and 25% on both questions. Assuming this 25% probability, even the 3-year-olds responded on both questions at a level that was above chance expectations ($z = 1.996$, $p = .023$, one-tailed binomial test). Within each group, there were no significant age differences between those who answered correctly and those who did not. Of the

17 3-year-olds who had one correct score, 10 said that both bears lied, and 7 that both bears had made a mistake. Comparable figures were 8 and 8 for the 4-year-old group and 6 and 4 for the 5-year-old group. The order in which the questions or alternatives were presented did not significantly influence the children's responses.

In support of our hypothesis, the results of Experiment 1 indicated that many 3-year-olds and more than half of 4- and 5-year-olds could distinguish between lies and mistakes in a setting that involved food and contamination. Few children in any of the age groups (10 out of 37 3-year-olds, 8 out of 45 4-year-olds, and 6 out of 28 5-year-olds) displayed evidence of lexical realism in claiming that the statements of both bears were lies.

Experiment 2

If children can accurately distinguish between lies and mistakes, they should be able to indicate that lying is accompanied by the deliberate concealment of secret information, whereas making a mistake is not. To replicate the results of Experiment 1 and to test whether children were aware that the onlooker bear had secret information that the other bear did not, we carried out a second experiment. We sought to determine the basis of their responses to questions about lies and mistakes by asking each child whether each bear knew the secret about the mold. Our hypothesis was that children who indicated that the onlooker bear had lied also would recognize that this bear had secret information and that this information was not known to the mistaken bear who had his back turned.

Method

Participants

These were 99 children divided into three age groups of 34 3-year-olds (mean age = 3 years 8 months; range = 3 years 5 months to 3 years 11 months), 34 4-year-olds (mean age = 4 years 5 months; range = 4 years 0 months to 4 years 10 months), and 31 5-year-olds (mean age = 5 years 3 months; range = 5 years 0 months to 5 years 7 months).

Table 8.2　Number of children in each age group correctly identifying bears' lies and mistakes in Experiment 2

Age group	n	Onlooker bear as lying		Onlooker bear as knowing secret		Bear with back turned as making a mistake		Bear with back turned as not knowing secret	
		No.	%	No.	%	No.	%	No.	%
3 years	34	24	70.6	23	67.6	25	73.5	27	79.4
4 years	34	24	70.6	31	91.2	26	76.5	29	85.3
5 years	31	22	71.0	28	90.3	22	71.0	31	100.0

Procedure

This was the same as in Experiment 1 except that the children were also questioned as to whether or not each bear knew the secret. Again the experimenter stated, "This bear didn't see (or did see) the mold on the bread. He told a friend" (at this point, the experimenter produced a stuffed animal toy) "that it was OK to eat." At this point, approximately half the children in each age group received the question, "Does this bear know or not know the secret about the mold? Following the questions about secrets, the experimenter restated what each bear had seen and had advised a friend and then posed the questions on lies and mistakes. The remainder of the children received the questions on lies and mistakes first and the those on secrets second. As in Experiment 1, the orders of the questions and the alternatives (mistake or lie) were alternated across the children in four formats.

Results and discussion

The numbers of correct responses for children in the three age groups are shown in table 8.2. On each of the four questions concerning whether the onlooker bear had lied and had known the secret and that the bear who had had his back turned made a mistake and did not know

Table 8.3   Number of children in each age group giving correct answers to both, one, or neither question on pairs of questions in Experiment 2

		Lies and mistakes			KS and NKS			Lies and KS			Mistakes and NKS		
Age group	n	Both	One	Neither	Both	One	Neither	Both	One	Neither	Both	One	Neither
3 years	34	16	17	1	18	14	2	19	8	7	20	12	2
4 years	34	17	16	1	27	7	0	23	9	2	23	10	1
5 years	31	18	8	5	28	3	0	22	6	3	22	9	0

KS = knows secret, NKS = does not know secret.

the secret, a clear majority in each group responded correctly. The levels of performance on the questions pertaining to lies and mistakes were similar to those in Experiment 1.

Two 3-point scales (0 = none correct, 1 = one correct, 2 = two correct) were created to reflect the numbers of correct answers for the two questions about mistakes and lies and the two questions about secrets. The scores were analyzed in a 3 (ages) × 2 (presentation orders: lie–mistake–secret vs. secret–lie–mistake) × 2 (question type: lie–mistake vs. secret) ANOVA. Only the main effect for question type was significant. The children were more likely to answer the questions involving secrets correctly than those involving lies and mistakes, $F(1, 92) = 7.53$, $p < .007$. Although performance improved with age, the difference among the groups again was not significant, $F(2, 92) = 2.499$, $p < .088$.

Table 8.3 shows the number of children correct on both, one, or neither question pertaining to four pairs of answers: (a) identifying the bear who lied and the one who made a mistake, (b) the bear who knew the secret and the one who did not, (c) the bear who both lied and knew the secret, and (d) the bear who both made a mistake and did not know the secret. Even the 3-year-olds responded correctly on each of the four pairs of questions at a level that was above chance expectations (e.g., for the pair of questions on lies and mistakes, $z = 6.43$, $p = .0001$, one-tailed binomial test, again assuming a 25% chance probability that the children could be right on both), although there was a significant increase with age in the numbers of children answering both questions on secrets correctly, $\chi^2(2, N = 99) = 12.58$, $p < .001$. Most children in all age groups identified the bear who lied as the one who knew the

Table 8.4 Pattern of responses for children giving one correct and one incorrect answer on pairs of questions in Experiment 2

	Lies and mistakes		*KS and NKS*		*Lies and KS*		*Mistakes and NKS*	
					L (cor)	*M (inc)*	*L (inc)*	*M (cor)*
Age group	*Both L*	*Both M*	*Both KS*	*Both NKS*	*NKS (inc)*	*KS (cor)*	*KS (cor)*	*NKS (cor)*
3 years	8	9	5	9	5	3	7	5
4 years	7	9	4	3	1	8	3	7
5 years	4	4	0	3	0	6	0	9

L = lie, M = mistake, KS = knows secret, NKS = does not know secret, cor = correct, inc = incorrect.

secret and identified that the bear who made a mistake as the one who did not know. For example, of the 24 3-year-olds who correctly identified the onlooker bear as having lied and the 23 who correctly identified this bear as knowing the secret, 19 were correct on both. Similarly, of the 25 3-year-olds who correctly identified the bear with his back turned as having made a mistake and the 27 who correctly identified this bear as not knowing the secret, 20 were correct on both. Those completely correct on all four questions in the 3-, 4-, and 5-year-old groups were 12 out of 34, 14 out of 34, and 18 out of 31, respectively. Again, the order in which the questions or alternatives were presented did not significantly influence the children's responses.

The patterns of responses for the children who gave one correct answer and one incorrect answer on a pair of questions is shown in table 8.4. With regard to the questions on lies and mistakes, the numbers of children who replied that both bears had lied and that both had made mistakes were about equal. In line with the result that performance on the questions referring to secrets was better than that those on lies and mistakes, many 4- and 5-year-olds correctly replied that the onlooker bear knew the secret that was not known to the bear who had his back turned; however, they incorrectly said either that the onlooker bear had made a mistake or that the bear who had his back turned had lied. In this regard, the 3-year-olds displayed no clear response pattern, reflecting their somewhat shakier knowledge of secrets.

Thus as in Experiment 1, few children in any age group said that both bears had lied. Moreover, although the numbers answering both questions on secrets correctly increased with age, most children, regardless of their age group, could indicate that the bear who lied knew the secret about the mold or that the bear who made a mistake did not know the secret. Their pattern of responses serves to dispel the possibility that the children were simply basing their judgments of lying on the perception of a bear as a naughty onlooker and demonstrates that their correct designations of lies and mistakes frequently corresponds to their understanding of the bear who did or did not know the secret.

Experiment 3

In Experiment 3, we examined three further aspects of children's performance on questions about lies and mistakes. First, despite their responses in Experiments 1 and 2, children might have believed that the behavior of the bear with his back turned who was deemed to have made a mistake was no less naughty than that of the onlooker bear, possibly because somehow the mistaken bear could have overheard the deception about the moldy bread. In this experiment, we emphasized that the bear with his back turned could not see or bear the experimenter. Our hypothesis was that, in this instance, children would be more likely to identify this bear as having made a mistake.

Second, we sought to compare the extent to which the domain of questioning facilitates children's performance. As Sweetser (1987) pointed out, the reprehensibility of the situation can influence judgments of lying. In the course of our earlier investigation, the reprehensibility of deceiving a companion about the edibility of a substance that creates the possibility of illness might have prompted children to distinguish mistakes from lies. If so, a secenario that is irrelevant to the domain of food and contamination but is perceived to be at least equally as dangerous should prompt a similar pattern of performance. However, if as we contend, children's correct responding is indeed facilitated specifically in the domain of food and contamination, their performance on questions about lies and mistakes in this domain should exceed that shown in other areas even when these areas are perceived to be at least equally dangerous.

The third aspect to the study concerned the relation between the children's responses on questions about lies and mistakes and the perceived naughtiness of the two bears in the scenarios. In view of the children's performance in the first two experiments, we hypothesized that children who could accurately distinguish between lies and mistakes would be able to indicate that the onlooker bear who lied was naughtier than the mistaken bear with his back turned.

Method

Participants

These were 64 children divided into two age groups of 32 3-year-olds (mean age = 3 years 7 months; range = 3 years 1 month to 3 years 11 months) and 32 5-year-olds (mean age = 5 years 3 months; range = 5 years 0 months to 5 years 10 months). This experiment was conducted by a different experimenter than in Experiments 1 and 2.

Procedure

The design followed that of previous research on adults' reasoning about food and contamination (Occhipinti & Siegal, 1994, Experiment 3). To test the effect of the domain of questioning on the children's answers, we exposed each child to a total of four scenarios. As in Experiments 1 and 2, the four scenarios all involved two bears. One was an onlooker who perceived relevant information and the other a bear who, because he was reading with his back turned, had no basis for knowing the true situation. Each bear gave the same factually false statement in response to a third companion.

The scenarios represented the following four conditions: food/safety (FS), food/safety-irrelevant (FSI), food-irrelevant/safety (FIS), and food-irrelevant/safety-irrelevant (FISI). The moldy bread scenario from Experiments 1 and 2 was used for the FS condition with the addition that the researcher handled the moldy bread with a thick gardening glove while spreading the vegemite to emphasize the presence of the contaminant. The FSI condition also involved a deception about bread that had an undesirable outcome. It focused on brown bread that had been deceptively hidden in a white bread bag. Brown bread was chosen to provide a distasteful food situation that, unlike the FS condition, was not associated with an element of contamination. At the outset of this scenario, the experimenter told the children, "Here are two slices of bread. Which one do you like to eat? Which one don't you like to eat?" All but I child chose the white bread as the one that was desirable to eat and the brown bread as the one that was not. In proceeding to present the scenario to the children, the experimenter pointed to each bear in turn and said, "This bear is watching what we're doing. This bear is sitting over here reading a book. He can't see us and he can't hear us." She continued, "Let's put the brown bread back in the white bag so we can't see it. This bear didn't see what color the bread was. He was reading a book and didn't see us. He told a friend it was white bread." For the child who preferred brown bread, the deception was enacted with white bread hidden in a brown bread bag.

The FIS condition involved a deception about a cubbyhouse that had a snake inside. The children were first asked if it was OK or not OK to touch snakes. (All children responded that it was not OK.) The experimenter then produced a miniature cubbyhouse (dimensions of 40 cm long, 18.5 cm high, and 21 cm wide) and a coiled snake (95 cm long; diameter when coiled = 12 cm) and handled it with the same gardening glove to emphasize its dangerousness. The snake was actually an "Authentic–Realistic Snake" that, through the startled reaction of the children, clearly lived up to the labeling on its package as "a real slick serpent" that "look alive!" and "feels alive." In addition, as is noted below, all but 1 child clearly recognized the snake's dangerousness by reporting that being bitten by it would make a person sick. Handling the snake cautiously with a thick gardening glove, the experimenter hid it inside the door of the dubbyhouse. Using the same wording as for the FSI condition, the experimenter informed the children that the onlooker bear had been watching whereas the other bear had not and that both bears told a friend that it was OK to go into the cubbyhouse.

The FISI condition also involved a deception about a cubbyhouse that had an undesirable outcome (inaccessibility for play). Unlike the FIS condition, this scenario was portrayed without an element of danger. The children were asked to check whether the door to the cubbyhouse was locked or unlocked. They all responded that it was unlocked. Then the experimenter locked the door and took away the key. The onlooker bear was described as having watched while the other had not and both bears had told a friend that the cubbyhouse was open.

For each condition, the experimenter asked the children, "Was that a lie or a mistake?" referring to the behavior of each bear. Then she asked, "Which bear was the naughtier? The bear who was watching us or the bear who couldn't see or hear us?" As in Experiments 1 and 2, the order of the alternatives for the questions about lies and mistakes and naughtiness were counterbalanced across children and conditions. Different bears were used for each scenario.

The FSI, FIS, and FISI conditions were chosen on the basis of pilot work with parents and preschool teachers who indicated that most 3-year-olds would be familiar enough with the situations to readily perceive the implications of the bears' deceptive statements. After the questions about lies and mistakes and naughtiness had been asked for the four conditions, we directly assessed children's familiarity with the type of context presented in each scenario by asking questions of the type, "Have you seen (moldy bread/brown bread/snakes/locked doors) before?" while pointing at the object in question. If children said "yes," they were asked to indicate whether they had seen the item "a little or a lot of the time." The children's perceptions of how dangerous it would be to heed the bears' statements in the two safety-relevant contexts were also assessed by asking. "If you (got bitten by a snake or ate moldy bread) would you get sick?" Those who said "yes" were asked, "Would you get a little bit sick or very sick?" For each child, the experimenter asked these questions about the four scenarios in the order in which they had been first presented.

Results and discussion

The numbers of correct responses for children on the test questions for the four conditions are shown in table 8.5. First, we report children's performance on questions in the FS condition in comparison with that in the two previous experiments. Then the children's responses are presented across conditions in relation to the perceived familiarity and danger of the scenarios and the perceived naughtiness of the bears' behavior.

Performance on each questions in FS condition

As was predicted, consistent with the emphasis in Experiment 3 that the bear with his back turned could not see or hear the deception, the number of 3-year-olds (28 out of 32) who correctly identified this bear as having made a mistake in the FS condition increased by 28% over those in Experiment 1 (22 out of 37) and 15% over those in Experiment 2 (25 out of 34). Similarly, the number of 5-year-olds (28 out of 32) in Experiment 3 who correctly identified this bear as having made a mistake increased by 25.5% over those in Experiment 1 (22 out of 37)

Table 8.5 Number of children out of 32 in each age group and condition correctly identifying the bears' lies and mistakes in Experiment 3

Age group and condition	Onlooker bear as lying		Onlooker bear as naughtiest		Bear with back turned as making a mistake	
	No.	%	No.	%	No.	%
3 years						
FS	19	59.4	28	87.5	28	87.5
FSI	18	56.3	25	78.1	23	71.9
FIS	16	50.0	26	81.2	21	65.6
FISI	9	28.1	27	84.3	23	71.9
5 years						
FS	30	93.8	31	96.9	31	96.9
FSI	31	96.9	32	100	29	90.6
FIS	28	87.5	29	90.6	24	75.0
FISI	29	90.6	32	100	25	78.1

FS = food–safety; FSI = food–safety-irrelevant; FIS = food-irrelevant–safety; FISI = food-irrelevant–safety-irrelevant.

and 22.8% over those in Experiment 2 (25 out of 34). The increase in Experiment 3 over that in Experiments 1 and 2 combined was significant for both 3-year-olds, $\chi^2(1, N = 103) = 4.04$, $p < .05$, and 5-year-olds, $\chi^2(1, N = 91) = 8.63$, $p < .001$.

In the case of the 5-year-olds in the FS condition of Experiment 3, the numbers (30 out of 32 or 93.8%) who correctly identified the onlooker bear as having lied increased by 15.2% over those in Experiment 1 (22 out of 28 or 78.6%) and 20.8% over those in Experiment 2 (22 out of 31 or 71.0%). The increase in their performance in Experiment 3 over that in Experiments 1 and 2 combined was also significant $\chi^2(1, N = 91) = 3.84$, $p < .05$. For the 3-year-olds, there were no significant differences in performance on Experiment 3 in comparison with Experiments 1 and 2.

Overall, out of the total of 103 3-year-olds tested in Experiments 1, 2, and 3, 66.0% (or 68) of the children answered correctly that the onlooker bear had lied, and 72.8% (or 75) answered correctly that the bear with his back turned had made a mistake. In both instances, performance was significantly greater than the 50% correct level that would be expected by chance ($zs \geq 3.153$, $ps < .001$).

Comparisons in performance on pairs of questions across conditions

Each child's correct answers to the two questions about mistakes and lies in the four conditions were scored on a 0–2 scale. Because preliminary analyses showed no effects attributable to the order in which the conditions were presented, the scores were analyzed in a 2 (ages) × 4 (conditions) ANOVA. The main effect for age was significant, $F(1, 62) = 33.00$, $p < .001$. The 5-year-olds ($M = 1.75$) outperformed the 3-year-olds ($M = 1.24$). There was also a significant main effect for condition, $F(1, 62) = 5.83$, $p < .001$. A planned comparison between scores in the FS condition ($M = 1.67$) and FSI condition ($M = 1.55$) yielded no significant difference, $F(1, 62) = 2.70$, $p > .10$. However, Newman-Keuls tests revealed that children performed significantly less well in the FIS ($M = 1.41$) and FISI ($M = 1.34$) conditions than in the FS condition ($ps < .01$) and the FSI condition ($ps < .05$). The Age × Condition interaction effect was no significant.

Figure 8.1 shows the percentages of children who correctly distinguished lies and mistakes in indicating both that the onlooker bear lied and that the bear with his back turned made a mistake. Of the 32 3-year-olds in the FS condition, 18 were correct on both questions, 10 on one question (8 showing an "MM" pattern in responding that both bears had made a mistake and 2 showing an "LL" in responding that both had lied), and 4 on neither. Only in this condition was performance by this age group above the 25% correct performance that would be expected by chance ($z = 3.89$, $p < .001$, binomial test). Comparable numbers for the other conditions respectively were as follows: FSI, 11 correct on both questions, 19 on one (12 MM and 7 LL), and 2 on neither; FIS, 8, 23 (14 MM and 9 LL), and 1; and FISI, 4, 24 (19 MM and 5 LL), and 4. As was predicted, the numbers who made lie–mistake distinctions were significantly greater in the FS condition than in any other. Of the 18 3-year-olds answering correctly in this condition, 8 were incorrect in the FSI condition, whereas only 1 child out of the 11 who was correct in the FSI condition was incorrect in the FS condition

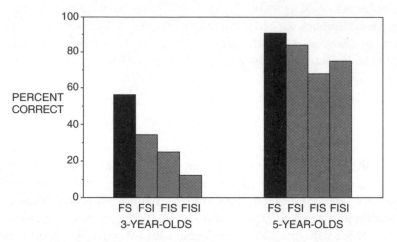

FS = food–safety, FSI = food–safety-irrelevant, FIS = food-irrelevant–safety,
FISI = food irrelevant–safety-irrelevant.

Figure 8.1   Percentage of children correctly distinguishing between lies and mistakes in the four conditions of Experiment 3

($p = .02$ by one-tailed sign test.) Performance in the FS condition also far exceeded that in the FIS and FISI conditions ($ps < .01$ by one-tailed sign tests).

In all conditions, there was significant increase with age in the numbers of children answering both questions correctly, $\chi^2(2, N = 64) \geq 8.01, ps < .001$. Most 5-year-olds in all conditions were able to respond correctly, although here also performance in the FS condition tended to have an edge over that in the others. Of the 32 5-year-olds in the FS condition, 29 were correct on both questions, 3 on one question (2 MM and 1 LL), and 0 on neither. Comparable numbers for the FSI, FIS, and FISI conditions respectively were 27, 4 (all LL), and 1; 22, 7 (1 MM and 6 LL), and 3; and 24, 6 (1 MM and 5 LL), and 2.

Understanding of lies and mistakes in relation to perceived familiarity and danger

Familiarity. The children's answers were unrelated to their reports of familiarity with the stimuli in the conditions. Of the 18 3-year-olds who were correct in the FS condition, 8 claimed that they had not seen moldy bread previously, 6 a little of the time, and 4 a lot of the time. Of the 14 incorrect children, the comparable numbers were 9, 4, and 1. For the three other conditions, the comparable breakdown of figures for correct children in contrast to incorrect children respectively were FSI: 5, 2, and 4 in contrast to 4, 8, and 9; FIS: 4, 3, and 1 in contrast to 9, 14, and 1; and FISI: 0, 3, and 1 in contrast to 0, 14, and 14. Of the 29 5-year-olds who were correct in the FS condition, only 1 reported having seen moldy bread a lot; 14 children either responded that they either had not seen moldy bread or that they had seen it a little. All 3 incorrect children reported that they had not seen moldy bread before. Of the 28 5-year-olds who were correct in the FSI condition, 5 claimed that they had not seen brown bread previously, 13 a little of the time, and 10 a lot of the time. Of the 4 incorrect children, the comparable numbers were 1, 1, and 2. For the two other conditions, the comparable breakdown of figures for correct children in contrast to incorrect children respectively were FIS: 9, 12, and 1 in contrast to 5, 5, and 0; and FISI: 0, 7, and 20 in contrast to 0, 1, and 4.

Danger. The children's judgments of lying the FS and FIS conditions were also unrelated to their perceptions of danger. However, this may have been in part because most children displayed an accurate grasp of both situations as dangerous. Of the 18 3-year-olds who were correct in the FS condition, 4 reported that eating moldy bread would not make them sick, 4 that it would make them a little sick, and 10 that it would make them a lot sick. Of the 14 incorrect children, the comparable numbers were 0, 6, and 8. For the 8 children correct in the FIS condition, none reported that being bitten by a snake would not make them sick, 3 that it would make them a little sick, and 5 that it would make them very sick. The comparable breakdown of figures for the 24 incorrect children were 1, 6, and 17, respectively.

These results show that differences in the 3-year-olds' performance between the FS and FIS conditions in distinguishing between lies and mistakes cannot be interpreted in terms of the greater perceived danger associated with the mold as there was actually a nonsignificant tendency for children to rate being bitten by a snake as a greater danger to health than eating moldy bread $\chi^2(1, 64) = 3.11$, $p < .10$, two-tailed. The same pattern was found in the 5-year-olds' responses. Of the 29 correct children in the FS condition, only 1 reported that eating moldy bread would not make them sick, 14 that it would make them a little sick, and 14 that it would make them very sick. Two of the 3 children who were incorrect reported that eating moldy bread would make them a little sick and 1 child that it would make him very sick. Regardless of performance, no 5-year-old indicated that being bitten by a snake would not result in illness. Only 5 out of 22 correct children and 1 out of 10 incorrect children said that it would make them become a little sick; the remainder said that it would make them very sick.

Thus the reprehensibility of the deception did not determine children's responses on lie–mistake tasks so much as the precise domain. Though children were equally familiar with moldy bread and snakes and saw being bitten by a snake to be at least as dangerous as eating moldy bread, the children were more successful at distinguishing mistakes from lies in the domain of food and contamination as represented in the moldy bread task in the FS condition than in the snake task in the FIS condition. Although the great majority of children clearly voiced their belief that both eating moldy bread and being bitten by a snake were dangerous, it is likely that food-irrelevant fears such as snake fear are learned primarily through associations generated by a heightened expectation of aversive outcomes following instances of exposure in the environment (Davey, 1995). By contrast, the domain of food and contamination constitutes a distinctive domain of food and contamination constitutes a distinctive domain of problem-solving knowledge that necessitates the application of criteria for classifying substances as edible or inedible. These criteria assist children's early preparedness to learn by channelling their selective attention to food attributes and can be seen to account for superior reasoning in the domain of food and contamination (for a discussion of learning within a knowledge domain, see Gelman, 1993).

Understanding of lies and mistakes in relation to perceived naughtiness

The children in Experiment 3 were quite proficient in judging the naughtiness of the two bears, similar to the results reported by Wimmer et al. (1984, 1985). The numbers of 3-year-olds out of 32 who judged the onlooker bear as naughtier in the FS, FSI, FIS, and FISI conditions were 28, 25, 27, and 27, respectively, with 23 children judging the onlooker bear as naughtiest in all four conditions. Of the 32 5-year-olds, 29 judged the onlooker bear to be naughtiest in all four conditions.

Three children judged the bear with his back turned to be naughtier in the FIS condition; 1 of these children also judged this bear to be naughtiest in the FS condition. Taking the sample as a whole, only in 4 out of 143 cases when children made a lie–mistake distinction was this followed by a failure to indicate that the onlooker bear was the naughtier: once in the FS condition for each age group and twice in the FIS condition for the 3-year-olds. A ceiling effect in the children's performance could have precluded significant effects on naughtiness judgments owing to food or safety. The success of the children in judging naughtiness may be due to the forced-choice format of the questioning in which they were required to make a simple comparison rather than evaluate each bear separately as in the case of the questions concerning lies and mistakes.

Bearing in mind that the four conditions were represented by only one scenario, the children's responses provide support for the position that an early understanding of the distinction between lies and mistakes is based on a notion of reprehensibility of intent and is specifically advanced in the domain of food and contamination. Most children in all conditions of Experiment 3 identified the onlooker bear as the naughtier bear, and in the FS condition, they frequently distinguished this bear from the bear who had his back turned as having lied, the same onlooker bear who in Experiment 2 was identified as having known the secret about the concealed mold.

Experiment 4

All the same, the children in Experiments 1–3 might have been judging the two bears not on the basis of their comparative access to secret information and their mistaken or deliberately deceptive behavior but on some initial perceived difference. For example, children's recognition of lies and mistakes might have been based on their prior judgments that the onlooker bear deserved more negative condemnation than the bear who had his back turned. If they interpreted onlooking behavior as an indication that a bear might have greedily wanted the bread for himself, they may see him as a mean bear who should be labeled a liar. By contrast, the children could conceivably construe the bear whose back was turned as disinterested in the bread. He would then be less likely to be seen by the children as a mean bear and to be labeled as a liar. In the case of chimpanzees' choices on related theory-of-mind tasks, the possibility that some prior preference could have influenced their performance has sparked considerable debate into the work that would be needed to rule out this alternative (Heyes, 1993; Povinelli, 1993). However, unlike chimpanzees, young children can readily be questioned beforehand to determine whether they have a prior preference that would influence their evaluations of the deliberate and mistaken behavior of informed and uninformed characters.

Thus our aim in Experiment 4 was to determine whether the children could have regarded the onlooker bear as naughtier even before the questions about lying had been asked. We asked 3-year-olds to indicate whether one bear was naughtier without describing how each of the bears incorrectly advised a friend that the moldy bread was OK to eat. On the basis of the results of our earlier studies, we hypothesized that children would not show a prior bias to choose the onlooker bear as naughtier.

Method

Participants

These were 19 children (mean age = 3 years 5 months; range = 3 years 0 months to 3 years 10 months).

Procedure

As in Experiment 3, the experimenter told each child, "Here are two teddy bears. This bear is watching what we're doing. This bear is sitting over here reading a book. He can't see us and he can't hear us. Here are two slices of bread. Which one is good to eat? Which one is not good to eat?" (All children said that the fresh bread was good to eat and the moldy one was not.) "Let's put some vegemite over the moldy part so we can't see it. This bear didn't see the mold on the bread. He was reading a book and didn't see us. This bear did see the moldy part on the bread. He was watching us."

The experimenter continued, "Right now, before I go on with the story, do you think one bear is naughtier?" If a child said yes, she asked, "Which one is the naughtier? Why?"

Results and discussion

Of the 19 children, 15 said that one bear was naughtier. When probed further, 13 said that this was the bear who had his back turned. Their justifications were that "He was reading" (8 children), "He wasn't watching" (3 children), "He was reading and wasn't watching" (1 child), and "He was hiding" (1 child). Only 2 children said that the informed bear was naughtiest and gave as their justification the reason, "He looked at the bread" or "He was looking." The 4 other children said they did not think one bear was naughtier than the other.

When asked in Experiment 3 to say which bear was naughtier after both bears had made false statements, the children were very quick to respond and overwhelmingly chose the onlooker bear. By contrast, pilot work for Experiment 4 had shown that nearly all children were puzzled and many remained silent when simply asked as soon as they had been shown the bears whether one was naughtiest. For that reason, we had to preface the question about naughtiness with the rationale "Right now, before I go on with the story, . . .". In comparing answers in Experiment 3 and 4, the question about naughtiness in both experiments had of course to remain similar. It clearly implied that children should make a choice, especially as the initial behavior of the two bears was described as different. Even so, as was predicted, the children's responses were consistent with our assumption that the children in our previous studies were highly unlikely to have tacitly prejudged the onlooker bear as naughtier. If anything, their prior, though reluctant, judgment was that the naughtier bear was the one who had his back turned and was not watching. Yet it was this bear in Experiments 1–3 who was liable to be judged correctly as having made a mistake once he wrongly advised that the bread with concealed mold was OK to eat.

Experiment 5

The results of our investigation so far attest to the genuine ability of many preschoolers to distinguish mistakes from lies in the domain of food and contamination. However, by asking the question, "Was that a lie or a mistake?" twice, some children might possibly have chosen one of the bears as having lied and then were prompted through repetition of the same question to use the other alternative (mistake) to label the second bear's behavior. Moreover, our previous studies did not provide a direct comparison with forms of questioning in which children have typically been found to display lexical realism. Thus Experiment 5 was designed to determine whether children placed in the four conditions used in Experiment 3 would respond any differently when asked the question, "Was that a lie or not a lie?" that has been used in other studies (e.g., Wimmer et al., 1985). Consistently with the position that this form of questioning conveys the implication that lying had indeed occurred, we predicted that children would show a pattern of lexical realism in their responses by claiming, despite repeated questioning, that all false statements were lies.

Method

Participants

These were 24 children (mean age = 3 years 9 months; range = 3 years 1 month to 3 years 11 months) drawn from the same selection of conters as the children in the previous studies but tested at a different time. The children were randomly drawn from the same population as those in the previous studies.

Procedure

The procedure for the children who were asked whether the bears had lied was the same as in the four conditions of Experiment 3 except that the children were asked, "Was that a lie or not a lie?" instead of "Was that a mistake or a lie?" or "Was that a lie or a mistake?"

Results and discussion

In sharp contrast to Experiment 3, in Experiment 5, of the total of 96 possible correct responses (on the basis of the 24 children in the four conditions), 91 were characterized by a lexical realism pattern in which the children responded that both bears had lied. Two children in the FIS condition and 1 child in the FSI condition correctly identified the informed bear as having lied and the bear who had his back turned as the one who had not lied. Two other children in the FS condition incorrectly claimed on both questions that the bear with his back turned had lied and that the informed bear had not.

The number of children out of 24 in the FS, FSI, FIS, and FISI conditions who correctly identified the onlooker bear as naughtier were 17, 14, 13, and 16, respectively. Although children responded similarly in the four conditions, only in the FS condition was the number above that which would be expected by chance ($p = .032$, one-tailed binomial test). Thus in response to the question "Was that a lie or not a lie?", preschoolers indicate that all false statements are lies even in the domain of food and contamination. However, they still judge the onlooker bear as naughtier, and their responses can be seen to reflect the form of questioning rather than a clear, genuine lexical realism.

The children's reports of their familiarity and danger of the events in the conditions were similar to those given in Experiment 3. Of the 24 children in the FS condition, 9 claimed that they had not seen moldy bread previously, 6 that they had seen it a little of the time, and 4 that they had seen it a lot of the time. For the three other conditions, the comparable figures were as follows: FSI, 5, 8, and 11; FIS, 2, 16, and 6; and FISI, 0, 15, and 9. In the FS condition, 10 children said that eating moldy bread would make them a little sick and 14 that it would make them very sick. In the FIS condition, 12 children said that being bitten by a snake would make them a little sick and 12 that it would make them very sick.

In our results overall, there was very little evidence for the interpretation that the children were merely response switching under repeated questioning in which they chose one alternative first (e.g., "lie") and then were prompted to choose the other ("mistake" in Experiments 1–3 or "not a lie" in Experiment 5) second. The children produced very few reversals of the correct pattern of responses in which they would reply that the onlooker bear had made a mistake (or not lied) and the other bear had lied. In fact, in all experiments when children were incorrect on the test questions, they were overwhelmingly consistent in responding either that both bears had lied or that both had made a mistake. Children who did give correct answers nearly always judged the onlooker bear as naughtier and often said that he was the one who knew the secret whereas the other bear did not.

Children's responses to repeated questioning can involve either answer consistency or answer switching, which in either case cannot be automatically equated with uncertainty (for a review of studies in which this issue has arisen, see Siegal & Peterson, 1994). We maintain that in tasks such as number conservation, at least some children may be certain of their initial conserving answer but switch their response because they do not share the relevance of the experimenter's purpose in questioning. By contrast, with regard to the edible–inedible distinction that is highly relevant to children's concerns and must be learned early, they enjoy being co-opted as a "food detective" and are likely to share the purpose of questioning should this be framed in the form of "Was that a lie or a mistake?"

General Discussion

Our investigation revealed that both conversational and domain-specific processes can influence preschoolers' answers to questions about lies and mistakes. Both the form and domain of questioning were responsible for the children's improved performance over previous studies and provide an illustration of how these factors together can influence children's success on cognitive developmental tasks. In response to questions that provided two viable alternatives in the form of a mistake and a lie in situations that involve detecting the edibility of food, preschoolers' local concerns are likely to coincide with those underlying an experimenter's questions, and they are more likely to reveal an ability to recognize mistakes and lies. Under these conditions, contrary to the results of previous studies of lexical realism (but in keeping with Wimmer et al.'s (1984, 1985) findings that have shown preschoolers' willingness to reward those who have unintentionally produced false statements), few children answered questions about lies and mistakes in a manner indicating that they believe that all false statements, mistaken or deliberate, are lies. Our findings instead suggest that many 4 and 5-year-olds and even a considerable number of 3-year-olds can often determine that a lie is based on a deliberate distortion of secret knowledge, whereas a mistake is based on a lack of knowledge that a protagonist falsely believes to be true.

In this respect, the domain of knowledge about food and contamination is central to survival. Not only do preschoolers have some substantial insight into the distinction between what appears good to eat and what in reality is contaminated, but adult reasoning is also apt to be facilitated in this domain. Occhipinti and Siegal (1994) presented adults with conditional reasoning tasks designed to compare the effects of safety on conditional reasoning in food and food-irrelevant contexts. Participants – whose ratings of their experience of contexts that were either relevant or irrelevant to food and safety were matched for plausibility, experience, and danger – were most likely to use formal logic in reasoning on tasks in which the safety issue (contamination) was relevant to food. Such results can be viewed to reflect an adaptive constraint or preparedness for learning about food and contamination that facilitates early reasoning (Rozin, 1990). By contrast, in studies in which young children have performed poorly, they have been asked more complex questions about lies and mistakes in areas that are less immediately relevant to survival such as reasoning about the causes of property damage (Strichartz & Burton, 1990).

Even with regard to questions about food and contamination, it could be thought that when asked, "Was that a lie or a mistake?", children select the term *lie* as best referring to a prototype use of the term (Coleman & Kay, 1981). By contrast, they reserve the alternative *mistake* to apply to a more peripheral instance that they regard as a "little" lie – the perpetrator of which preschoolers are less likely than older children and adults to criticize by use of the stronger, more prototypical term *lie* owing to a "charitable" orientation toward others. However, we believe that this interpretation is highly unlikely. Preschoolers are not generally unwilling to punish or criticize, and they do not hesitate to choose the critical term "not X" (e.g., "not OK") in questions of the form of "Was that (individual's behavior) X or not X?" (Siegal & Storey, 1985; Smetana, 1981). Moreover, in ongoing work (Siegal & Peterson, 1995), 3-year-olds have been asked to choose between pairs of photographs of faces with neutral and angry expressions to match the thoughts of a target figure who is described as thinking that a story character has made a mistake. In this respect, most 3-year-olds match the neutral expression with thoughts that the character made a mistake and reserve the angry expression for thoughts that a character has lied. Therefore, we maintain that the interviewer's use of the term *lie* conveys the implication that he or she presupposes that lying is liable to have occurred. If not counteracted by a viable alternative such as *mistake*, children who are inexperienced in the scientific purposes of conversation in experiments are likely to assent to this implication. They are prompted to indicate that even a mistaken perpetrator has told a lie, although they have implicitly judged that this perpetrator lacks the knowledge to deceive deliberately and is not as naughty in comparison with one who know-ingly lies.

The present series of studies was limited to single instances of situa-tions that are relevant or irrelevant to food and safety. Using a wider variety of stimuli, it remains to be determined whether children's precocious understanding in the domain of food and contamination results, for example, from perceptions of danger or disgust or both. Moreover, food and contamination may not be the only domain in which children's understanding of the lie–mistake distinction can be wit-nessed. Nevertheless, our position is that the element of disgust is likely to be seen as essential to very early moral development. Haidt, Koller, and Dias (1993) and Shweder, Mahapatra, and Miller (1987) have shown that an "ethics of divinity" is pre-eminent in the moral judg-ments of children in many parts of the world, including in such heavily populated representations of humanity as Brazil and India. According to this system of ethics, the self is seen as a spiritual entity that strives to avoid pollution and to attain purity and sanctity. The disgust associ-ated with early contamination sensitivity jeopardizes adherence to this code. Recognition of deception about food may therefore engender an incipient awareness of the lie–mistake distinction. Disgust such as that that occurs when deceived about the presence of contaminants can translate into a moral emotion of anger directed toward a protagonist (Nemeroff & Rozin, 1994; Rozin, Lowery, & Ebert, 1994). In this sense, we believe that the contamination disgust that is reflected in an early understanding of the lie–mistake distinction may be an initial source of reasoning about health and morality. Demonstrating instances of lies and mistakes in these disgust settings may have instructional value in enhancing preschoolers' awareness of health risks through highlight-ing the fact that others may provide deceptive information on the edibility of substances.

Apart from the above-chance level of group performance on ques-tions about lies and mistakes in the domain of food and contamination, there were substantial numbers of children in all age groups who made errors. However, in this connection, it is worthwhile to note that there can be sizeable disagreement as to what constitutes a lie among older children and adults who at times themselves can define exaggerations, guesses, and other accidentally false statements as lies (Peterson, Peterson, & Seeto, 1983). It is possible that such responses are due to differences in the background knowledge of speakers and listeners that can lead to difficulties in communication (Clark, 1992). For example, even with the precautions that we took to maintain relevance in conversation, some child listeners may not have clearly shared the premises that the bear with his back turned lacked the information that was possessed by the onlooker bear. They might have thought that this bear somehow could have heard about what had happened to the moldy bread and be just as liable as the onlooker bear to have lied or that this bear was negligent in not ensuring that he or she told the truth and avoided telling a lie (cf. Shultz, Wright, & Schleifer, 1986). In the many experiments on false belief knowledge (e.g., Sodian, 1991), substantial efforts have had to be made to encourage children to accept the premises of the experiment (e.g., that in searching for a treasure, a robber should be prevented from finding it and a king should be helped). There is no guarantee that children's behavior reflects this acceptance (Siegal & Peterson, 1994; Sullivan & Winner, 1993). In the present experiments as well, we gained the impression that some of the younger children responded that the secret was either known or not known to both of the bears. They did not fully accept that the onlooker bear maintained access to information that was unavailable to the bear whose back was turned.

To account for the transition between a rudimentary understanding of lies and mistakes that is tied to a specific domain and form of question and one that is domain-free and emerges in response to many question forms requires consideration of both cultural and biological factors. Cultural factors such as the amount of conversation directed at children to consider mental states can heighten children's awareness of both the potential for deception in many domains and the implications of questions (Dunn, Brown, Slomkowski, Tesla, & Youngblader, 1991; Peterson & Siegal, 1995; Siegal & Peterson, 1994). At the same time, neuropsychological accounts have often been proposed for changes with age on theory of mind tasks (Sodian, Taylor, Harris, & Perner, 1991; Thatcher, 1992). In our view, changes such as those associated with right-hemisphere maturation in early childhood may also underlie pragmatic understanding, enabling insight into the implications of questions (Siegal, Carrington, & Radel, in press). Further research is required to determine the interplay of cultural and biological factors in children's recognition of lies and mistakes and to examine their role in the development of a general theory of mind.

References

Au, T. K., Sidle, A. L., & Rollins, K. B. (1993). Developing an intuitive understanding of conservation and contamination: Invisible particles as a plausible mechanism. *Developmental Psychology, 29*, 286–99.

Brown, R., & Hanlon, C. (1970). Derivational complexity and the order of
acquisition in child speech. In J. R. Hayes (ed.), *Cognition and the development
of language* (pp. 155–207). New York: Wiley.

Bussey, K. (1992). Lying and truthfulness: Children's definitions, standards, and
evaluative reactions. *Child Development, 63*, 129–37.

Clark, H. H. (1992). *Arenas of language use*. Chicago: University of Chicago
Press.

Coleman, L., & Kay, P. (1981). Prototype semantics: The English verb 'lie'.
Language, 57, 26–44.

Davey, G. (1995). Preparedness and phobias: Specific evolved associations or a
generalized expectancy bias. *Behavioral and Brain Sciences, 18*, 289–304.

De Villiers, J. G., & De Villiers, P. A. (1978). *Language acquisition*. Cambridge, MA:
Harvard University Press.

Donaldson, M. (1978). *Children's minds*. Glasgow, Scotland: Fontana.

Dunn, J., Brown, J., Slomkowski, C., Tesla, C., & Youngblader, L. (1991). Young
children's understanding of other people's feelings and beliefs: Individual
differences and their antecedents. *Child Development, 62*, 1352–66.

Ekman, P. (1985). *Telling lies*. New York: Norton.

Ferguson, C. (1977). Baby talk as a simplified register. In C. Snow & C. A.
Ferguson (eds.), *Talking to children: Language input and acquisition*
(pp. 209–35). Cambridge, UK: Cambridge University Press.

Gelman, R. (1993). A rational-constructivist account of early learning about
numbers and objects. *Psychology of Learning and Motivation, 30*, 61–95.

Grice, H. P. (1975). Logic and conversation. In P. Cole & J. L. Morgan (eds.),
Syntax and semantics: Vol. 3. Speech acts (pp. 41–58). New York: Academic
Press.

Haidt, J., Koller, S. H., & Dias, M. G. (1993). Affect, culture, and morality, or is
it wrong to eat your dog? *Journal of Personality and Social Psychology, 63*,
613–28.

Hart, H. L. A., & Honoré, T. (1985). *Causation in the law* (2nd edn). Oxford,
England: Clarendon Press.

Heyes, C. M. (1993). Anecdotes, training, trapping and triangulating: Can
animals attribute mental states? *Animal Behaviour, 46*, 177–88.

Kalish, C. W. (in press). Preschoolers' understanding of germs as invisible
mechanisms. *Cognitive Development*.

Leekam, S. R. (1992). Believing and deceiving: Steps to becoming a good liar.
In S. J. Ceci (ed.), *Social and cognitive factors in preschool children's deception*.
Hillsdale, NJ: Erlbaum.

Leslie, A. M. (1994). *Pretending* and *believing*: Issues in the theory of ToMM. *Cognition, 50,* 211–38.

Nemeroff, C., & Rozin, P. (1994). The contagion concept in adult thinking in the United States: Transmission of germs and of interpersonal influence. *Ethos, 22,* 158–86.

Occhipinti, S., & Siegal, M. (1994). Reasoning about food and contamination. *Journal of Personality and Social Psychology, 66,* 243–53.

Peterson, C. C., Peterson, J. L., & Seeto, D. (1983). Developmental changes in ideas about lying. *Child Development, 54,* 1529–35.

Peterson, C. C., & Siegal, M. (1995). Deafness, conversation, and theory of mind. *Journal of Child Psychology and Psychiatry, 36,* 459–74.

Piaget, J. (1977). *The moral judgement of the child.* Harmondsworth, England: Penguin Books. (Originally published 1932)

Povinelli, D. J. (1993). Reconstructing the evolution of mind. *American Psychologist, 48,* 493–509.

Rozin, P. (1990). Development in the food domain. *Developmental Psychology, 26,* 555–62.

Rozin, P., Lowery, L., & Ebert, R. (1994). Varieties of disgust faces and the structure of disgust. *Journal of Personality and Social Psychology, 66,* 870–81.

Shultz, T. R., Wright, K., & Schleifer, M. (1986). Assignment of moral responsibility and punishment. *Child Development, 57,* 177–84.

Shweder, R. A., Mahapatra, M., & Miller, J. (1987). Culture and moral development. In J. Kagan & S. Lamb (eds.), *The emergence of morality in young children* (pp. 1–83). Chicago: University of Chicago Press.

Siegal, M. (1991a). A clash of conversational worlds: Interpreting cognitive development through communication. In L. B. Resnick, J. M. Levine, & S. Behrens (eds.), *Perspectives on socially shared cognition* (pp. 23–40). Washington, DC: American Psychological Association.

Siegal, M. (1991b). *Knowing children: Experiments in conversation and cognition.* Hillsdale, NJ: Erlbaum.

Siegal, M. (in press). Conversation and cognition. In R. Gelman & T. Au (eds.), E. C. Carterette & P. Friedman (gen. eds.), *Handbook of perception and cognition: Vol. 13. Perceptual and cognitive development.* San Diego, CA: Academic Press.

Siegal, M., & Beattie, K. (1991). Where to look first for children's knowledge of false beliefs. *Cognition, 38,* 1–12.

Siegal, M., Carrington, J., & Radel, M. (in press). Theory of mind and pragmatic understanding following right hemisphere brain damage. *Brain and Language.*

Siegal, M., & Peterson, C. C. (1994). Children's theory of mind and the conversational territory of cognitive development. In C. Lewis & P. Mitchell (eds.), *Children's early understanding of mind: Origins and development* (pp. 427–55). Hillsdale, NJ: Erlbaum.

Siegal, M., & Peterson, C. C. (1995). *Preschoolers' abilities to match facial expressions to thoughts about lies and mistakes.* Manuscript in preparation.

Siegal, M., & Share, D. L. (1990). Contamination sensitivity in young children. *Developmental Psychology, 26*, 455–8.

Siegal, M., & Storey, R. M. (1985). Day care and children's conceptions of moral and social rules. *Child Development, 56*, 1001–8.

Smetana, J. G. (1981). Preschool children's conceptions of moral and social rules. *Child Development, 52*, 1333–6.

Sodian, B. (1991). The development of deception in young children. *British Journal of Development Psychology, 9*, 173–88.

Sodian, B., Taylor, C., Harris, P. L., & Perner, J. (1991). Early deception and the child's theory of mind: False trails and genuine markers. *Child Development, 62*, 468–83.

Strichartz, A. F., & Burton, R. V. (1990). Lies and truth: A study of the development of the concept. *Child Development, 61*, 211–20.

Sullivan, K., & Winner, E. (1993). Three-year-olds' understanding of mental states: The influence of trickery. *Journal of Experimental Child Psychology, 56*, 135–48.

Sweetser, E. E. (1987). The definition of *lie*: An examination of the folk models underlying a semantic prototype. In D. Holland & N. Quinn (eds.), *Cultural models in language and thought* (pp. 43–66). New York: Cambridge University Press.

Thatcher, R. W. (1992). Cyclic cortical reorganization during early childhood. *Brain and Cognition, 20*, 24–50.

Wellman, H. M., & Bartsch, K. (1988). Young children's reasoning about beliefs. *Cognition, 31*, 438–56.

Wimmer, H., Gruber, S., & Perner, J. (1984). Young children's conception of lying: Lexical realism-moral subjectivism. *Journal of Experimental Child Psychology, 37*, 1–30.

Wimmer, H., Gruber, S., & Perner, J. (1985). Young children's conception of lying: Moral intuition and the denotation and connotation of "to lie." *Developmental Psychology, 21*, 993–5.

NINE

Discussing Truth and Lies with Children

Introduction

In the past legal personnel have been very concerned about whether children, especially younger ones, have an appropriate appreciation of what lying is and of the consequences (for example, in court) of lying. Recently it has been realized that the reliability of children's accounts, say in investigative interviews, may well be very much influenced by whether the adult questioning the child has sufficient skill (see part II of this book). In the 1990s Amye Warren's research contributed to this realization and her study (with colleagues) of discussions with children of truth/lying in real-life sexual abuse interviews is a landmark paper.

Though it is important that any person interacting with the law appreciates the importance of telling the truth, the whole truth, and nothing but the truth, such an appreciation does not necessarily mean that such a person will give a more reliable account. Some adults, though taking an oath in court, nevertheless purposely lie!

A crucial study would be to see how skilled child protective service personnel usually are at discussing truth/lies with children (for example to what extent their approach was commensurate with modern-day developmental psychology). Also important would be to determine if improvements in such skills would increase the accuracy of children's responses to questioning about an event.

If a judge or jury saw a child answering truth/lie questions inaccurately, when these questions were asked by an unskilled interviewer, this could well affect their judgement of the child's credibility. This is especially likely to be the case if the judge and jury did not have sufficient knowledge of developmental psychology to realize that the questioning was poor, and this is likely to be the case even if such a child goes on to give a reliable (i.e. truthful) account.

Suggested reading

Memon, A., Vrij, A., & Bull, R. (1998). *Psychology and law: Truthfulness, accuracy and credibility*. Maidenhead: McGraw-Hill.

Discussing Truth and Lies in Interviews with Children: Whether, Why, and How?

Mary Lyn Huffman, Amye R. Warren, and Susan M. Larson

As more children are participating in forensic interviews, researchers have begun focusing on factors that enhance or diminish children's interview performance. Although various researchers and practitioners have developed interview protocols designed to elicit accurate reports from children, little empirical research has demonstrated which, if any, of these protocols or their components are necessary or sufficient for achieving this end.

One commonly recommended interview technique is to ask children to distinguish between truth and lying (N. E. Walker & Hunt, 1997). There appear to be two primary reasons for using this technique: (a) to demonstrate the child's competency or reliability as a witness and (b) to increase the likelihood of telling the truth during the interview.

Regarding the first reason, most states require that a witness be able to understand the difference between truth and lying and to understand the obligation to tell the truth in legal proceedings. In the past, children's competency often was challenged, and children were required to pass formal competency tests before testifying in court (Haugaard, Reppucci, Laird, & Nauful, 1991). However, formal competency testing requirements have been abolished by most states, and children typically are presumed competent to testify in sexual abuse cases (Poole & Lamb, 1998).

Even if a truth–lie discussion (TLD) is not deemed necessary for formal competency testing purposes, interviewers may wish to demonstrate children's competency to increase the likelihood that their interview statements will be accepted into evidence. If a child is not available to testify at trial, and under certain hear-say exceptions, the child's out-of-court interview statements may be allowed (e.g., McGough, 1994). In determining whether to accept a child's out-of-court statements, judges may partly rely on evidence of that child's competency and reliability. Thus, if forensic interviewers do engage children in TLDs, it is important that they do so in a way that allows children to demonstrate their full abilities. Clearly, the "optimal" TLD differs according to children's ages, linguistic and cognitive abilities, and levels of moral understanding.

A review of the literature on children's understanding of truth and lying reveals that even 4-year-olds can distinguish between facts (truth) and non-facts (lies), if asked to do so in a concrete manner (Bussey, 1992), that is, using concrete examples with tangible, ordinary objects. Although past research (see Strichartz & Burton, 1990, for a review) suggested that young children do not take speaker intentions into account when classifying statements as truths or lies, other evidence (Wimmer, Gruber, & Perner, 1984) indicates that they can, if asked to assign consequences to the speaker's statement (i.e., worse consequences are assigned to deliberate false statements). Moreover, recent research shows that preschoolers are capable of differentiating lies from mistakes (Siegal & Peterson, 1996).

A. G. Walker (1994) proposed that in a competency *voir dire*, young children (below school age) should be given truth (factual) and lie (non-factual) examples from their everyday lives; for example, "What if your [brother/sister/friend] ate up all your mom's cookies and said *you* did it. Is he/she telling the truth or is he lying?" (p. 106). Interviewers also should ask if it is a good thing or a bad thing to tell a lie and what the consequences of telling a lie are. Furthermore, preschoolers should promise to tell only the truth during the interview.

The second primary assumption behind discussing truth and lying with child witnesses is that such discussions will increase the truthfulness of children's interview statements. Although there is an obvious intuitive appeal to this reasoning, Poole and Lamb (1998) warned that currently there is no evidence that TLDs increase accuracy. Furthermore, whether a TLD can increase accuracy depends on which of many proposed underlying mechanisms are responsible for producing children's false statements. Children may make false statements due to social pressures, faulty memories, or other cognitive factors (Ceci & Bruck, 1993). If a child makes a false statement knowingly, for example, to please an authority figure or under pressure from an insistent interviewer, then a TLD may be effective in encouraging truthfulness. Although no direct research on this topic has yet been conducted, prior studies in which children have been "warned" against compliance with tricky interviewers and difficult or leading questions have shown that warnings can reduce suggestibility and increase accuracy (e.g., Warren, Hulse-Trotter, & Tubbs, 1991). However, few researchers or practitioners believe that the majority of children's false statements during interviews are deliberate lies. Instead, children's errors frequently are attributed to faulty memories – whether inadequately encoded, more quickly forgotten, or easily "overwritten" by later conflicting suggestions (see Ceci & Bruck for a review). If a child's memory for an event has been impaired by subsequent misleading information, then a TLD would be unable to repair the child's memory (but see Zaragoza, 1991, for a discussion of the evidence for and against true memory impairment as the cause of children's suggestibility).

Another cognitive mechanism thought to underlie children's errors is poor source monitoring. Source monitoring refers to the ability to recall the context as well as the content of a memory; for example, to remember not only that an event took place, but whether one only heard or read about that event as opposed to directly witnessing or experiencing it (Ceci, Huffman, Smith, & Loftus, 1994). If source-monitoring errors are responsible for children's false statements, then perhaps a TLD would encourage children to sort out actually experienced (true) from suggested (only heard about) events. However, according to Poole and Lindsay (1995), source-monitoring abilities improve with age, and children, especially preschoolers, are more prone than adults to commit source-monitoring errors (Lindsay, Johnson, & Kwon, 1991). In sum, the likelihood of TLDs increasing accuracy probably depends on factors such as how well the original event is remembered, how long it has been since the occurrence of the event, how strong any misleading suggestions are, the social relationship (i.e., status differential) between the interviewer and the child, and the child's age and cognitive abilities.

Finally, Poole and Lamb (1998) warned that TLDs could make children appear less accurate to factfinders or jurors if the children are

unable to answer the truth–lie questions correctly, even if their memories of the target events are accurate. Given no demonstrated benefits
and the potential resultant harm, Poole and Lamb thus suggested that
interviewers should conduct a "truth–lie ceremony" only if local regu-
lations or customs require it.

Even so, many currently followed interviewing protocols advocate a
discussion of the difference between truth and lying (see Poole & Lamb,
1998, or N. E. Walker & Hunt, 1997, for reviews of interviewing protocols). For example, in the initial stages of the "Step-Wise Interview,"
developed by Yuille, Hunter, Joffe, and Zaparniuk (1993), interviewers
are advised to discuss telling the truth before asking the child about the
event in question. They are directed to begin the discussion in a very
general manner, and only if such general questions yield inappropriate
answers should more specific questions be used. Vignettes of characters
telling lies and the truth may be helpful. Questions about consequences
are also important, and the child should agree to tell the truth during
the interview.

In summary, it appears that many practitioners and researchers
believe that determining a child's ability to distinguish truth from lying
remains an important task for interviewers. Though many protocols
recommend including a TLD in children's interviews, it is unknown
whether most interviewers actually include them, and if so, how they
are conducted and whether they are effective in increasing children's
accuracy.

Only one other study (A. G. Walker & McKinley-Pace, 1995) has analyzed actual TLDs. However, these researchers focused primarily on the
linguistic form of questions employed, and they did not look for potential developmental differences in children's responses. They found
that most of the interviewer's questions expected only "yes" or "no"
responses from the children. Thus, these interviewers probably were not
allowing children to demonstrate their full understanding of truth and
lying.

Our first study, therefore, was designed to examine the presence and
characteristics of TLDs during actual investigative interviews, focusing
on the types of questions asked and developmental differences in children's definitions of truth and lies. Our first study assessed TLDs in
actual interviews, and our second study examined the effectiveness of
TLDs in increasing accuracy of children's reports about past events. We
compared the typical TLD seen in Study 1 to either no TLD or a more

elaborate TLD in their effects on preschooler's accuracy during interviews about an interactive event.

Study 1

Method

Transcript sample. Transcripts of videotaped forensic interviews from different counties in one southern state were analyzed. These transcripts were obtained from two sources. One set of 20 interviews from one county was obtained from the county child protective services (CPS) office. A caseworker went through the files pulling the first 20 videotaped sexual abuse interviews found, with the only criterion being that 10 of the interviews were with children below the age of 6 years (preschool) and the other 10 with children over age 6 (school-age). No other selection criteria (e.g., race, gender, abuse disclosure, case outcomes, or apparent interview quality) were employed (see Warren, Woodall, Hunt, & Perry, 1996, for a more detailed description). The second sample was obtained with permission from state officials and researchers with a grant from the National Center on Child Abuse and Neglect (Boat & Everson, 1996). These interview transcripts came from the same and other counties in the same state and represented about 60% of all counties that videotape their interviews. This sample was selected by asking CPS professionals in each county to send the first videotaped sexual abuse interview with a child under 6 years old and the first with a child over 6 years old conducted after a given date. No other selection criteria were used (see Boat & Everson, 1996, for a more detailed description).

The total sample included 132 transcripts from 33 different counties. The majority of the counties submitted between 1 and 3 interviews for analysis, but 2 counties were overrepresented, with 23 and 19 transcripts. Overall, there were 33 boys and 100 girls interviewed (one interview included 2 children). Ages were indicated for 116 of the children, who ranged from 1 year 10 months to 14 years 8 months, with a mean age of 6 years 7 months (SD = 3 years 4 months). The ages appeared evenly distributed across the range, with 58 children below the age of 6 and 58 age 6 or older. One hundred and eight children were White and 5 were African America (19 transcripts lacked racial information).

Eleven of the interviews included more than 1 interviewer, for a total of 145 interviewers. The interviewers were predominantly White ($N = 114$) and female ($N = 112$). Interviewers were caseworkers and police officers. One hundred and fifteen of the children at least partially disclosed some form of abuse during the interviews ($114 =$ sexual abuse, $1 =$ physical abuse), according to our minimal definition of disclosure, which required only assenting if asked about being touched inappropriately.

Coding. For a transcript to be coded as containing a TLD, the interviewer must have attempted to have the child distinguish between the truth and a lie. Although some interviewers proceeded with the interview without establishing that the child understood these terms, if a TLD was attempted then a Discussion was coded as present.

Although the focus of the analyses was on the characteristics of TLDs, truth and lies appeared in some transcripts without any explicit discussion. For example, in one transcript the interviewer just reminded the child to tell the truth, and in another case, a child stated that her sister lied a lot. The interviewer did not have the child define these terms or discuss the difference between truths and lies. Thus, these interchanges were not coded as TLDs.

For each TLD, the researchers recorded the location of the discussion in the transcript (beginning, middle, or end), who initiated the discussion (interviewer, child, or someone else), whether examples were present or not, characteristics of these examples, whether the interviewer initiated a moral judgment (e.g., asking the child if it is right or wrong to tell the truth), intentions (i.e., "Did he mean to say something that wasn't true?"), or consequences (i.e., "What happens when you tell a lie?") concerning the truth or a lie. It was also noted whether the child answered all the interviewer's questions before proceeding with the interview and whether the interviewer asked the child to tell the truth in the interview.

Additionally, the transcripts were analyzed to determine whether the interviewers referred back to the TLD at the end of the interview. For example, at the end of the interview an interviewer might say, "Now is everything you told me the truth?" Thus, this question ties the initial discussion to the abuse-related testimony.

For each discussion, the type of question asked to initiate it was coded. "Yes–no" questions always require a "yes" or "no" response;

"wh-" question include who, what, when, where, or how and require more than merely yes or no responses; and "forced choice" questions request a specific response suggested within the question.

Examples used to define truth and lies were categorized. If the child was asked to make a truth–lie judgment about the color of an object (e.g., hair, clothing, objects in the room), it was coded as a color judgment. Examples also were categorized as referring to clothing, bodily characteristics, identity of interviewer or child (e.g., name, gender, or occupation), objects in room, environment (e.g., weather), time (e.g., time of day, day of the week, or time of the year), action (e.g., "If I said I was going to a friend's house and then didn't go, is that a lie?"), or other (e.g., whether the interview was being videotaped).

Results

We first examined the presence or absence of TLDs in the transcripts. Then we examined the characteristics of TLDs when present. Furthermore, when TLDs were present, we compared their characteristics across two age groups; preschool children under 6 years ($N = 32$) versus those 6 years and older ($N = 35$). These broad age groups were chosen based on the original transcript selection criteria. (Both samples were selected such that approximately one half of the interviews came from children under 6 years and one half from children aged 6 years and over.)

The presence of TLDs. TLDs were present in 56% of the transcripts (74 of 132). Using the presence or absence of a TLD as a grouping variable and age (when available, $N = 116$) as a continuous dependent measure, we found no significant relation between the child's age and presence of a TLD, $t(107) = 1.10$, $p = .27$. In a more detailed analysis, we examined the presence of TLDs in six age groups (determined by sample size); under 4 years old ($n = 24$), 4 years old ($n = 20$), 5 years old ($n = 14$), 6–7 years old ($n = 22$), 8–10 years old ($n = 20$), and 11 years and older ($n = 16$). The chi-square analysis was not significant. However, it was interesting to note that for 2-year-olds, TLDs were present in 29% (2 of 7) of the interviews versus 41% (7 of 17) for the 3-year-olds and 63% (12 of 19) for the 4-year-olds. For all interviews with older children, this figure varied between 60% and 70%.

The presence of a TLD did not significantly relate to the child's gender, $\chi^2(1, N = 132) = 1.03$, $p = .31$, but marginally related to whether the child disclosed abuse, $\chi^2(1, N = 132) = 3.42$, $p = .07$. When a child did not disclose abuse ($n = 17$), TLDs were present in 35% ($n = 6$), but when a child did disclosed abuse ($n = 115$), 59% contained TLDs. Of course, the extremely small sample of nondisclosers and our inability to verify the accuracy of disclosures renders any clear interpretation of these results impossible.

Characteristics of TLDs. As expected, most TLDs occurred at the beginning of the interview. Out of 74 transcripts, 58 (78%) were at the beginning, 6 (8%) were in the middle, and 10 (14%) were at the end of the interviews. The interviewer initiated all TLDs.

When initiating the discussion, 91% of interviewers asked a yes–no question. Only 5% ($n = 2$) asked a wh- question and 4% initiated with a forced choice question. Interviewers did not ask significantly different types of introductory questions of younger and older children. Overall, 60% of all questions asked in the TLDs were yes–no questions, 22% were wh- questions, and 18% were forced choice questions.

Examples of truths and lies. Sixty-six percent (49 of 74) of all TLDs contained examples of either truth or a lie. Ninety-four percent (46 of 49) of these examples were provided by the interviewer. Of interviews containing examples, all contained an example of a lie and only 49% (24 of 49) contained an example of the truth. Fifteen (31%) contained more than one example of a lie, whereas only 4 (8%) contained more than one truth example. Combining examples of truths and lies, 55% of all examples were color judgments (i.e., "If I said that my hair was purple, is that a truth or a lie?").

Most of the examples the interviews employed concerned tangible objects visible to the child at the time of questioning. It is interesting to note that 32% of the examples used clothing, 20% used the child's or interviewer's identity, and 18% used objects in the room. Only 4% of all examples were more abstract (one child stated that saying that you were going to a friend's house when you were not would be a lie).

Definitions of truth and lies. Only 22% (16 of 74 children) of all TLDs elicited children's definitions of truth or lies. Five children were asked to define both a truth and a lie and 10 were asked to define only a truth.

None were asked to define just a lie. Three other transcripts contained definitions of truths and lies but the interviewer provided these. One transcript contained only a lie definition, one only a truth definition, and one contained both. The following are example definitions provided by children:

> A lie is something that is not true, and true is something that is the real thing. (10-year-old girl)

> The truth, like if you asked me if wha- if we were inside or outside, I'd – I'd say inside and it wou-wouldn't be a lie, it would be tellin' the truth, and if I said outside that would be lyin'. (10-year-old boy)

When defining a lie, 62.5% of the children used circular reasoning by saying that a lie is not telling the truth. They also equated lying with receiving punishment, not admitting one's actions, or omitting information (each 12.5%). Thirty-one percent state that telling the truth was telling what really happened. Sixteen percent used circular reasoning saying that truth is not telling a lie. Others said it is the same as telling the right thing (16%). Overall, 8 children gave a definition of a lie and 19 gave a definition of the truth.

Moral judgments and consequences. Out of the 74 TLDs, only 16 (22%) elicited a moral judgment about telling the truth or telling a lie, and this did not differ between the two age groups. None of the interviewers asked the children about the intentions of someone who lies or tells the truth.

Only 31% of the TLDs (23 of 74) contained a dialogue about the consequences of lying or truth-telling. When eliciting consequence information, 17% (4 of 23) were yes–no questions (e.g., "Do you get in trouble for telling a lie?") and 83% (19 of 23) were wh- questions (e.g., "What happens when you tell a lie?"). Older children were not asked about consequences more than younger children. Even young children seemed to understand the consequences of lying and truth-telling when asked. This 4-year-old girl explains:

> I: What happens when you tell a lie?
> C: I don't know. [pause] Get a whooping.
> I: Do you? What happens when you tell the truth?
> C: Don't get no whooping.

> I: Don't get whooping.
> C: No.

In fact, 32% (7 of 22) stated physical punishment as the consequence of lying. Five other children (23%) mentioned a more general punishment, such as getting into trouble. One child even believed that "the police come to get you" when someone tells a lie. Fewer children provided a consequence for truth-telling. The most popular, though, was religious reward or the avoidance of punishment. Three children (out of 7) said they do not get in trouble, and two children said they would go to heaven.

Concluding the TLDs. Twenty-two percent (16 of 74) of the interviews progressed without the child having answered all the interviewer's questions. Eight percent (6 of 74) of all children remained confused about the definition of the truth and a lie when the interviewer ended the TLD and moved into a discussion of the abuse. Only 50% (37 of 74) of interviewers tied the TLD to the child's abuse testimony by asking the child to tell the truth. Five percent (4 of 74) indirectly told the child to tell the truth in the interview (i.e., "Today we are only going to deal with what is true and not a lie").

At the end of the interview, only 43% (32 of 74) of interviewers related the child's testimony to the TLD by asking the child if he or she had told the truth in the interview. When the interview was tied to the TLD, 81% (26 of 32) of the interviewers asked a yes–no question (i.e., "Was everything you told me today the truth?"), and 19% (6 of 32) asked a forced choice question (i.e., "All that you told me was that a truth or the lie?").

Example TLD narratives. TLDs were attempted even with the youngest children in the sample. For example, the following narratives demonstrate the difficulty of interviewing this age group about the truth and a lie. The following exchange is between the interviewer and a child 1 your 10 months old (the youngest child in the sample):

> I: Now, B., do you know the difference between the truth and a lie?
> C: [Nods]
> I: If I told you that – that you were standing on your head right now, what would I be telling you?

C: Old McDonald said that at the police station.
I: Uh-huh. At the police station?
C: You've got to take his shirt off. [Referring to small boy doll]

This 2-year-old child also seemed to have great difficulty understanding the questions.

I: John. Okay. John, do you know the difference between the truth and a lie?
C: [shakes head affirmatively] Uh-huh.
I: You do? What happens if you tell a lie?
C: [looks to grandmother]
I: What happens if you tell a lie? Huh? Do you know what happens?
C: Huh?
I: What happens if you tell a lie? Can you tell me what happens? Do you know your colors? Do you know your colors pretty good?
C: Uh-huh.
I: If I told you this was blue, is that the truth or is that a lie?
C: That's lying.
I: That's a lie? Is that what you said?
C: That's lying.
I: What color is that? Do you know what color this is, this sweater? What color is that?
C: Color is that? [child looks at grandmother, rubs her stomach]

One 3-year-old boy had difficulty distinguishing between a truth and a lie.

I: If I said [holding up one finger] I'm holding up three fingers, what's that, a truth or a lie?
C: Truth.
I: Okaaay. If I said there wasn't any pizza here [rubs top of the table], what's that, a truth or a lie?
C: Truth.
I: [Laughs] Okay. Uhm. [pause] let's seeeee. Okay. We don't really know the difference between the truth and a lie. . . .

Study 2

Overall, the findings of Study 1 show that children were often (i.e., more than 50% of the time) asked to distinguish truth and lying during forensic interviews. The discussions of truth and lying did not appear to substantially differ based on the age of the child being interviewed. Even the youngest children (2- and 3-year-olds) sometimes were asked to distinguish truth and lying when research indicates they may have difficulty doing so.

The typical TLD proceeded as follows: first, children were asked some variant of the question, "Do you know the difference between the truth and a lie?" Second, they were asked to judge a concrete example (e.g., "If I said that my hair was purple, would that be the truth or a lie?"). Last, they were told to tell only the truth during the remainder of the interview. These TLDs were brief, concrete, and primarily closed-ended, calling for yes–no answers from the children. The interviewers did not ask the children to distinguish lies from mistakes or to take a speaker's intentions into account when judging a false statement. Thus, these typical discussions may have been challenging to the very youngest children but may have failed to reveal the older children's complete understanding of truths and lies.

Whether these brief discussions actually facilitated children's truth-telling during the subsequent interviews cannot be determined from the transcripts. Thus, our second study was designed to assess the effects of TLDs on children's accuracy in reporting events. By using staged events, we could readily measure the children's accuracy and compare accuracy rates across different types of TLD conditions.

Based on the findings of Study 1, a "standard" protocol for interviewing children about truth and lying was developed. If more than 50% of the transcripts contained a TLD element, then it was included in the standard TLD. Therefore, the standard TLD contained one question asking if the child understood the difference between the truth and a lie, two questions requiring the child to make a truth–lie judgment about a concrete example (i.e., "If I said that you were a boy, would that be a truth or a lie?"), and one statement by the interviewer requesting the child to only tell the truth in the interview.

We also developed an elaborated or extended TLD including more of the "advanced" questions not usually asked in the typical TLD. This extended discussion (presented in the method section) included more open-ended questions, focused on examples and definitions of lies (because the concept of "truth" is too abstract), included a question regarding consequences of lying, and presented three scenarios involving lying or truth-telling that our participants were asked to judge. We hypothesized that having children discuss truth and lying more extensively might make them more accurate when asked to recall events. Thus, Study 2 was designed to compare the effects of no TLD, the standard TLD, and the extended TLD on children's accuracy about a previous event.

Method

Participants. Sixty-seven children (41 boys and 26 girls) from three preschools in a midsized southern town participated in the research. Their ages ranged from 4 years 6 months to 6 years 9 months, with a mean age of 5 years 4 months ($SD = 6.5$ months). Most of the children were White and from middle-class families. Children participated if parental consent was obtained. Initially, 75 children began the experiment, but during the course of the experiment, 8 children were dropped due to missing the initial staged event or one or both of the subsequent interviews.

Procedures. The preschool classrooms were visited by Sam Stone, a fictitious character played by an experimental confederate. He greeted the children and did two of three events all focusing on a theme of circles. He drew circles of different sizes with the children, gave them streamers made of red paper to twirl in circles in the air, or gave them paper pizzas and asked them to put only round paper foods on them. The two events actually performed in each classroom were determined randomly.

Prior to conducting any interviews, the interviewers spent 1–2 hours with each classroom acclimatizing to the children in their school environment. After a week following Sam Stone's visit, children were interviewed about the events of that visit. The purpose of the interview was to introduce misleading information about the prior events. The type of questions asked about each event varied according to which two of the three events each classroom had experienced. Straightforward questions were asked about one of the actual, experienced events (termed the true event); for example, "Did Sam Stone do a dance with you?" Misleading questions were asked about the other actual event (called the manipulated event). For example, if Sam Stone asked the children to draw different sizes of circles, a question might be asked leading the child to think Sam Stone asked them to draw circles of the same size: "Someone said they drew all small circles, were all your circles the same size?" Questions also were asked about the remaining event that the child never experienced (termed the false event), such as, "Did Sam Stone play a game with pizza?"

The second interview was conducted by a different interviewer 2 days after the first interview. All of these interviews were videotaped. Children in each classroom were randomly assigned to one of three lie discussion conditions. Children in the no TLD condition did not answer any questions about the truth and a lie before being asked specific questions about Sam Stone's visit. Children in the standard TLD were asked only a few questions about the difference between truth and lying, derived from TLDs observed in Study 1. Children in the extended TLD were asked more questions about the difference between truth and lying, were asked to make judgments about other children telling the truth and lies, and were asked about moral consequences of lying. Finally, all children were asked to recall all that Sam Stone did during his visit and were then asked specific questions about details not previously mentioned in their free-recall accounts; for example, "How many circles did you draw?" No misleading questions were asked during this second interview.

The TLDs. As mentioned previously, the standard TLDs were developed based on findings from Study 1. They were conducted as follows:

> Do you know the difference between a truth and a lie?
> If I said your shirt was red, is that the truth or a lie? (actually true)
> If I said you were a girl/boy, is that the truth or a lie? (actually false)
> I want you to tell me the truth about when Sam Stone visited your classroom. Okay?

The extended TLDs were conducted as follows:

> I want to ask you a few questions about what it means to tell the truth and what it means to tell a lie. I want to learn what you think about a truth and a lie.
> What is a lie?
> what could you say that would be a lie?
> What should you say instead?
> Is it a good thing or a bad thing to tell a lie? Why?
> What happens when your mom or dad finds out you said a lie?

Is it ever okay to lie? When?
If yes, why is it okay to lie? If no, why not?
Is it better to tell what really happened? Why?

I am going to give you some examples of what some of my friends have said, and I want you to tell me if he/she said a truth, a lie, or something else. My friend's name is Jim/Jane and he/she is your age.

One day Jane/Jim and his/her mother were at home and the phone rang. Jim/Jane's mother did not want to talk on the phone and asked Jim/Jane to answer the phone but say she was not at home. When Jim/Jane answered the phone and the person asked for Jim/Jane's mother, Jim/Jane said, "My mother is not at home." Did Jim/Jane tell the truth, a lie, or something else? Why is that a ——? Was it okay for Jim/Jane to say his/her mother was not at home? Why/Why not?

[In conclusion] We are going to talk about what Sam Stone did during his visit and I want you to tell me what really happened Okay? Remember to tell me the truth about what Sam Stone did.

In addition to this story about lying to protect a parent, children were asked about a child who broke a teapot but claimed that the cat did it (lie for self-protection) and another about a child who ate a cookie without permission but told the truth about it (true story). These vignettes were chosen to represent the categories of lies children may be most likely to commit under forensic circumstances.

During the extended TLD, interviewers asked the children to provide examples of lies to elicit more discussion from the children. Lies were targeted because it has been suggested that they are more readily understood and discussed by young children (A. G. Walker, 1994).

Scoring. For each of the three events, there were five specific questions the child answered. Therefore, accuracy for each event ranged from 0 (*no questions answered correctly*) to 5 (*all questions answered correctly*). Interrater reliability was 98% for two raters independently coding each response.

Results

We first performed an analysis of the children's responses during the first (suggestive) interview to confirm that randomization into subsequent TLD conditions for the final interview was successful. There was no significant difference in the children's total accuracy in the first interview according to TLD condition, $F(2, 66) = 0.783$, $p = .461$. The children were 66% accurate in this first interview, with an average score of 11.9 out of 18 questions. They averaged just over one (1.07) "don't know" response during this first interview, which did not differ significantly according to TLD condition, $F(2, 66) = 0.388$, $p = .680$.

A 3 (types of discussion: none, simplistic, or extended) × 3 (type of event: true, false, or manipulated) repeated measures analysis of variance was conducted on children's accurate responses to final interview questions. Main effects of both the type of discussion, $F(2, 64) = 3.43$, $p = .04$, and the event condition, $F(2, 128) = 4.08$, $p = .02$, were significant, but their interaction was not. Overall across conditions, the average accuracy for the true events was 4.06, for manipulated events it was 3.61, and for false events it was 3.34. A Fisher's least significant difference (LSD) post hoc comparison revealed that the true event was significantly more accurately recalled than the false event, whereas the accuracy scores on the manipulated event fell in between (but did not significantly differ from) these extremes. Across events, the mean accuracy for the no TLD condition was 10.9, for the standard TLD condition was 10.2, and for the extended TLD was 12.5. According to a Fisher's LSD post hoc comparison, children in the extended TLD group were more accurate than children given the standard TLD or no TLD, who did not differ from one another (see table 9.1)

Of course, it is important to determine whether the children involved in the extended TLDs were, in fact, capable of answering the questions posed to them during the discussions. Interpretation of the results would be quite problematic if the extended TLD increased accuracy, even though the children were incapable of answering its questions appropriately. When responding to the three vignettes included in the extended TLD, the children were successful at categorizing them as truths or lies. For vignette 1 (selfish lie), 91% of the children correctly categorized it as a lie, and 96% of the children said that what the story character did was not okay. For vignette 2 (altruistic lie), 77% of the children correctly categorized this as a lie. Almost 82% of the children said it was wrong for the story character to have told this lie to protect a parent. Vignette 3, in which a child told the truth about committing a misdeed, was correctly labeled as the truth 68% of the time, and 82% of the children believed that it was okay to tell the truth in this vignette.

Table 9.1   Children's accuracy for true, false, and manipulated events by TLD condition

	Truth–Lie Discussion		
	No TLD	Standard TLD	Extended TLD
Event Condition			
True			
M	3.87	3.86	4.46
SD	1.22	1.25	0.96
False			
M	3.30	2.50	4.22
SD	2.23	2.43	1.54
Manipulated			
M	3.48	3.55	3.82
SD	1.62	1.77	1.22
Don't know responses			
M	.65	.36	.86
SD	1.07	.79	1.58

TLD = truth–lie discussion. Accuracy scores ranged from 0 (*low*) to 5 (*high*).

To ensure that the children in the extended TLD condition were not more accurate simply because they became more cautious about reporting all information, we conducted an analysis of "don't know" responses to the 15 specific question (5 about each event). Twenty-one children (out of all 67 in the study) gave a "don't know" response at least once. Eight of these children were in the no TLD condition (*n* = 23), 5 were in the standard TLD condition (*n* = 22), and 8 were in the extended TLD condition (*n* = 23). No significant effect of TLD condition on number of "don't know responses" emerged.

Discussion

As predicted, children asked to fully discuss truth and lying were more accurate when later asked questions regarding both experienced and suggested but nonexperienced events. This increase in accuracy did not come at the expense of an increase in "caution" and omission errors; children in the extended TLD condition were no more likely than those in the standard or no TLD conditions to answer "I don't know." Children given the "standard" TLDs, however, were no more accurate than those who did not discuss truth or lying at all.

We must note several caveats and limitations to our results. First, the ecological validity of our events and interviews is limited. Our findings may be bound by the types of events and questions used in our study. We used three relatively neutral events and asked only five specific questions about each event. Second, the children who engaged in the extended TLDs spent the greatest amount of time with the interviewers prior to being questioned about the target events. The children in the standard TLD condition spent somewhat less time talking with the interviewers, whereas the children with no TLD spent the least. Thus, our differences may be due as much to amount of time spent as to *how* that time was spent. Perhaps the children in the extended TLD condition had developed better rapport with the interviewer prior to target questioning. Unfortunately, we could not control for total amount of time spent in the interviews without further confounding the results – having the children in the standard and no TLD conditions doing other things with the interviewers might also have influenced their performance during target event questioning. In future research, perhaps we can include children who spend equivalent amounts of time with the interview in rapport-building or in other forms of competency assessment (e.g., vocabulary or other language skills testing) and then compare these preinterview techniques to TLDs in their impact on performance. If the extended TLD is effective partially due to its facilitation of rapport-building, then the time spent in an extended TLD may be even more effective, by accomplishing two critical objectives simultaneously.

General Discussion

This series of studies represents the first step in establishing the necessity of, and the necessary ingredients for, TLDs in forensic interviews. We first provided descriptive analysis of the TLDs typically found in actual abuse interviews, and then empirically demonstrated that these "standard" interview techniques were ineffective for increasing children's accuracy during an interview about an interactive, past event.

Instead, we proposed an extended lie discussion and demonstrated that it did increase children's accuracy during a subsequent interview. Because children involved in a standard TLD were no more accurate than those who did not discuss truth and lying at all, it appears that if an interviewer's goal is to increase the validity of a forensic interview, then a TLD should be included only if the discussion is conducted in greater depth than those we found to be typical of current practice. Given the limited attention spans of young children and the time constraints under which interviewers typically must work, devoting time to ineffective techniques is counterproductive. As already mentioned, there are additional reasons for conducting TLDs with preschoolers (e.g., establishment of competency). The effectiveness of the standard and extended TLDs in fulfilling these other purposes is unclear from this study. However, it is always important to elicit accurate testimony from child witnesses regardless of an interviewer's other goals.

What made the extended TLDs effective? We know that they did *not* make children more cautious about reporting information, but otherwise, our results do not allow us to make any definitive statements regarding underlying causal mechanisms. However, we propose two plausible, complementary explanations. First, the extended discussions may have led children to focus on possible negative consequences of "lying" or reporting false information. The extended TLD questioned children about intentions, the consequences of lying and truth-telling, and why it is important to tell the truth, whereas the standard discussions ask children only to make fact versus non-fact judgments (e.g., about the color of objects). Perhaps it is only when asked to discuss the moral implications of truth and lying that the child becomes more likely to report the truth (or less likely to report false information). Another possible explanation is that the extended TLDs encouraged source monitoring or separating actual events from those only suggested in the first interviews.

This latter explanation runs counter to much of the current thinking on young children's suggestibility and source-monitoring skills. For example, Ceci et al. (1994) repeatedly questioned preschoolers about both actual and false events. Despite initially correctly denying the false events, over time and repeated interviews, many of the children came to believe that the false events had happened to them. Even when the children's parents explained to them that the suggested events had not actually happened, the children continued to insist that the events had indeed occurred. Ceci et al. thus postulated that when children report a false event after repeated or leading questions, they maintain their false stories because they have come to earnestly believe them to be true. If a child earnestly believes an event to have happened, then a TLD should not affect the child's testimony.

One critical difference in the studies may be the number of suggestive interviews. Ceci et al. (1994) focused on children's inability to distinguish false from true events after repeated (10 or so) interviews, whereas in this study, only two interviews were conducted. Perhaps the children in our study still were able after only a week to separate the actual from the suggested events, and the extended lie discussions encouraged them to make such distinctions during subsequent questioning about the events. After many more suggestive interviews or after a longer delay, however, it is possible that the children would no longer have been able to separate truth from falsehood, rendering any TLDs ineffective.

Despite the apparent success of the extended discussions in increasing children's accuracy, there are several limitations that make practical application problematic. Our findings may not hold for delayed interviews about traumatic events. Furthermore, use of extended TLDs, though improving accuracy, could have unforeseen detrimental effects. For example, when we examined children's performance during the extended TLDs themselves, we noted that a few of the children appeared confused about the difference between truth and lies. Those children might have appeared more competent during the simpler, standard discussions. Thus, although the extended discussions resulted in increased accuracy for some children, others might have been disadvantaged by the same procedure. Furthermore, if fact-finders or jurors viewed taped testimony of children given extended TLDs, these children might appear less competent, and thereby less credible, than when only interviewed with the standard TLD or no TLD. For example, Lyon and Saywitz (1999) found that children's perceived competency was affected by the way in which their understanding of truths and lies was assessed. They also found that children seemed reluctant to discuss lying and its consequences and often failed to answer questions on these topics. Given that our extended TLD focuses on lying and its consequences, it may result in lower apparent competency and/or credibility for some children. On the other hand, children who can successfully answer questions in an extended TLD may appear more competent and credible.

In future research, we plan to test the effectiveness of the extended TLD after longer delays, after more suggestive interviews, and with children of varying ages and from varying backgrounds. Additionally, although the extended TLD in its entirety increased children's accuracy, it remains unclear what specific features and underlying mechanisms (e.g., social or cognitive) were responsible for this effect. Thus, in future studies, we will be examining the components of the extended TLD separately. Finally, it is unclear how differing forms of TLDs may affect children's believability, regardless of their accuracy. We currently are conducting a study in which mock jurors are shown videotapes of children (from our second study), engaging in standard, extended, and no TLDs, then answering the target event questions. We expect that, regardless of actual accuracy in responding to target event questions, children engaged in extended TLDs will appear more truthful and believable than the other children. Until these and other studies are completed, interviewers should be cautious, given the potential benefits and drawbacks of discussing truth and lying with children during forensic interviews.

References

Boat, B. W., & Everson, M. D. (1996). Concerning practices of interviewers when using anatomical dolls in Child Protective Service investigations. *Child Maltreatment, 1*, 96–104.

Bussey, K. (1992). Children's lying and truthfulness: Implications for children's testimony. In S. J. Ceci, M. D. Leichtman, & M. Putnick (eds.), *Cognitive and social factors in early deception* (pp. 89–109). Hillsdale, NJ: Lawrence Erlbaum Associates, Inc.

Ceci, S. J., & Bruck, M. (1993). Suggestibility of the child witness: A historical review and synthesis. *Psychological Bulletin, 113*, 403–39.

Ceci, S. J., Huffman, M. L. C., Smith, E., & Loftus, E. F. (1994). Repeatedly thinking about a non-event: Source monitoring misattributions among preschoolers. *Consciousness and Cognition, 3*, 388–407.

Haugaard, J. J., Reppucci, N. D., Laird, J., & Nauful, T. (1991). Children's definitions of the truth and their competency as witnesses in legal proceedings. *Law and Human Behavior, 15*, 253–71.

Lindsay, D. S., Johnson, M. K. & Kwon, P. (1991). Developmental changes in memory source monitoring. *Journal of Experimental Child Psychology, 52*, 297–318.

Lyon, T. D., & Saywitz, K. J. (1999). Young maltreated children's competence to take the oath. *Applied Developmental Science, 3*, 16–27.

McGough, L. S. (1994). *Child witnesses: Fragile voices in the American legal system.* New Haven, CT: Yale University Press.

Poole, D. A., & Lamb, M. E. (1998). *Investigative interviews of children: A guide for helping professionals.* Washington, DC: American Psychological Association.

Poole, D. A., & Lindsay, D. S. (1995). Interviewing preschoolers: Effects of non-suggestive techniques, parental coaching, and leading questions on reports of nonexperienced events. *Journal of Experimental Child Psychology, 60,* 129–54.

Siegal, M., & Peterson, C. C. (1996). Breaking the mold: A fresh look at children's understanding of questions about lies and mistakes. *Developmental Psychology, 32,* 322–34.

Strichartz, A. F., & Burton, R. V. (1990). Lies and truth: A study of the development of the concept. *Child Development, 61,* 211–20.

Walker, A. G. (1994). *Handbook on questioning children: A linguistic perspective.* Washington, DC: American Bar Association on Children and the Law.

Walker, A. G., & McKinley-Pace, M. J. (1995, June). Questioning children on truth and lies: A real-world look at the problems. *Third National Colloquium of the American Professional Society on the Abuse of Children,* Tucson, AZ.

Walker, N. E., & Hunt, J. S. (1997). Interviewing child victim–witnesses: How you ask is what you get. In C. P. Thompson, D. J. Herrmann, J. D. Read, D. Bruce, D. G. Payne, & M. P. Toglia (eds.), *Eyewitness memory: Theoretical and applied perspectives* (pp. 55–87). Mahwah, NJ: Lawrence Erlbaum Associates, Inc.

Warren, A. R., Hulse-Trotter, K., & Tubbs, E. (1991). Inducing resistance to suggestibility in children. *Law and Human Behavior, 15,* 273–85.

Warren, A. R., Woodall, C. E., Hunt, J. S., & Perry, N. W. (1996). "It sounds good in theory, but . . .": Do investigative interviewers follow guidelines based on memory research? *Child Maltreatment, 1,* 231–45.

Wimmer, H., Gruber, S., & Perner, J. (1984). Young children's conception of lying: Lexical realism – Moral subjectivism. *Journal of Experimental Child Psychology, 37,* 1–30.

Yuille, J. C., Hunter, R., Joffe, R., & Zaparniuk, J. (1993). Interviewing children in sexual abuse cases. In G. S. Goodman & B. L. Bottoms (eds.), *Child victims, child witnesses: Understanding and improving testimony* (pp. 95–115). New York: Guilford.

Zaragoza, M. S. (1991). Preschool children's susceptibility to memory impairment. In J. Doris (ed.), *The suggestibility of children's recollections* (pp. 27–39). Washington, DC: American Psychological Association.

Part IV

Children and the
Legal System

TEN

Closed-Circuit Television and Children's Testimony

Introduction

With society's increasing awareness that the frequency of children being victimized or being witnesses to crime is not as low as people had previously thought, there has come a concern that our legal procedures have not been designed with children in mind. While in most countries children are not required to testify in civil cases, in criminal courts they are usually required to do so. Children often had to give their evidence in criminal trials right in front of the defendant, with many other adults present who were strangers. In one study, some children who gave evidence even thought that the jury were friends of the defendant!

In such trials in the recent past many children seemed to find it difficult to give their version, and some just broke down in tears or literally hid under a table. While some aspects of criminal proceedings were designed (often long ago) in the belief that they aided justice (for example, having to give evidence in front of the person one is accusing in a very large room designed to intimidate adults), a number of these aspects were developed in ignorance of the needs and emotions of children, and of the findings from developmental psychology in general.

During the 1990s a number of countries brought in legislation to allow children to give their evidence, not right in the courtroom, but from a room in the same building, linked to the courtroom by closed-circuit television (CCTV). While this could be developmentally appropriate, some people, especially defence lawyers, argued that having the child testify away from the defendant(s) presumed the defendant's guilt and denied the defendant(s) the right to confront witnesses against them. In the face of such defence arguments some countries only allow

CCTV in special circumstances, whereas others allow it as a matter of routine for all children.

The new laws allowing the use of CCTV in cases where children are witnesses were often brought in as a result of media criticism of the existing procedures designed for adults, rather than as a result of research directly showing the benefits of children giving their evidence via CCTV. What was then needed was studies of the effectiveness of this usage of CCTV, and the 1998 study by Gail Goodman and her colleagues is the most extensive of these.

Suggested reading

Spencer, J., & Flin, R. (1993). *The evidence of children: The law and the psychology*, 2nd edn. London: Blackstone.

Face-to-Face Confrontation: Effects of Closed-Circuit Technology on Children's Eyewitness Testimony and Jurors' Decisions

Gail S. Goodman, Ann E. Tobey,
Jennifer M. Batterman-Faunce,
Holly Orcutt, Sherry Thomas,
Cheryl Shapiro, and Toby Sachsenmaier

Increases in the reporting and prosecution of child sexual abuse over the past decade have resulted in many children testifying in criminal court, accompanied by attempts to protect them from the stress of face-to-face confrontation. Children's potential vulnerability coupled with defendants' rights to confrontation makes the use of protective measures a matter of social science and legal concern. A number of controversial trial convictions have been appealed based on psychological assumptions regarding the use of protective measures, such as closed-circuit television (CCTV), when children testify. For example, in a highly publicized case, Kelly Michaels' conviction in New Jersey was overturned in part because the judge improperly permitted the children to testify via CCTV (Rosenthal, 1995). Alternatively, in a less-publicized case, a 9-year-old who watched his mother kill his siblings, and was almost killed by her himself, was required to testify face-to-face with his mother at trial (*Buffalo News*, 1989).

Surprisingly little scientific research exists on the possible advantages and disadvantages of CCTV when children take the stand. Proponents of CCTV reason that if children do not have to face the defendant or enter the courtroom, children will be less traumatized by testifying. They also assert that a more comfortable child may provide more complete and accurate reports, and thus enhance the truth-seeking function of trials. In contrast, opponents of CCTV contend that use of such technology violates defendants' Fourteenth Amendment rights to due process by eroding the presumption of innocence and impeding fact-finders' abilities to assess the credibility of child witnesses, and violates defendants' Sixth Amendment right to face-to-face confrontation of witnesses.

The present research was designed to address a number of such claims that arise when a child testifies with the aid of closed-circuit technology. Are children more accurate when testifying in open court or when testifying via CCTV? Does the testimony setting affect children's experience of pretrial anxiety? Is it possible to predict which children will refuse to testify in open court versus via CCTV? Are jurors better able to evaluate the accuracy of child witnesses in live or closed-circuit trials? Are the effects of the employment of closed-circuit technology different for younger versus older witnesses? Are jurors biased by use of closed-circuit testimony, leading them to view the defendant as guilty when, in fact, he or she is not guilty? Likewise, does the use of closed-circuit technology bias jurors for or against child witnesses? We attempted to answer these questions in an elaborate mock-trial study in which children either testified live or via CCTV.

Protective Measures and Children's Testimony

By 1995, 34 states had statutorily authorized judges to allow certain child witnesses to testify via CCTV (National Center for the Prosecution of Child Abuse, 1995). Nevertheless, most prosecutors prefer to present a live witness (Goodman, Pyle-Taub, Jones, England, Port, Rudy, & Prado, 1992). A live witness is thought to have greater influence on the jury, enhancing the immediacy and emotional impact of the testimony compared to that of a televised witness (Davies & Noon, 1991; MacFarlane, 1985). Prosecutors also believe that appeals of convictions are less likely with live testimony (Quas, DeCicco, Bulkley, & Goodman, 1996).

Indeed, when the US Supreme Court first became involved in determining the constitutionality of such measures at trial, defendants' rights were highlighted. In *Coy v. Iowa* (1988), the defendant argued that the use of a screen to shield two child victim/witnesses violated his Sixth and Fourteenth Amendment rights. In writing the majority decision overturning Coy's conviction, Justice Scalia argued that face-to-face presence "may, unfortunately, upset the truthful rape victim or abused child; but, by the same token it may confound and undo the false accuser, or reveal the child coached by a malevolent adult" (p. 1020). He further reasoned that by observing the child testify in front of the defendant, jurors can better factor nonverbal cues (e.g., eye contact) into their overall impressions.

However, in *Maryland v. Craig* (1990), the US Supreme Court ruled in favor of use of CCTV in child sexual abuse cases when the trauma of face-to-face confrontation would not permit the child to reasonably communicate. This ruling, written by Justice O'Connor, specified the need for a "particularized" (case by case) judicial determination of a child's ability to reasonably communicate in the presence of the defendant. Despite the US Supreme Court ruling permitting use of CCTV, a number of state supreme courts (e.g., Pennsylvania's) have determined that CCTV violates rights to face-to-face confrontation as laid out in state constitutions.

Effects of confrontational and courtroom stress on children's reports

If children's testimony is compromised by confrontation or courtroom stress, then jurors' duty as factfinders may be impeded. In his dissenting opinion in *Coy v. Iowa* (1988), Justice Blackmun argued that the fear and trauma associated with testifying in front of the defendant may traumatize the child and undermine the truth-finding function of the trial by inhibiting effective testimony. Indeed, confronting the accused is a major stress factor for child witnesses (Goodman et al., 1992; Murray, 1995; Sas, 1991; Spencer & Flin, 1990; Whitcomb, Shapiro, & Stellwagen, 1985) and the completeness and accuracy of children's testimony can be seriously hampered by intimidation and/or heightened emotion. When confronted with the accused, children may show signs of anxiety (e.g., crying, shaking, attempting to leave the courtroom), refuse to testify, be unable to verbalize answers or state accusations, and have difficulty making person identifications (e.g., Bussey, Ross, & Lee, 1991; Dent, 1977; Goodman et al., 1992; Peters, 1990; see Goodman, Levine, Melton, & Ogden, 1991, for a review). Absence of a face-to-face encounter does not seem to increase children's commission errors (e.g., false identification rate; Dent, 1977; Peters, 1990), although more research on this important issue is needed.

Experiments to examine courtroom stress, as opposed to confrontational stress per se, have also been conducted. Saywitz and Nathanson (1993) found that 8- to 10-year-olds interviewed in a courtroom displayed impaired memory performance and provided higher stress ratings as compared to children questioned at their own school (see also Hill & Hill, 1987). Other stressors include lack of legal knowledge, insensitive interviewing techniques and inadequate protection during cross-examination, and lack of social support for the child giving evidence (Spencer & Flin, 1990). Thus, several aspects of legal involvement are stressful for children. In contrast, a supportive atmosphere can have a positive effect on children's reports, especially to decrease suggestibility (Carter, Bottoms, & Levine, 1996; Goodman, Bottoms, Schwartz-Kenney, & Rudy, 1991; Moston & Engelberg, 1992).

Taken together, studies indicate that it may be difficult for children to recount events fully and accurately when the perpetrator is physically present. In addition, the courtroom setting and several legal practices seem to be related to heightened stress in children, which may in turn affect accuracy.

Individual differences in reactions to confrontational stress and willingness to testify

Factors that determine how children respond to the stress of testifying are still largely unexplored. Literature on children's reactions to other stressful events suggests substantial variation in children's responses (Rutter, 1993). Similarly, regarding the stress of testifying, some children react quite negatively to taking the stand, while others show considerable resilience (Goodman et al., 1992). The former category includes children who are so distressed at even the thought of testifying that they refuse to enter the courtroom. If CCTV helps relieve children's stress, reluctant children should be more willing to testify via CCTV than in open court.

Given the opportunity to testify via CCTV or not, it is likely that individual differences in children will affect their willingness to testify. Although we know of no studies examining predictors of children's agreement to testify in regular court or over CCTV (but see Cashmore, 1992), individual difference factors related to cognitive and socioemotional development may moderate children's ability to cope with testifying. For example, older compared to younger children express greater negativity about testifying (Goodman et al., 1992), perhaps because of the former's understanding of the implications (e.g., defendant incarceration, witness cross-examination). In contrast, younger children may be more likely to refuse because of fear about the unknown: lack of legal knowledge resulting in misunderstanding and fear is a major stress factor for child witnesses (Berliner & Conte, 1995; Spencer & Flin, 1990). Individual differences in memory or language skills may result in children who lack sufficient memory or verbal skills being hesitant to testify. Socioemotional factors may also be important: children with pre-existing psychological problems or deficits in self-esteem may be too disturbed or timid to testify. Underlying many of these hypothetical trends may be heightened anxiety about performance, leading to refusal to take the stand. In contrast, children of authoritarian parents may feel compelled to testify despite the children's own feelings. We were interested in examining if CCTV leads fewer children to refuse to testify and if we could identify individual difference predictors of children's agreement to take the stand. Such findings could aid the courts in making particularized case-by-case determinations (*Maryland v. Craig*, 1990) as to which child may be too frightened to testify in open court.

Jurors' Perceptions of Child Witnesses

From a legal perspective, the accuracy of courtroom testimony is only as important as factfinders' (e.g., jurors') abilities to reach the truth because it is factfinders' perceptions of testimony that directly affect the outcome of a trial. How do jurors' perceive children's testimony? Are there individual differences among children or jurors that might affect perceptions of children when they testify via CCTV?

Jurors' views of children's testimony

Characteristics of children may affect jurors' perceptions of children's credibility as witnesses. A number of studies indicate that as age increases up through early adulthood, perceived witness credibility also increases (Goodman, Golding, Helgeson, Haith, & Michelli, 1987; Leippe & Romanczyk, 1987, 1989). Nevertheless, other studies show the reverse or no relation (Bottoms & Goodman, 1994; Duggan, Aubrey, Doherty, Isquith, Levine, & Scheiner, 1989; Nightingale, 1993). Contrasting trends may reflect juror's stereotypes of children as applied to different kinds of cases. Jurors may find young children particularly credible in sexual assault cases under the stereotype that children are basically honest and lack sufficient sexual knowledge to make false claims, whereas jurors may find children less credible than adults in cases were strength of memory is a key issue under the stereotype that children's memory is unreliable (Bottoms & Goodman, 1994; Leippe & Romanczyk, 1989). Interaction effects of age with other variables (e.g., communication style) have been documented (e.g., Schmidt & Brigham, 1996). It is thus possible that children of different ages will be seen as more or less credible when they testify via CCTV. For instance, jurors might think that younger children need protective measures to testify accurately, whereas older children may be viewed as capable of testifying in open court.

Another child characteristic concerns children's confidence and consistency. Perceptions of confidence and consistency have been found to influence jurors' views of child witnesses (e.g. Leippe, Manion, & Romanczyk, 1992). If CCTV promotes confident and consistent testimony, then jurors' views of children may be affected.

In addition, juror characteristics may influence perceptions of open court versus CCTV testimony, especially when case evidence is ambiguous (Goodman et al., 1984). For example, Duggan et al. (1989) found that mock jurors who were more experienced with children were less likely to attribute responsibility to the child victim/witness in a sexual assault case and more confident of the defendant's guilt. Likewise, Leippe et al. (1992, Experiment 3) reported that couples with parenting experience were better able to discriminate accurate from inaccurate reports by 5- to 6-year-olds than couples without the benefit of similar parenting experience. Gender is another potentially important juror characteristic. In child sexual abuse cases, women on average are more "pro-victim," express more empathy toward child witnesses, and rate child witnesses more favorably, whereas men on average tend to be more pro-defense (e.g., Bottoms, 1993). To the extent that women tend to be more pro-victim in child witness cases, they may also be more approving of CCTV since the goal of such technology is to protect children from the stress of testifying. To the extent that men are more pro-defense, they may be more disapproving of CCTV testimony for children.

In summary, characteristics of children, such as age, confidence, and consistency, may interact with testimony setting (open court vs. CCTV) to influence jurors' perceptions of child witnesses. Juror characteristics are likely to be important as well. For example, women may react more favorably than men to children's testimony via CCTV.

Jurors' abilities to discern accurate child testimony

Does CCTV interfere with jurors' abilities to assess witness accuracy? Only a handful of studies have investigated jurors' abilities to distinguish accurate from inaccurate child testimony (e.g., Goodman, Bottoms, Herscovici, & Shaver, 1989; Leippe, Manion, & Romanczyk, 1992; Wells, Turtle, & Luss, 1989), none involving use of CCTV. In general, these studies indicate that mock jurors have difficulty assessing children's accuracy, especially that of young children. The strongest predictors of mock jurors' perceptions of believability and accuracy are their ratings of witness confidence and consistency, attributes that are not necessarily associated with accurate child witnesses (Leippe et al., 1992). It is unknown whether CCTV will strengthen or diminish jurors' discernment abilities.

Children's and Jurors' Reactions to CCTV

Use of CCTV in child sexual abuse trials has been adopted in a number of countries where confrontation rights are not constitutionally guaranteed. In the United Kingdom, Davies and Noon (1991) found that children who gave evidence via CCTV versus open court were rated as more resistant to leading questions, more consistent, more confident, and less unhappy (e.g., shed fewer tears). However, testimony via CCTV appeared to have less immediacy and emotional impact for the jury. Murray (1995) replicated some (e.g., children shed more tears in open court than in CCTV trials), but not all of Davies and Noon's findings. Importantly, in these studies, no significant differences in conviction rates emerged for CCTV versus regular trials. Finally, Cashmore (1992) found that some children preferred facing the accused in court. No studies have examined if knowledge of a child's choice of CCTV affects jurors' reactions (e.g., if choosing CCTV implies fear and thus guilt).

Two laboratory studies compared adults' perceptions of children's testimony presented in traditional courtroom settings versus via CCTV. In Swim, Borgida, and McCoy's (1993) study, mock jurors watched either a videotaped trial in which a child witness testified or the child's videotaped deposition. Jurors remembered more of the child's testimony in the latter case. Jurors did not see the child as more or less credible (e.g., believable, accurate) as a result of medium of presentation. Guilt ratings did not significantly differ across testimony condition; if anything, jurors were less likely to view the defendant as guilty when the child testified via CCTV. Ross, Hopkins, Hanson, Lindsay, Hazen, and Eslinger (1994) also examined effects of CCTV on mock jurors' perceptions in a videotaped re-enactment of a child sexual abuse trial. Compared to open trial testimony, testimony via CCTV resulted in ratings of lesser likelihood of defendant guilt when the child was the only witness but not when the child was one of several witnesses. However, use of a videotaped trial to depict the live-trial conditions in both Swim et al.'s and Ross et al.'s studies may limit generalizability. In essence, both conditions were presented on videotape. Thus, results might differ given a live child witness rather than a videotaped witness. Furthermore, reactions to the child witness are qualified by the fact that in both studies, the child was an actress following a script.

In summary relatively little is known about effects of closed-circuit technology on stereotypes of or biases about child witnesses, or on the ability to discriminate accurate from inaccurate child witnesses. One might expect that, if facing the defendant limits the amount of detail children are willing to report and inhibits the appearance of confidence and consistency, then children may be viewed as less credible when testifying in the presence of the defendant than when testifying via CCTV. In addition, if jurors are biased against the defendant by use of CCTV, then perhaps these procedures would create an imbalance in favor of the prosecution and therefore should not be permitted or only employed in extreme circumstances. However, if jurors do not experience a negative bias toward the defendant as a result of protective measures, then they might be used with less controversy when children testify.

The Present Research

The present study was designed to determine the effects of CCTV on children's eyewitness testimony and mock jurors' perceptions of child witnesses. Each child individually participated in a play session with an unfamiliar male confederate. In the "defendant guilty" condition, the confederate had the child place stickers on exposed body parts (i.e., the child's arm, toes, and bellybutton). In the "defendant not guilty" condition, the confederate had the child place stickers on the child's clothing rather than on bare skin. Each child then testified in a separate mock trial held in an actual courtroom. Eighty-eight complete trials were held, each involving a different child. Prior to each trial, the child answered questions about her or his legal knowledge and anxiety level. At each trial, actors played the parts of the judge, attorneys, and bailiff. Mock juries of community recruits viewed the trials, with the child's testimony being presented either live in open court ("regular trial" condition) or over CCTV ("closed-circuit" condition). Mock jurors made ratings concerning the child witness and defendant, and deliberated to reach a verdict.

Several predictions were made. First, based on former research, it was predicted that older children and children who testified on CCTV would make fewer omission errors and be less suggestible than younger children and children who testified in open court. The latter prediction should particularly hold for younger children who may be more intimidated by confrontation and public performance. Second, it was predicted that children would experience greater pretrial stress at the thought of testifying in court than via CCTV, and third, that more children would refuse to testify in the former than the latter condition. Fourth, individual differences related to cognitive (e.g., legal knowledge) and socioemotional (e.g., self concept) factors were expected to affect children's willingness to testify.

Predictions concerning jurors' reactions were also advanced. If children provide more detailed and accurate testimony in the CCTV versus regular trial condition, then jurors may be more likely to rate the

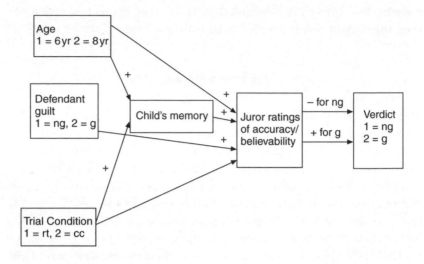

rt = regular trial, cc = closed-circuit trial

Figure 10.1 Path model: Proposed influence of experimental conditions, children's testimony, and jurors' rating of accuracy/believability on jurors' verdicts for guilty (g) and not-guilty (ng) conditions

children as credible witnesses. Moreover, if when a child testifies via CCTV, negative defendant impressions result, jurors might be prone to vote guilty. Alternatively, if CCTV causes loss of testimonial impact, then children may be perceived as less credible and defendants as more likely innocent in the CCTV than in the regular trial condition. Our fifth prediction was based on these latter possibilities because loss of impact and no negative bias toward the defendant have been reported in several studies (e.g., Davies & Noon, 1991; Ross et al., 1994). Our sixth prediction was that if jurors are biased to believe older rather than younger children (especially when memory and suggestibility are at issue), jurors should rate older children as more accurate and believable, even when actual accuracy is statistically controlled, regardless of testimony condition. A number of these predictions are captured in the path model presented in figure 10.1.

Seventh, concerning discernment, it was predicted that jurors would have particular difficulty assessing the accuracy of younger compared to older children (Leippe et al., 1992). Based on previous research, our eighth prediction was that jurors' perceptions of child confidence and consistency would be positively related to jurors' perceptions of accuracy and believability. Finally, women and people with more experience with children were expected to view child witnesses more favorably than would men and people with less experience with children.

Method

Participants

One hundred and eighty-six children participated: 85 5–6-year-olds ($M = 6$ years, 1 month; range = 5 years, 0 months to 6 years, 8 months) and 101 8–9-year-olds ($M = 8$ years, 4 months; range = 7 years, 6 months to 9 years, 1 month). Eighty-eight of these children testified, specifically, 42 5–6-year-olds ($M = 6$ years, 0 months; range 5 years, 0 months to 6 years, 10 months) and 46 8–9-year-olds ($M = 8$ years, 5 months; range 7 years, 8 months to 9 years, 1 month). For both the total sample and testifiers, children were randomly assigned to experimental condition with an approximately equal number of boys and girls included in each experimental group. Families were offered between $35 and $50 for their participation.

A total of 1,201 community subjects served as mock jurors. Jurors were recruited by calling people on voter registration lists and by placing announcements in local classified newspaper advertisements. Mock jurors had to meet eligibility requirements often used for actual jury participation (e.g., US citizenship; over 17 years of age; not being a felon or judge), enhancing the comparability of the sample to actual jury pools. Jurors were approximately evenly distributed across age (21% 18–29-year-olds, 21% 30–39-year-olds, 20% 40–49-year-olds, 19% 50–64-year-olds, 18% 65 years and above) and gender (e.g., 594 women and 607 men). Eighty-three percent of the sample was Anglo, and the next largest category was African American (13%). These percentages closely reflected community rates. Four percent of the participants had not completed high school, 53% had either a high school education or some college, and approximately 37% of subjects reported having at least one college degree, with less than 1% of the latter holding a graduate school degree. Half of the sample was employed, 21% were retired, and the remainder were unemployed, homemakers, or students.

Approximately 65% of the mock jurors reported having children of their own. Jurors were paid between $25 and $30 for their participation.

Predeliberations, the mock juries ranged in size from 9 to 20 jurors. During deliberations and after, each mock jury was composed of 9–12 jurors balanced as much as possible for gender. In 13 of the 88 trials, there were fewer than 12 participants. When more than 12 jurors showed up, all of them completed predeliberation questionnaires, but randomly determined "alternates" did not deliberate or contribute post-deliberation data to the study.

Materials

Peabody Picture Vocabulary Test-Revised (PPVT-R)

Form L of the PPVT-R (Dunn & Dunn, 1981) measured children's receptive vocabulary. Standard score equivalents ($M = 100$, $SD = 15$) were employed.

Pictorial Scale of Perceived Competence and Social Acceptance for Young Children (PCSA)

Harter and Pike's (1984) scale assesses children's self concept. A higher mean score indicates a more positive self concept.

Child Behavior Checklist (CBCL)

The parent version of the CBCL (Achenbach & Edelbrock, 1983) was used to index problem behavior. Parents rate the frequency in the last 6 months of 118 problem behaviors on a 3-point scale (0 = not true and 2 = often true). The scale provides T scores for total behavior problems, externalizing behaviors (e.g., delinquency, hyperactivity), and internalizing behaviors (e.g., depression, somatic complaints).

Parental authoritarian scale

A subset of 15 questions from the Traditional Family Ideology Scale was used to measure parental authoritarianism (Levinson & Huffman, 1955). Parents self-report on a 1–6 scale, with a higher score indicating stronger authoritarian attitudes.

Legal knowledge questionnaire

Similar to questionnaires used by Flin, Stevenson, and Davies (1989) and Saywitz, Jaenicke, and Camparo (1990), this questionnaire consisted of eight questions concerning children's knowledge of court, various courtroom personnel, and the consequences of telling the truth versus a lie in court.

The Spielberger State Anxiety Scale (SAS)

Children's precourt anxiety was assessed through a mean score from the 20-item A-State scale from the State-Trait Inventory for Children (Spielberger, 1973). For each item (e.g., "I feel not nervous, nervous, very nervous"), a 3-point scale is generated, with higher scores indicating greater anxiety.

Courtroom Anxiety Questionnaire (CAQ)

The CAQ uses open-ended questions (scored as 1 = positive to 4 = negative) and then a "faces scale" ("very happy" to "very unhappy," creating a 4-point scale) to measure pre- and postcourt anxiety (Goodman et al., 1992). The questions probed children's feelings about being a witness, talking to the judge and lawyers, and speaking in front of the jury and defendant. Higher scores indicate greater anxiety.

Pretrial memory questions

Intended to assess children's memory for the Session 2 event, this questionnaire included two free recall questions (i.e., "Tell me everything you can remember about what happened when you were with that man" and "Did you do anything else") and 21 direct questions. The direct questions consisted of 15 specific (e.g., "Did he show you any pictures?"), 2 correctly leading (e.g., "You met him before that day, right?" which was true), and 4 misleading questions (e.g., "What color were the gloves that you put on?" when in fact the child did not put on gloves). The pretrial memory questions helped prepare children for testifying (similar to "refreshing" a child's memory, as often occurs for actual child witnesses; Myers, 1992) and tested for possible pretestimony memory differences across the guilt and trial condition groups.

Child trial questionnaire

For the courtroom questioning, a script was written that included two free recall questions asked during direct examination (i.e., "Tell me everything you can remember about what happened when you made the movie," along with the prompt "Did you do anything else?," and "Is there anything else you feel comfortable telling me about what happened when you were with Greg?") and 105 questions constituting the direct, cross-, and redirect examination about the events that occurred and the elements of the crime (e.g., "Did he have you put a sticker on your belly button, on the belt buckle, or on your shirt over where your belly button is?" and "Did he film that while making the video?"). The 105 questions were of three types, specific (e.g., "Where were you when you made the movie?"), misleading (e.g., "You had to take off some of your clothes to put the costume on, right?" when in fact children did not remove their clothes to put on the costume), and correctly leading (e.g., "And didn't Greg turn the TV and camera off before your Mom or Dad came back?" when in fact he did turn the equipment off). A subset of the direct questions were particularly relevant to physical or sexual abuse cases (e.g., "Did Greg kiss you?"). The questionnaire also contained one defendant identification question (i.e., for subjects in the regular trial condition, "That man who was there with you, is he in the courtroom today?," and for subjects in the closed-circuit condition, "That man who was there with you, is this a picture of him?") Response bias was controlled by approximate equating of the number of correct "yes" and "no" responses for each question category.

Jury questionnaires

A demographic questionnaire included questions regarding the mock jurors' age, gender, race/ethnicity, martial status, income, education, religious orientation, experience with children, support of the death penalty, experience of victimization, and prior jury experience.

Pre- and postdeliberation questionnaires included a question concerning the guilt of the defendant (guilty vs. not guilty judgment), certainty of guilt (6-point scale), and a yes/no question concerning whether the prosecutor proved his case beyond a reasonable doubt. A higher score implied greater guilt. The questionnaires also included a variety of questions concerning the trial, each followed by a series of

6-point Likert scales. Predeliberation questionnaires included questions concerning the child witness's believability, accuracy, honesty, suggestibility, likelihood of making up the story, likelihood of misunderstanding the defendant's actions, degree of influence by the prosecutor's and defense attorney's questions, ability to provide testimony based on fact rather than fantasy, attractiveness, intelligence, consistency, and confidence. Also included were questions about the degree to which the juror empathized with the defendant and child, how positively the juror felt about the defendant and the child, the child's tress level while testifying overall fairness of the trial, fairness of the trial to the child and defendant, and how realistic the trial appeared. A higher score indicated more of the dimension in question (e.g., for suggestibility, 1 = not at all suggestible and 6 = extremely suggestible). Additionally, questions were included concerning the juror's confidence of the main elements of the crime and of the child's age being under 11 years old. A higher number indicated a greater degree of confidence. Questions also assessed how easy it was for juror and defendant to see and hear the child witness. A higher number indicated more ease in seeing and hearing.

Postdeliberation questions included jurors' ratings of verdict, guilt, certainty of guilt, certainty that the crime took place, ability of the prosecutor to prove the case, degree of confidence of the main elements of the crime, and confidence the child was under 11 years of age (these items and their scales were the same as the corresponding ones above). Additional questions involved the degree to which the following factors influenced the decision to vote guilty or not guilty: child testimony, defendant's decision not to testify, knowledge the crime was not real, belief that children make unreliable witnesses, and arguments of prosecutor or defense. A higher number indicated the decision was based highly on the factor.

Procedure

Families were recruited from respondents to a mailing concerning participation in developmental research. Interested families were contacted by phone and given an overview of the study. When parent and child arrived for the first session, the study was explained to the parent in detail, and informed consent was obtained from the parent. Assent was obtained from children at relevant points throughout the study. The child was administered the PRVT-R and PCSA; the parent completed the CBCL and the authoritarian scale. The child and parent were then escorted to a room where an adult male "baby-sitter" was waiting. The child was told that the baby-sitter would watch the child while the parent and research assistant (RA) finished their paperwork. The parent and RA then left the room and observed the interaction through a one-way mirror. During the interaction the child and confederate played a standardized set of games (e.g., Trouble, Balance) for 20 min. This play session allowed the confederate to build rapport with the child. At the end of the session the parent and RA returned, and the child chose a small toy to take home. Parents were asked not to discuss the events or the nature of the research with their child until after the final session. The interaction of the child and confederate was surreptitiously videotaped.

Session 2 was scheduled for 1–2 days later. Upon arrival, the child was told that the RA and parent had to go to another building, but that the baby-sitter from last time would watch the child. The child was escorted to the room where the confederate was waiting, the parent and RA once again watched the interaction through a one-way mirror, and the interaction was surreptitiously videotaped. During this session the confederate suggested making a movie with the child. The room was equipped with a camcorder and TV so that the child was able to watch him or herself on TV. The confederate told the child that they would make a movie in which the child would be the movie star and the confederate would be the director. The child received a nickel every time he or she did as the confederate instructed. During the course of the movie the confederate filmed the child putting on a costume over the child's clothes, placing stickers on various parts of his or her body, and examining the items in a toy medical bag.

While making the movie, the child participated in either the defendant-guilty or defendant-not-guilty condition. Within each age group and gender, children were randomly assigned to one of these two conditions. In the defendant-guilty condition, the confederate instructed the child to place a sticker on his or her exposed upper arm, exposed toes, and exposed bellybutton. In the defendant-not-guilty condition, the confederate had the child place stickers on the child's shirt-sleeve rather than the arm, on the child's shoes rather than the toes, and on the buckle of a belt worn by the child rather than the bellybutton. Thus, the defendant was either guilty or not guilty of the mock crime of videotaping a child displaying exposed body parts (i.e., upper arm, toes, and belly button). Regardless of condition, after making the movie, the confederate and child looked at a set of art reproductions. A final game of Balance was played, which the confederate always let the child win. The session lasted approximately 18 min.

The parent and RA then returned, and the child chose another small toy to take home. Next, the child was left alone with the parent, who was instructed to question the child briefly about what happened, using a standardized set of questions (e.g., "Did you have fun?"). In this way, all parents and children had a chance to discuss the event. Parents were then asked to refrain from further discussion of the event with the child.

Session 3 was the mock trial. Resembling theatrical productions involving actors and a video crew, mock trials were staged in a real courthouse on weekend mornings. The specifics of our mock-trial procedure were agreed upon after considerable ethical discussion, and 9 months of pilot testing and refinement to ensure that adequate preparation of the children was accomplished so that the task was not too stressful. Such pilot testing revealed the necessity of employing staff who could establish rapport quickly and well with children, the chance for children to tour the courtroom and answer questions on the witness stand before being asked to testify, the opportunity for children to meet and have a friendly exchange with the prosecutor and judge before the trial, a chance for children to adjust to the courtroom and answer simple questions posed by the judge before the jury entered, and maintenance of an emotionally supportive atmosphere by the judge and attorneys toward the children. The critical importance of the children's parents staying in the courtroom when the children testified also became apparent, a privilege often denied actual child witnesses. Additionally, the fact that the children had not been hurt or threatened by the defendant (who had been kind to the children) undoubtedly made the experience less stressful than that of many actual child witnesses.

The mock trial took place after a 2-week delay ($M = 15$ days; range = 4–40 days) from Session 2. On the morning of Session 3, the child was told by the parent that they were going to go downtown to talk to some people about when the child made the movie with the man. Minimizing the parental explanation was intended to reduce variation in what parents told children and to reduce the amount of time during which a child might become anxious about answering questions in public. For the mock trial, parent(s) brought the child to the City Court Building, where they were greeted by an RA and escorted to an interview room adjacent to the courtroom. A separate mock trial was conducted for each of the 88 child testifiers. To ensure that a witness would testify, two children were scheduled for each mock trial. The testifier was chosen randomly with the restriction that the child agreed to testify and that delays across conditions were approximately equal. Graduate RAs and clinical social workers were trained to act as child interviewers (similar to a child advocate role).

The interview began with questioning concerning the child's expectations for the session and the child's legal knowledge. The parent, interviewer, and RA then led the child into an empty courtroom for a tour. Throughout the tour the interviewer and RA explained the courtroom process, including the roles of judge, lawyers, jury, and witness. The RA led role-plays with parents and children to enhance familiarity with the courtroom process. During this time actors playing the roles of judge and prosecuting attorney wandered into the courtroom and engaged the child in friendly conversation. Court tours, provision of legal information, and meetings with legal personnel are often rendered for actual child witnesses (Myers, 1992; Sas, 1991).

For children testifying in the CCTV condition, a further tour of a closed-circuit witness room occurred. The child was told that sometimes witness testify from a different room. The child, accompanied by the interviewer, initially sat in a juror's seat and watched the RA and parent go to the witness room and appear on the TV set. The child then went to the witness room and role-played being a witness while the parent and RA watched on the TV.

After the tour, the child, parent, and interviewer returned to the interview room. The interviewer asked the child the pretrial memory questions concerning making the movie. No feedback as to the accuracy of the child's response was given. The interviewer then told the child that the baby-sitter was *perhaps* not supposed to make the movie and *might* be in a little bit of trouble because of it. The child was reassured that he or she was not in any trouble, but that a judge wanted to find out what happened with the baby-sitter and that he was going to hold a trial in which he wanted the child to testify. The child was asked if he or she would be willing to be a witness and testify (either in open court or via CCTV, depending on trial condition). The child then answered questions from the Spielberger SAS and the CAQ concerning how he or she was feeling.

Forty-seven out of the 186 children who appeared at the courthouse refused to testify, either by outright refusal or by appearing distressed so that the RA judged that the child should not continue. Eight-year-olds were more likely to refuse to testify in the regular trial condition ($n = 14$) than in the CCTV condition ($n = 4$). Interestingly, the difference in refusal rate across conditions was not as pronounced for the younger children ($n = 17$ in regular trials; $n = 12$ in CCTV trials). Thus, a selection bias may have led to more "brave" 8-year-olds appearing in regular trials, and the results of the present study should be considered in that light. Although eliminating these children from the study may limit generalizability, children who are too frightened to testify in actual trials are often excluded from such trials as well. On a random basis, an additional 52 children were not asked to take the stand because only one child could testify per trial. Exceptions to random dismissal from testifying occurred when standardization across conditions was considered necessary (e.g., equalizing delays between Sessions 2 and 3 across trial conditions). Children who did not testify were thoroughly debriefed.

If the child agreed to testify and was chosen to take the stand, the actor serving as the prosecutor briefly instructed the child to tell the truth, speak loudly, and to say "I don't know" if the child was unsure of the answer to a particular question. Attorneys were naive to the guilt or innocence of the defendant.

As the questioning of the child and the court tour were being conducted, mock jurors arrived at the courthouse. Jurors were escorted to a jury room where jurors were informed that the study concerned jury decision-making, and that they would view a simulated trial in which they would hear testimony of a young child about events experienced with the "defendant," our confederate. Jurors were asked to pretend that "videotaping a child exposing body parts" was a real crime, and that they should determine if our confederate was guilty or not guilty of that mock crime. Jurors were told that the study's results would likely influence decisions about fair ways to hold trials when children serve as witnesses, but jurors were not told of our specific interest in CCTV. Jurors provided informed consent, completed the demographic questionnaire, entered the courtroom, and then the trial commenced. Except for the child's answers to questions, the entire trial was scripted.

We describe the regular trial condition first, and then only what differed from it for the CCTV trials. For the regular trials, the jury received standard initial instructions from the judge, including information about the court process, the charges, and the jurors' duties. They were further instructed that to find the defendant guilty the prosecution would have to prove beyond a reasonable doubt that on or about the date of Session 2, the defendant videotaped a child under age 11 years while the child displayed at least one of the following body parts: bare feet, bare shoulder, bare upper arm, bare back, or bare belly button. The judge also explained that the jurors were not to consider intent or consequences of the act. Finally, the judge randomly selected a foreperson. The jury then heard opening arguments from the prosecutor and defense attorney, after which they left the room while the competence of the child witness was determined. The child was then escorted to the witness stand in the courtroom, and the parent was instructed to sit in the audience. The judge briefly built rapport with the child and then proceeded to ask 16 qualifying questions concerning the child's awareness of the nature of truth and lie (such questions are typically asked to determine the competency of child witnesses). All children answered the questions accurately.

When competency questioning was complete, the jury was escorted back to the courtroom. The bailiff brought the Bible to the child witness, who stood while the judge administered the oath. After the child was sworn in, direct, cross-, and redirect examination of the child witness proceeded. The actors had been trained to work with children and to avoid being harsh or accusatory in their questioning; the child testified for approximately 20 min. Once back at the interview room, children were given positive feedback on their performance, thoroughly debriefed (e.g., shown the videotape of themselves with the baby-sitter, told that nothing wrong happened and that they were merely in a study), and rewarded with $10 and a toy. No other witnesses testified, including the defendant.

After the child left the witness stand, the attorneys presented their closing arguments, and the judge presented his final instructions to the jury, stating that: the indictment was not evidence of guilt; jurors should focus on witness credibility, not sentencing; there is a presumption of innocence; and the defendant's decision not to testify could not be held against him. The judge also reminded jurors of the reasonable doubt burden, the charges, and the four elements in question: the date of the alleged acts, the child's age, videotaping a child's exposed body part(s), and exposure of at least one body part. Upon returning to the jury room, jurors completed predeliberation questionnaires and were then given a copy of judge's final instructions to review. Jurors deliberated as a group to reach a unanimous verdict of guilty or not guilty for up to 30 min.[1] When the deliberation period was over, jurors completed postdeliberation questionnaires, were debriefed, and were paid.

In the CCTV condition, the procedure was the same, except that a large TV monitor was present in the courtroom. The child and parent were escorted to the witness room, which was directly behind the courtroom, from which the child testified. The child was seated on a couch with a videocamera in full view, and the parent and RA were seated off camera and out of the child's direct line of sight. After the opening arguments, the judge entered the witness room, built rapport with the child, and asked the competence questions. He then returned to the courtroom and ordered the TV monitor to be turned on. Jury, defendant, attorneys, and judge viewed the child's testimony on the TV screen. The bailiff brought the Bible to the child and the judge administered the oath from the courtroom. The attorneys entered the witness room one at a time to conduct the direct, cross-, and redirect examination of the child. When questioning was completed, the TV monitor was turned off, and the procedure from that point was the same as that for the regular trial, with the exception that in the judge's final instructions, he added that no implications should be drawn from use of CCTV, that it is not evidence in itself, and that it should not be considered during deliberations. Courtroom proceedings in both conditions were videotaped, as were jury deliberations.[2]

Results

We first describe scoring and preliminary analyses. We then turn to evaluation of children's testimony in the CCTV versus regular court conditions. Relations between children's testimony and legal knowledge are also explored, as are relations between children's anxiety and trial condition, age, and legal knowledge. Logistic regression permitted examination of predictors of children's refusal to testify. We then focus on analyses of jurors' reactions, including pre- and postdeliberation judgments. A path analysis tested relations between children's CCTV versus regularcourt testimony and jurors' reactions to such testimony. Across the various analyses, all significant effects are reported.

Scoring and coding

For pretrial and trial testimony, free recall was scored for units of correct and incorrect information based on a system commonly used in child witness research (e.g., Tobey & Goodman, 1992). For example, the statement "We played with stickers" received five units of correct information, two units for "we," one for "played," and two for "stickers" (plurals received two units). If the child said, "We only played with stickers," the child received one unit of incorrect information for "only." Due to actor error, one child was not asked free recall questions. Responses to directive questions (i.e., specific, misleading, and correctly leading) were scored for proportion correct answers as well as proportion of omission errors (child omitted information), commission errors (child indicated that something happened when in fact it did not, or indicated a feature that was not present), and "don't know" responses. About 20% of the protocols were scored by independent raters. Proportion of agreement was at least .80 for all memory variables.

Legal knowledge questionnaire

A scoring system was devised to code children's answers to the eight legal knowledge questions. The first question concerned children's general knowledge of a courtroom and was scored on a 3-point scale for accuracy: 0 = "I don't know," irrelevant, or incorrect response; 1 = accurate information, but with little detail, descriptive, or partial response (e.g., people, chairs); 2 = accurate information with greater detail than for number 1; characteristic features mentioned (e.g., place where you prove something, solve problems). Four of the questions related to children's knowledge of courtroom roles (judge, lawyer, witness, jury; e.g., What is a judge? What is a judge's job in court?) and were scored on 4-point scales, guided by Saywitz et al.'s (1990) scoring system: 0 = "I don't know," irrelevant, or incorrect response, and 3 = responses including more than one defining feature (e.g., "A judge is someone who makes decisions and keeps order"). An analogous scoring system was used to code the question dealing with reasons people go to court. The last two questions dealt with the ramifications of telling a lie or the truth in court. These were scored on a 3-point scale: 0 = "I don't know," irrelevant, or incorrect response, 1 = responses indicating that the witness goes to jail if a lie is told (for the lie question) or that the witness does not go to jail or is set free if the truth is told (for the truth question), 2 = responses mentioning that the lie would have to be detected (for the lie question) or that the witness would have to be believed to be telling the truth (for the truth question). Three raters independently scored 25% of 6- and 8-year-olds' responses. Proportion of agreement was 84% or above. Disagreements were discussed and resolved. Then one of the raters scored the remaining responses. An average score for each child created.

Preliminary analyses

Preliminary analyses indicated that delay between the child's experience with the baby-sitter and the trial did not significantly differ across experimental or age groups for the children's memory performance. Delay is thus not considered further. However, some pre-existing differences among the experimental groups were uncovered when 2 (age) × 2 (trial condition) × 2 (guilt) analyses of variance (ANOVAs) were conducted on children's pretrial memory data (see Batterman-Faunce, 1993). As a result, for relevant analyses of the children's trial performance reported below, analyses of covariance (ANCOVA) controlling for these pretrial memory differences were conducted in addition to the ANOVA. ANCOVA results are reported only when they differ from those of the ANOVAs.[3]

The large number of mock jurors included in the study resulted in considerable statistical power in juror-level analyses. For example, correlations as low as .07 were statistically significant at the .05 alpha level (two-tailed). Instead of using traditional alpha levels, a cutoff of .30 was employed as an index of significance for the correlational analyses of the juror data. This cutoff represents a value typically statistically significant in social science research.

Initial analyses of the juror data explored possible confounding variables. Correlational analyses revealed that participants recruited via voter registration roles tended to be older than those recruited through newspaper advertisement, $r = .45$, $p < .001$, and to be more likely to have children, $r = .33$, $p < .001$. These variables were associated with constellations of other related variables, such as contact with children, marriage, and previous jury service. However, juror age and parenthood were not significantly associated with juror questionnaires judgments, trial condition, guilt condition, or child age.

Children's testimony performance

We predicted that children who testified via CCTV rather than in open court would make fewer errors of omission and be less suggestible. Means and standard deviations for the children's testimony performance (responses to free recall questions, directive questions overall, and the subset of misleading questions) are presented in table 10.1. A series of 2 (age) × 2 (trial condition) × 2 (guilt) ANOVAs was conducted to test our first prediction and examine children's performance generally. The first of these analyses concerned the number of correct and incorrect units of information to the free recall questions. In addition, similar analyses separately involving proportion correct, omission, commission, and "don't know" responses to trial questioning as a whole (i.e., combined responses to specific, misleading, and correctly leading questions) and to misleading questions are reported.

Free recall

A significant main effect of trial condition for pretrial correct free-recall responses, $F(1, 76) = 6.43$, $p < .025$, warranted an ANCOVA. When the number of correct units of information each child recalled at trial was entered as a dependent variable, the main effect of age was significant, $F(1, 73) = 5.20$, $p < .05$, with 8-year-olds, adjusted $M = 25.79$, recalling more correct information than 6-year-olds, adjusted $M = 12.98$. (The nonadjusted means were: older children, adjusted $M = 25.22$, $SD = 22.86$, and younger children, $M = 12.93$, $SD = 9.76$.) The trial condition × guilt interaction was not significant, $F(1, 73) = 3.06$, $p = .08$. An ANOVA on the number of incorrect units of information recalled by each child during the trial revealed unexpectedly that 8-year-olds recalled a larger number of incorrect units of information, $M = 2.82$, $SD = 3.24$, than 6-year-olds, $M = 1.07$, $SD = 2.20$; age effect, $F(1, 79) = 8.33$, $p < .01$. In summary, in response to the free-recall questions asked at trial, older children recalled more correct and more incorrect information than younger children. There were no significant effects for trial or guilt condition.

Directive questions overall

ANOVAs were also conducted on the children's responses to specific, misleading, and correctly leading questions combined (see table 10.1). For proportion of correct answers provided by each child, 8-year-olds provided a higher proportion of correct information overall, $M = .78$, $SD = .06$, than 6-year-olds, $M = .69$, $SD = .08$; age effect, $F(1, 80) = 34.74$, $p < .001$. At trial, 8-year-olds also made a lower proportion of omission errors, $M = .06$, $SD = .03$, than 6-year-olds, $M = .09$, $SD = .06$; age effect, $F(1, 80) = 11.55$, $p = .001$. Analyses of the proportion of commission errors to the trial questions yielded several significant effects. Older children made fewer commission errors, $M = .06$, $SD = .03$, than younger children, $M = .08$, $SD = .03$; age effect, $F(1, 80) = 7.79$, $p < .01$. Although the mean difference was small, it fell in the predicted direction. In addition, there was a significant but uninterpretable age × trial condition × guilt interaction, $F(1, 80) = 7.76$, $p < .01$. Analyses of simple effects revealed that in the closed-circuit, not-guilty condition 6-year-olds made more commission errors than older children, $F(1, 21) = 5.23$, $p < .05$. Similarly, when the defendant was guilty and the children testified in a regular trial, younger children made more commission errors than older children, $F(1, 23) = 12.88$, $p < .01$. Why significant age effects appeared in these two trial conditions is unclear, although it is interesting that the two effects reinforce concerns of opponents and proponents of CCTV, respectively. The total proportion of "don't know" responses to the trial interview was entered into an ANCOVA, with proportion of "don't know" answers to pretrial memory questions entered as a covariate. There were no significant effects. In summary, when children's responses to specific, misleading, and correctly leading questions were combined, a consistent set of effects emerged showing older children to be generally more accurate witnesses regardless of trial condition. Older children provided a higher proportion of correct information and a lower proportion of commission and omission errors than younger children.

Misleading questions

To examine children's suggestibility, ANOVAs were conducted on the children's responses to misleading questions. Six-year-olds, $M = .56$, $SD = .16$, provided a lower proportion of correct responses to

Table 10.1 Performance on free recall, directive overall, and misleading questions (*SD*s)

	Closed-circuit		Regular	
	8-year-olds	*6-year-olds*	*8-year-olds*	*6-year-olds*
Number correct free recall				
Not guilty	17.33 (11.34)	9.10 (4.65)	30.09 (23.46)	17.00 (13.16)
Guilty	33.00 (32.62)	15.50 (12.14)	22.17 (20.82)	10.58 (5.87)
Number incorrect free recall				
Not guilty	2.92 (3.42)	.50 (.71)	2.55 (1.57)	.60 (.84)
Guilty	3.40 (4.62)	1.90 (3.87)	2.50 (3.15)	1.25 (1.91)
Proportion correct directive				
Not guilty	.78 (.08)	.69 (.09)	.80 (.04)	.70 (.05)
Guilty	.75 (.06)	.69 (.10)	.80 (.04)	.69 (.10)
Proportion omission directive				
Not guilty	.06 (.05)	.08 (.05)	.05 (.04)	.10 (.06)
Guilty	.07 (.03)	.07 (.05)	.05 (.02)	.11 (.06)
Proportion commission directive				
Not guilty	.06 (.02)	.09 (.03)	.07 (.03)	.07 (.03)
Guilty	.07 (.02)	.07 (.03)	.05 (.03)	.09 (.03)
Don't know directive				
Not guilty	.10 (.08)	.13 (.11)	.07 (.05)	.12 (.07)
Guilty	.10 (.09)	.17 (.14)	.09 (.06)	.10 (.08)
Proportion correct misleading				
Not guilty	.63 (.10)	.54 (.16)	.66 (.09)	.59 (.15)
Guilty	.67 (.11)	.57 (.19)	.71 (.11)	.55 (.14)
Omission misleading				
Not guilty	.09 (.07)	.12 (.08)	.09 (.06)	.13 (.04)
Guilty	.07 (.04)	.08 (.05)	.07 (.03)	.16 (.06)
Proportion commission misleading				
Not guilty	.15 (.06)	.18 (.08)	.16 (.10)	.14 (.09)
Guilty	.15 (.07)	.15 (.07)	.11 (.06)	.21 (.10)
Don't know misleading				
Not guilty	.14 (.12)	.16 (.16)	.09 (.08)	.13 (.15)
Guilty	.11 (.11)	.20 (.20)	.10 (.10)	.07 (.11)

misleading questions than 8-year-olds, $M = .67$, $SD = .10$; age effect, $F(1, 80) = 13.80$, $p < .001$. Omission errors to the misleading questions constituted a measure of suggestibility (e.g., a response of "No, it wasn't," to, "The camera wasn't on when you played doctor, was it?") Six-year-olds, $M = .12$, $SD = .07$, made more omission errors than 8-year-olds, $M = .08$, $SD = .05$; age effect, $F(1, 80) = 14.79$, $p < .001$. The age × trial condition interaction was also significant, $F(1, 80)$ 4.22, $p < .05$. Simple effects showed that younger, $M = .10$, $SD = .07$, and older children, $M = .08$, $SD = .05$, had similar rates of error when testifying via CCTV, but the error rate of younger, $M = .15$, $SD = .05$, but not older children, $M = .08$, $SD = .05$, increased when testifying in open court, $Fs (1, 40) \geq 7.00$, $ps < .05$.

Proportion of commission errors to misleading questions was another index of suggestibility. The ANOVA produced a significant age × trial condition × guilt interaction, $F(1, 80) = 5.25$, $p = .025$. Simple effects analyses revealed that when the defendant was guilty and children testified in the regular trial condition, younger children made significantly more commission errors than older children; $F(1, 23) = 9.41$, $p < .01$. There were no other significant simple effects. For proportion of "don't know" responses to the misleading questions, no significant effects emerged.

In summary, when children's responses to misleading questions were considered, older children were less suggestible witnesses. They answered a higher proportion of misleading questions correctly and made a lower proportion of omission errors. Interestingly, age differences, particularly relevant to younger children's errors to misleading questions, were affected by trial condition. When testifying in regular trials, younger compared to older children made significantly more commission errors when the defendant was guilty. In regular trials, younger children also made more omission errors than older children. Furthermore, younger children testifying in regular trials made more errors of omission than their agemates who testified in a closed-circuit setting. The only adverse effect of CCTV on children's accuracy (i.e., an increase in commission errors to directive questions for younger compared to older children in the not-guilty condition) that we detected appeared in an uninterpretable interaction, and thus may be a spurious effect. Overall, the results supported our first prediction, at least as it applies to younger children.

Effects of legal knowledge on testimony performance

Although age differences in children's legal knowledge are well documented, little is known about the effects of legal knowledge on children's testimony. A number of courtroom preparation programs teach children about the legal system under the assumption that greater knowledge will facilitate children's ability to testify accurately and completely (MacFarlane, 1992; Sas, 1991). To explore this issue, we first examined whether older compared to younger children possessed greater legal knowledge, as would be expected. A 2 (age) × 2 (guilt) × 2 (trial condition) ANOVA was conducted for each child's average legal knowledge score. Older children, $M = 1.06$, $SD = .55$, had higher legal knowledge scores than younger children, $M = .31$, $SD = .30$; age effect, $F(1, 78) = 63.39$, $p < .001$. Correlations were then conducted to examine the relation between legal knowledge and children's testimony, with age partialed. Although the correlations between children's average legal knowledge score and free recall performance were nonsignificant, the former was significantly correlated with the proportion of direct questions overall answered correctly, $r = .24$, $p < .05$, $n = 82$, as well as with specific questions answered correctly, $r = .23$, $p < .05$, $n = 82$. Thus, children with greater legal knowledge at the start of Session 3 were more correct in their responses to direct questions (especially specific questions) than those who knew less initially about the legal system, even with age controlled.[4]

Children's anxiety

One purpose of CCTV is to reduce children's anxiety about testifying. We therefore predicted that children who believed they would testify in open court would be more anxious than children who believed they would testify via CCTV. A series of separate 2 (age) × 2 (guilt) × 2 (trial condition) ANOVAs was conducted with the following scores for each child serving as a dependent measure: average Spielberger SAS score, CAQ open-ended scale score, and CAQ faces scale score.[5] In addition, to examine possible effects of child gender on anxiety, a series of separate 2 (age) × 2 (gender) ANOVAs was also conducted on the same three dependent measures. For these analyses, it was possible to include all children who participated in the study, as well as the subgroup that testified.

Table 10.2 Means and standard deviations (in parentheses) for overall pretrial anxiety as a function of age, guilt, and trial condition (testifiers only)

	6-year-olds	8-year-olds
Regular trial		
Guilty	1.56 (.60)	2.34 (.55)
Not guilty	1.79 (.49)	1.86 (.34)
Closed-circuit		
Guilty	1.73 (.46)	1.83 (.30)
Not guilty	1.40 (.41)	1.90 (.31)

When the total sample of children was included, the average score on the Spielberger SAS was significantly higher for children in the regular trial than the CCTV condition, $F(1, 167) = 6.62$, $p < .01$, $n = 175$; thus, children who expected to testify in open court, $M = 1.65$, $SD = .27$, felt more negatively about testifying than children who expected to testify via CCTV, $M = 1.55$, $SD = .23$. Older children expressed a greater level of anxiety than younger children as measured by both the CAQ open-ended scale, $M = 2.11$, $SD = 1.02$, and $M = 1.58$, $SD = .85$, respectively, $F(1, 136) = 10.50$, $p < .01$, $n = 140$, and faces scale, $M = 2.14$, $SD = .55$, and $M = 1.92$, $SD = .76$, respectively, $F(1, 172) = 5.29$, $p < .05$, $n = 176$. The overall anxiety level of girls was higher than that for boys as indexed by the CAQ open-ended scale, $M = 2.08$, $SD = 1.08$, and $M = 1.76$, $SD = .90$, respectively, $F(1, 136) = 4.18$, $p < .05$, $n = 140$, and faces scale, $M = 2.20$, $SD = .66$, and $M = 1.90$, $SD = .63$, respectively, $F(1, 172) = 10.76$, $p < .001$, $n = 176$.

For children who testified, there were no significant effects when the Spielberger SAS scores or the CAQ open-ended scores were entered in to separate analyses. However, for the CAQ faces scale, a significant age effect replicated that reported above, $F(1, 84) = 15.01$, $p < .001$, $n = 88$, with older children, $M = 2.00$, $SD = .44$, expressing more anxiety than younger children, $M = 1.61$, $SD = .50$. The only other significant effect was an age × guilt × trial condition interaction on the CAQ faces scale, $F(1, 80) = 8.21$, $p < .01$, $n = 88$ (see table 10.2). Eight-year-olds who testified in the regular courtroom when the defendant was guilty expressed more pretrial anxiety than their agemates who testified in the same courtroom setting when the defendant was not guilty, $F(1, 22) = 6.24$, $p < .05$, or than those who testified via CCTV when the defendant was guilty, $F(1, 21) = 6.86$, $p < .05$, as well as than the younger children who testified via CCTV when the defendant was guilty, $F(1, 23) = 11.66$, $p < .01$ (simple effects). Thus, 8-year-olds who were to testify in open court when the defendant was guilty expressed the most pretrial anxiety.[6] These results emerged despite the fact that the bravest 8-year-olds were the ones to agree to testify in the open-court condition. When children testified via CCTV, older children expressed more anxiety than younger children, perhaps because older children still realized the implications of testifying even if they were to do so from a separate room.

In court preparation programs, it is often assumed that legal knowledge will help children be less frightened of testifying. Interestingly, when the total sample of children was considered, there was an inverse relation between legal knowledge and anxiety (as assessed on the CAQ faces scale), even with age partialed, $r = -.17$, $p < .05$, $n = 163$. Thus, children with a better understanding of the legal system expressed the least anxiety about taking the stand.

Refusal to testify

We predicted that individual differences related to children's cognitive and socioemotional levels would influence refusal to testify. The criterion variable, refusal or agreement to testify, was dichotomous (0 = agree; 1 = refuse), and thus logistic regression was employed. The predictor variables were age in months, gender, parental authoritarianism, self concept, verbal ability, behavior problems, pretrial memory correct (free recall and direct questions), legal knowledge score, anxiety (CAQ faces score), defendant guilt condition, and trial condition. Nine children were dropped due to missing data. Also, four children were excluded because they became upset on the stand or on their way to it; they did not continue in the study and were immediately debriefed. Inclusion of them in either the refusal or nonrefusal group is problematic because technically, they agreed to testify at first, but they later "refused" by becoming upset. Of the 179 children included in the analysis, 136 (76%) agreed to testify, while 43 (24%) refused.

For the logistic regression, order of entry was determined based on causal priority, temporal occurrence, and stability (Pedhazur, 1982).[7] Age and gender were entered on the first step. Younger compared to older children were significantly more likely to refuse to testify ($b = -.03$, $p < .01$). The effect for gender was not significant. Parenting style (authoritarianism) was entered on the second step. Although not statistically significant, the trend was for children with parents scoring lower in parental authoritarianism to be more likely to refuse to testify ($b = -.67$, $p = .07$). The child's PCSA total score, PPTV-R standard score equivalent, and CBCL internalizing and externalizing T scores were entered on the third step. Children who scored lower on the PPVT-R were more likely to refuse to testify ($b = -.03$, $p = .01$). CBCL and PCSA scores were not significant predictors.

Proportions correct for pretrial free recall and pretrial direct questions, mean legal knowledge score, and mean CAQ faces score were entered on the fourth step. Children who scored lower on proportion correct for pretrial direct questions were significantly more likely to refuse to testify ($b = -7.35$, $p < .01$). In addition, children who scored higher on mean courtroom anxiety were significantly more likely to refuse ($b = 2.43$, $p < .001$). For the courtroom anxiety measure, the ROR (odds ratio) was 11.35. Thus, a child with a score of 3 (unhappy) was 11 times more likely to refuse than one who scored 2 (happy), and 22 times more likely to refuse than a child who scored 1 (very happy). Effects of legal knowledge and proportion correct recall were not significant. Although it is unclear why the two memory measures led to different results, their correlation was only .21, suggesting different underlying processes.

Guilt and trial condition were entered on the fifth step. Guilt condition did not significantly predict children's refusal to testify. The effect of trial condition approached significance ($b = -.93$, $p = .08$). Children asked to testify in open court were more likely to refuse to testify than children asked to testify via CCTV. Entered on the seventh step were two- and three-way interactions representing all combinations of the following variables: age, gender, guilt, and trial condition. None of the interactions was significant.

Thus, in summary, children who were younger, evidenced poorer memory for direct questions, expressed more anxiety about testifying, and had lower verbal ability were more likely to refuse to testify. In addition, there were trends for children who had less authoritarian parents and, as predicted, who were asked to testify in regular court to be more likely to refuse to take the stand.

Jurors' Reactions

Predeliberation judgments

Analyses of jurors' responses to a number of predeliberation-questionnaire items are reported elsewhere (Tobey, Goodman, Batterman-Faunce, Orcutt, & Sachsenmaier, 1995). Here we present analyses of particular concern to the legal system regarding use of CCTV, as well as analyses relevant to individual differences (e.g., juror gender). Several sets of ANOVAs were conducted. One set involved a series of 2 (age) × 2 (trial condition) × 2 (guilt) × 2 (juror gender) ANOVAs, with all factors varied between subjects and with each juror's rating entered as the dependent measure ("juror analyses"). Because jurors' predeliberation judgments were independent (i.e., jurors did not yet have a chance to discuss their impressions), jurors' individual ratings could be entered as the dependent measures in these predeliberation analyses. Predicted interactions were further analyzed into simple effects, followed by planned comparisons. It could be argued, however, that these analyses do not take into account the fact that different children testified at each trial and thus that the stimulus condition varied for jurors across trials. Therefore, when the above analyses produced significant effects, a 2 (age) × 2 (trial condition) × 2 (guilt) × 10 (child) × 2 (juror gender) ANOVA was conducted with each juror's rating again entered as the dependent measure, but with the child factor nested within the three other factors ("child nested analyses").[8] In addition, analyses were conducted at the "jury level." That is, for each jury, separate means for all female and male jurors were entered as dependent measures. One reason for conducting this set of analyses concerns the postdeliberation judgments. Once jurors deliberated, their judgments were no longer independent. A second reason concerns the above argument that the jurors were in different stimulus conditions by virtue of having viewed different children.

Juror-level analyses are used as the primary basis for the predeliberation findings reported here. When results were significant in juror-level analyses but not in jury-level and child nested analyses, the lack of correspondence is noted. However, in virtually all cases, findings reported here were significant in all three types of analyses.

Guilt judgments

An important question for the legal system is whether CCTV biases jurors to believe the defendant is guilty. For the dichotomous guilt judgments, jurors were more likely to vote guilty when an older child, $M = .45$, $SD = .50$, rather than a younger child, $M = .35$, $SD = .48$, testified; child age effect, $F(1, 1171) = 14.02$, $p < .001$. As would be hoped, jurors were more likely to view the defendant as guilty when he was indeed guilty, $M = .59$, $SD = .49$, as opposed to when he was not guilty, $M = .23$, $SD = .42$; $F(1, 1171) = 183.95$, $p < .001$. However, guilt interacted with age, $F(1, 1171) = 11.43$, $p = .001$. When the defendant was guilty, mock jurors were more likely to vote guilty when an 8-year-old testified, $M = .67$, $SD = .47$, than when a 6-year-old testified, $M = .48$, $SD = .50$, $p < .05$. When the defendant was not guilty, the age effect was not significant: 8-year-olds, $M = .23$, $SD = .42$, 6-year-olds, $M = .22$, $SD = .42$. Results were very similar when judgments about certainty of guilt and whether the prosecutor proved his case, as measured on 6-point scales, were analyzed. In all cases, there were no significant effects involving trial condition.

Ratings of fairness

Three questions addressed the perceived fairness of the mock trials: fairness of the trial overall, fairness to the defendant, and fairness to the child. When these ratings were entered into separate ANOVAs (as described above), the following significant effects emerged. In regard to fairness of the trial, women, $M = 4.70$, $SD = 1.40$, viewed the trial as less fair than did men, $M = 4.92$, $SD = 1.27$: gender effect, $F(1, 1166) = 7.42$, $p < .01$. In regard to fairness to the child, jurors who heard an older child's testimony viewed the trial as more fair to the child, $M = 5.56$, $SD = .78$, than jurors who heard a younger child's testimony, $M = 5.41$, $SD = .93$: child age effect, $F(1, 1166) = 8.62$, $p < .01$. Trial condition significantly interacted with juror gender in regard to judgments of how fairly the child was treated. As predicted, women who observed closed-circuit trials, $M = 5.58$, $SD = .82$, viewed the proceedings as more fair to the child than did women who observed regular trials, $M = 5.44$, $SD = .87$, $F(1, 585) = 3.94$, $p < .05$, whereas trial condition did not significantly affect men's ratings (regular, $M = 5.52$, $SD = .78$, and closed-circuit, $M = 5.45$, $SD = .93$; simple effects). The magnitude of the differences was relatively small, however. Analyses were also conducted on each juror's rating of fairness of the trial to the defendant. Men, $M = 5.07$, $SD = 1.25$, viewed the trial as more fair to the defendant than did women, $M = 4.89$, $SD = 1.33$; $F(1, 1166) = 5.29$, $p < .025$. However, there was also an uninterpretable age $\times$ guilt $\times$ gender interaction concerning jurors' views of how fairly the defendant was treated, $F(1, 1166) = 5.33$, $p < .025$.

The important legal point to be taken from these findings is that jurors did not view closed-circuit trials as more or less fair to the defendant. Women, however, viewed the trials as less fair to the defendant and less fair overall. Women also viewed regular trials as less fair than closed-circuit trials to children. Other gender effects on jurors' judgments are reported next.

Juror gender

It was predicted that women would view child witnesses more favorably than would men. To examine this hypothesis, a series of 2 (age) $\times$ 2 (guilt) $\times$ 2 (trial condition) $\times$ 2 (juror gender) ANOVAs was performed with relevant items from the juror questionnaire serving as dependent measures. A number of significant main effects of juror gender emerged (see table 10.3), in general confirming the prediction. For instance, women were more likely than men to see the defendant as guilty, were more certain that the crime occurred, and felt less empathy for the defendant. Men more than women seemed suspicious of the children's testimony, rating the children as more likely to have misunderstood the intentions of the defendant, more easily influenced by the prosecutor, and more suggestible.

When considering the significant guilt $\times$ gender interaction concerning the degree to which the child's testimony was influenced by the prosecutor, $F(1, 1173) = 4.95$, $p < .05$, simple effects revealed that men observing trials in which the defendant was guilty were more likely to rate the child's testimony as having been influenced by the prosecutor,

Table 10.3 Mock jurors' mean predeliberation ratings for significant main effects of juror gender from juror-level analyses of variance (*SD*s in parentheses)

	Women	Men	
Guilty[a]	.45 (.50)	.37 (.48)	$F(1, 1171) = 8.52, p < .001$
Certainty of guilt	3.51 (1.19)	3.16 (1.94)	$F(1, 1146) = 10.34, p = .001$
Certainty crime occurred	3.80 (1.91)	3.44 (1.98)	$F(1, 1166) = 10.83, p = .001$
Child misunderstood	3.05 (1.57)	3.30 (1.58)	$F(1, 1174) = 7.51, p < .01$
Influenced by prosecutor	2.64 (1.48)	2.87 (1.48)	$F(1, 1173) = 7.40, p < .01$
Suggestibility[b]	2.69 (1.44)	2.88 (1.47)	$F(1, 1173) = 5.06, p < .025$
Empathy for defendant[c]	3.45 (1.45)	3.66 (1.53)	$F(1, 1165) = 5.18, p < .025$

Higher score indicates more of the attribute or dimension in question.

[a] Jury-level analyses, $p = .07$.
[b] Child nested analyses, $p < .10$.
[c] NS in child nested analyses.

$M = 3.07$, $SD = 1.48$, than were women who observed the same trials, $M = 2.65$, $SD = 1.44$, $F(1, 6.07) = 12.97$, $p < .001$, and than were men who observed trials in which the defendant was not guilty, $M = 2.66$, $SD = 1.46$, $F(1, 603) = 12.03$, $p = .001$. However, the simple effect across guilt condition was not significant for women (not guilty, $M = 2.63$, $SD = 1.51$). Thus, men observing trials in which the defendant was guilty perceived more influence by the prosecutor than did men observing trials in which the defendant was not guilty.

An age × gender interaction was significant for ratings of the believability of the children's testimony, $F(1, 1182) = 5.23, p < .025$. A similar pattern emerged for both male jurors, $F(1, 602) = 37.21, p < .001$, and female jurors, $F(1, 592) = 7.67, p < .01$, in that they tended to find the younger children's testimony (men, $M = 4.22$, $SD = 1.31$; women, $M = 4.48$, $SD = 1.18$) less believable than the testimony of older children (men, $M = 4.83$, $SD = 1.15$; women, $M = 4.76$, $SD = 1.25$). When it came to rating the believability of the 6-year-olds' testimony, however, women were more likely to rate the younger children as believable than were men, $F(1, 519) = 5.75$, $p < .025$.

To summarize, men tended to be slightly, but significantly, more sympathetic to the defense than were women on all measures. Men were less likely to see the defendant as guilty, less certain the crime occurred, more likely to feel empathy for the defendant, and more likely to think that the child misunderstood the defendant's acts and was suggestible. Both men and women viewed younger children as less believable than older children, although women were more likely than men to believe the younger children.

Discernment

It was possible to examine with correlational analyses whether jurors discerned the accuracy of children's testimony in the regular versus CCTV condition. If jurors can discern accuracy better when children testify via CCTV, this finding would produce support for use of closed-circuit technology. Alternately, if CCTV interferes with jurors' abilities to discern accuracy (e.g., masks subtleties of children's expressions), then jurors may be less able to discriminate accurate from inaccurate testimony in the CCTV versus regular-trial condition. Correlations between measures of children's accuracy overall and jurors' judgments of children's accuracy are presented in table 10.4 as a function of trial condition and children's age. As can be seen, jurors' ability to discern the accuracy of the children's testimony was less than might have been hoped for. Proportion of children's correct responses overall was the accuracy measure most strongly associated with jurors' ability to correctly discern children's accuracy. Nevertheless, for that measure, significance was reached only when 8-year-olds testified over CCTV and 6-year-olds testified in open court. Furthermore, jurors evinced little ability to discern children's suggestibility as assessed by children's accuracy in answering misleading questions, $r = -.09$, $n = 1192$. When jurors' ability to do so was considered for each trial condition and age, there was little if any improvement: CCTV condition, 8-year-olds, $r = -.07$, $n = 336$, and 6-year-olds, $r = .13$, $n = 238$; regular-trial condition, 8-year-olds, $r = .06$, $n = 339$, and 6-year-olds, $r = .14$, $n = 279$. Thus, there was no indication that jurors discerned children's accuracy better in the CCTV or regular-trial condition.

Table 10.4 Correlations between children's total accuracy and jurors' judgments of accuracy (number of subjects in parentheses)

	Closed-circuit		Regular	
	8-year-olds	6-year-olds	8-year-olds	6-year-olds
Free recall correct	−.02 (337)	.06 (239)	.10 (329)	.28 (282)
Free recall incorrect	−.05 (337)	−.01 (239)	.06 (326)	.07 (282)
Proportion correct (Direct questions)	.32* (337)	.24 (239)	.19 (342)	.31* (282)
Proportion omission (Direct questions)	−.04 (337)	−.01 (239)	.11 (342)	−.22 (282)
Proportion commission (Direct questions)	.06 (337)	.02 (239)	.08 (342)	.16 (282)
Proportion don't know (Direct questions)	−.28 (337)	−.19 (239)	−.23 (342)	−.18 (282)

$*p < .05.$

Confidence and consistency

It was predicted that jurors' perceptions of child confidence and consistency would be positively related to jurors' perceptions of accuracy and believability. These predictions were confirmed by the following correlation coefficients: jurors' judgments of child confidence and accuracy, $r = .59$, $n = 1,194$, child consistency and accuracy, $r = .62$, $n = 1,192$, child confidence and believability, $r = .52$, $n = 1,192$, and child consistency and believability, $r = .62$, $n = 1,190$. Thus, the often-cited correlations of perceptions of confidence and consistency with perceptions of accuracy and believability appeared in the present study, indicating that jurors use confidence and consistency as credibility cues.

Interestingly, jurors' ratings of confidence and consistency at times significantly correlated with measures of children's actual accuracy, but not systematically so. When jurors viewed younger children in regular trials, a positive correlation emerged for children's proportion correct scores to direct questions with both ratings of confidence, $r = .34$, $n = 278$, and consistency, $r = .47$, $n = 277$, and a negative correlation emerged for children's overall omission errors to direct questions with confidence, $r = -.37$, $n = 278$ and consistency, $r = -.51$, $n = 277$. Furthermore, when jurors viewed older children in closed-circuit trials, a significant positive correlation was revealed for children's proportion correct scores to direct questions with consistency, $r = .39$, $n = 337$. Thus, in some instances perceptions of confidence and consistency did relate to children's actual accuracy, but it is unclear why these particular correlations and not others were significant.

Demographic characteristics

Correlations were examined to determine if jurors' demographic characteristics predicted their predeliberation ratings of the children or the trial. None were significant, including the degree of contact jurors had with children and whether or not jurors were parents, countering our prediction.

Path analysis

Path analyses tested the model depicted in figure 10.1. First, two endogenous variables related to children's accuracy of testimony were created through factor analysis. The first factor, Memory 1, reflects the amount of information children provided to free recall questions. Both free recall correct (.83) and incorrect (.88) scores loaded positively on this factor. The second factor reflects children's accuracy to directive questions overall (Memory 2). Children's direct-question accuracy scores loaded positively on this factor (.74) and their inaccuracy scores loaded negatively (−.85). Factor scores were created for these two factors. Furthermore, due to significant effects involving juror age and pretrial correct and incorrect information for both free recall and direct questions (reported above), these variables were statistically controlled, as appropriate, in the following regressions, but were not depicted in the model.

Standard path analysis, employing ordinary least squares regression to predict a unidirectional path, was used to estimate the fully saturated model depicted in figure 10.2 ($n = 1,110$). To assess the contributions of nonoverlapping variance for each term in the model, all variables postulated as effects were regressed simultaneously on those postulated as

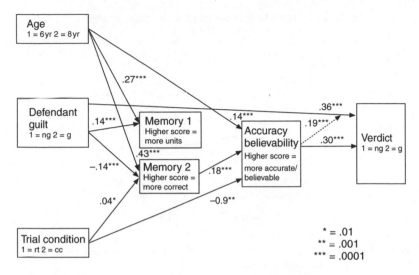

ng = not guilty, g = guilty, rt = regular trial, cc = closed-circuit trial,
Memory 1 = amount of free recall, Memory 2 = accuracy on direct questions

Figure 10.2 Results of the path analysis predicting predeliberation verdicts

causes. As expected, older children provided more information in free recall and answered direct questions more accurately. Unexpectedly, when the defendant was guilty, children provided more information in free recall and answered fewer direct questions correctly than when he was not guilty. Of particular interest, children who testified via CCTV rather than in open court were more accurate in answering direct questions.

How did the above factors relate to jurors' ratings of the accuracy and believability of child witnesses? Ratings of accuracy and believability, which were highly correlated ($r = .65$), were combined to form a mean of the two variables. There was a significant direct effect, with older children viewed as more accurate/believable than younger children. Age also had an indirect effect on jurors' views of children's accuracy/believability that was mediated through children's accuracy in answering direct questions. Age positively predicted accuracy in answering direct questions, which in turn predicted jurors' views of accuracy/believability.

As predicted, children in the regular trial condition were viewed as more accurate/believable than children in the CCTV condition.

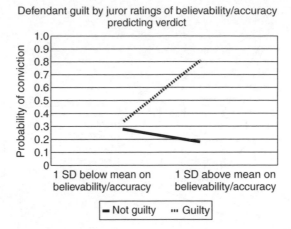

Figure 10.3 Interaction of guilt condition and accuracy/believability in predicting predeliberation verdicts

However, trial condition also exerted an indirect effect on jurors' views of child accuracy/believability, which was mediated by children's accuracy in answering direct questions. In contrast to the direct effect, the indirect effect indicated that children who testified via CCTV were more accurate in answering direct questions, which led them to be viewed as more accurate/believable.

There was one additional indirect effect. Children's accuracy in answering direct questions mediated a relation between guilt condition and ratings of children's accuracy/believability. Specifically, children's decreased accuracy in the guilty condition led in turn to jurors rating the children as more accurate/believable. This may reflect jurors' bias toward not-guilty verdicts (see below).

Finally, guilt condition strongly predicted verdict. When the defendant was guilty, jurors were more likely to rate him as guilty, independently of their ratings of the accuracy/believability of the children. There was also a direct effect of ratings of children's accuracy/believability on jurors' predeliberation verdicts. However, for interpreting this direct effect, a significant accuracy/believability × guilt condition interaction is relevant (see figure 10.3). In the guilty condition, higher ratings of children's accuracy/believability were associated with guilt judgments. In the not-guilty condition, the opposite pattern existed: higher ratings of children's accuracy/believability were associated with not-guilty judgments. A number of indirect effects were also apparent (see figure 10.2). There were indirect effects of trial condition and age on verdict that were mediated through the accuracy/believability judgments. Moreover, age, guilt condition, and trial condition had indirect effects on verdict mediated by children's accuracy on direct questions and accuracy/believability ratings.

In summary, although children were more accurate when testifying over CCTV, jurors' views of children's accuracy/believability were affected by trial condition in two ways. The direct effect of testifying over CCTV was to lower children's credibility in the eyes of the jurors. However, an indirect effect of trial condition was that when children provided more accurate testimony, it led jurors to believe the children more.

Postdeliberation judgments

It was of interest to examine jurors' votes of guilty or not guilty after deliberation, as well as how certain they felt about the defendant's guilt. Jury-level ANOVAs were performed. Regarding votes of guilty or not guilty, juries in not-guilty trials were far less likely to vote guilty, $M = .09$, $SD = .20$, than juries in guilty trials, $M = .33$, $SD = .37$: guilt condition effect, $F(1, 154) = 25.74$, $p < .001$. Thus, the false-conviction rate was only 9%, whereas the false-acquittal rate was 67%. Moreover, jurors more often "hung" when the defendant was guilty than when he was not guilty, again indicating a reluctance to convict. Four juries indicated a hung verdict in the not-guilty condition, whereas 15 juries indicated a hung verdict in the guilty condition. When considering certainty of guilt, juries in not-guilty trials were far less certain of the defendant's guilt, $M = 1.87$, $SD = 1.02$, than juries in guilty trials, $M = 3.29$, $SD = 1.43$: guilt condition effect, $F(1, 154) = 52.11$, $p < .001$. There were no significant effects associated with child age, trial condition, or juror gender. Thus, after deliberation only guilt mattered. [The general decrease in pre- versus postdeliberation guilty verdicts, although suggestive of a "leniency effect" associated with deliberations (Kerr, 1981), was not significant in jury-level analyses.]

Although it is encouraging that few false convictions of the defendant occurred when he was innocent, it is somewhat disconcerting that when he was guilty, he was infrequently convicted. Jurors apparently felt quite hesitant to convict based on the testimony of a child.

Discussion

When children testify, judgments of the importance of face-to-face confrontation involve a careful balancing of the interests of the defendant,
the child witness, and the state. The research presented here reflects
an attempt to shed light on current debates regarding the use of CCTV
when children testify. Proponents of protective measures argue for shel-
tering the child from further trauma and reducing stress to allow the
best testimony possible. Opponents of protective measures claim that
use of such measures infringes on defendant's rights by biasing jurors
against the defendant and impeding factfinders' abilities to reach the
truth.

The present study addressed a number of questions posed by the
current debate. The first question considered possible effects of testimony setting (i.e., open court versus CCTV) on children's accuracy
when testifying. Results of initial analyses indicated that use of CCTV
interacted with children's age to produce some benefits for the testimony
of younger children. Although, in general, older children were more
accurate witnesses than younger children, the use of CCTV functioned
to decrease suggestibility for younger children. Misleading questioning,
which sometimes occurs in court (especially but not exclusively in cross-
examination), has been found to be particularly detrimental to the accuracy of young children's reports (Luss & Wells, 1992). In the present
study, young children who testified in open court made more errors to
misleading questions than other children their age who testified in the
closed-circuit courtroom. However, the effects of testifying via CCTV
were not completely positive in regard to young children's accuracy.
Specifically, the closed-circuit condition was also associated with more
commission errors overall for younger than older children when the
defendant was not guilty. However, this expected age difference appeared
in an uninterpretable interaction and is thus possibly spurious in regard
to the effects of CCTV. In any case, the path analysis revealed a small
but significant positive effect of closed-circuit technology on children's
answers to the direct questions overall. Thus, CCTV generally promoted
more accurate testimony in children.

Second, the study assessed the relation between the court setting and
children's experience of anxiety. Not surprisingly, the prospect of testifying in open court rather than via CCTV was associated with children

experiencing greater pretrial anxiety. Thus, CCTV served a protective function for children even before they testified. In addition, girls and older children were more likely to express pretrial anxiety, findings consistent with those from studies in which children awaiting actual trials were interviewed (Goodman et al., 1992; Whitcomb et al., 1991). Pretrial anxiety and a younger age were associated with children refusing to testify or becoming too upset to testify, as were lower verbal skills and a poorer memory for the target event. These findings may be useful to the courts, attorneys, and mental health professionals in attempting to determine the subset of children who may be too frightened to testify in a regular trial. However, in light of the *Maryland v. Craig* decision, it should be kept in mind that we did not measure inability to reasonably communicate, but rather refusal (including being upset). Nevertheless, refusal to testify could arguably be considered one form of inability to reasonably communicate.

Consistent with former studies (e.g., Flin et al., 1989; Saywitz et al., 1990), older compared to younger children possessed greater understanding of the legal system. Interestingly, children who articulated greater legal knowledge expressed less pretrial anxiety. Greater legal knowledge was associated with answering direct questions correctly at trial, even when effects of age were controlled. These results support the practice common in court preparation programs of teaching children about the legal system in an effort to quell their anxieties and promote optimal testimony (e.g., Sas, 1991). It is unclear, however, whether these latter two findings represent causal effects. It is possible, for instance, that smarter children possessed greater legal knowledge and more accurate memorics.

Third, the degree to which jurors may be better able to evaluate the accuracy of child witnesses in live or closed-circuit trials was examined. Opponents of protective measures have contended that use of these measures interferes with jurors' abilities to discern accurate from inaccurate testimony. Findings based on the present research do not support the notion that factfinders' discernment abilities are impaired by the use of CCTV. Unfortunately, jurors' abilities to discern accurate from inaccurate testimony was less than perfect across the board. Jurors tended to base their impressions of witness credibility on perceived confidence and consistency, rather than on actual accuracy, although in some cases actual accuracy and confidence and consistency ratings were significantly related.

Another concern addressed was the possibility that jurors may be biased by use of closed-circuit testimony leading them to regard the defendant more negatively or view the defendant as guilty when, in fact, he or she was not guilty. The present study did not uncover direct negative biases toward the defendant due to the employment of CCTV (cf. Ross et al., 1994). In general, when CCTV was used, the defendant was no more likely to be convicted and the trial was not viewed as more unfair to the defendant. However, these results must be interpreted cautiously because of limits on the generalizability of our study. For instance, the defendant was not accused of having performed a violent or abusive action and only one witness testified, which could affect the trends we uncovered. Moreover, medium of testimony produced an indirect effect on perceptions of defendant guilt that was not favorable to the defendant.

It was also of interest to determine if the use of closed-circuit technology biases jurors for or against child witnesses. In fact, closed-circuit technology was associated with a negative bias. Children who testified via CCTV were viewed as less believable than children who testified in regular trials, despite the fact that, if anything, children who testified via CCTV were more accurate. As reported elsewhere, children who testified via CCTV rather than in regular trials were also viewed as less attractive, less intelligent, more likely to be making up a story, and less likely to be basing their testimony on fact versus fantasy (Tobey et al., 1995). However, there was one positive effect of CCTV in regard to jurors' perceptions of the child witnesses: to the extent that CCTV promoted more accurate child testimony, jurors viewed the children as more accurate and believable. This latter finding supports the use of CCTV not only in promoting children's accuracy, but in facilitating jurors' accurate assessment of such testimony.

Based on former research, we predicted that, on average, women would be more pro-victim and men would be more pro-defense (Bottoms, 1993). This prediction was confirmed. Moreover, women considered testifying via CCTV to be more fair for young children, whereas men did not. These findings may reflect women's more protective stance toward children and men's identification with the defendant. However, as argued by Bottoms (1993), underlying these gender effects may also be differences in attitudes and empathy toward children and child victims.

Overall, the present study has important implications for the use of closed-circuit technology when children testify. The protective nature of the closed-circuit arrangement helped children feel less anxious about testifying, helped them agree to testify, and reduced suggestibility in younger children. Nevertheless, due to jurors' negative biases toward child witnesses when CCTV was employed, attorneys may choose to leave closed-circuit testimony for the most extreme circumstances, such as when children have been severely injured or threatened and refuse to testify unless they can do so via CCTV. In regard to arguments made by opponents of protective measures (e.g., *Coy v. Iowa*, 1988), the defendant's chances of acquittal in our study were not handicapped as a result of closed-circuit technology. The defendant was not viewed more negatively by jurors and there were not more guilty verdicts rendered when children testified via CCTV (although the fact that children were more accurate in the CCTV condition, which led them to be viewed as more believable, could be construed as a negative consequence for defendants). Additionally, jurors were no better at discerning accurate testimony when children testified in open court than when they testified over CCTV. Importantly, it should be noted that the present research did not address the question of jurors' ability to detect overt deception when protective measures are used. However, in a related study, Orcutt (1995) found that jurors were essentially no better at detecting overt deception in child witnesses when testimony was viewed directly in open court versus when the child testified over CCTV.

Relative to former experimental research on the effects of CCTV on children's testimony and jurors' reactions, the degree of ecological validity of the present study is notable. Child subjects testified in a courtroom setting about an event in which they had actually participated. A community sample of potential jurors watched each trial and deliberated to reach a verdict. The staging of the trial was very realistic and captivating for both child witnesses and jurors. However, caution should be employed in applying our findings to actual cases or in using them as the basis for social policy. Although this research attempted to attain greater ecological validity than heretofore obtained in experiments on jurors' perceptions of children's testimony, it is not without its problems. Ethical constraints rightfully dampened the realistic nature of the study. Although the child witnesses testified in a fairly realistic setting, they were not nearly as stressed as they undoubtedly would have been in an actual trial. The fact that the defendant had been kind to the children and the alleged inappropriate behavior was neither stressful nor thought of as "bad" at the time also presumably reduced children's distress and placed limits on generalizability of our findings. Specifically, it could be argued that these qualities of the children's experiences are likely to result in an *under*estimation of any facilitative effects of CCTV on the accuracy of their testimony and on the lessening of their fear because children probably felt less fear or anxiety in facing the defendant in the present study than in more typical child sexual abuse cases. In addition, children in actual cases, such as those concerning child sexual abuse, may be coached or told to keep a secret. Neither of these factors played a role in the present research. Moreover, only one witness testified in our mock trials – the child. Presumably, in a real trial, more evidence and testimony would be presented to jurors.

The fact that the "crime," limited by ethical constraints, lacked harmful and salacious components may have affected not only children's behavior, but also jurors' judgments. Jurors may have been less willing to convict the defendant because the acts (exposing toes, upper arm, and belly button) were not at all heinous. Although jurors were instructed to pretend that the alleged acts were criminal, it is difficult to speculate on how the relative innocuousness of the case affected jurors' perceptions of the child witness. That jurors only deliberated for 30 min is another important limit on the study's ecological validity, especially in relation to the verdict and postdeliberation findings. Also, subject jurors knew that they were part of a research project and that the trial was not real. This knowledge may have affected their perceptions; if they believed they were making decisions that affected people's lives, their responses might have been different.

However, when the findings of the present study are considered in conjunction with those of several others (e.g., Davies & Noon, 1991; Ross et al., 1994), a relatively consistent picture begins to emerge. Testifying via CCTV may be beneficial for some child witnesses, but it may also limit the impact of children's testimony on jurors' initial decisions. Fortunately, our results indicate that after deliberations, the actual guilt of the defendant was the primary basis on which verdicts were reached. Although in predeliberation ratings, nearly a quarter of the jurors judged the defendant guilty when he was not guilty (even though children in the not-guilty condition were presumably trying to communicate his innocence), less than 10% of the jurors falsely convicted the defendant after deliberations, a finding that highlights the importance of deliberation when conducing research of this kind. In the end, for better or for worse, jurors seemed disinclined to convict a defendant based solely on the word of a child.

Notes

1 Time to deliberate was restricted because of limitations on our use of the courthouse. This restriction also affected how many witnesses could testify.

2 It should be noted that in the not-guilty condition, most children correctly denied that their bare upper arm, toes, or belly button had been exposed and videotaped, although for some children, errors and/or inconsistent testimony were elicited. Thus, jurors in the not-guilty condition were faced largely with denial that the mock crime took place. We included the not-guilty condition because of assumptions about children's suggestibility. That is, given inclusion at trial of leading questions about the crime (e.g., "Didn't he have you put them [stickers] on your toes?" asked with permission of the judge during direct examination), it was expected that false reports of the crime would be elicited. In fact, they occurred with a surprisingly low frequency. Inclusion of such leading questions necessitated that a few questions were misleading for children in the not-guilty condition but correctly leading for children in the guilty condition. However, these were balanced by questions that were misleading for children in the guilty condition and correctly leading for children in the not-guilty condition ("Didn't you keep your socks on when you played with the toe stickers?" asked during cross-examination). Out of the 108 questions asked, only 8 varied in this way.

Also, part way through the study jurors were observed making their verdict based on a specific element of the crime (i.e., the requirement that the child's body was videotaped for the defendant to be "guilty"). Because the videotape was not present at the trial and the questioning of the child did not adequately address this point, some juries seemed to base their verdicts on the fact that they were unsure that the camera had actually functioned and that the incident was actually taped. To correct for this problem, a modification was made part way through the study. Child subjects in Phase 2 of the study were told by the confederate to wave "goodbye" to the camera just before it was turned off, and then watched themselves waving in a brief play back. In court, Phase 2 children were asked two additional questions during the trial, whereas Phase 1 children were not asked these questions. There were no significant interactions involving phase, and phase had no effect on the results of the ANOVAs. Thus, phase is not discussed further.

3 For inferences concerning effects of trial and guilt conditions on children's testimony, analyses of covariance controlling for pretrial differences in memory performance are pertinent. This is so because the pretrial differences may reflect a possible confound (e.g., random assignment that failed to equate memory performance; the fact that certain children chose not to testify at trial). For considering effects of children's testimony on jurors' perceptions, analyses of variance that do not control for pretrial differences apply because they reflect the children's performance as viewed by jurors.

4 Legal knowledge was measured at the outset of Session 3. Subsequently, children were provided with legal knowledge during the tour of the courtroom. The fact that children's initial legal knowledge still predicted their pretrial anxiety and the accuracy of their testimony is of interest.

5 Rather than providing responses to the open-ended scale of the CAQ, a number of children preferred to point to the faces, resulting in more missing data for the open-ended than the faces scale.

6 Children were not told the specific nature of the "crime," and thus 8-year-olds in the guilty/open-court condition presumably inferred that videotaping exposed rather than nonexposed body parts was more suspect.

7 Variables with higher causal priority and greater stability were entered earlier than other variables. For instance, the cluster of variables associated with the child were viewed as having greater stability than the variables entered in later steps. In general, however, if the variables within a block are causally prior and highly correlated, then their contribution may be underestimated. Also, it should be noted that internal consistencies for the parent authoritarian scale and PCSA were relatively low, .70 and .71, respectively, which may affect detection of significant effects for these variables.

8 To conduct the univariate nested analyses, a MANOVA program had to be used and the analyses required equal n across cells. To equalize the number of subjects, only 10 trials per cell could be included. We thus had to randomly eliminate 8 trials. It is possible that removing these 8 trials from the analyses decreased somewhat the comparability of the ANOVA and MANOVA results.

References

Achenbach, T. M., & Edelbrock, C. S. (1983). *Manual for the Child Behavior Checklist and Revised Child Behavior Profile*. Burlington, VT: University of Vermont, Department of Psychiatry.

Batterman-Faunce, J. M. (1993). *Closed-circuit versus open courtroom testimony: Effects on the accuracy and suggestibility of child witnesses.* Doctoral dissertation, State University of New York at Buffalo, NY.

Berliner, L., & Conte, J. R. (1995). The effects of disclosure and intervention on sexually abused children. *Child Abuse and Neglect, 19,* 371–84.

Bottoms, B. L. (1993). Individual differences in perceptions of child sexual assault victims. In G. S. Goodman, & B. L. Bottoms (eds.), *Child victims, child witnesses* (pp. 229–62). New York: Guilford Press.

Bottoms, B. L., & Goodman, G. S. (1994). Perceptions of children's credibility in sexual assault cases. *Journal of Applied Social Psychology, 24,* 702–32.

Buffalo News. (1989).

Bussey, K., Lee, K., & Grimbeek, E. (1993). Lies and secrets: Implications for children's reporting of sexual abuse. In G. S. Goodman, & B. L. Bottoms (eds.), *Child victims, child witnesses* (pp. 147–68). New York: Guilford Press.

Carter, C., Bottoms, B. L., & Levine, M. (1996). Linguistic and socio-emotional influences on the accuracy of children's reports. *Law and Human Behavior, 20,* 335–58; Correction, *20,* 579.

Cashmore, J. (1992). *The use of closed-circuit television for child witnesses in the ACT.* Sydney, Australia: Australian Law Reform Committee.

Coy v. Iowa, 56 USLW 4931 (1988).

Davies, G., & Noon, E. (1991). *An evaluation of the live link for child witnesses.* London: Home Office.

Dent, H. (1977). Stress as a factor influencing person recognition in identification parades. *Bulletin of the British Psychological Society, 30,* 339–40.

Duggan, L. M., Aubrey, M., Doherty, E., Isquith, P., Levine, M., & Scheiner, J. (1989). The credibility of children as witnesses in a simulated child sex abuse trial. In S. Ceci, D. Ross, & M. Toglia (eds.), *Perspectives on the child witness* (pp. 71–99). New York: Springer-Verlag.

Dunn, L. M., & Dunn, L. M. (1981). *Manual for the Peabody Picture Vocabulary Test – Revised.* Circle Pines, MN: American Guidance Services.

Flin, R. H., Stevenson, Y., & Davies, G. M. (1989). Children's knowledge of court proceedings. *British Journal of Psychology, 80,* 285–97.

Goodman, G. S., Bottoms, B., Herscovici, B. B., & Shaver, P. (1989). Determinants of the child victim's perceived credibility. In S. Ceci, D. Ross, & M. Toglia (eds.), *Perspectives on children's testimony* (pp. 1–22). New York: Springer-Verlag.

Goodman, G. S., Bottoms, B., Schwartz-Kenney, B., & Rudy, L. (1991). Children's testimony about a stressful event: Improving children's reports. *Journal of Narrative and Life History, 7,* 69–99.

Goodman, G. S., Golding, J., & Haith, M. M. (1984). Jurors' reactions to child witnesses. *Journal of Social Issues, 40,* 139–56.

Goodman, G. S., Golding, J., Helgeson, V., Haith, M. M., & Michelli, J. (1987).

When a child takes the stand: Jurors' perceptions of children's eyewitness testimony. *Law and Human Behavior, 11*, 27–40.

Goodman, G. S., Levine, M., Melton, G. B., & Ogden, D. (1991). *Craig v. Maryland*. Amicus Brief to the US Supreme Court on behalf of the American Psychological Association, *Law and Human Behavior, 15*, 13–30.

Goodman, G. S., Pyle-Taub, E., Jones, D. P. H., England, P., Port, L. P., Rudy, L., & Prado, L. (1992). Emotional effects of criminal court testimony on child sexual assault victims. *Monographs of the Society for Research in Child Development, 57* (Serial No. 229).

Harter, S., & Pike, R. (1984). The pictorial scale of perceived competence and social acceptance for young children. *Child Development, 55*, 1969–82.

Hill, P., & Hill, S. (1987). Videotaping children's testimony: An empirical view. *Michigan Law Review, 85*, 809–33.

Kerr, N. (1981). Social transition schemes: Charting the group's road to agreement. *Journal of Personality and Social Psychology, 41*, 684–702.

Leippe, M. R., Manion, A. P., & Romanczyk, A. (1992). Eyewitness persuasion: How and how well do fact finders judge the accuracy of adults' and children's memory reports? *Journal of Personality and Social Psychology, 63*, 181–97.

Leippe, M. R., Manion, A. P., & Romanczyk, A. (1993). Discernability or discrimination? Understanding jurors' reactions to accurate and inaccurate child and adult witnesses. In G. S. Goodman, & B. Bottoms (eds.), *Understanding and improving children's eyewitness testimony*. New York: Guilford Press.

Leippe, M. R., & Romanczyk, A. (1987). Children on the witness stand: A communication/persuasion analysis of jurors' reactions to child witnesses. In S. J. Ceci, M. P. Toglia, & D. F. Ross (eds.), *Children's eyewitness memory* (pp. 155–77). New York: Springer-Verlag.

Leippe, M. R., & Romanczyk, A. (1989). Reactions to child (versus adult) eyewitnesses: The influence of jurors' preconceptions and witness behavior. *Law and Human Behavior, 13*, 103–32.

Levinson, D. J., & Huffman, P. E. (1955). Traditional family ideology and its relation to personality. *Journal of Personality, 23*, 251–74.

Limber, S. P., & Castrianno, L. M. (1990, August). *Lay persons' perceptions of sexually abused children*. Paper presented at the meeting of the American Psychological Association, Boston, MA.

Luss, C. A., & Wells, G. L. (1992). The perceived credibility of child eyewitnesses. In H. Dent & R. Flin (eds.), *Children as witnesses* (pp. 73–92). Chichester, UK: Wiley.

Maryland v. Craig, 47 CrL 2258 US SupCt (1990).

MacFarlane, K. (1992). *Children's court school*. Colloquium, SUNY-Buffalo, NY.

MacFarlane, K. (1985). Diagnostic evaluations and the use of videotapes in child sexual abuse cases. *University of Miami Law Review, 40*, 135–65.

Moston, S., & Engelberg, T. (1992). The effects of social support on children's eyewitness testimony. *Applied Cognitive Psychology, 6*, 61–75.

Murray, K. (1995). *Live television link: An evaluation of its use by child witnesses in Scottish criminal trials.* Scottish Office: Central Research Unit.

Myers, J. E. B. (1992). *Evidence in child abuse and neglect cases: Vol. 1* (2nd edn). New York: Wiley.

National Center for the Prosecution of Child Abuse (1995). *Child witnesses: The use of closed-circuit television testimony.* Washington, DC: US Department of Health and Human Services.

Nightingale, N. (1993). Juror reactions to child victim witnesses: Factors affecting trial outcome. *Law and Human Behavior, 17,* 679–94.

Orcutt, H. (1995). *Detecting deception: Factfinders' abilities to assess the truth.* Doctoral dissertation, State University of New York at Buffalo, NY.

Pedhazur, E. J. (1982). *Multiple regression in behavioral research: Explanation and prediction* (2nd edn). Chicago: Holt, Reinhart, and Winston.

Peters, D. (1990, March). Confrontational stress and children's testimony: Some experimental findings. In S. Ceci (Chair), *Do children lie? Narrowing the uncertainties.* Symposium presented at the American Psychology and Law Society Meetings, Williamsburg, VA.

Quas, J., DeCicco, V., Bulkley, J., & Goodman, G. S. (1996). District attorneys' views of innovative practices for child witnesses. *APLS Newsletter, 16,* 5–8.

Rosenthal, R. (1995). *State of New Jersey v. Margaret Kelly Michaels*: An overview. *Psychology, Public Policy, and Law, 1,* 246–71.

Ross, D. F., Hopkins, S., Hanson, E., Lindsay, R. C. L., Hazen, K., & Eslinger, T. (1994). The impact of protective shields and videotape testimony on conviction rates in a simulated trial of child sexual abuse. *Law and Human Behavior, 18,* 553–66.

Rutter, M., (1993). Stress, coping, and development: Some issues and some questions. In N. Garmezy, & M. Rutter (eds.), *Stress, coping, and development in children* (pp. 1–41). New York: McGraw-Hill.

Sas, L. (1991). *Reducing the system-induced trauma for child sexual abuse victims through court preparation, assessment, and follow-up.* Ontario, Canada: London Family Court Clinic.

Saywitz, K. J., Jaenicke, C., & Camparo, L. (1990). Children's knowledge of legal terminology. *Law and Human Behavior, 14,* 523–35.

Saywitz, K. J., & Nathanson, R. (1993). Children's testimony and their perceptions of stress in and out of the courtroom. *Child Abuse and Neglect, 17,* 613–22.

Schmidt, C., & Brigham, J. (1996). Jurors' perceptions of child victim-witnesses in a simulated sexual abuse trial. *Law and Human Behavior, 20,* 581–606.

Spencer, J. R., & Flin, R. (1990). *The evidence of children: The law and the psychology.* London: Blackstone.

Spielberger, C. D. (1973). *Preliminary manual for the State-Trait Anxiety Inventory for Children ("How I Feel" questionnaire).* Palo Alto, CA: Consulting Psychologists Press.

Swim, J., Borgida, E., & McCoy, K. (1993). Videotaped versus in-court witness testimony: Does protecting the child witness jeopardize due process? *Journal of Applied Social Psychology, 23,* 603–31.

Tobey, A., & Goodman, G. S. (1992). Children's eyewitness memory: Effects of participation and forensic context. *Child Abuse and Neglect, 16,* 779–96.

Tobey, A. E., Goodman, G. S., Batterman-Faunce, J. M., Orcutt, H. K., & Sachsenmaier, T. (1995). Balancing the rights of children and defendants: Effects of closed-circuit television on children's accuracy and jurors' perceptions. In M. S. Zaragoza, J. R. Graham, G. C. Hall, R. Hirschman, & Y. S. Ben-Porath (eds.), *Memory and testimony in the child witness* (pp. 214–39). Thousand Oaks, CA: Sage.

Warren-Leubecker, A., Tate, C. S., Hinton, I. D., & Ozbek, I. N. (1989). What do children know about the legal system and when do they know it? First steps down a less traveled path in child witness research. In S. J. Ceci, D. F. Ross, & M. P. Toglia (eds.), *Perspectives on children's testimony* (pp. 131–57). New York: Springer-Verlag.

Wells, G. L., Turtle, J. W., & Luss, C. A. E. (1989). The perceived credibility of child eyewitnesses: What happens when they use their own words? In S. J. Ceci, D. F. Ross, & M. P. Toglia (eds.), *Perspectives on the child witness* (pp. 23–46). New York: Springer-Verlag.

Whitcomb, D., Runyan, D., De Vos, E., Hunter, W. M., Cross, T., Everson, M., Peeler, N., Porter, C., Toth, P., & Cropper, C. (1991). *"Child victim as witness" research and development program.* Final report to the Office of Juvenile Justice and Delinquency Prevention, U.S. Department of Justice.

Whitcomb, D., Shapiro, E., & Stellwagen, L. (1985). *When the victim is a child: Issues for judges and prosecutors.* Washington, DC: US Department of Justice.

ELEVEN

The Effect of 'Lawyerese' on Children

Introduction

When I began my own research on children and the law, one of the first things I did was attend a criminal trial in which children were giving evidence as alleged victims. To one 6-year-old the prosecuting lawyer said 'I put it to you that a response like that in a court of law such as this is inappropriate. Do you agree?' This was a lawyer examining a 6-year-old witness, supposedly for his own side of the case!!

In much the same way that most courtrooms have been designed much more for adults than for children, so much lawyer training has been devoted to the questioning of adults, rather than children. Thus many lawyers, when questioning children, employ practices that have been developed in virtual ignorance of the findings from developmental psychology. However, in some countries a number of lawyers, like police officers and social service personnel before them, are now taking the trouble to learn about relevant developmental issues so that they can question children appropriately. Unfortunately, the rate of improvement among, and training provision for, lawyers usually lags behind that provided in some countries for police officers.

The paper by Nancy Perry and her colleagues makes it clear that 'Lawyerese' (the kinds of complex questions and terminology often employed by attorneys and lawyers) confuses children. Does this impede courts in carrying out their duties? Should such questioning be prohibited, and if so, how? How could lawyers become more aware of the psychology of questioning children?

Suggested reading

Westcott, H. (1995). Children's experiences of being examined and cross-examined: The opportunity to be heard? *Expert Evidence*, 4, 13–19.

When Lawyers Question Children: Is Justice Served?

Nancy W. Perry, Bradley D. McAuliff,
Paulette Tam, Linda Claycomb,
Colleen Dostal, and Cameron Flanagan

Lawyers are students of language by profession, and they exercise their power in court by manipulating the thoughts and opinions of others through the skillful use of language (Philbrick, cited in O'Barr, 1982). As one forensic linguist noted, "The most powerful weapon an attorney has in the war of words he wages with the witness is manipulation of question form, and it is a tool frequently referred to in articles and manuals on deposition and trial practice" (Walker, 1987, p. 64).

Consider the case of a 9-year-old child who alleged that an adult had attempted to abduct her. She provided descriptions of the individual, the car, and the license plate number. On the basis of that information, a suspect was arrested and brought to trial. During legal proceedings the child performed competently and credibly. However, one attorney repeatedly confronted her with convoluted questions. For example, with regard to truth-telling he asked,

> You don't know if any of your brothers or sisters or if I was your brother – well, any of your brothers or sisters didn't really tell what happened, didn't quite tell the truth once, you don't know of any of that happening in your family?

With regard to the license plate number he queried,

> Did you just pick that up just because you talk – you plan your time to fill your space, the spacing off or riding your bike, or did anybody tell you you should read license plates?

And, with regard to the suspect he asked,

> Prior to seeing Mr. B. in his front yard on that night – on that day – And the individual in the car, did you ever see Mr. B. get into his car before that, or get out of his car?

As those examples illustrate, when we ask unnecessarily complex questions, we risk miscarriage of justice. Yet, despite the importance of language as a strategic resource to lawyers, its role in courtroom chemistry is poorly comprehended (O'Barr, 1982, p. 12), especially when children serve as witnesses. Thus, McGough (1993) argued, "Today's challenge is to evaluate what changes, if any, should be made to legal rules which take into account the demonstrable developmental differences between children and adults" (p. 1).

Certainly, any professionals who question children – psychologists, social workers, police officers, and others – may engage in poor questioning techniques (e.g., Boyd, 1993; Dent, 1982). In one recent study, for example, Boyd (1993) found that the complexity of questions posed by a small sample of Child Protective Service workers did not vary as a function of child's age, although developmental theory argues that it should.

However, the language of attorneys seems particularly ill-suited to children's comprehension (Brennan & Brennan, 1988; Flin, Stevenson, & Davies, 1989; Pierre-Puysegur, 1985; Saywitz, 1989; Saywitz & Goodman, in press; Saywitz, Nathanson, Snyder, & Lamphear, 1993; Saywitz et al., 1990; Walker, 1993; Warren-Leubecker et al., 1989). The complex terminology and convoluted sentence forms (e.g., negatives, double negatives, tag questions, rapid shifts, multiple components, unclear references) often present in legal questioning tend to be particularly problematic for child witnesses (Brennan & Brennan, 1988; Danet, 1980; O'Barr, 1982), who understand precious little about the legal system.

Flin et al. (1989), for example, asked 105 Britons (children aged 6, 8, and 10 years, and adults) to complete a legal knowledge questionnaire designed to measure subjects' recognition, description, and conception of court-related terminology. Respondents performed best on vocabulary recognition, while encountering more difficulty with descriptions and concepts. Moreover, a clear developmental trend in children's performance emerged, replicating previous research findings from other countries.

For example, in the United States, Warren-Leubecker et al. (1989) developed a series of studies designed to investigate developmental trends in children's conceptions of the legal system. In the first study, 563 children ranging from 3 to 14 years of age completed a questionnaire containing court-related questions (e.g., "Do you know what a courtroom is?," "Who is in charge of a courtroom?," "What do lawyers do?"). Data analysis revealed fairly straightforward age trends in which older children possessed more knowledge of legal concepts than younger children. In a second study on an older population of 326 subjects ranging in age from 13 to 18 years, Warren-Leubecker et al. (1989) observed that although adolescents appeared to possess "accurate conceptions of most basic legal terms (e.g., judge, jury, lawyer), . . . their knowledge of more technical legal concepts and terms (e.g., perjury, manslaughter) was lacking" (p. 179).

Saywitz (1989) also examined developmental differences in children's conceptualizations of the judicial system. However, unlike Warren-Leubecker et al., Saywitz's sample included children with varied amounts of direct legal experience. In that study, 48 children ranging from 4 to 14 years of age participated in interviews focusing on knowledge of court-related concepts (e.g., jury, judge, truth-seeking process, witness credibility). Results indicated that children of different ages and varying amounts of experience bring different expectations to the courtroom, and that maturational processes play an important role in the development of children's legal knowledge. For example, children in the 8- to 11-year-old age range demonstrated an adequate understanding of the terms *court, judge, witness*, and *lawyer*, but few appeared to have mastered the concept of *jury*.

Recognizing the lack of empirically sound research investigating the relationship between children's development of communication skills and the task of testifying, Saywitz et al. (1990) examined age-related patterns in children's ability to communicate their understanding of commonly used legal terms. Using transcripts from actual legal proceedings, the researchers created a list of 35 legal terms which were used frequently in cases involving child witnesses. The legal terms were randomly assigned to two lists and administered to 60 public school students (20 of each grade: kindergarten, third, and sixth grades). Data analysis revealed grade-related patterns in children's knowledge of legal terms and in their misunderstanding of terms. Consider, for example, this case provided by Saywitz et al. (1990):

In court a child asked "to identify" an assailant failed to do so. Her failure damaged her credibility and surprised the adults. Previously, they had asked her "to point" to the person who hurt her and she had performed the task readily. (p. 523)

The authors concluded that "age-appropriate word choice in the examination of child witnesses may be an important factor in eliciting accurate testimony" (p. 531), and suggested that normative data should be gathered on age-related patterns of the use and understanding of legal terms commonly encountered by child witnesses.

The results of those research studies raise the question of whether children can be expected to understand and respond appropriately to the vocabulary and question forms typically employed by lawyers. Although increasing numbers of children are appearing as witnesses in court, few researchers have investigated the hypothesis that use of complex question forms actually subverts the truth-seeking function of the court (Danet, 1980; O'Barr, 1982). Two recently published studies systematically investigated that question (Brennan & Brennan, 1988; Walker, 1993).

Walker (1993) conducted a linguistic analysis of courtroom transcripts involving the testimony of a 5-year-old who had purportedly witnessed the murder of another child. Faced with the challenge of determining whether or not the child satisfied the legal requirements for competency, Walker found essentially no problems. The child demonstrated competence as both a speaker and a witness. However, there were serious problems with the adults' competence at asking questions. Walker's linguistic analysis revealed three potential problem areas when lawyers question children: (a) age-inappropriate words and expressions, (b) complex syntactic constructions, and (c) general ambiguity. Moreover, Walker noted that the most troublesome question form was one that presented more than one proposition but asked for only one yes-or-no answer. Review of Walker's case study suggests that additional studies involving more children of different ages must be conducted in order to assess developmental trends in children's ability to comprehend and respond to complex questions framed in the legal context.

Brennan and Brennan (1988) also conducted a study that addressed the issue of children's ability to process lawyers' questions. They analyzed 26 Australian transcripts in which children between 6 and 15 years of age gave evidence under cross-examination. From those transcripts, the researchers selected a representative list of attorneys' questions. Those questions, as well as representative questions from teachers and counselors, were orally presented to 30 children of varying language ability. The children heard legal and nonlegal questions of varying complexity, and then were asked to repeat them verbatim. Based upon a tradition of testing comprehension via repetition (e.g., Fraser, Bellugi, & Brown, 1963; Gleason, 1993), the researchers reasoned that ability to accurately reproduce language is the foundation of comprehension. For each question Brennan and Brennan calculated the number and type of repetition errors made by each child, and also assessed whether the child's version retained the general sense of the original question. Brennan and Brennan found that as questions became more courtroom specific and combative, children were less able to attend to and repeat the language of the questions. The researchers speculated that, under such circumstances, children would be less likely to respond in a meaningful and truthful way in court. However, Brennan and Brennan did not assess the children's ability to answer the questions posed, only their ability to repeat them.

Our study expands upon the Australian study in three important ways: First, we questioned children about a witnessed event, an experimental situation that more closely simulates the actual legal context. Second, children provided a self-assessment of their comprehension of each question, a technique that allowed us to test their metacognitive skills in a mock legal context. Third, children not only repeated question forms but also provided answers to the questions posed, an approach that assesses comprehension more completely than mere verbatim repetition. Thus, our study is a significant extension of Brennan and Brennan's work. To our knowledge, it is the first study of its kind to simultaneously (a) test children's understanding of typical courtroom question forms, (b) measure the accuracy of children's beliefs about whether or not the questions asked were comprehended, and (c) measure the accuracy of children's responses to both complex and simply phrased question forms.

We hypothesized that developmentally inappropriate questioning would significantly reduce the accuracy of witnesses' responses. Review of the extant literature on the development of language and metacognitive skill served as the basis for our predictions.

Language development

Children under the age of 6 have limited comprehension of negatives (Gaer, 1969; Gleason, 1993; Hopmann & Maratsos, 1977; Walker, 1994), and even for adults, a negative question is more difficult to understand than a positive one (deVilliers & deVilliers, 1979; Walker, 1994). Gleason (1989) reported that children can use both negative and simple sentences, but negative questions are much more difficult to understand, and generally are not fully comprehended before the age of 8. In addition, questions containing more than one negative are substantially more confusing than are single negative questions (Charrow & Charrow, 1979; Matthews & Saywitz, 1992; Walker, 1994). Moreover, many common legal terms are unfamiliar to or misinterpreted by children under 10 years of age (Flin et al., 1989; Pierre-Puysegur, 1985; Saywitz, 1989; Saywitz et al., 1990), and lengthy or complex compound sentences with embedded clauses typically are beyond the comprehension and memory of children younger than 8 years of age (Charrow & Charrow, 1979; Danet, 1980; Reich, 1986; Walker, 1993, 1994). When children answer compound questions, they often respond to only part of the question and seem not to realize that their answers may be interpreted by the listener as applying to other parts of the question as well (Dickson, 1981; Saywitz, 1995).

Metacognitive development

The ability to monitor one's mental processes, such as memory and knowledge, is known as metacognition. Even preschool-age children display some sensitivity in memory-monitoring activities (Cultice, Somerville, & Wellman, 1983), but metacognitive skill improves substantially with age (Markman, 1979; Wellman, 1977). Moreover, young children do not routinely ask for clarification, perhaps because they do not recognize when adult questions are confusing (Flavell, Speer, Green, & August, 1981; Markman, 1977, 1979; Saywitz, 1995; Saywitz & Snyder, 1991). For example, in one study, children were given instructions that omitted vital information. Nevertheless, 6-year-olds claimed to understand the directions, whereas 8-year-olds were likely to ask for more information (Markman, 1977, 1979). Yet, even when children do not understand questions about past events, they are likely to try to answer them anyway (Saywitz & Snyder, 1993). In fact, even when children are told that they may ask for clarifying information, they seldom do so (Cosgrove & Patterson, 1977; Patterson, Massad, & Cosgrove, 1978). Indeed, skill in knowing whether or not one understands a question and in using strategies for coping with noncomprehension develops quite gradually (Dickson, 1981; Flavell, 1981; Saywitz et al., 1990; Singer & Flavell, 1981), although recent research suggests that children's ability to detect and cope with noncomprehension may be enhanced through instruction and preparation (Saywitz, Nathanson, Snyder, & Lamphear, 1993).

The legal implication of the developmental literature on language and metacognitive development seems clear: Young children are likely to have communication and metacognitive difficulties when they serve as witnesses during legal proceedings because the typical language of lawyers is developmentally mismatched with the abilities of children. Therefore, we predicted that (a) younger children would have more difficulty answering lawyerlike questions (i.e., those involving negatives, double negatives, multipart constructions, difficult vocabulary, or complex syntax) than would older children or adults, and (b) children would have difficulty assessing whether or not they comprehended the complex questions they heard.

Method

Participants

One hundred twenty students participated in our study. We included 15 male and 15 female white, middle-class students from each of four populations: kindergarten, fourth grade, ninth grade, and college. Kindergarteners ranged in age from 5 years 4 months to 7 years 2 months ($M = 6$ years 0 months), fourth graders from 9 years 5 months to 10 years 8 months ($M = 9$ years 11 months), ninth graders from 14 years 1 month to 16 years 6 months ($M = 15$ years 0 months), and college students from 18 years 0 months to 22 years 3 months ($M = 19$ years 2 months).

Materials

We created two sets of materials: (a) a videotaped incident and (b) two sets of questions.

Videotaped incident. We videotaped a very brief incident (less than two minutes in duration) in which a 5-year-old girl (Katie) built several towers of blocks. A college-age male (Sam) entered the room, complained about his bad day, and asked Katie what she was doing. When she replied, Sam said he didn't care about her "stupid towers," and angrily left the room after knocking over her blocks. The incident ended with Katie wiping tears from her eyes.

Question forms. We also prepared two sets of questions concerning the people, actions, dialogue, and feelings involved in the videotaped incident (see table 11.1). One set (Lawyerese) included five forms of complex questions commonly used by attorneys (Brennan & Brennan, 1988; Danet, 1980; Goodman et al., 1992):

1   Negatives – that is, questions involving the word "not" (e.g., "Did Sam *not* knock over Katie's blocks?")

2   Double negatives – that is, questions involving the word "not" two times (e.g., "Did Sam *not* say he was *not* having a good day?")

3   Multipart – that is, questions involving two parts that have different answers (e.g., "At the end of the video, was Sam mad [yes] or was Katie happy? [no]")

4   Specific/difficult vocabulary – that is, questions including advanced vocabulary and/or legal terminology (e.g., "In the incident depicted, was the perpetrator in chartreuse apparel?")

5   Complex syntax – that is, sentence structure that is difficult to process (e.g., "At any time before or after she cried did the blocks fall down?")

In contrast, as table 11.1 also shows, in the second set of questions (Simplified), we eliminated those complicated forms and substituted simply phrased questions regarding the same content. For four of the five categories, simplified questions were of the same length (plus or minus one word). Questions that included complex syntax used two to three times as many words as their simplified counterparts. Questions asking for information about people, actions, dialogue, and feelings were counterbalanced across question type, as was the correctness of "yes" and "no" responses.

To summarize, we included four questions in each of five lawyerese categories and matched each one with a simplified version.

Table 11.1 Lawyerese and simplified questions

Lawyerese categories and questions	Simplified questions	Question reference	Correct response
1. Questions including a negative			
Did you not see a woman in the video? (9)	Did you see a woman in the video? (8)	Person	Yes/No
Did Sam not knock over Katie's blocks? (7)	Did Sam knock over Katie's blocks? (6)	Action	No/Yes
Did Sam not say, "I like your pretty towers"? (9)	Did Sam say, "I like your pretty towers"? (8)	Words	Yes/No
Was Sam not in a bad mood when he came in? (11)	Was Sam in a bad mood when he came in? (10)	Interpretation	No/Yes
2. Questions including a double negative			
Would you not say Katie did not have a red sweatshirt? (11)	Would you say that Katie had on a red sweatshirt? (10)	Person	Yes
Is it not true that Sam did not knock over the blocks? (12)	Is it true that Sam knocked over the towers of blocks? (11)	Action	Yes
Did Sam not say he was not having a good day? (11)	Did Sam say that he was having a very good day? (11)	Words	No
Is it not true that Katie did not make Sam cry? (11)	Is it true to say that Katie made Sam cry? (10)	Interpretation	No
3. Multipart questions			
Did you see a man and did he have gray hair? (11)	Did you see a man?	Person	Yes
	Did he have gray hair? (5 + 5 = 10)		No
Did Sam drink a glass of milk and did he knock over the towers? (14)	Did Sam drink a glass of milk?	Action	No
	Did Sam knock over the towers? (7 + 6 = 13)		Yes

Did Sam say he'd had a great day and say he didn't care about her stupid towers? (17)	Did Sam say he'd had a great day?	Words	No
	Did Sam say he didn't care about her stupid towers (8 + 10 = 18)		Yes
At the end of the video was Sam mad or was Katie happy? (13)	Was Sam mad at the end?	Interpretation	Yes
	Was Katie happy at the end? (6 + 6 = 12)		No
4. Questions including difficult vocabulary			
In the incident depicted, was the perpetrator in chartreuse apparel? (10)	In the video, was the bad guy wearing green clothes? (10)	Person	No
Was there a display of affection between the participants? (9)	Did you see Katie and Sam hug each other? (9)	Action	No
Did the victim acknowledge Sam's presence? (6)	Did Katie say "hi" to Sam? (6)	Words	Yes
Was the aggressor cantankerous? (4)	Did Sam seem grumpy? (4)	Interpretation	Yes
5. Questions involving complex syntax			
Would it be correct to suggest that the man in the video wearing red was named John? (17)	Was the man named John? (5)	Person	No
At any time before or after she cried did the blocks fall down? (13)	Did the blocks ever fall down? (6)	Action	Yes
Did the young man after the towers were built say his day was good? (14)	Did the man say he'd had a good day? (9)	Words	No
Was Katie, before everything happened at the beginning of the video, happy about her towers? (15)	Was Katie happy about her towers at first? (8)	Interpretation	Yes

Word count for each question appears in parentheses.

We intermingled all questions and presented them to students in random order.

Metacognitive assessment form. We made a two-dimensional mock stoplight by pasting red, yellow, and green circles on construction paper. Participants used the stoplight to indicate their level of comprehension for each question asked (green = *easy to comprehend*, yellow = *unsure*, red = *difficult to comprehend*).

Coding forms. We developed several forms to record data:

1   The Data Recording Sheet provided spaces for demographic information (e.g., date of birth, date of assessment, gender, year in school) and listed each question as well as its code and correct answer. That form also included spaces to record (a) whether the student had pointed to the red, green, or yellow light on the mock stoplight, (b) whether the student had responded "yes," "no," or "don't know" to each question, and (c) whether the student's response was correct, incorrect, or neither (i.e., "don't know").

2   The Question Repetition Form listed each question and its code, and provided space to record students' verbatim repetitions of the questions. We used that form to mark where the students' responses included additions, deletions, substitutions, and/or transpositions of words.

3   The Individual Subject Data Summary Form summarized the data from the other record forms and provided spaces to indicate for each question whether students' repetitions (a) retained the original sense of the question, (b) provided a sense of the question that was related to, but different from, the original, or (c) was unrelated to the original sense of the question.

Procedure

After establishing rapport, we trained each student in the method for answering questions: First, we asked the student to repeat the question verbatim. Second, using the mock stoplight made of construction paper, we asked the student to indicate whether the question was understood and could be answered. Specifically, we pointed to each color on the spotlight and said:

Green means the question is easy and you know how to answer it. Red means the question is hard and it can't be answered. Yellow means the question is easy, but you do not know how to answer it.

Third, we instructed the student to answer the question using one of three responses: (a) Yes, (b) No, or (c) I don't know. After explaining the process, we provided a trial run with questions unrelated to the study's purpose. When we were satisfied that the participant understood the procedure, we played the videotaped incident involving Katie and Sam.

Next, each student provided a free recall description of what had happened in the videotaped incident. We then reviewed the three-step procedure for answering questions (repeat, indicate comprehension, and answer) and asked the 44 questions listed in table 11.1.

We videotaped each student's responses for later coding, and used the coding forms to record data for each subject. Two individuals scored and evaluated each student's responses. For the several thousand data points, rater disagreements occurred on only a few occasions. When that happened, we discussed the responses as a research team and came to consensus about the appropriate way to score the responses.

We completed a series of 11 repeated measures analyses of variance with four levels for the between-subjects variable (age) and five levels for the withinsubjects variable (question type). We used Fisher's PLSD technique for post-hoc analyses of main effects, and Tukey's HSD procedure for post-hoc analyses of significant interactions. We analyzed data for several dependent measures: (a) errors in verbatim repetition, (b) retention of the sense of the questions asked, (c) comprehension of each question form, and (d) accuracy of students' responses.

Results

Collectively, the results confirmed our hypothesis that developmentally inappropriate questioning significantly reduces the accuracy of witnesses' responses. Table 11.2 provides a comparison of means for correct responses by question form and grade, and table 11.3 provides the same information for "don't know" responses.

Table 11.2 Means (and standard deviations) for correct responses by question type and grade

Question type	Kindergarten	Fourth grade	Ninth grade	College
Negative form	1.3 (1.0)	1.8 (1.2)	2.1 (1.3)	2.3 (1.2)
Simplified	3.2 (0.7)	3.7 (0.5)	3.7 (0.6)	3.7 (0.7)
Double negative form	1.8 (0.9)	1.7 (0.9)	1.4 (1.3)	1.6 (1.0)
Simplified	2.6 (0.9)	3.5 (0.9)	3.6 (0.5)	3.4 (0.9)
Multifaceted form	0.5 (1.0)	0.6 (0.9)	1.3 (1.5)	0.1 (0.4)
Simplified	3.1 (0.8)	3.7 (0.4)	3.6 (0.4)	3.5 (0.8)
Difficult vocabulary form	1.2 (1.1)	1.2 (1.0)	1.8 (0.7)	2.2 (1.0)
Simplified	2.8 (0.8)	3.1 (0.8)	3.2 (0.7)	3.3 (0.7)
Complexly embedded proposition form	2.2 (1.0)	3.2 (0.7)	3.0 (0.9)	3.0 (0.8)
Simplified	2.8 (1.0)	3.6 (0.9)	3.5 (0.6)	3.6 (0.6)

Table 11.3 Means (standard deviations), and percentages for "don't know" responses by question type and grade

Question type	Kindergarten	Fourth grade	Ninth grade	College
Lawyerese ($n = 20$)	3.0 (2.3)	4.1 (2.6)	4.9 (3.3)	3.8 (2.6)
	14.8%	20.3%	24.5%	19.2%
Simplified ($n = 20$)	1.2 (1.9)	1.0 (1.1)	2.2 (1.8)	1.8 (2.7)
	5.8%	5.1%	11.1%	8.8%

How well could witnesses of each age repeat various question forms?

Regardless of age, students made significantly more errors – including additions, deletions, substitutions, and transpositions – when repeating lawyerese ($M = 58.4$) as opposed to simply phrased questions

(M = 11.2), $F(1,113)$ = 735.6, p < .0001. We found a predictable developmental trend in children's ability to repeat the questions verbatim, with kindergarteners making significantly more repetition errors (M = 71.4) than the older students (M = 36.8, 16.7, 16.7, for fourth grade, ninth grade, and college students, respectively), $F(3,113)$ = 62.6, p < .0001. Fisher's PLSD revealed significant mean differences (p < .0001) for all pairwise comparisons except the comparison of ninth graders with college students.

The question type by grade interaction also was significant for the errors analysis, $F(3,113)$ = 55.6, p < .0001. Tukey's HSD procedure for simple effects demonstrated that, at all grade levels, students made significantly more errors when repeating lawyerese (M = 112.1, 64.4, 31.3, and 29.4 for kindergarten, fourth, ninth, and college students, respectively) as opposed to simple questions (M = 30.7, 9.3, 2.1, 4.1 for kindergarten, fourth, ninth, and college students, respectively). The mean differences (81.5, 55.1, 10.3, and 25.3 for kindergarten, fourth, ninth, and college students, respectively) were significant, with p < .01 in all cases. Moreover, on the lawyerese questions, kindergarteners produced significantly more errors than did fourth graders (mean difference = 47.7, p < .01), ninth graders (mean difference = 80.9, p < .01), and college students (mean difference = 82.8, p < .01). Similarly, on the lawyerese questions, fourth graders produced significantly more errors than did ninth graders (mean difference = 33.1, p < .01) and college students (mean difference = 35.0, p < .01). Finally, kindergarteners produced significantly more errors on the simplified questions (M = 30.7) than did the older students (M = 9.3, 2.1, and 4.1 for fourth-grade, ninth-grade, and college students, respectively). The mean differences between kindergarteners and older students were significant, p < .01 (mean difference = 21.4, 28.6, and 26.6 for fourth, ninth, and college comparisons, respectively). Thus, the simple effects analyses revealed that although students of all grade levels had more difficulty repeating lawyerese questions than simplified questions, grade level served as a mediating variable. Kindergarteners had significant difficulty repeating both types of questions, whereas fourth graders had more difficulty with lawyerese than simplified questions; ninth graders and college students demonstrated no significant differences in error rates for either lawyerese or simplified question forms.

How often did witnesses repeat the sense of the questions?

We calculated a score for the sense of the question by examining the number and type of errors (additions, deletions, substitutions, and transpositions) made by each student in repeating each question. If the original meaning of the question was preserved in the student's repetition (regardless of errors in verbatim repetition), we scored the response as 1; however, if the original meaning of the question was changed, we scored the response as 0. For example, one student's addition of two important words to a question resulted in a score of 0 (Did Sam not say, "I *do not* like your pretty towers?"), whereas the same student's addition of one unimportant word to another question resulted in a score of 1 (Did the young man after the towers were built say *that* his day was good?).

The main effect for question type was significant, $F(1,110) = 753.9$, $p < .0001$, indicating that the sense of simply phrased questions ($M = 17.6$) was preserved significantly more often than the sense of lawyerese questions ($M = 10.9$). The main effect for grade also was significant, $F(3,100) = 57.5$, $p < .0001$, demonstrating a significant developmental trend ($M = 9.6$, 13.9, 16.5, and 16.3 for kindergarteners, fourth graders, ninth graders, and college students, respectively). Fisher's PLSD revealed that all pairwise comparisons except the ninth grade–college comparison were significant, $p < .0001$.

The age by question type interaction also was significant, $F(3,110) = 31.0$, $p < .0001$. Regardless of question type, kindergarteners retained the sense of the question significantly less often than did older students (lawyerese $M = 4.5$, 9.9, 13.9, 14.3 for kindergarten, fourth-grade, ninth-grade, and college students; simplified $M = 14.6$, 18.0, 19.1, 18.4 for kindergarten, fourth-grade, ninth-grade, and college students). For the lawyerese questions, Tukey's HSD procedure for simple effects produced significant mean differences ($p < .01$) for the comparisons between kindergarteners and fourth graders (mean difference $= -5.4$), ninth graders (mean difference $= -9.4$), and college students (mean difference $= -9.8$); and between fourth graders and ninth graders (mean difference $= -4.0$) and college students (mean difference $= -4.4$). For the simplified questions, Tukey's HSD produced significant mean differences ($p < .01$) for the comparisons between kindergarteners and older students (mean differences = −3.4, −4.4, and −3.8 for fourth-grade, ninth-grade, and college students, respectively). When questions were phrased simply, on average, fourth-grade, ninth-grade, and college students maintained the original sense of the question more than 90% of the time, whereas kindergarteners conveyed the sense of the question only about 70% of the time. In contrast, with lawyerese questions, performance averaged only 70% for older students, with fourth graders and kindergarteners performing at less than 50% and 25% accuracy, respectively. Thus, regardless of question type, kindergarteners had significantly more difficulty than older students retaining the original sense of the questions asked, whereas fourth graders had more trouble retaining the sense of only the lawyerese questions; older students demonstrated no significant differences in their ability to retain the original sense of the questions asked.

How well could witnesses of each age assess comprehension of the questions?

We focused on only one color of the mock stoplight (green) in the comprehension analysis. When a student indicated green on the spotlight, he or she essentially was saying, "the question is easy and I know how to answer it," thus indicating confidence in correctly answering the question. For purposes of assessing comprehension, we defined a metacognitive hit as the match between a student indicating that the question was easy to answer and answering the question correctly. We scored hits as 1. Whenever the student touched green on the spotlight (indicating that the question was easy and could be answered), but answered the question incorrectly, we scored the miss as 0. In order to control for response set (i.e., the tendency to prefer one color on the stoplight), we divided the number of hits by the number of green responses, resulting in a score for percent hits.

When collapsed across ages, students had a mean metacognitive hit rate of 90% for simplified questions, but a mean hit rate of only 54% for lawyerese questions (barely above the 50% chance level), $F(1,111) = 587.8, p < .0001$. In other words, regardless of age, students were well able to assess when they comprehended simply worded questions, but demonstrated very poor performance in assessing their comprehension of complex question forms. The repeated measures ANOVA and Fisher's PLSD post-hoc analysis revealed a significant developmental trend,

$F(3,111) = 27.9$, $p < .0001$. Collapsed across question type, kindergarteners ($M = 54.8\%$) were significantly less likely to earn hits than were older students ($M = 72.9\%$, 80.3%, and 76.5% for fourth graders, ninth graders, and college students, respectively). The age by question type interaction was not significant.

Two conclusions regarding metacognitive skill seem appropriate. First, kindergarteners performed significantly more poorly than their older counterparts regardless of question type. This result suggests that, not surprisingly, the youngest children had difficulty using our metacognitive strategy to indicate level of comprehension. Second, regardless of age, students had difficulty with metacognitive monitoring for the lawyerese questions. In other words, students of all ages frequently were fooled into thinking that the lawyerese questions were easy to answer when, in fact, they were not; rarely did such a result occur for the simplified questions.

How well could witnesses of each age answer the questions?

We scored a response as accurate if the student gave the correct answer to the dichotomous (yes–no) question, or as inaccurate if the student gave the wrong answer. We analyzed "don't know" responses separately because they fell into neither the correct nor the incorrect category.

"Don't know" responses. Table 11.3 provides the means, standard deviations, and mean percentages of "don't know" responses by grade and question type. As inspection of the table reveals, students gave significantly more "don't know" responses to the 20 lawyerese questions ($M = 3.9$) than to the 20 simplified questions ($M = 1.5$), $F(1,116) = 137.9$, $p < .0001$. The main effect for grade also was significant, $F(3,116) = 2.8$, $p < .05$ ($M = 2.1$, 2.5, 3.6, 2.8, for kindergarten, fourth-grade, ninth-grade, and college students, respectively), although the interaction was not. Fisher's PLSD revealed that the significant effect for grade was accounted for by the mean difference (-1.5) between kindergarteners and ninth graders.

Incorrect responses. For questions answered, the number of incorrect responses was inversely proportional to the number of correct responses. Therefore, we analyzed only correct responses.

Correct responses. On average, students correctly answered twice as many simply phrased questions ($M = 16.8$) as lawyerese forms ($M = 8.7$), $F(1,113) = 1013.0$, $p < .0001$. The main effect for grade also was significant, $F(3,113) = 11.3$, $p < .0001$ ($M = 10.9$, 13.1, 13.6, 13.3 for kindergarten, fourth-grade, ninth-grade, and college students, respectively), although the interaction was not. Fisher's PLSD revealed that the significant main effect for grade was accounted for by the kindergarten students, with mean differences of -2.1, -2.7, and -2.4 for the comparisons with fourth-grade, ninth-grade, and college students, respectively.

The analysis assessing the ability to correctly answer negative questions – that is, those involving the word "not" – revealed that the main effects for both question type, $F(1,115) = 194.1$, $p < .0001$ ($M = 1.9$ and 3.6 for negative and simplified questions, respectively), and grade, $F(3,115) = 7.0$, $p = .0002$, were significant. Simple questions were relatively easy for all ages to answer ($M = 3.2$, 3.7, 3.7, and 3.7 for kindergarten, fourth-grade, ninth-grade, and college students, respectively), whereas questions involving the word "not" were more difficult ($M = 1.3$, 1.8, 2.1, and 2.3 for kindergarten, fourth-grade, ninth-grade, and college students, respectively). The interaction was not significant.

The analysis of double negative questions – that is, those including two negative expressions within one question – produced no significant main effect for age. However, the main effect for question type was significant ($M = 1.6$ and 3.3 for lawyerese and simplified forms, respectively), $F(1,114) = 230.3$, $p < .0001$, as was the interaction of grade and question type, $F(3,114) = 7.5$, $p = .0001$. Tukey's HSD revealed significant differences between the mean number of correct responses to double negative and simplified question forms at all ages ($M = 1.8$ versus 2.6 for kindergarteners, 1.7 versus 3.5 for fourth graders, 1.4 versus 3.6 for ninth graders, and 1.6 versus 3.4 for college students). Although the older children answered the simplified questions quite well ($M = 3.5$, 3.6, and 3.4 for fourth-grade, ninth-grade, and college students, respectively), kindergarteners ($M = 2.6$) did not fare so well. In fact, kindergarteners showed significantly poorer performance that students from each of the other grade levels, $p < .01$ in all cases.

All age groups experienced difficulty trying to answer questions containing two contradictory clauses. No age group scored over 33% accuracy on that lawyerese style, and the college students scored an abysmally low 2% accuracy, a finding that baffled us. The main effect for grade was significant, $F(3,115) = 7.0$, $p = .0002$ ($M = 1.8$, 2.1, 2.5, 1.8 for kindergarten, fourth-grade, ninth-grade, and college students, respectively). Fisher's PLSD revealed that the effect for age was accounted for by the ninth-grade students, with mean differences of -0.7, -0.3, and 0.7 for the kindergarten, fourth-grade, and college student comparisons, respectively. The main effect for question type also was significant, $F(1,115) = 812.7$, $p < .0001$ ($M = 0.6$ and 3.5 for multipart and simplified questions, respectively). All age groups showed marked improvement when the two question parts were asked separately as opposed to in the combined form ($M = 3.1$ versus 0.5 for kindergarteners, 3.7 versus 0.6 for fourth graders, 3.6 versus 1.3 for ninth graders, and 3.5 versus 0.1 for college students, respectively), $p < .01$ in all cases. The grade by question type interaction also was significant for the multipart questions analysis, $F(3,115) = 6.7$, $p = .0003$. Tukey's HSD procedure revealed that the significant interaction effect was accounted for primarily by the ninth-grade students' performing significantly better on the multipart questions ($M = 1.3$) than the other students ($M = 0.5$, 0.6, 0.1 for kindergarteners, fourth graders, and college students, respectively), $p < .01$ for kindergarten and college comparisons, and $p < .05$ for fourth grade comparison.

The analysis of questions involving difficult or specific vocabulary produced a predictable developmental trend ($M = 2.0$, 2.2, 2.5, 2.7 for kindergarten, fourth-grade, ninth-grade, and college students, respectively), $F(3,114) = 5.9$, $p = .0009$. Three of the pairwise comparisons obtained using Fisher's PLSD were significant: kindergarten versus ninth grade (M difference $= -0.5$), kindergarten versus college (M difference $= -0.7$), and fourth grade versus college (M difference $= -0.5$). The question type analysis also was significant, $F(3,114) = 225.1$, $p < .0001$. Replacing difficult vocabulary ($M = 1.6$) with simple, nontechnical terms ($M = 3.1$) was associated with significantly improved performance. The age by question type interaction also was significant, $F(3,114) = 2.9$, $p < .04$. Tukey's HSD procedure revealed that, at all grade levels, students correctly responded to questions including difficult vocabulary significantly less often ($p < .01$) than to simplified questions ($M = 1.2$ versus 2.8 for kindergarteners, 1.2 versus 3.1 for fourth graders, 1.8 versus 3.2 for ninth graders, and 2.2 versus 3.3 for college students). For questions including difficult vocabulary, kindergarteners and fourth graders responded correctly significantly less often than college students (mean difference $= -0.9$, $p < .01$).

Students seemed less confused by questions we devised that included complex syntax than by any other lawyerese form. That finding could be an artifact of our question design, because many of our syntactic complexities did not concern event-salient points. Even so, that question type analysis still was significant (M = 2.9 and 3.4 for lawyerese and simplified forms, respectively), $F(1,114)$ = 29.6, $p < .0001$, as was the main effect for age (M = 2.5, 3.4, 3.3, 3.3 for kindergarten, fourth-grade, ninth-grade, and college students, respectively), $F(3,114) = 11.5$, $p < .0001$. Fisher's PLSD showed that the main effect for age was accounted for by the relatively poor performance of the kindergarten students (M difference $= -0.9$, -0.8, and -0.8 for the comparisons with fourth-grade, ninth-grade, and college students, respectively). The grade by question type interaction was not significant.

Figure 11.1 summarizes the overall results. As the figure suggests, kindergarten children could correctly answer the simply phrased questions approximately 70% of the time; whereas almost 90% accuracy was achieved by older students. Moreover, students of all ages had difficulty answering lawyerese questions. Across age groups, children were relatively adept at answering questions involving complex syntax. In contrast, students of all ages had considerable difficulty answering other forms of lawyerese questions. Specifically, students of all ages had difficulty correctly answering questions with multiple parts having mutually exclusive answers (e.g., "At the end of the video, was Sam mad [yes] or was Katie happy? [no]"). Indeed, correct answers to that question form never exceeded 35%. On average, children and young adults produced correct responses to questions involving negatives, double negatives, or difficult vocabulary only 50% of the time at best.

What was the relationship between ability to accurately repeat questions and to correctly answer them?

In order to assess the relationship between repetition and response accuracy, we calculated four Pearson correlation coefficients. The number of repetition errors committed was negatively related to accuracy of response, $r = -.657$, $p < .0001$, and positively correlated with inaccuracy, $r = .544$, $p < .0001$. Conversely, maintenance of the original meaning of the question was positively related to response accuracy,

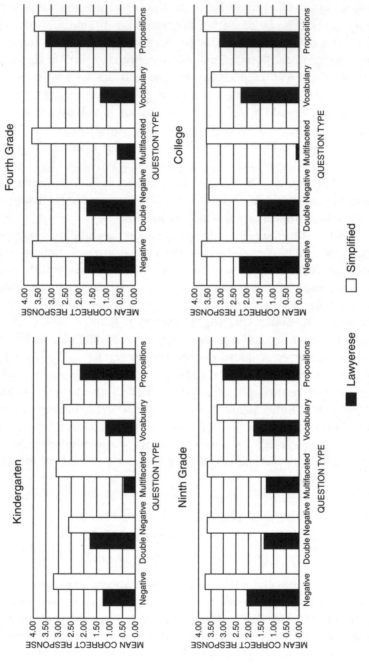

Figure 11.1 Mean correct responses by question type and grade

$r = .678$, $p < .0001$, but negatively correlated with incorrect responses, $r = -.606$, $p < .0001$.

Discussion

Our results strongly support the hypothesis that developmentally inappropriate questioning reduces both witness comprehension and the accuracy of witnesses' responses. When questions are difficult and/or complex, children's comprehension suffers, as does that of adolescents and young adults. In other words, the mismatch between the language capacities of child witnesses and the courtroom language commonly employed by attorneys does, indeed, obfuscate communication. The likely result is that, under such circumstances, witnesses – especially those who are children – cannot tell "the truth, the whole truth, and nothing but the truth."

Thus, our results add to a data base supporting the assertion made by Saywitz et al. (1993):

> Lying, fantasizing, and coaching are not the *only* reasons why a child's testimony might seem unbelievable or unreliable. Another plausible reason is the mismatch between the linguistic, cognitive, and emotional worlds of children and adults, a mismatch that obfuscates communication with child witnesses. (p. 76)

Our results also suggest that even 5- to 6-year-old children can correctly answer most simply phrased, straightforward questions regarding a recently viewed event of short duration, although their ability is less well developed than that of individuals aged 9 years or older. In contrast, children, adolescents, and young adults alike are befuddled by convoluted question forms, whether they know it or not.

Finally, some forms of lawyerese seem to be more pernicious than others. For example, questions that include multiple parts with mutually exclusive answers seem particularly difficult to answer, a finding that replicates the results of Walker's (1993) linguistic case study. Questions that include negatives, double negatives, or difficult vocabulary also pose significant problems, a finding that supports the conclusions of several researchers (e.g., Cashmore & Bussey, 1990; Charrow & Charrow, 1979; Flin et al., 1989; Gaer, 1969; Melton, Limber, Jacobs,

& Oberlander, 1992; Pierre-Puysegur, 1985; Saywitz, 1989; Saywitz et al., 1990; Saywitz & Snyder, 1993; Stevens & Berlinger, 1980; Walker, 1993; Warren-Leubecker et al., 1989).

Our results also indicate that the ability to accurately repeat a question is related to the ability to correctly answer it. This finding provides some corroboration for Brennan and Brennan's (1988) assumption that skill in accurately reproducing language is the foundation of comprehension. Of course, ability to parrot back a short sentence is not necessarily an indication that the sentence was comprehended, so this result should be applied very cautiously, especially in legal contexts where witness responses may have serious consequences for defendants.

Certain factors limit the generalizability of our results to the courtroom setting. First, our witnessed incident was very brief, and questioning occurred immediately after participants watched the videotaped event. In actual investigations, witnessed events may be long, complex, and emotionally compelling; moreover, questioning may be delayed by hours, days, weeks, or even years (Flin, Boon, Knox, & Bull, 1992). Second, we asked only four questions per category of lawyerese, certainly a minimal number. Third, our questions required only dichotomous yes–no responses, which some researchers have found problematic (e.g., Boyd, 1993; Dent & Stephenson, 1979; Poole & White, 1991; White, 1990). Although forced-choice questioning is common in the courtroom (Brennan & Brennan, 1988), children often are asked to provide more complex free narrative as well.

Although these factors reduce the ecological validity of our laboratory study, real-world conditions (e.g., open-ended and more complex questions, greater time delays between event and questioning, stressful conditions, multiple interviewers) should serve to exacerbate rather than reduce communication difficulties. Therefore, the fact that we found highly significant results in a laboratory study suggests that the miscommunication effects may be quite robust.

Despite the limitations inherent in our study, our results add to a growing body of literature regarding communication with children in forensic contexts. The results of investigations completed to date provide support for the contention that changes in questioning procedures used in legal proceedings involving children are long overdue. Stafford (1962) noted more than 30 years ago that "Questions should be kept within the grasp of the child's mind. . . . Interrogators should remember that questions which seem simple and direct to them may be confusing or absolutely meaningless to a child" (p. 314). More recently, Hafemeister (1994) surveyed 227 state trial court judges regarding the appropriateness of a variety of methods designed to reduce the traumatization of child witnesses. The survey revealed that 99.2% of the judges surveyed believed that "specific attention should be paid to posing questions at a level the child can understand" (p. 12).

Our study provides empirical support for the recommendations offered by Stafford (1962) and Hafemeister (1994) and calls into question the assumption that such purportedly communicative procedures as examination and cross-examination necessarily get at the truth of the case when children testify. Although the US Supreme Court opined that "cross-examination is beyond any doubt the greatest legal engine ever invented for the discovery of the truth" (*California v. Green*, 1970, cited in McGough, 1993), others disagree. For example, Whately (cited in McGough, 1993) suggested that "the kind of skill by which the cross-examiner succeeds in alarming, misleading, or bewildering an honest witness may be characterized as the most, or one of the most, base and depraved of all possible employments of intellectual power" (p. 1).

Courtroom justice requires congruity between the language of the courtroom and the language capacities of witnesses, whether those witnesses are children, adolescents, or adults. The results of our study point toward specific strategies for remediation. Thus, we offer the following recommendations:

1   The language of the courtroom should be simplified. Judges should insist that attorneys (and other professionals) ask witnesses simply phrased questions.

2   Specifically, courts should require professionals to eliminate the use of the following question forms: negatives, double negatives, questions with multiple parts, and questions that employ difficult vocabulary. Our results suggest that eliminating such question forms is imperative when young children give evidence, and clearly is advisable even when older children, adolescents, and adults testify.

3   Lawyers and judges, as well as other professionals who work with child witnesses, should receive specialized training in developmentally appropriate questioning techniques. Saywitz (1994; 1995) and Walker (1994) provide excellent descriptions of such techniques.

Additional investigation into children's communication in forensic contexts also is warranted. Specifically, it would be fruitful to investigate the following areas: (a) Children's comprehension of questions concerning longer and/or more complex witnessed events involving longer postevent delays; (b) the comprehension of 3- and 4-year-olds, and of those from different cultural and socioeconomic backgrounds; (c) the effect of follow-up questions designed to encourage children to justify, clarify, and elaborate on responses to forced-choice questions; and (d) the effect of skeptical or combative questioning on child witnesses' comprehension and responses.

References

Boyd, C. J. (1993). *Questioning techniques of Child Protective Service workers.* Unpublished master's thesis, The University of Tennessee at Chattanooga.

Brennan, M., & Brennan, R. E. (1988). *Strange language: Child victims under cross examination* (3rd edn). Wagga Wagga, NSW: Charles Sturt University – Riverina.

California v. Green, 399 U.S. 149 (1970).

Cashmore, J., & Bussey, K. (1990). Children's conceptions of the witness role. In J. Spencer, G. Nicholson, R. Flin, & R. Bull (eds.), *Children's evidence in legal proceedings: An international perspective* (pp. 177–88). Cambridge: University of Cambridge.

Charrow, R. P., & Charrow, V. R. (1979). Making legal language understandable: A psycholinguistic study of jury instruction. *The Columbia Law Review, 79,* 1307–74.

Cosgrove, J. M., & Patterson, C. J. (1977). Plans and the development of listener skills. *Developmental Psychology, 13,* 557–64.

Cultice, J. C., Somerville, S. C., & Wellman, H. M. (1983). Preschoolers' memory monitoring: Feeling-of-knowing judgments. *Child Development, 54,* 1480–6.

Danet, B. (1980). Language in the legal process. *Law & Society Review, 14,* 445–564.

Dent, H. R. (1982). The effects of interviewing strategies on the results of interviews with child witnesses. In A. Trankell (ed.), *Reconstructing the past: The role of psychologists in criminal trials* (pp. 279–97). Stockholm: Norstedt.

Dent, H. R., & Stephenson, G. M. (1979). An experimental study of the effectiveness of different techniques of questioning child witnesses. *British Journal of Social and Clinical Psychology, 18,* 41–51.

deVilliers, P., & deVilliers, J. (1979). *The developing child.* Cambridge, MA: Harvard University.

Dickson, W. P. (1981). *Children's oral communication skills.* New York: Academic Press.

Flavell, J. H. (1981). Cognitive monitoring. In W. P. Dickson (ed.), *Children's oral communication skills* (pp. 35–60). New York: Academic Press.

Flavell, J. H., Speer, J. R., Green, F. L., & August, D. L. (1981). The development of comprehension monitoring and knowledge about communication. *Monographs of the Society for Research in Child Development, 46* (5, Serial No. 192).

Flin, R., Boon, J., Knox, A., & Bull, R. (1992). The effect of a five month delay on children's and adults' eyewitness memory. *British Journal of Psychology, 83*, 323–36.

Flin, R., Stevenson, Y., & Davies, G. M. (1989). Children's knowledge of court proceedings. *British Journal of Psychology, 80*, 285–97.

Fraser, C., Bellugi, U., & Brown, R. (1963). Control of grammar in imitation, comprehension, and production. *Journal of Verbal Learning and Verbal Behavior, 2*, 121–35.

Gaer, E. P. (1969). Children's understanding and production of sentences. *Journal of Verbal Learning and Verbal Behavior, 8*, 289–94.

Gleason, J. B. (1989). *The development of language.* Columbus, OH: Merrill.

Gleason, J. B. (1993). Language development: An overview and a preview (pp. 1–37). In J. B. Gleason (ed.), *The development of language* (3rd edn). New York: Macmillan.

Goodman, G. S., Taub, E. P., Jones, D. P. H., England, P., Port, L. K., Rudy, L., & Prado, L. (1992). Testifying in criminal court. *Monographs of the Society for Research in Child Development, 57* (5, Serial No. 229).

Hafemeister, T. L. (1994, March). *Efforts to minimize trauma to child witnesses: A judicial appraisal of the best means to bring related information to their attention.* In M. J. Saks (Chair), *Disseminating information to the judiciary.* Presented to the biennial meeting of the American Psychology–Law Society, Santa Fe, NM.

Hopmann, M. R., & Maratsos, M. P. (••). A developmental study of factivity and negation in complex syntax. *Journal of Child Language, 5*, 295–309.

Markman, E. M. (1977). Realizing that you don't understand: A preliminary investigation. *Child Development, 48*, 986–92.

Markman, E. M. (1979). Realizing that you don't understand: Elementary school children's awareness of inconsistencies. *Child Development, 50*, 643–55.

Matthews, E., & Saywitz, K. (1992). Child victim witness manual. *CJER Journal, 12*, 1–69.

McGough, L. (1993, March). Policy implications. In N. W. Perry (Chair), *The child witness: Does legal policy reflect empirical evidence?* Symposium conducted at the biennial meeting of the Society for Research in Child Development, New Orleans, LA.

Melton, G., Limber, S., Jacobs, J., & Oberlander, L. (1992). *Preparing sexually abused children for testimony: Children's perceptions of the legal process* [Final report to the National Center on Child Abuse & Neglect, Grant No. 90-CA-1274]. Lincoln, NE: University of Nebraska–Lincoln.

O'Barr, W. M. (1982). *Language, power, and strategy in the courtroom.* New York: Academic Press.

Patterson, C. J., Massad, C. M., & Cosgrove, J. M. (1978). Children's referential communication: Components of plans for effective listening. *Developmental Psychology, 14,* 401–6.

Pierre-Puysegur, M. (1985, July). *The representations of the penal system among children from six to ten years.* Presented at the 8th biennial meeting of the International Society for the Study of Behavioral Development, Tours, France.

Poole, D. A., & White, L. T. (1991). Effects of question repetition on the eyewitness testimony of children and adults. *Developmental Psychology, 27,* 975–86.

Reich, P. (1986). *Language development.* Englewood Cliffs, NJ: Prentice-Hall.

Saywitz, K. J. (1989). Children's conceptions of the legal system: Court is a place to play basketball. In S. J. Ceci, D. F. Ross, & M. P. Toglia (eds.), *Perspectives on children's testimony* (pp. 131–57). New York: Springer-Verlag.

Saywitz, K. J. (1994). Children in court: Principles of child development for judicial application. In J. Bulkley, & C. Sandt (eds.), *A judicial primer on child sexual abuse.* Washington DC: American Bar Association.

Saywitz, K. J. (1995). Improving children's testimony: The question, the answer, and the environment. In M. S. Zaragoza, J. R. Graham, G. C. N. Hall, R. Hirschman, & Y. S. Ben-Parath (eds.), *Memory and testimony in the child witness.* Thousand Oaks, CA: Sage.

Saywitz, K. J., & Goodman, G. S. (in press). Interviewing children in and out of court: Current research and practical implications. In L. Berliner, J. Briere, & J. Bulkley (eds.), *APSAC Handbook on Child Maltreatment.* Newbury Park, CA: Sage.

Saywitz, K., Jaenicke, C., & Camparo, L. (1990). Children's knowledge of legal terminology. *Law and Human Behavior, 14,* 523–35.

Saywitz, K. J., Nathanson, R., & Snyder, L. (1993). Credibility of child witnesses: The role of communicative competence. In L. S. Snyder, & K. J. Saywitz (eds.), *Topics in Language Disorders, 13,* 59–78.

Saywitz, K. J., Nathanson, R., Snyder, L., & Lamphear, V. (1993). *Preparing children for the investigative and judicial process: Improving communication, memory and emotional resiliency* (Report No. 90CA1179). Washington DC: National Center on Child Abuse and Neglect.

Saywitz, K. J., & Snyder, L. (1991, April). *Preparing child witnesses: The efficacy of comprehension monitoring training.* Paper presented at the biennial convention of the Society for Research in Child Development, Seattle, WA.

Saywitz, K. J., & Snyder, L. (1993). Improving children's testimony with preparation. In G. Goodman, & B. Bottoms (eds.), *Child victims, child witnesses* (pp. 117–46). New York: Guilford Publications.

Singer, J., & Flavell, J. (1981). Development of knowledge about communication: Children's evaluations of explicitly ambiguous messages. *Child Development, 52,* 1211–15.

Stafford, C. E. (1962). The child as a witness. *Washington Law Review, 37,* 303–24.

Stevens, D., & Berlinger, L. (1980). Special techniques for child witnesses. In L. G. Shulz (ed.), *The sexual victimology of youth* (pp. 246–56). Springfield, IL: Thomas.

Walker, A. G. (1987). Linguistic manipulation, power, and the legal system. In L. Kedar (ed.), *Power through discourse* (pp. 57–80). Norwood, NJ: Ablex.

Walker, A. G. (1993). Questioning young children in court: A linguistic case study. *Law and Human Behavior, 17,* 59–81.

Walker, A. G. (1994). *Handbook on questioning children: A linguistic perspective.* Washington, DC: American Bar Association Center on Children and the Law.

Warren-Leubecker, A., Tate, C., Hinton, I., & Ozbek, I. (1989). What do children know about the legal system and when do they know it? First steps down a less traveled path in child witness research. In S. Ceci, D. Ross, & M. Toglia (eds.), *Perspectives on children's testimony* (pp. 158–83). New York: Springer-Verlag.

Wellman, H. M. (1977). The early development of intentional memory behavior. *Human Development, 20,* 86–101.

White, S. (1990). The investigatory interview with suspected victims of child sexual abuse. In A. M. La Greca (ed.), *Through the eyes of the child: Obtaining self-reports from children and adolescents* (pp. 368–94). Boston: Allyn & Bacon.

Children as Perpetrators

TWELVE

The Development of Offending

Introduction

The papers in parts II, III and IV have involved experimental or quasi-experimental designs in which the investigators have manipulated some variables and examined the effects of these and other pre-existing variables (for example gender) on the participants in these studies. Although it is not possible experimentally to manipulate whether children offend and, if so, by how much, a lot nevertheless can be learned from longitudinal developmental studies, as was the case for aspects of part I of this book on victimization. (Longitudinal studies are those where the *same* children are tested several times over a period of time, often years.)

Thus, learning more about the developmental psychology of offending (like that of victimization) requires somewhat different investigatory skills from those typically employed in studies of children as (usually mock) victims/witnesses. However, what developmental psychology has learned about child victims in terms of the reliability of their accounts (part II), of their appreciation of truth/lies (part III), and of their treatment by the legal system (part IV) could be generalized to child perpetrators. Unfortunately, such generalization is very slow to take place in many countries.

What many countries are becoming ever more aware of, thanks to developmental research, is the factors that put children at risk of offending. The study by Rolf Loeber and colleagues is a fine example of what can be achieved if sufficient resources are made available for the large, complex studies that seem necessary.

Suggested reading

Farrington, D. (1999). Criminal careers of two London cohorts. *Criminal Behaviour and Mental Health*, 9, 91–106.

The Development of Male Offending: Key Findings from the First Decade of the Pittsburgh Youth Study

Rolf Loeber, David P. Farrington, Magda Stouthamer-Loeber, Terrie E. Moffitt, and Avshalom Caspi

Although there are a plethora of longitudinal studies on the development of antisocial and delinquent behavior (for a recent overview, see Loeber, Farrington, Stouthamer-Loeber, & Van Kammen, 1988a), many of them have serious limitations. First, although it has been long known that an early onset of offending during the elementary school period predicts later chronic offending (Loeber, 1982), few studies started with preadolescent samples. Second, many studies did not start by measuring lifetime delinquent behavior at the first assessment; as a result, it is often impossible to gauge whether the measured onset of delinquent acts (e.g., in the previous year) was truly an onset, or a mere repetition of behavior. Third, many studies had relatively small samples, making it difficult to trace the antecedents and causes of relatively low prevalence, serious delinquency. Fourth, attrition in many studies is often relatively high (Capaldi & Patterson, 1987), which by necessity affects statistical power and casts doubts on the validity of conclusions drawn from the data. Lastly, many studies have only two or three assessments spaced over many years. This makes it impossible to trace the development of deviancy and the duration of exposure to risk factors, which only can be achieved by regular assessments of risk factors *and* outcomes at frequent (e.g., yearly) intervals. These were the main reasons to start the Pittsburgh Youth Study, which is a prospective longitudinal survey of the development of juvenile offending, mental health problems, and drug use, and their risk factors in three samples of inner-city boys. The current paper concentrates on the development of delinquency.

Participants in the study included preadolescent and adolescent boys: the first assessment included lifetime measurements up to that point; subsequent assessments were carried out at half-yearly intervals (later changed to yearly intervals) without interruption in data collection (table 12.1); sample size was large, and attrition has been low. Lastly, the study regularly measured risk and protective factors and antisocial behavior at all follow-up assessments. These aspects and other features of the Pittsburgh Youth Study will be discussed later.

A crucial activity over the past ten years has been to see that the study's funding remained intact. It was originally funded by the Office of Juvenile Justice and Delinquency Prevention (OJJDP), and data collection began in 1987–88. Since that time the participants have been followed up regularly, and two books (Loeber, Farrington et al., 1998a; Stouthamer-Loeber & Van Kammen, 1995) and over 50 papers have been published. The study is currently supported by the Office of Juvenile Justice and Delinquency Prevention, the National Institute of Mental Health (NIMH), and the National Institute of Drug Abuse (NIDA). Since not all publications are easily accessible to readers, this report summarizes the major findings from the first ten years of the study with reference to the original publications.

In addition to the main study, a few substudies have been executed to examine specific issues in more detail than was possible in the main study. Two should be mentioned in particular: In the summer of 1990 boys from the middle sample were intensively assessed on neuropsychological, impulsivity and personality measures (principal investigator Terrie E. Moffitt). Also, a study of psychophysiological and biological risk factors for violence was undertaken in 1996–98 on the middle sample (principal investigator: Adrian Raine), but since the data collection has only just been completed, the results of that study are not yet available. The principal investigator for the main study is Rolf Loeber, with Magda Stouthamer-Loeber and David P. Farrington, as co-investigators.

Table 12.1 Sequence of assessments in the Pittsburgh Youth Study

	1987 Sp	Fa	1988 Sp	Fa	1989 Sp	Fa	1990 Sp	Fa	1991 Sp	Fa	1992 Sp	Fa	1993 Sp	Fa	1994 Sp	Fa	1995 Sp	Fa	1996 Sp	Fa	1997 Sp	Fa	1998 Sp	Fa	1999 Sp	Fa	2000 Sp
C1	1987		1988		1989		1990		1991		1992		1993		1994		1995		1996		1997		1998		1999		2000
C2	1988		1989		1990		1991		1992		1993		1994		1995		1996		1997		1998		1999		2000		2001
	Sp	Fa	Sp	Fa	Sp	Fa	Sp	Fa	Sp	Fa	Sp	Fa	Sp	Fa	Sp	Fa	Sp	Fa	Sp	Fa	Sp	Fa	Sp	Fa	Sp	Fa	Sp
Youngest Sample																											
Age	7	7.5	8	8.5	9	9.5	10	10.5	11		12		13		14		15		16		17		18		19		20
As	S	A	B	C	D	E	F	G	H		J		L		N		P		R		T		V		X		Z
Middle Sample																											
Age	10	10.5	11	11.5	12	12.5	13																				
As	S	A	B	C	D	E	F																				
Oldest Sample																											
Age	13	13.5	14	14.5	15	15.5		16.5		17.5		18.5		19.5		20.5		21.5		22.5		23.5		24.5		25.5	
As	S	A	B	C	D	E		G		I		K		M		O		Q		SS		U		W		Y	

C1 = Cohort 1 assessments (third of sample); C2 = Cohort 2 assessments (other two-thirds of sample); Sp = Spring; Fa = Fall; As = Assessment.

Design and Methods

Participants

Participant selection and methods have been described in detail else-where (Loeber, Stouthamer-Loeber, Van Kammen & Farrington, 1991; Loeber, Farrington et al., 1998a), and are only summarized briefly here. Boys attending the first, fourth, and seventh grades in the public school system in inner-city Pittsburgh were randomly selected for participation in a longitudinal study of the development of disruptive and delinquent behaviors. Of those families contacted, 84.7% of the boys and their parents agreed to participate. An initial screening (S) assessment then followed to identify high-risk participants. About 850 boys were screened in each grade. Boys in the youngest and middle samples were given the Self-Reported Antisocial Behavior (SRA) questionnaire (Loeber, Stouthamer-Loeber, Van Kammen, & Farrington, 1989), while those in the oldest sample completed the Self-Reported Delinquency (SRD) questionnaire (adapted from the National Youth Survey, see Loeber, Farrington et al., 1998a). Parents and teachers were given the respective forms of the Child Behavior Checklist (Loeber, Farrington et al., 1998a).

The information from this screening assessment was used to identify approximately 30% of the boys with the most severe disruptive behavior problems (approximately 250 boys in each of the three samples). Additionally, a random selection of boys from the remaining 70% of each sample was made (approximately another 250 boys in each follow-up sample). This selection process resulted in approximately 500 boys in each sample (503, 508, 506, in the youngest, middle, and oldest samples, respectively), half high risk and half average or low risk. Just over half were African American boys, and just under half were white boys.

The boys in the follow-up samples, as well as their parents and teachers, were initially followed up at half-yearly intervals (9 assessments for the youngest sample, 7 for the middle sample, and 6 for the oldest sample), after which only the youngest and oldest samples were followed up at yearly intervals (see table 12.1). The middle sample was discontinued when the youngest sample began to overlap it in age. Funding is currently in place to follow up the youngest sample until age 20, and the oldest sample until age 25.5.

The term *parent* is used to describe the person who was interviewed, and is defined as the individual who claimed to have the principal responsibility for looking after the boy in the household. In the follow-up sample, the parent was in 91.1% of the cases the biological, step-, or adoptive mother, with another 4.0% being aunts, grandmothers or foster mothers. The remainder of the respondents were male parents. For simplicity of exposition, we will refer to the parent using the female gender.

Measures

The aim was to measure key constructs that were thought to be causes or correlates of delinquency. As far as possible, we used existing measures; however, a large number of measures had to be specially developed or modified using language suitable for an urban, generally lower socio-economic class sample. Some of these new measures were derived from earlier work at the Oregon Social Learning Center, and we are greatly indebted to the input from staff there. In addition, several measures resulted from collaboration among investigators of the OJJDP Program of Research on the Causes and Correlates of Delinquency (Terence P. Thornberry, Alan J. Lizotte, Margaret Farnworth, and Susan B. Stern in Rochester; David Huizinga, Finn Esbensen, and Delbert S. Elliott in Denver). A listing of the measures can be found in Loeber, Farrington et al. (1998a). That source also contains a detailed description of many of the constructs used in analyses to date.

Official records of offending were searched in the Juvenile Court of Allegheny County, covering the period up to the date of the first follow-up assessment (A) for participants in that county and, prospectively, for a period of about six years subsequent to that assessment. Allegheny County covers the city of Pittsburgh and the surrounding area. In addition, California Achievement Test data on reading, language, and mathematics were collected yearly from the schools (see Loeber, Farrington et al., 1998a for details).

The interviewing process

Practical aspects of data collection and management in the Pittsburgh Youth Study have been described in several publications (Stouthamer-Loeber, 1993; Stouthamer-Loeber & Van Kammen, 1995;

Stouthamer-Loeber, Van Kammen, & Loeber, 1992; Van Kammen & Stouthamer-Loeber, 1997). Many analyses show that the most elusive and uncooperative respondents tend to be disproportionately delinquent and antisocial (e.g., Farrington et al., 1990). Hence the loss of respondents is especially serious and likely to produce misleading and invalid results in studies focussing on delinquent and antisocial behavior. Methods of dealing with missing data (e.g., by imputation) are a very poor substitute for collecting as complete data as possible in the first place. Therefore, we felt it was essential to maximize the initial response rate and also the rate of retaining participants subsequently in the study.

The initial response rate in the screening assessment (S) in the Pittsburgh Youth Study, which required cooperation from *both* the parent and the boy, was 84.7%. Subsequent retention rates were high. For example, 92.0% and 89.7% of the participants in the youngest sample completed the assessments at waves N and P, respectively (the 12th and 13th waves).

Data collection in the Pittsburgh Youth Study was organized and controlled in-house (Stouthamer-Loeber & Van Kammen, 1995). We believe that the quality and completeness of data would have been lower if the interviewing process had been contracted out to an agency. It seems unlikely that any data collection agency – however experienced, reputable and professional – could be as passionately concerned as we are about the quality and completeness of the data and the well-being of our participants. Furthermore, we believe that it is important for principal investigators and analysts to have close and continuing contact with the data-collection process, in order to become fully aware of all the decisions made at key choice points as well as the strengths and weaknesses inherent in the data.

The data-collection process, especially in the early years, was a daunting and very labor-intensive task. Each year, there were 9,000 assessments (500 boys × 3 samples × 2 assessments × 3 informants), each containing several different questionnaires and hundreds of variables. It was necessary to coordinate about 30–40 part-time interviewers and 10 data entry staff, in addition to other staff involved in data checking and making constructs and documentation. All these people were organized by three supervisors, and ultimately by Magda Stouthamer-Loeber and Welmoet van Kammen, who shared the major responsibility for data collection. From 1994 to 1995, the information from participants was entered directly on laptop computers carried by interviewers, but the transition from paper-based to fully computerized data collection was a painful process that consumed many more person-hours than anticipated.

Interviewers

Interviewers were carefully selected and trained. Generally, the best interviewers were street-wise, self-confident people who had some previous experience at interviewing. Students were unsuitable because their studies and other time commitments (e.g., to complete term papers and vacations) conflicted with the requirements of interviewing (e.g., to be available to conduct interviews at unpredictable times according to the convenience of participants). Interviews were generally conducted in the participants' homes. Interviewers included males and females and whites and African Americans; there was no attempt to match characteristics of interviewers to characteristics of participants. Despite the fact that many interviews were carried out in high-risk areas such as housing projects, where violence and even shoot-outs were not uncommon, no interviewer was ever a victim of violence while interviewing. This was partly attributable to the safety training which was given to the interviewers.

In order to contain costs of the interviews, interviewers were paid per interview, not per hour, and the fee included an element of expenses to cover the average mileage required to track down the participant and complete the interview. Names of participants were released to interviewers in batches; the interviewers were not given the next batch until the supervisor was satisfied that they had tried all possible avenues for interviewing the more difficult to find and the more difficult to schedule participants. This was done to maximize the response rate and to prevent interviewers from concentrating on the "easy" cases in order to maximize their fees and minimize their efforts.

Interviewers were very carefully supervised using a computerized scheduling system. They had regularly scheduled weekly meetings with supervisors and also had to call the supervisor's answering machine every day for messages. All contacts and attempts to contact participants were recorded. At least 10% of all interviews were randomly selected for validation telephone calls to check that the interview really happened, and to collect information on interviewer behavior. Data entry and checking occurred within one week of each interview in order to detect missing data. It was then the responsibility of the interviewer to re-contact the participant to obtain the missing data. Two interviewers were dismissed after we found that they had taken shortcuts in retrieving missed questions. Interviewers were not paid until the interview information was complete.

Boys and parents were paid for each interview, and we believe that this was important in maximizing the response rate. The parents were initially paid $12.50, with an additional $5 for boys in the oldest sample, and these fees were increased gradually. Currently, we pay $60 to the parent and $60 to the boy per assessment.

More interviewers were hired than were actually needed, and those whose performance did not reach the specified standards (e.g., number of completed interviews, percentage of errors, percentage of refusals, missed mandatory contacts with supervisors) were let go after one month. Over the years, a cadre of reliable interviewers was gradually assembled who were used repeatedly for several waves of data collection. In order to minimize interviewer bias, interviewers did not interview the same participants at consecutive assessments and, therefore, our group of interviewers needed constant replenishment.

Many of the more delinquent boys were difficult to locate because their living circumstances were not stable. They might be sleeping at the home of their operative mother on some days, at the home of a father figure on other days, and on a friend's floor on other days. Some participants had a bewildering variety of names and aliases. A child might be listed on his birth certificate as Nathaniel Augustus Jones, but Mr Jones senior may have disappeared soon after Nathaniel's birth and the child may then have used his mother's maiden name as his last name, or some of the last names of his mother's male partners. Or he may hardly know what his real name is, since everyone calls him Skinny Beanstalk or EsBe for short.

Interviewers were required to search diligently for participants and were trained in methods of overcoming their reluctance to cooperate. Fortunately, Pittsburgh is a relatively stable city, but sometimes the tracking process was long and frustrating. Overall, we have been highly successful in retaining participants in the study. After ten years, we have lost only one participant because of our inability to trace him. Even when participants moved long distances away from Pittsburgh, interviews were accomplished by telephone.

Overall, in an atmosphere where accuracy and completeness of the data were emphasized and highly valued, staff took great pride in going to extraordinary lengths to do the best possible job. We are very grateful to both interviewers and participants for their invaluable efforts.

Development of Offending

Prevalence, frequency, and onset

Several publications contain information about the prevalence, frequency, and onset of delinquency (Farrington, Loeber, Stouthamer-Loeber, & Van Kammen, 1996a; Farrington, Loeber, Stouthamer-Loeber, Van Kammen, & Schmidt, 1996b; Huizinga, Loeber, & Thornberry, 1993; Loeber, Farrington et al., 1998a). We will first highlight the findings from boys', parents', and teachers' information on delinquency reported by Farrington, Loeber et al. (1996a) since they are the most extensive. It should be kept in mind that, because of their young age, boys in the youngest and middle samples up to age 10 responded to the Self-Reported Antisocial Behavior questionnaire, after which they were given the Self-Reported Delinquency question-naire. Since the two questionnaires are only partly overlapping, the results for ages 6 to 10 are only partly comparable to those for ages 11 to 16.

Figure 12.1 shows the yearly prevalence of serious delinquency (the percentage committing acts at each age) between ages 6 and 16. Serious delinquency includes car theft, breaking and entering, strongarming, attack to seriously hurt or kill, forced sex, or selling drugs. At age 6, there were no differences between African American and white boys, but the differences gradually increased, with the prevalence at age 16 reaching 26.6% for African Americans and 18.7% for whites. As prevalence increased, so did the mean frequency of serious offending, accelerating more steeply for African American than for white boys (figure 12.2). Figure 12.3 shows the cumulative onset of serious delinquency, indicating a steeper age of onset curve for African American compared to white boys. By age 15, 51.4% of African American boys had engaged in serious delinquency, compared to 28.1% of white boys.

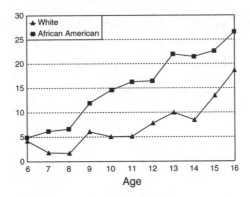

Figure 12.1 Prevalence of serious delinquency (percentage committing at each age)

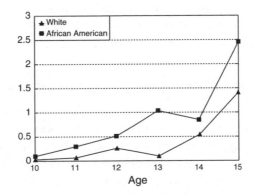

Figure 12.2 Frequency of serious delinquency (mean number of acts committed at each age)

Prevalence of delinquency in court records

Court records were searched for the period between each boy's 10th and 18th birthday in the oldest sample, and each boy's 10th birthday and about age 16 for the middle sample (Farrington et al., 1996b; Loeber, Farrington et al., 1998a). In the middle sample, 29.7% of the boys had been petitioned to the court for a delinquent offense, compared to 44.6% of the boys in the oldest sample (boys in the youngest sample were too

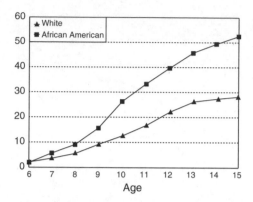

Figure 12.3 Age of onset of serious delinquency (cumulative percentage committing acts)

young at this time for many of them to be petitioned to the court). Comparable figures for index offenses in the middle and oldest samples were 22.2% and 34.1%, and for index violence were 11.9% and 14.7%.

Development of delinquency, aggression and violence

We were interested in specifying the age at which formerly nonviolent boys engaged for the first time in violent acts and in establishing when less serious forms of aggression first emerged. As shown in Loeber and Hay (1997), the onset of minor aggression (arguing, bullying) tended to occur first, followed by the onset of physical fighting (including gang fighting), and then by the onset of violence. These results were replicated, across the three samples. Further, the onset curves based on prospective information from the youngest sample largely overlapped with data collected retrospectively in the middle and oldest samples. We also created onset curves for minor delinquency, moderate delinquency, and serious delinquency (Loeber, DeLamatre et al., 1998; Loeber, Farrington et al., 1998a), which showed that minor delinquency emerged first, followed by moderate delinquency, which in turn was followed by serious delinquency. Again, the results applied to all three samples.

In summary, the seriousness of aggression and the seriousness of delinquency both appear to develop in an orderly fashion, with the onset of less serious behaviors occurring before the onset of more serious behaviors. Severity of delinquency was correlated with the variety of delinquent acts (.58, .59, and .65, for the three samples, respectively), and less strongly with frequency (.26 and .30, for the middle and oldest samples, respectively), see Loeber, Farrington et al., 1998a.

Typologies of offenders

We devoted a separate article to typologies of offenders over four waves of data (Loeber, Stouthamer-Loeber et al., 1991). We made a distinction between four seriousness levels of delinquency: nondelinquency, minor delinquency, moderate delinquency, and serious delinquency. On the basis of the seriousness classification at four data points, seven types of offenders were identified: stable nondelinquents, starters, stable moderates, escalators, stable highs, de-escalators, and desisters. We found substantial differences among the three samples in the most common types, with the nondelinquents and starters the most prevalent in the youngest sample, the nondelinquents and escalators in the middle sample, and the stable moderates, escalators, and de-escalators in the oldest sample. The shifts in the most common types with age represent the beginning, worsening, and decreasing of delinquent activities from middle childhood to adolescence (see also Loeber & Le Blanc, 1990).

Stability of delinquency and aggression

Zhang, Loeber, and Stouthamer-Loeber (1997) examined the stability of minor and serious forms of theft and violence over eight assessment waves covering a period of four years. For example, they found that the year-to-year odds ratios for minor theft offenses in the youngest sample amounted to 4.9, 7.6, and 7.1, while the odds ratios for serious violence were 5.4, 7.0, and 6.7. Similar figures were observed for other delinquent behavior, and also in the middle sample. Thus, the continuity of delinquent involvement across different forms and severity levels of delinquency was substantial. Loeber and Hay (1997) showed that the prevalence of physical fighting decreased in adolescence, especially between ages 12 and 17. They also found some indication that the stability of physical fighting increased between ages 6–7 and 9–10. Year-to-year odds ratios in the youngest sample increased from 10.6 to 18.6, likewise, Zhang et al. (1997) found that year-to-year odds ratios for minor violence increased with age from 5.6 to 8.2; serious violent offenses occurred at a rate too low to compute stability estimates. It should be noted, however, that violence in the older samples was often intermittent from year to year in most of the active violent offenders (Huizinga, Loeber, & Thornberry, 1993).

Developmental pathways

The above findings on the onset of various levels of delinquency seriousness suggested that individuals' development toward serious forms of delinquency may be orderly. We investigated whether a single or a multiple pathway model would best represent delinquency development, and if a multiple pathway model was best what would be the dimensions on which to distinguish different pathways. The rationale for identifying dimensions of overt and covert antisocial acts, and to a lesser extent, conflict with authority figures, was supported by meta-analyses of parent and teacher ratings from many other studies (Frick et al., 1993; Loeber & Schmaling, 1985).

After initial research comparing single versus multiple pathways (Loeber, Wung et al., 1993), a model of three pathways (figure 12.4) was found to fit the data in the oldest sample, using retrospective data collected at the beginning of the study and six waves of prospective assessments covering three years: (a) an Authority Conflict Pathway prior to the age of 12, that starts with stubborn behavior, and has defiance as a second stage, and authority avoidance (e.g., truancy) as a third stage; (b) a Covert Pathway that starts with minor covert acts, has property damage as a second stage, and moderate to serious delinquency as a third stage; and (c) an Overt Pathway that starts with minor aggression, has physical fighting as a second stage, and violence as a third stage.

Each of the three pathways represents different developmental tasks. The Overt Pathway represents aggression as opposed to positive problem solving; the Covert Pathway represents lying, vandalism, and theft versus honesty and respect for property; the Authority Conflict Pathway represents conflict with and avoidance of authority figures versus respect for authority figures. This conceptualization implies that the fact that a juvenile achieves one developmental task (such as honesty) does not necessarily mean that he will achieve another developmental task. Alternatively, youth may fail to achieve several of these developmental tasks. This implies that pathways in disruptive behavior can be conceptualized as different lines of development with some boys advancing on

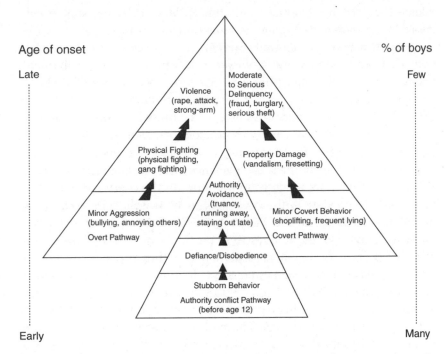

Figure 12.4 Three developmental pathways toward serious juvenile offending

several pathways at the same time. This has the advantage that the pathway model can help to account for multi-problem boys.

We were able to replicate the pathway findings on the middle and youngest samples using data collected over six and eight assessments, respectively (Loeber, Wung et al., 1993; Loeber, DeLamatre et al., 1998). A refinement was to distinguish boys whose antisocial behavior was temporary (called experimenters) and those who persisted in their anti-social acts. Research showed that persisters fitted the pathways better than experimenters (Loeber, Keenan, & Zhang, 1997). The majority of those who escalated to the highest stage in a pathway tended to begin committing less serious behaviors in the hypothesized order. The pathway analyses were replicated for African American and white boys. Recently, Tolan, Gorman-Smith and Loeber (1998) have replicated the pathway findings in a sample of African American and Hispanic adolescents in Chicago and in a nationally representative US sample of adolescents (see also Elliott, 1994, and Le Blanc, 1997, for similar evidence for developmental sequences toward violence).

The pathway model allowed several conceptualizations of the development toward increasing seriousness of antisocial and delinquent behavior: (a) escalation within a pathway; (b) persistence of problem behavior over time; and (c) a multiplicity of pathways. The results showed that with age more boys progressed on two or three pathways, indicating an increasing variety of problem behavior over time (Kelley, Loeber et al., 1997; Loeber, Wung et al., 1993; Loeber, Keenan, & Zhang, 1997). We found some evidence that development in more than one pathway was orderly, in that boys in the overt pathway were more likely to escalate in the covert pathway as well, compared to the probability of boys in the covert pathway escalating in the overt pathway. Thus, aggressive boys were particularly at risk of also committing covert acts. Further, escalation in either the overt or covert pathway was often preceded by boys' escalation in the authority conflict pathway (Loeber, Wung et al., 1993). In other words, conflict with authority figures was either a precursor or a concomitant of boys' worsening in overt or covert acts. The pathway model accounted for the majority of the most seriously affected boys, that is the self-reported high-rate offenders (Loeber, Keenan, & Zhang, 1997; Loeber, Wung et al., 1993) and court reported delinquents (Loeber, Keenan, & Zhang, 1997).

In summary, the pathway model that we developed for boys shows that the warning signs of early onset of disruptive behavior must not be dismissed with a "this soon will pass" attitude (Kelley, Loeber et al., 1997). However, we cannot yet distinguish accurately between those boys whose problem behavior will get worse over time and those who will improve. We see the pathway model as a way to help identify youth at risk and optimize early interventions before problem behavior becomes more stable and worse over time.

Risk Factors

Child risk factors

Impulsivity. A detailed multisource, multimethod battery of impulsivity measures was administered to the boys in the middle sample in the summer of 1990 when they averaged 12 to 13 years of age (White, Moffitt, Caspi, Bartusch, Needles, & Stouthamer-Loeber, 1994). The goals of this project were (a) to examine the interrelations among a variety of different measures of impulsivity, (b) to identify different possible underlying dimensions of impulsivity tapped by a variety of different impulsivity measures, and (c) to determine if different measures of impulsivity are differentially related to self-reported delinquency. The boys were invited to the come to the university, along with a parent, for a testing session. We collected data on 11 different measures of impulsivity, representing the most reliable and valid published methods to date.

- *Time perception.* We operationalized the concept of cognitive tempo by using time estimation and production tasks.
- *Stroop Color and Word Association Test.* The Stroop test assesses the ease with which a participant can inhibit an automatic overlearned response, substituting a competing novel response.
- *Trail Making Test.* This is a neuropsychological test of the ability to initiate, switch, and stop a sequence of complex purposeful behavior that requires attention and concentration skills.
- *Circle-tracing Task.* This motor task is a simple way of testing motor inhibition in which participants are directed to trace over a 9-inch circle as slowly as they can.
- *Delay of Gratification.* This task is a computer game designed to pit a less desirable but immediate monetary outcome against a more desirable but delayed one.
- *Card Playing Task (CPT).* This task, also presented as a computer game, operationalizes a disinhibited response style under circumstances that establish a strong positive response set.
- *Eysenck Impulsiveness Scale* is a self-report questionnaire measure of impulsive behavior.
- *Teacher-reports of Impulsivity* were obtained from teachers who rated each boy on six items that measured impulsive behavior (e.g., "fails to finish things he starts," "wants to have things right away").
- *Ego Undercontrol* was measured via parent reports on the Common Language version of the California Child Q-Sort (CCQ), a language-simplified personality assessment procedure intended for use with nonprofessional lay observers.

- *Videotape Observations.* Testing sessions were videotaped and observed by three trained coders who rated each boy on two dimensions: *motor restlessness* and *impatience/impersistence.* The coders had no knowledge about the participants or hypotheses.

In general, the correlations among the 11 impulsivity measures were low, and ranged from −.08 to .33, suggesting that the construct of impulsivity is not unidimensional. However, certain subsets of impulsivity measures were more highly interrelated than others. Exploratory and confirmatory factor-analysis techniques pointed to two correlated but distinct forms of impulsivity.

The first factor (labelled Behavioral Impulsivity) appeared to measure impulsivity that was associated with lack of behavioral control. This interpretation is consistent with the finding that the variables with the highest loading on this factor were those that tapped disinhibited, undercontrolled behavior. These variables were parent-reported undercontrol, observer-rated motor restlessness, teacher-reported impulsivity, self-reported impulsivity, and observer-rated impatience/impersistence.

The second factor (labelled Cognitive Impulsivity) appeared to measure impulsivity that was associated with effortful and planful cognitive performance. This interpretation is consistent with the finding that the variables with the highest loadings on this factor were those that tapped mental control and the mental effort required to switch adaptively between mental sets. These variables were Trail Making Test time, Stroop errors, time perception, number of cards played on the CPT, circle tracing, and delay of gratification.

Both cognitive and behavioral impulsivity were significantly and positively related to delinquency when it was measured cross-sectionally, as well as when it was measured across time. However, the links between behavioral impulsivity and the self-reported delinquency outcome measures (average $r = .43, p < .001$) were stronger than those between cognitive impulsivity and the delinquency outcome measures (average $r = .18, p < .01$). To assess the unique contribution of impulsivity to the variance in delinquency, we also statistically controlled for effects of individual differences in SES and IQ. Cognitive and behavioral impulsivity together accounted for 16% of the variance in delinquency, with the effects of SES and IQ controlled. However, whereas cognitive impulsivity was not related to delinquency independently of IQ, individual differences in behavioral impulsivity continued to exert a strong effect on delinquency above and beyond individual differences in IQ.

Because it has been hypothesized that stable and severe antisocial behavior is especially associated with poor impulse control, we compared the self-reported delinquency of three groups of boys: (a) stable nondelinquents, (b) stable, serious delinquents, and (c) all other delinquent boys (i.e., delinquent boys who did not meet criteria for the stable, serious delinquency group). Stable serious delinquents showed the highest levels of cognitive and behavioral impulsivity. Indeed, they were nearly 1 standard deviation above the sample norm and almost 2 standard deviations more impulsive than were the boys who had never been delinquent. Stable nondelinquents had the lowest mean scores, and the impulsivity of the non-serious delinquent group fell in between the scores of the two other groups.

Futher follow-up research revealed that impulsivity interacts with neighborhood context to influence juvenile offending (Lynam, Caspi, Moffitt, Wikström, & Loeber, in review). Impulsive boys were at greatest risk for juvenile offending in Pittsburgh's poorest neighborhoods. The effects of impulsivity may be potentiated in poorer neighborhoods because these neighborhoods are characterized by lower levels of informal social controls. It is possible that impulsive boys in these poor neighborhoods may encounter and take advantage of more opportunities to commit delinquent acts than impulsive boys in better-off neighborhoods. These results emphasize that accounts of antisocial behavior that rely on trait explanations alone are incomplete. Although impulsivity has emerged as one of the strongest individual-level predictors of antisocial behavior in our research, its effects on delinquent offending are clearly shaped by the social context of development.

Intelligence. A robust finding in many studies is that delinquents score 8–10 IQ points lower than non-delinquents (Wilson & Herrnstein, 1985), but researchers have disagreed about the correct interpretation of this finding, and its possible implications for prevention. Data from the middle sample of boys shed light on this issue (Lynam, Moffitt & Stouthamer-Loeber, 1993). In the summer of 1990, when these boys were aged 12–13, they were given the WISCR, which is a standardized intelligence test. An initial analysis showed that the self-reported delinquent boys scored on average 8 points lower than the nondelinquent boys, and the most serious among the delinquents scored 11 points lower.

Some critics who are skeptical of the link between IQ and delinquency have objected that the observed relation between IQ and delinquency could be an artefact of social class or race. In the study, a measure of social class was entered as a control in analysis of the relation between IQ scores and self-reported delinquency scores, but this reduced the difference between delinquents and nondelinquents by only one IQ point. Race was addressed by analyzing the data separately for African American and white boys, which revealed that delinquents scored 8 points below nondelinquents within *both* ethnic groups.

Critics have also argued that delinquents score poorly on IQ tests because they are not interested in doing well, they are oppositional to the tester, or they come from a subculture that does not value intellectual performance. In the study, the boys were videotaped while taking the IQ test, and later research assistants who were blind to the nature of the study watched the videos and rated each boy on interest, effort, boredom, impatience, and impersistence during the test. For example, raters watched for boys who lay their heads on the table, yawned often, or refused to attempt parts of the test. Although there was quite a range of scores on this rating, entering it as a control reduced the difference between delinquents and nondelinquents by only 2 IQ points.

A further study addressed the question of whether the relation between IQ and delinquency depended on the boys' neighborhood to see if the relation were different in a local youth subculture that does not value intellectual performance (Moffitt, Caspi, Silva, & Stouthamer-Loeber, 1995). The relation was the same in good and bad Pittsburgh neighborhoods. A further artefactual possibility that was also checked was whether impulsivity mediated the relation between IQ and delinquency. Many measures of impulsive self-control are known to correlate with IQ scores, and thus perhaps a delinquent boy's impulsiveness is the important ingredient in the link between his IQ score and his delinquency. However, analyses showed that only about one fifth of the effect of IQ on delinquency operated via impulsivity.

Critics have argued that the subset of delinquents who get caught for their delinquent acts (and thus complete an IQ test in jail) may have lower IQ scores than boys who are just as delinquent but who cleverly evade detection. The study proved that this was not the sole explanation of the IQ–delinquency link by showing that IQ relates to self-reports of delinquency (Lynam et al., 1993), as well as to mothers' and teachers' reports of delinquent acts (Moffitt et al., 1995).

These analyses appeared to rule out the current major artefactual explanations of the relation between IQ and delinquency. Having ruled out the alternatives, the study turned to testing a causal explanation. A plausible theory is that low IQ leads to frustration, failure, and humiliation at school, and that these alienating experiences prompt youth to engage in delinquency. Using cross-sectional data, the study found evidence (Lynam et al., 1993) that this correlational pathway is at least partially true, primarily for the African American boys. For these boys, 75% of the relation between IQ and delinquency operated through the boys' school achievement, as reported by their teachers. Bright boys may enjoy favor from teachers and may find that the rewards school has to offer are more attractive than delinquency. Research has shown that it is not easy to improve children's IQ scores permanently, but these findings suggest that the refractory nature of IQ need not be a source of pessimism. It is not necessary to change IQ if it is feasible to improve the reception that low IQ children experience in schools. If all children found school as rewarding as the brightest children do, schools could be a powerful delinquency prevention tool.

Personality. Studying the middle sample, we developed an assessment instrument to describe the personalities of the boys. In the summer of 1990, the parents complete the "Common Language" version of the California Child Q-Sort (CCQ), a language-simplified personality assessment procedure intended for use with lay observers (Caspi et al., 1992). The CCQ contains 100 statements written on individual cards that describe a wide range of personality attributes. The boys' parents (primarily mothers) were asked to sort these item-cards into a forced nine-category distribution along a continuum ranging from "most like this boy" to "not at all like this boy". The CCQ can be used to obtain scores for children on three of the most important "superfactors" of personality: Constraint, Negative Emotionality, and Positive Emotionality (Tellegen et al., 1988). Individuals high on Constraint endorse conventional social norms, avoid thrills, and act in a cautious and restrained manner. Individuals high on Negative Emotionality have a low general threshold for the experience of negative emotions such as fear, anxiety, and anger, and tend to break down under stress. Individuals high on

Positive Emotionality have a low threshold for the experience of positive emotions and for positive engagement in their social environments, and view life as essentially a pleasurable experience.

The results revealed robust personality correlates of delinquency. Whether delinquency was measured using self-, parent, or teacher reports, and whether delinquency was assessed among African American or white boys, greater delinquent participation was associated with greater negative emotionality and less constraint (Caspi et al., 1994; Moffitt et al., 1995).

Related work on personality and delinquency has focussed on psychopathy. Borrowing from the adult literature, Lynam (1997) operationalized psychopathy using extensive data collected on the middle sample. The results showed that psychopathy had a childhood manifestation which could be measured reliably. Psychopathic children, like their adult counterparts, were the most frequent, severe, aggressive, and temporally stable offenders. Psychopathic children were also impulsive, as assessed with a multimethod, multisource battery of measures. They were also prone to externalizing behavior disorders and comparatively immune to internalizing disorders. Most important, childhood psychopathy provided incremental validity in predicting serious stable antisocial behavior in adolescence over and above other known predictors and other classification approaches. This work provides clear support to the growing body of evidence attesting to the importance of personality as a contributor to delinquency.

Attitudes. It is well known that delinquents tend to have attitudes favorable to delinquency. It is less clear, however, to what extent attitudes favorable to delinquency predict later delinquent acts, to what extent delinquent acts predict favorable attitudes, whether both delinquent acts and attitudes are symptoms of the same underlying construct, and whether relations vary for violent compared to nonviolent forms of delinquency. Zhang et al. (1997) showed that in most cases delinquent attitudes predicted delinquency as well as the reverse. However, attitudes increasingly predicted delinquency with increasing age. The findings also showed some specificity: on average, a delinquent attitude had a stronger concurrent association with its counterpart behavior than with other behaviors (e.g., tolerance of minor violence was more strongly related to minor violence than to minor theft).

Drug dealing. We examined drug dealing by boys in the oldest sample over a period of three years. Drug dealing was defined as dealing in marijuana or hard drugs, independently from drug use (Van Kammen & Loeber, 1994; Van Kammen, Maguin, & Loeber, 1994). At the age of about 15, 12.8% of the boys had initiated drug dealing, with the typical age of onset being later than the onset of illicit drug use and serious delinquency. Having friends involved in drug dealing increased the risk of boys drug dealing by a factor of 10.

Event history analyses showed that prior repeated property or violent offenses, and repeated drug use increased the risk of onset of drug dealing. Once initiated, drug dealing was associated with an increase in violent offenses and in carrying a concealed weapon. Further, initiation of drug dealing was uniquely related to an increased frequency of property offenses, particularly car-related theft and fraud. Discontinuation of drug dealing was associated with a decrease in delinquent activities. In summary, results show the reciprocal interactions between delinquency and drug dealing, with one being a risk factor for the other.

Other child risk factors. We examined the relation between several other risk factors and delinquency (Loeber, Farrington et al., 1998a). The dichotomized delinquency seriousness score at waves S and A was the outcome: dichotomized to identify serious delinquents in the middle and the oldest samples, and dichotomized to identify moderate and serious delinquents in the youngest sample. Information on delinquent acts was provided by the boy, his mother and teacher. We found that the following child factors were related to delinquency: boy's lack of guilt feelings, old for grade (being held back because of low achievement), high Attention Deficit-Hyperactivity Disorder (ADHD) score, low achievement (ratings by boy, parent, and teacher), and depressed mood. In hierarchical multiple regressions, the most important child predictor was lack of guilt, a finding which was consistent across samples. Also, among the next most important predictors were being old for grade (all samples) and depressed mood (youngest and oldest samples). In addition, a high ADHD score contributed in the youngest and middle samples, and HIA problems (hyperactivity, impulsivity, and attention problems as rated by parents and teachers) in the middle and the oldest samples. Low (academic) achievement only entered for the oldest sample.

Academic factors. The relationship between poor academic performance and delinquency was examined further in several papers (Maguin & Loeber, 1996a; Maguin, Loeber, & LeMahieu, 1993). Maguin et al. (1993) in cross-sectional analyses showed that the likelihood of delinquency for boys with poor reading performance was similar for African Americans and whites, even though African Americans had a higher prevalence of delinquency. The worse the reading performance in any ethnic group, the more serious the delinquency. However, further analyses showed that the relationship between poor reading performance and delinquency could be explained by the presence of attention problems as rated by parents and teachers. This was further confirmed in a large meta-analysis (Maguin & Loeber, 1996a).

Family factors

Of the family variables, Loeber, Farrington et al. (1998a) found that poor supervision was the best explanatory variable for delinquency, increasing the risk of delinquency by a factor of 2.6 for the oldest sample, but somewhat less for the other samples (Odds Ratios: 1.9 and 1.5). Next came poor parent–boy communication, which increased the risk of delinquency by a factor of 2.4 in the middle sample, and 1.5 in the oldest sample (this was not measured in the youngest sample). Physical punishment by the mother increased the risk of delinquency by a factor of about 2 in each of the three samples. Several other parent variables increased the risk of delinquency, but only for the youngest and the middle samples, such as the mother's high stress, substance use problems, and anxiety/depression.

In hierarchical regression analyses, physical punishment predicted delinquency for the middle and oldest samples, while poor supervision predicted for the oldest sample only. Parent anxiety/depression entered into the equation, but for the middle sample only, while unhappy parents were most relevant for the youngest sample. Remarkably, no other parent variable predicted delinquency in the youngest sample; other parent variables only entered the equation for children at an older age.

Macro factors

Loeber, Farrington et al. (1998a) also found that of the socio-economic factors, the family on welfare was associated with the highest risk of delinquency in all three samples (Odds Ratios: 2.1, 2.5, and 2.4), followed by low socioeconomic status (1.5, 2.2, and 1.5). Other variables which increased the risk of delinquency in two out of the three samples were a small house, an unemployed father, and a poorly educated mother. Among the demographic variables, the most strongly related were a broken family (2.0, 2.9, and 2.8), and African American ethnicity (1.9, 2.5, and 2.3). A young mother (under age 20 at the time of the boy's birth) about doubled the risk of delinquency, but only for the middle and oldest samples. Finally, bad neighborhood, either measured through census data or by means of the mother's report, doubled the risk for delinquency in all three samples.

The hierarchical regression analyses showed that having a young mother, an unemployed father and living in a bad neighborhood were significant independent predictors in two of the three samples. African American ethnicity was a less consistent predictor (middle sample only). The relative unimportance of ethnicity in the explanation of delinquency was remarkable, especially since African American boys tended to commit more serious delinquency. However, Peeples and Loeber (1994), reporting on the oldest sample, demonstrated that, when African American boys did not live in underclass neighborhoods, their delinquent behavior was similar to that of white boys. Once individually measured factors (such as single parent family and poverty/welfare) were included in hierarchical regression analyses predicting serious delinquency, residence in an underclass neighborhood was still significantly related to serious delinquent behavior, while ethnicity was not.

Considerably more work was done on neighborhood classification, using the 1980 census data, and distinctions were made between low, medium, and high socio-economic status neighborhoods (Loeber & Wikström, 1993). That work investigated to what extent boys' advancement on the overt and covert pathways was different in various neighborhoods. The results for the middle and oldest samples showed that more boys in low than in high SES areas, especially at younger ages, were involved in overt behavior. Moreover, a higher proportion of boys living in low SES areas tended to advance on the overt pathway and engage in violence than those living in high SES neighborhoods. More boys in the low SES areas had been involved in covert behaviors, and more boys in those areas, compared to boys in high SES areas, had penetrated to the highest step in the covert pathway, but this was more true for the middle than for the oldest sample. Thus, deviant development, known to be associated with later serious delinquency, tended to occur more quickly in the worse neighborhoods, and in the case of overt behaviors tended to occur at a relatively young age in those areas.

Replication of findings

Most of the findings on explanatory factors for delinquency observed in one sample of the Pittsburgh Youth Study were replicated in the other two samples. This applied both to univariate relationships and to logistic regressions (Loeber, Farrington et al., 1998a). Further, many of the predictors of delinquency and violence in the middle sample of the Pittsburgh Youth Study were identical to predictors of the same outcomes in the Cambridge Study on Delinquent Development (Farrington, 1998; Farrington & Loeber, 1998). Finally, many of the risk factors identified in the Pittsburgh Youth Study are corroborated in the existing literature on risk factors (see reviews by Farrington, 1996, and Loeber, Farrington et al., 1998a).

Peer factors

In the analyses of risk factors reported by Loeber, Farrington et al. (1998a), peer factors were not taken into account as explanatory factors. Such factors are highly correlated with delinquency because of the high rate of co-offending of juveniles and their peers. Arguably, peer delinquency could simply be an indicator of the boy's own delinquency. However, Keenan et al. (1995) examined the temporal relations between boys' exposure to deviant peer behavior and the boys' own initiation of disruptive and delinquent behavior. The results showed that exposure to deviant peers was significantly followed by initiation of disruptive/delinquent behaviors characteristic of the overt and covert pathways.

Predictors of self-reported violence and court referred violence

For the middle sample in the Pittsburgh study (and the London sample), Farrington (1998) compared the predictors of reports of violence (based on information from the boy, parent and teacher) and those of court referred violence over a period of six years. The following factors predicted either outcome, often with the same magnitude: low guilt, low achievement, young mother, broken family, single mother, low SES, family on welfare, and bad neighborhood, measured either by census data or by parent report. Examples of unique predictors of court violence were: poorly educated mother and large family.

These analyses did not include African ethnicity, because of the very low prevalence of this in the London sample. However, a study on the validity of reports of delinquency (Farrington et al., 1996b) showed that in logistic regression analyses, ethnicity predicted the probability of future petitions to the juvenile court for delinquency independently of the combined delinquency scale (based on boy, mother, and teacher reports). Ethnicity was a stronger predictor of court petitions than of the combined delinquency measure. We will return to this in the section on Methodological Issues.

Comorbidity

It is important to investigate how far different types of problem behavior are inter-related, and hence are all symptoms of the same underlying syndrome. Another important topic is how far risk factors are the same for all types of problem behavior. To the extent that different types of problem behavior are inter-related, it is useful to identify multiple problem boys, and to study risk factors for multiple problem boys. Eight problem behaviors were studied in the youngest, middle and oldest samples at screening (S) and wave A (Loeber, Farrington et al., 1998b): delinquency, substance use, attention deficit, conduct problems, physical aggression, covert behavior, depressed mood, and shy/withdrawn behavior. All risk factors and problem behaviors were dichotomized.

All eight problem behaviors were significantly inter-correlated in most cases, and there was no tendency for the strength of relationships to vary with age. In a factor analysis, all eight problem behaviors had substantial weightings on the first factor. These results support the idea that all eight behaviors are symptoms of the same underlying syndrome. However, it was noticeable that depressed mood, shy/withdrawn behavior, and substance use had the lowest correlations with the other five problem behaviors, which were highly inter-correlated. Also, weightings on the second factor distinguished delinquency and physical aggression at one extreme from depressed mood and shy/withdrawn behavior at the other. Therefore, the results also supported the idea of distinct (but inter-correlated) internalizing and externalizing syndromes.

When 40 key explanatory risk factors were studied, there was no indication that the strength of relationships between risk factors and problem behaviors varied with age. Delinquency and conduct problems were related to the largest number of risk factors (over 50%), while shy/withdrawn behavior and substance use were related to the smallest number (less than 40%). Generally, the child and family risk factors were related to a variety of different problem behaviors: low achievement, lack of guilt, hyperactivity-impulsivity-attention deficit (HIA) problems, poor parent–boy communication, and poor parental supervision were related to almost all problem behaviors at all ages. The macro risk factors tended to be more specific; in particular, African American ethnicity, bad neighborhood, and young mother were especially related to delinquency.

Boys with four or more problem behaviors (20–25% of boys) were identified as multiple problem boys. In general, these boys were characterized more by externalizing problems than by depressed mood, shy/withdrawn behavior, or substance use. They were predicted especially by lack of guilt, HIA problems, low achievement, poor parent–boy communication, and parental stress. Macro factors did not predict them independently of child and family factors, suggesting that any effect of macro factors in producing multiple problem boys operated indirectly through child and family factors. When the multiple problem boys were excluded from the analysis, relationships between single risk factors and single problem behaviors were attenuated but not eliminated. Uniquely, the strength of the relationship between African American ethnicity and delinquency was *greater* among boys who did *not* have multiple problems, suggesting that white boys who were delinquents were *more* likely to have multiple problems.

Delinquency, conduct problems, physical aggression, attention deficit, and covert behavior were particularly closely inter-related. These five externalizing behaviors were predicted by a variety of child and family risk factors, and they were particularly characteristic of the multiple problem boys. These results should be investigated longitudinally, to see how far risk factors at S and A predict *later* multiple problem behaviors.

Cumulative effects of risk factors

Using information from waves S and A, we computed the cumulative effects of risk factors on serious delinquency (Loeber, Farrington et al., 1998a). The risk score was based on 12 key explanatory variables: lack of guilt, old for grade, low achievement (parent, boy, teacher ratings), ADHD score, depressed mood, poor supervision, physical punishment, ethnicity, broken family, low SES, family on welfare, and bad neighborhood (mother rating). Especially in the oldest sample, there was a linear relation between the number of risk factors and the probability of serious delinquency.

Differences in risk factors with age

Loeber, Stouthamer-Loeber et al. (1991) in their investigation of predictors of initiation, escalation, and desistance found several shifts in risk factors over four data waves. For example, they found that physical aggression and social withdrawal decreased with age in their strength of prediction of delinquency, while school problem behaviors, peer deviance, and boys' positive attitude to deviancy increased in predictive efficiency. Some factors were especially associated with the early initiation of offending before age 12, including social withdrawal and depression, a positive attitude to problem behavior, association with deviant peers, and family problems. In contrast, the later onset of offending (between ages 13 and 14) was associated with low school motivation. Nearly all (90%) of the stable high offenders in the youngest sample scored high on physical aggression, compared to 51% and 44% in the middle and oldest samples, respectively. In the middle and oldest samples, predictors of escalation were: poor school functioning, disruptive behaviors, a positive attitude to deviant behavior, and some aspects of family functioning. In summary, the results indicate some common risk factors at different ages, but also some risk factors whose impact becomes more pronounced at an early compared to a later age.

Protective factors

Protective factors have often been conceptualized as processes that interact with risk factors in reducing the probability of a negative outcome (Rutter, 1985; 1990). However, we argue that, as with the study of main effects of risk factors, we need to study the *main effects* of protective factors before investigating the interaction effects between protective and risk factors.

To that end, we examined the effects of protective and risk factors as represented by opposite poles of the same variable (Stouthamer-Loeber, Loeber, Farrington, Zhang, Van Kammen, & Maguin, 1993). All variables were trichotomized as closely as possible at the 25th and 75th percentiles within each sample. In the case of the delinquency classification, groups of nondelinquents, minor delinquents, and serious delinquents were formed. Similarly, the independent variables were trichotomized into positive (potentially protective), neutral, and negative (potentially risk) sections of the score distribution. Analyses were carried out cross-sectionally at waves S and A.

The results showed that protective and risk effects often co-occurred in the same variables, that few variables had risk effects only, and none had protective effects only. Overall, protective effects were as likely to promote nondelinquency as to suppress serious delinquency. In contrast, risk effects were as likely to suppress nondelinquency as to promote serious delinquency. Several variables were mostly associated with distinctions between nondelinquency and minor delinquency. Examples are parental stress, and social interactional variables, such as supervision, communication, peer delinquency, and boys' attitude to antisocial behavior. Only two variables (age of the mother at the birth of the child and mother's education) were exclusively associated with the distinction between minor and serious delinquency. In contrast, all of the externalizing behaviors (e.g., accountability, oppositional defiant behavior, attention deficit/hyperactivity, and the ability to feel guilt) were about equally associated with the lower *and* the upper ends of the delinquency categorization. Finally, the results showed that the magnitude of protective and risk effects, as judged from the contingency coefficients and number of significant odds ratios, increased with age. There is an obvious need to replicate these analyses using longitudinal data.

In separate analyses over four data waves, Loeber, Stouthamer-Loeber et al. (1991) found the following correlates of desistance in offending: low social withdrawal, low disruptive behavior, and positive motivational and attitudinal factors.

Help-seeking

We investigated the extent that parents of delinquent boys received help for dealing with their problems (Stouthamer-Loeber, Loeber, & Thomas, 1992; Stouthamer-Loeber, Loeber, Van Kammen, & Zhang, 1995). We considered help received from anyone (including lay people) and from professionals (especially mental health professionals). In addition, delinquents are often referred to the juvenile court, and the question is to what extent parents have received help to deal better with the behavior problems of their boys. In general, help-seeking for behavior problems was twice as common for the oldest compared to the youngest boys (20.7% vs. 11.1%). However, help-seeking very often resulted in only one contact with a help provider.

Delinquency seriousness

The percentage of parents having sought any help (help for behavior problems, or help from mental health professionals) increased with increasing seriousness of delinquency. Less than half of the parents of seriously delinquent boys had received help, and only one-quarter of the parents of these boys had received help from a mental health professional. Surprisingly, three quarters of the parents of seriously delinquent boys had never sought help from a mental health professional (Stouthamer-Loeber, Loeber, & Thomas, 1992).

Steps in developmental pathways

Stouthamer-Loeber et al. (1995) compared which delinquent and problem behaviors according to the developmental pathways model (Loeber, Wung et al., 1993) distinguished between those who received help compared to those who did not. In general, the higher the advancement in multiple pathways, the higher the frequency of help-seeking. The age of onset of any disruptive behavior or serious disruptive behavior was inversely related to the frequency of help-seeking. This finding indicates that early-onset problem behavior, even of a serious nature, in general does not trigger help-seeking or the provision of professional services.

Court contact

A comparison between boys with and without court contact showed that court delinquents received more intensive help than non-court delinquents. It may well be possible that court intervention brought the necessity for help to the parents' attention. This is reinforced by the fact that only 16.9% of the boys' parents sought help *before* the year in which their boy was referred to the juvenile court. The average age of onset for any disruptive behavior was 7.4 and the average age at which the first help was sought was 9.9, which shows that there was a two-and-a-half-year gap between when the problems first appeared and when help was sought.

We also examined (Office of Juvenile Justice and Delinquency Prevention, 1998) how long disruptive behaviors had been apparent in boys who eventually were referred to the juvenile court for an index offense. The results showed that the onset of the first step in any of the pathways tended to take place at age 7.0, moderately serious problem behavior at age 9.5, serious delinquency at age 11.9, while the age of first contact with the juvenile court was 14.5. This showed that about seven and a half years elapsed between the earliest emerging disruptive behavior and the first contact with the juvenile court. It should be noted that delinquent boys who were not referred to the juvenile court also tended to have a long history of problem behaviors.

In summary, the development of disruptive and delinquent behaviors was largely left unchecked. These findings have important implications for preventive interventions, and for policy makers. Preventive interventions can take place in the relatively long time window between the onset of early problem behaviors of a minor kind and the first contact with the juvenile court. Second, such interventions are relevant for policy makers since they should realize that eventual index offenders have had the unchecked opportunity to commit delinquent acts for many years.

Methodological Issues

Dichotomization of constructs

For many analyses of the Pittsburgh Youth Study, explanatory and outcome variables were dichotomized, contrasting the "worst" quarter of boys with the remaining three-quarters. Dichotomization has often been criticized, on the grounds that it loses information (since sub-threshold cases are treated as indistinguishable) and that it reduces the measured strength of association and statistical power. However, Loeber, Farrington et al. (1998a) argued that in some cases the benefits of dichotomization could outweigh the costs. They illustrated their points using analyses of the oldest sample at waves S and A.

First, they showed that there was no decrease in the measured strength of association if appropriate indices were used. In particular, the average value of tetrachoric correlations with dichotomous variables was the same as that of product-moment correlations with continuous variables. Second, they argued that the odds ratio was a more useful and realistic measure of strength of association with dichotomous variables than was the (phi) correlation. Whereas phi correlations suggested that relationships with delinquency were weak, odds ratios suggested that relationships with delinquency were strong. Third, they demonstrated that several relationships with delinquency were non-linear. For example, boys were particularly likely to be delinquents if they had very young or old mothers, and least likely if they had mothers who were of an average age. Dichotomization was a simple and understandable way of dealing with non-linear relationships. Fourth, the results were not greatly affected by different dichotomization splits. Fifth, the relative importance of explanatory variables was very similar irrespective of whether they were continuous or dichotomous and whether ordinary least squares or logistic regression was used. Sixth, it was easy to investigate interaction effects using dichotomous variables. Seventh, it was also easy to identify boys with multiple risk factors.

Loeber, Farrington et al. (1998a) concluded that dichotomization was useful when explanatory and outcome variables were crudely measured in a small number of categories, when variables had skewed distributions (as was often the case with delinquency), and when explanatory variables were non-linearly related to outcome variables. Overall, dichotomization facilitated the study of risk factors, encouraged a focus on individuals as well as variables, greatly simplified the presentation of results, yielded findings that were easily understandable by a wide audience, and showed no signs of producing misleading conclusions.

Validity of measures

Self-reports are widely used to measure delinquent behavior. A crucial issue concerns their concurrent and predictive validity, which is usually assessed by comparing self-reports with official records of delinquent behavior. Farrington, Loeber et al. (1996b) compared self-reports at waves S and A with juvenile court petitions before wave A and in the following six years. The middle sample was studied from an average age of 10.7 years at A to an average age of 16.6 years, and the oldest sample was studied from an average age of 13.9 years at A up to their eighteenth birthdays. The main measure of validity that was used was the AROC (Area under the Receiver Operating Characteristic curve), scaled from 0 = chance, to 1 = perfect discrimination between petitioned and non-petitioned boys.

The results showed that the self-reports had concurrent validity in relation to past petitions. For example, AROC = .366 for criminal delinquency (excluding status, traffic, drunkenness, and other minor offenses) and AROC = .478 for index offenses in the oldest sample. The self-reports also had predictive validity in relation to future petitions, although predictive validity was generally lower than concurrent validity; AROC = .332 for criminal delinquency and AROC = .288 for index offenses in the oldest sample. Importantly, predictive validity was similar for white and African American boys, although concurrent validity was higher for white boys. Ethnicity predicted future petitions independently of self-reported delinquency. When self-reports of being arrested were studied, it was found that petitioned African American boys were more likely to admit being arrested than petitioned white boys.

Multiple informants

It might be expected that measures based on multiple data sources would be more valid than measures based on only a single data source. Farrington et al. (1996b) tested this by comparing the validity of self-reported delinquency with the validity of the combined delinquency scale (based on reports by mothers, boys and teachers). They found that the combined scale had similar concurrent validity to the self-report scale, but higher predictive validity. For example, for predictive validity of the combined scale in the oldest sample, AROC = .425 for criminal delinquency and AROC = .385 for index offenses. The combined scale had higher predictive validity than the self-report scale for both African American and white boys.

The combined scale identified more serious delinquents than the self-report scale, especially in the middle sample. In this sample, 10% of African American boys and 7% of white boys were serious delinquents at A according to self-reports, but 35% of African American boys and 18% of white boys were serious delinquents at A according to the combined scale. The predictive validity of the combined scale was similar for white and African American boys for criminal delinquency, but higher for white boys for index offenses. Ethnicity predicted future petitions independently of the combined delinquency scale.

The main conclusions from this analysis were that there was an increase in predictive validity by combining self-report data with information from mothers and teachers, and that the self-report and combined delinquency scales had significant predictive validity for both white and African American boys. The most perplexing result was why, at any given level of delinquency seriousness, African American boys were more likely to be petitioned in the future. Possible reasons included objectively more serious offending by African American boys (e.g., index violence committed with weapons), biases in police and court processing, differences in demeanor between African American and white boys when apprehended by the police, differences in police patrolling in African American compared to white areas, and a more intense or more speedy escalation of delinquency for African American boys.

Comparison between informants

We compared how well parents and children, compared to teachers, reported on the child's academic performance. Maguin and Loeber (1996b) addressed this issue in the youngest, middle, and oldest samples. They found that mothers' ratings of the academic performance of their son correlated with final grades as well as or better than did teachers' ratings. However, mothers' ratings, compared to teachers' ratings, correlated more poorly with achievement test scores. In comparison with mothers and teachers, the boys' ratings correlated more poorly with final grades or achievement test scores. Correlates, however, do not reveal biases in raters' judgment. The results showed that mothers and boys in the oldest sample tended to over-estimate rather than under-estimate the final grade. This information is useful in deciding whether to use, for example, parents' ratings as a proxy for teachers' ratings, because the results show the limitations of such an approach.

Conclusions and Future Priorities

The Pittsburgh Youth Study has a unique combination of features. Three different samples of boys have been followed up at frequent (6-month or 1-year) intervals, making it possible to assess how far results are replicable. The youngest and oldest samples have so far been followed up for 10 years with no gaps in data collection, and the middle sample was followed up for three years. Information has been collected from different sources (the boy, mother, and teacher) about explanatory variables from different domains (boy, family, peer, school, neighborhood) and many different types of outcome variables (not only delinquency but also substance use, sexual behavior, and externalizing and internalizing mental health problems). Over time, the attrition rate has been very low.

The Pittsburgh Youth Study had a high-risk design to maximize the yield of serious delinquency. Even so, the prevalence of serious delinquency was surprisingly high. According to boys, mothers and teachers, 51% of African American boys and 28% of white boys had committed serious delinquency up to age 17. One third of the oldest sample were petitioned to the court for index offenses as juveniles. While the prevalence of index violence increased between ages 12 and 17, the prevalence of physical fighting decreased (Loeber & Hay, 1997), suggesting that the boys were becoming more clearly divided into high and low violence categories. Physical aggression was particularly related to stable high offending in the youngest sample. There was considerable year-to-year stability in antisocial behavior. While all the outcomes were inter-related, delinquency was particularly associated with externalizing problems such as attention deficit and conduct problems. Three developmental pathways to serious delinquency (Covert, Overt and Authority Conflict) were replicated over the three samples.

Delinquency was related to measures of impulsivity, IQ, and personality. Two types of impulsivity underlay 11 measures, namely cognitive and behavioral impulsivity, and delinquents were especially characterized by behavioral impulsivity (restless, poorly controlled behavior). Low IQ was related to self-reported delinquency independently of socioeconomic status, ethnicity, neighborhood, and impulsivity. Delinquents tended to have high negative emotionality (i.e., showing negative emotions such as anger and fear) and low constraint (i.e., not cautious, seeking thrills and taking risks).

Child, family and macro (socio-economic, demographic, and neighborhood) explanatory variables were related to delinquency in all three samples. The most important risk factors were lack of guilt, low achievement, poor parental supervision, poor parent–boy communication, family on welfare, broken family and living in a bad neighborhood. The probability of delinquency increased with increasing numbers of risk factors. Multiple problem boys were especially predicted by the first four (child and family) of these risk factors. Many univariate and multivariate relationships between risk factors and delinquency were replicated not only between the combined (boy, mother, teacher) scale and court referrals but also between Pittsburgh and London. Deviant peers were not considered as an explanatory variable, but they predicted the onset of delinquency.

Many analyses were based on dichotomized variables, and systematic comparisons showed that dichotomization did not produce incorrect or misleading results. Self-reports and the combined scale both had predictive validity in relation to future court petitions for African American and white boys, but predictive validity was higher for the combined scale. The probability of future court petitions was higher for African American boys after controlling for past delinquency (on self-reports or the combined scale). However, controlling for poor reading ability, there were no differences between African American and white boys on the combined delinquency scale. The relationship between poor reading and delinquency was mediated by attention problems. Also, there were no differences in (self-reported) delinquency between African American and white boys who did not live in underclass neighborhoods. The pathways to delinquency were accelerated in the worst neighborhoods.

Theoretical considerations

When we started the Pittsburgh Youth Study, we were aware, of course, of key criminological theories (Elliott et al., 1985; Gottfredson &

Hirschi, 1990; Wilson & Herrnstein, 1985), and many constructs from such theories have been incorporated in the measurements of our study. At the same time, we realized that none of the existing theories covered all important risk factors but, instead, usually focussed on a small subset of such factors. Our approach has been to include a wide variety of known and potential risk factors in our measurements, to permit the testing of a wide variety of current and future theories. Our conceptualization takes into account that offending has both long-term and immediate antecedents, and that both are necessary for persisting delinquency. Examples of long-term antecedents are poor parental monitoring over extended periods of time, and low birth weight. Examples of more immediate antecedents of offending are the use of drugs prior to the commission of a delinquent act, and provocation by others prior to a violent act.

With the exception of a few theories (Farrington, 1996; Catalano & Hawkins, 1996; Le Blanc & Fréchette, 1989), most theories tend to be adevelopmental, and do not view serious offending as caused by the accumulation of deviancy processes from childhood through adulthood. Our own conceptualization has added several important theoretical aspects. First, we developed and expanded the concept of developmental criminology (Loeber & Le Blanc, 1990; Le Blanc & Loeber, 1998), in which we laid out key developmental aspects of offending and how to operationalize them. Second, we conceptualized developmental criminology as an interdisciplinary effort to integrate knowledge about the development of predelinquent problem behavior and knowledge of the development of delinquent offending. In that way, we expanded the inquiry to account better for the slow but steady growth in deviancy in some and not in other youth. Our findings support the notion that a dichotomy between early- and late-onset offenders can be defended, but at the same time it constitutes a simplification of a gradual entry of youth into delinquent offending between childhood and adolescence. As a corollary of the developmental approach to offending, we want to document different causal processes for the onset, escalation, and desistance of deviance.

A basic premise that organizes our research is that offending by most juveniles results from forces within the individual and forces in the individual's social environment (parents, siblings, and peers) in different contexts (family home, school, neighborhood). Examples of individual factors (such as impulsivity, lack of guilt), but also distal individual factors such as birth complications, are known to affect later functioning. Examples of family risk factors include parental pathology, and parents' child rearing practices. Examples of peer risk factors are rejection by peers, and association with deviant peers. These social factors operate differently in different settings. The life-course approach to juvenile delinquency takes into account that social interactions relevant to the development of offending initially take place within the family, but are subsequently broadened to include the school and the neighborhood as youth become more mobile and face different problems of adaptation in each setting. We are interested not only in the impact of early risk factors on delinquency in childhood and adolescence, but also how later risk factors influence offending through the life-course into adulthood.

Whereas many theories of juvenile offending appear to imply that causes are invariant with age, we assumed that causes are likely to differ for those with different ages of onset of offending. Specifically, we believe that similar risk factors may affect all youth, but that causal processes represented by risk factors vary by age of onset of offending. Thus, we expect that individual factors may dominate causal processes affecting early-onset offenders, but psychosocial factors may affect late-onset offenders.

Most theories are correlational in nature and tend to use data from all juveniles in a sample, while not distinguishing between those who engage in serious versus less serious forms of offending. As a result, most of these theories emphasize relationships between risk factors and delinquency (usually indicated by low correlations), but do not yield information about the causes that differentiate why some juveniles and not others escalate to serious offending. Our approach is not to construct a single theory attempting to explain offending in all juveniles. Instead, we attempt to explain why some youth escalate to serious offending after an early onset, why others reach such behaviors while starting later in life, and why some youth desist from offending. Thus, in the best of circumstances we will eventually produce specific explanations for developmentally defined subgroups of offenders. Our conceptualization of developmental pathways in offending constitutes a first step in this process toward specific rather than general theoretical explanations. Our approach is based on the assumption that empirical knowledge relevant for interventions and sanctions has to be based on the life-course of *individuals* rather than the usually weak relationships between *variables*, while recognizing that knowledge about relationships between variables can inform knowledge about individuals.

Eventually, juvenile justice personnel, therapists, and public health planners, need to know what are the main causes that apply to specific groups of juveniles. This brings us to the last point relevant to theories. We see our empirical efforts as part of an attempt to intervene in delinquency processes *prior to* juveniles getting arrested or brought before the court. Advances in the prevention of serious juvenile delinquency are predicated on improving our knowledge of causes for youth at risk for serious delinquency, especially those causes that are potentially modifiable.

Future research

Key priorities for future research in the Pittsburgh Youth Study include the following. First, we need to better address the development of serious offending as a function of the persistence and change in risk and protective factors from childhood to adolescence. Second, we need to better understand factors contributing to gun wounding and homicide victimization. Particularly, we will focus on the relatively high percentage of boys in the oldest sample who have been shot and/or killed (9.4% of the boys in that sample). Third, we will examine the consequences of delinquent offending, and address the relationship between self-reports and court petitions at different ages, to estimate the probability of an offense leading to a court petition and factors related to this probability. Fourth, we need to investigate why some boys develop patterns of multiple problems and others do not.

Fifth, we plan to investigate how far ethnic differences in violence (on court petitions and the combined scale) hold up after controlling for all explanatory variables. Sixth, we aim to study how far the relationship between the number of risk factors and delinquency holds up in different contexts (neighborhoods and public housing). Seventh, we need to examine factors that influence boys' successful transition from adolescence to adulthood, including desistance from delinquency. Also, we aim to study the effect of gangs, by measuring delinquency before, during and after gang membership.

Currently, the funding of the oldest sample (by NIMH) is assured until 2000, and the funding of the youngest sample (by NIDA) is assured until

2001. By then, the youngest sample will have been followed up from age
7 to age 20, and the oldest sample will have been followed up from age
13 to age 25. In addition, plans are underway to carry out a single
follow-up of the middle sample at ages 22–23.

Hopefully, the Pittsburgh Youth Study will have contributed even
more by then to knowledge about the development of offending and
antisocial behavior in boys. Its sister longitudinal study of girls (funded
by NIMH, and the Office of Research on Women's Health) is scheduled
to begin in 1998. In due course, it should be possible to establish how
far risk factors for girls are similar to or different from risk factors already
established for boys. In both studies, one of the greatest challenges is
to translate research findings into practice that is relevant to juvenile
justice, mental and public health, and public policy. Along that line,
challenges include the development of screening methods and preventive interventions, and the dissemination of easily understandable
results to policy makers and practitioners.

References

Capaldi, D., & Patterson, G. R. (1987). An approach to the problem of recruit-
ment and retention rates for longitudinal research. *Behavioral Assessment* 9:
169–177.

Caspi, A., Black, J., Block, J. H., Klopp, B., Lynam, D., Moffitt, T. E., & Stouthamer-
Loeber, M. A. (1992). A "common-language" version of the California Child
Q-Set for personality assessment. *Psychological Assessment* 4: 512–523.

Caspi, A., Moffitt, T. E., Silva, P. A., Stouthamer-Loeber, M., Krueger, R. F., &
Schmutte, P. S. (1994). Are some people crime-prone? Replications of the
personality-crime relationship across countries, genders, races, and methods.
Criminology 32: 163–195.

Catalano, R. F., & Hawkins, J. D. (1996). The social development model: A theory
of antisocial behavior. In: Hawkins, J. D., ed. *Delinquency and crime: Current
theories*. New York: Cambridge University Press.

Elliott, D. S. (1994). Serious violent offenders: Onset, developmental course,
and termination – The American Society of Criminology 1993 Presidential
address. *Criminology* 32: 1–21.

Elliott, D. S., Huizinga, D., & Ageton, S. S. (1985). *Explaining delinquency and drug
use*. Beverly Hills: Sage Publications.

Farrington, D. P. (1996). The explanation and prevention of youthful offending.
In: Hawkins, J. D., ed. *Delinquency and crime: Current theories*. New York: Cambridge University Press.

Farrington, D. P. (1998). Predictors, causes and correlates of male youth violence. In: Tonry, M., & Moore, M., eds. *Youth violence* (Crime and Justice, vol. 24). Chicago: University of Chicago Press, in press.

Farrington, D. P., Gallagher, B., Morley, L., St. Ledger, R., & West, D. J. (1990). Methods of tracing and securing cooperation in a 24-year follow-up study. In: Magnusson, D., & Bergman, L., eds. *Data quality in longitudinal research.* Cambridge: Cambridge University Press.

Farrington, D. P., & Loeber, R. (1998). Transatlantic replicability of risk factors in the development of delinquency. In: Cohen, P., Slomkowski, C., & Robins, L. N., eds. *Where and when: Geographical and generational influences on psychopathology.* Mahwah, N.J.: Lawrence Erlbaum, in press.

Farrington, D. P., Loeber, R., Stouthamer-Loeber, M., & Van Kammen, W. B. (1996a). *Prevalence of delinquent acts between ages 6 and 16.* Paper presented at the annual meeting of the American Society of Criminology, Chicago (November).

Farrington, D. P., Loeber, R., Stouthamer-Loeber, M., Van Kammen, W. B., & Schmidt, L. (1996b). Self-reported delinquency and a combined delinquency seriousness scale based on boys, mothers, and teachers: Concurrent and predictive validity for African-Americans and Caucasians. *Criminology* 34: 501–525.

Frick, P. J., Lahey, B. B., Loeber, R., Tannenbaum, L., Van Horn, Y., Christ, M. A. G., Hart, E. A., & Hanson, K. (1993). Oppositional defiant disorder and conduct disorder: A meta-analytic review of factor analyses and cross-validation in a clinic sample. *Clinical Psychology Review* 13: 319–340.

Gottfredson, M., & Hirschi, T. (1990). *A general theory of crime.* Stanford, CA: Stanford University Press.

Huizinga, D., Loeber, R., & Thornberry, T. (1993). Longitudinal study of delinquency, drug use, sexual activity, and pregnancy among children and youth in three cities. *Public Health Reports: Journal of the U.S. Public Health Service* 108: Supplement 1: 90–96.

Keenan, K., Loeber, R., Zhang, Q., Stouthamer-Loeber, M., & Van Kammen, W. B. (1995). The influence of deviant peers on the development of boys' disruptive and delinquency behavior: A temporal analysis. *Development and Psychopathology* 7: 715–726.

Kelley, B. T., Loeber, R., Keenan, K., & DeLamatre, M. (1997). Developmental pathways in disruptive and delinquent behavior. *Juvenile Justice Bulletin, Office of Juvenile Justice and Delinquency Prevention* (November).

Kelley, B. T., Huizinga, D., Thornberry, T. P., & Loeber, R. (1997). Epidemiology of serious violence. *Juvenile Justice Bulletin, Office of Juvenile Justice and Delinquency Prevention:* 1–11 (June).

Le Blanc, M. (1997). *The development of interpersonal violence: Gradation in relation to other problem behavior and delinquency and the social and personal characteristics of various trajectories of violent behavior.* Paper presented at the annual meeting of the American Society of Criminology, San Diego (November).

Le Blanc, M., & Fréchette, M. (1989). *Male offending from latency to adulthood.* New York: Springer-Verlag.

Le Blanc, M., & Loeber, R. (1998). Developmental criminology updated. In: Tonry, M., ed. *Crime and Justice* (vol. 23). Chicago: Chicago University Press.

Loeber, R. (1982). The stability of antisocial and delinquent child behavior. *Child Development* 53: 1431–1446.

Loeber, R., & Le Blanc, M. (1990). Toward a developmental criminology. In: Tonry, M., & Morris, N., eds. *Crime and Justice* Vol. 12. Chicago, IL: University of Chicago Press.

Loeber, R., DeLamatre, M., Keenan, K., & Zhang, Q. (1998). A prospective replication of developmental pathways in disruptive and delinquent behavior. In: Cairns, R., ed. *The Individual as a Focus in Developmental Research.* Thousand Oaks, CA: Sage, in press.

Loeber, R., Farrington, D. P., Stouthamer-Loeber, M., & Van Kammen, W. B. (1998a). *Antisocial Behavior and Mental Health Problems: Explanatory Factors in Childhood and Adolescence.* Mahwah, NJ: Lawrence Erlbaum.

Loeber, R., Farrington, D. P., Stouthamer-Loeber, M., & Van Kammen, W. B. (1998b). Multiple risk factors for multiproblem boys: Co-occurrence of delinquency, substance use, attention deficit, conduct problems, physical aggression, covert behavior, depressed mood, and shy/withdrawn behavior. In: Jessor, R., ed. *New perspectives on adolescent risk behavior.* Cambridge: Cambridge University Press, in press.

Loeber, R., & Hay, D. F. (1997). Key issues in the development of aggression and violence from childhood to early adulthood. *Annual Review of Psychology* 48: 371–410.

Loeber, R., Keenan, K., & Zhang, Q. (1997). Boys' experimentation and persistence in developmental pathways toward serious delinquency. *Journal of Child and Family Studies* 6: 321–357.

Loeber, R., & Le Blanc, M. (1990). Toward a developmental criminology. In: Tonry, M., & Morris, N., eds. *Crime and Justice* Vol. 12. Chicago: University of Chicago Press.

Loeber, R., & Schmaling, K. (1985). Empirical evidence for overt and covert patterns of antisocial conduct problems. *Journal of Abnormal Child Psychology* 13: 337–352.

Loeber, R., Stouthamer-Loeber, M., Van Kammen, W. B., & Farrington, D. P. (1989). Development of a new measure of self-reported antisocial behavior for young children: Prevalence and reliability. In: Klein, M. W., ed. *Cross-National Research in Self-Reported Crime and Delinquency*. Boston: Kluwer-Nijhoff.

Loeber, R., Stouthamer-Loeber, M., Van Kammen, W. B., & Farrington, D. P. (1991). Initiation, escalation and desistance in juvenile offending and their correlates. *Journal of Criminal Law and Criminology* 82: 36–82.

Loeber, R., & Wikström, P-O. (1993). Individual pathways to crime in different types of neighborhood. In: Farrington, D. P., Sampson, R. J., & Wikström, P. O., eds. *Integrating Individual and Ecological Aspects of Crime*. Stockholm: National Council for Crime Prevention.

Loeber, R., Wung, P., Keenan, K., Giroux, B., Stouthamer-Loeber, M., Van Kammen, W. B., & Maughan, B. (1993). Developmental pathways in disruptive child behavior. *Development and Psychopathology* 5: 101–132.

Lynam, D. R. (1997). Pursuing the psychopath: Capturing the fledgling psychopath in a nomological net. *Journal of Abnormal Psychology* 106: 425–438.

Lynam, D. R., Caspi, A., Moffitt, T. E., Wikström, P-O. H., & Loeber, R. (in review). The effects of impulsivity on delinquency are stronger in poor neighborhoods.

Lynam, D. R., Moffitt, T. E., & Stouthamer-Loeber, M. (1993). Explaining the relation between IQ and delinquency: Class, race, test motivation, school failure, or self-control? *Journal of Abnormal Psychology* 102: 187–196.

Maguin, E., & Loeber, R. (1996a). Academic performance and delinquency. In: Tonry, M., ed. *Crime and Justice*, Vol. 20. Chicago: University of Chicago Press.

Maguin, E., & Loeber, R. (1996b). How well do ratings of academic performance by mothers and their sons correspond to grades, achievement test scores, and teachers' ratings? *Journal of Behavioral Education* 6: 405–425.

Maguin, E., Loeber, R., & LeMahieu, P. (1993). Does the relationship between poor reading and delinquency hold for different age and ethnic groups? *Journal of Emotional and Behavioral Disorders* 1: 88–100.

Moffitt, T. E. (1993). Life-course-persistent and adolescence-limited antisocial behavior: A developmental taxonomy. *Psychological Review* 100: 674–701.

Moffitt, T. E., Caspi, A., Silva, P. A., & Stouthamer-Loeber, M. (1995). Individual differences in personality and intelligence are linked to crime: Cross-context evidence from nations, neighborhoods, genders, races, and age-cohorts. In: Hagan, J., ed. *Current perspectives on aging and the life cycle. Volume 4: Delinquency and disrepute in the life course*. Greenwich, CT: JAI Press.

Peeples, F., & Loeber, R. (1994). Do individual factors and neighborhood context explain ethnic differences in juvenile delinquency? *Journal of Quantitative Criminology* 10: 141–157.

Rutter, M. (1985). Resilience in the face of adversity: Protective factors and resistance to psychiatric disorder. *British Journal of Psychiatry* 147: 598–611.

Office of Juvenile Justice and Delinquency Prevention, *Serious and violent juvenile offenders* (1998, April). Washington, DC: OJJDP Juvenile Justice Bulletin.

Stouthamer-Loeber, M. (1993). Optimizing data quality of individual and community sources in longitudinal research. In: Farrington, D. P., Sampson, R. J., & Wikström, P. O., eds. *Integrating Individual and Ecological Aspects of Crime*. Stockholm, Sweden: National Council for Crime Prevention.

Stouthamer-Loeber, M., Loeber, R., Farrington, D. P., Zhang, Q., Van Kammen, W. B., & Maguin, E. (1993). The double edge of protective and risk factors for delinquency: Interrelations and developmental patterns. *Development and Psychopathology* 5: 683–701.

Stouthamer-Loeber, M., Loeber, R., & Thomas, C. (1992). Caretakers seeking help for boys with disruptive delinquent behavior. *Comprehensive Mental Health Care* 2: 159–178.

Stouthamer-Loeber, M., Loeber, R., Van Kammen, W. B., & Zhang, Q. (1995). Uninterrupted delinquent careers: The timing of parental helpseeking and juvenile court contact. *Studies on Crime and Crime Prevention* 4: 236–251.

Stouthamer-Loeber, M., & Van Kammen, W. B. (1995). *Data collection and management: A practical guide*. Newbury Park, CA.: Sage.

Stouthamer-Loeber, M., Van Kammen, W. B., & Loeber, R. (1992). The nuts and bolts of implementing large-scale longitudinal studies. *Violence and Victims* 7: 63–78.

Tellegen, A., Lykken, D., Bouchard, T. J., Wilcox, K. J., Segal, N. L., & Rich, S. (1988). Personality similarity in twins reared apart and together. *Journal of Personality and Social Psychology* 54: 1031–1039.

Tolan, P. H., Gorman-Smith, D., & Loeber, R. (1998). Developmental timing of onset of disruptive behaviors and later delinquency level. Unpublished manuscript, University of Illinois, Chicago, IL.

Van Kammen, W. B., & Loeber, R. (1994). Are fluctuations in delinquent activities related to the onset and offset of juvenile illegal drug use and drug dealing? *Journal of Drug Issues* 24: 9–24.

Van Kammen, W. B., Maguin, E., & Loeber, R. (1994). Initiation of drug selling and its relationship with illicit drug use and serious delinquency in adolescent boys. In: Weitekamp, E. G. M., & Kerner, H. J., eds. *Cross-National Longitudinal Research on Human Development and Criminal Behavior*. Dordrecht, The Netherlands: Kluwer.

Van Kammen, W. B., & Stouthamer-Loeber, M. (1997). Practical aspects of data collection and data management. In: Bickman, L., & Rog, D., eds. *Handbook of applied social research methods*. Thousand Oaks, CA: Sage.

White, J., Moffitt, T. E., Caspi, A., Bartusch, D. J., Needles, D., & Stouthamer-Loeber, M. (1994). The measurement of impulsivity and its relationship to delinquency. *Journal of Abnormal Psychology* 103: 192–205.

Wilson, J. Q., & Herrnstein, R. J. (1985). *Crime and human nature*. New York: Simon & Schuster.

Zhang, Q., Loeber, R., & Stouthamer-Loeber, M. (1997). Developmental trends of delinquency attitudes and delinquency: Replication and synthesis across time and samples. *Journal of Quantitative Criminology* 13: 181–216.

THIRTEEN

Children as Abuse Perpetrators

Introduction

In my introduction to the first paper in this book I made the point that until fairly recently many people falsely believed that the victimization of children was a rare phenomenon. Even more difficult for most of us to assimilate is the idea that children can themselves be the perpetrators of victimization, especially of sexual abuse. Given society's unawareness of this issue, the interaction between such children and the law usually does not go that well.

There is much that developmental psychology needs to learn about the prevalence of such behaviour and its causation. Also pressing is a need for more knowledge about possible treatment for such perpetrators and the actual effectiveness of various treatments. Although developmental aspects of children's own sexuality, and their evolving sexual relationships, is no longer such a taboo subject in several societies, we know considerably less about children as sex abusers.

While developmental psychology is rich in theory we need more cogent ideas regarding children as perpetrators of sexual abuse. In this pioneering paper Eileen Vizard and her colleagues review the limited literature and discuss important problems such as the definition of abuse. In a case I was recently involved in (to comment on the quality of the interviewing) a neighbour said she had seen the 7-year-old girl who lived next door playing with 'the willy' of another neighbour's 4-year-old son. Would such behaviour constitute the perpetration of sexual abuse?

Suggested reading

Bailey, S. (1996). Adolescents who murder. *Journal of Adolescence*, **19**, 199–239.

Child and Adolescent Sex Abuse Perpetrators: A Review of the Research Literature

Eileen Vizard, Elizabeth Monck,
and Peter Misch

Introduction

Acknowledgement of the existence of child and adolescent perpetrators of sexual abuse is relatively recent and followed several years after the recognition of adult sexual abuse of children in the USA (Kempe & Kempe, 1978), and the UK (Mrazek, Lynch & Bentovim, 1981).

In this relatively new area of work, the factual knowledge base is sparse and theoretical understanding of the problem is limited. New treatment approaches for adolescent abusers are developing, even though treatment outcome studies are still rare. Nevertheless, a sanguine clinical view prevails about the effectiveness of early intervention with child and adolescent sexual abusers. Existing theoretical models in relation to adolescent sex offending are based on work with adults, and seldom take into account the physical, emotional, and social developmental factors, which are an integral part of the psychopathology of child and adolescent sexual abusers.

This paper will describe definitional issues, what is currently known about the common characteristics of adolescent sexual abusers, theories of aetiology, and critically review the current literature on the outcome of treatment programmes. The implications for research and clinical practice will be discussed.

Definitions

Problems of defining abusive behaviour are more frequently mentioned in the literature on adolescent abusers than on adult abusers, and no doubt spring from the continued lack of information about normal psychosexual development in children and young people (NCH, 1992: p. 3). But they also spring from confusion about what expectations society should have of adolescent sexual behaviour. Becker (1988) has described nondeviant sexual behaviour in adolescence as "noncoercive sexual interaction with a peer" (p. 197). By extrapolation, deviant sexual behaviour may be defined as having three elements: the use of coercion or force, sexualized interactions which are age-inappropriate for the partner, and partners who are not peers. If any of these elements are present, the behaviour of the subject may be defined as abusive, but we would acknowledge that even these guidelines leave open the question of what constitutes "coercion", and "age-appropriate sexual interactions", and even (at the margins) who are peers, and who are not. Even with more uniform practice of eliciting information, cultural, religious and individual attitudes and practices would mean that some variations of what was acceptable behaviour would continue.

Normal Child and Adolescent Psychosexual Development

Large-scale studies of sexual behaviour in normal children have been rare. Friedrich, Grambsch, Broughton, Kuiper and Beilke (1991) reported a survey of 880 2–12-year-olds. Those with a history of sexual abuse, or physical or mental handicap were excluded. Mothers completed behaviour checklists, one of which was specifically designed to elicit information on their children's sexual behaviour. The results showed that increased sexualized behaviour in the child was linked to a measure of family nudity, and with increased general behaviour problems. It is pointed out that such links may be variously interpreted: parents who themselves see nothing wrong in family nudity, may also allow greater freedom for sexualized behaviour in their children, or indeed be more comfortable in reporting it. Sexualized behaviour in the children was not associated with sociodemographic variables. The authors emphasize that a variety of sexual behaviours in these age groups "appear to be normal" (p. 463). They also argue that when several of the least frequent behaviours are present, the child should be assessed in greater detail.

Money and Ehrhardt (1972) claimed that pre-teen children were probably as "sexual" as younger children could be observed to be, but sought to conceal their behaviour in order to conform to society's rules on modesty and manners. Friedrich et al. (1991) also observed a decline in children's overt sexual behaviour with age and in both sexes. In each age-group it is recognized that a small proportion of children and adolescents show behaviour which is unacceptable or dangerous to others. Sexual aggression in children and young people is easier to categorize as both unacceptable and dangerous, which perhaps makes it all the more surprising that such behaviour was accepted as abusive so late.

When it comes to describing normal adolescent sexual development the picture becomes much more confused. Downs and Hillje (1993) point out that systematic studies of sexual behaviour in this age-group were not undertaken until the 1940s, and accurate sex education is still lacking in most cultures. Biological processes associated with sexual maturation combine with social processes to influence the age at which sexual activities start, and the type of activity. Smith and Udry (1985) reported that the prevalence of different types of sexual behaviour in 12–15-year-olds followed different developmental patterns in black and white youths, and in boys and girls, but for the large majority the sequences of behaviour moved from touching and kissing through sexual petting to full intercourse. An increase with age of sexual intercourse has been found in innumerable studies (e.g., Elliott & Morse, 1989). Billy, Landale, Grady and Zimmerle (1988) noted that age at first intercourse itself had consequences for later sexual behaviour. Among other associated factors, early intercourse led to selecting friends who were also sexually active. Much coercive or nonconsensual behaviour shades into acts which are partially agreed between the partners, or in which one partner (usually the male in heterosexual relationships) subscribes to beliefs that certain actions give a "right" to sexual favours: for example, accepting an invitation to another's home or spending a lot of money on someone (Check & Malamuth, 1983; Goodchilds, Zellman, Johnson & Giarusso, 1988).

The paucity of observational or experimental data on childhood sexuality is being, in part, attributed to ethical considerations where the mere act of observing induced sexual responses in children could lay the experimenter open to charges of child abuse (Bancroft, 1989). The point has been made that "there is no universal standard for optimal child rearing or for child abuse and neglect" (Korbin, 1981), and that there is a danger that ethnocentric judgements may become incorporated in psychosexual definitions of normality.

Professional interpretations of the meaning of sexualized interactions between children may vary between cultures and over time. Gundersen, Melas and Skar (1981) conducted individual interviews with 60 Norwegian preschool teachers about their perceptions or direct observations of the sexual knowledge and behaviour of their pupils. Half of the teachers reported seeing "direct sexual behaviour, such as body exploration, genital manipulation, and coitus training" (p. 52) and one third of the teachers reported that children were "often" interested in other children's genitals. In the USA Cantwell (1988) later described the same behaviours in very young children as molestation and warned that "An educational effort is needed to take child perpetrators of inappropriate sexual activities seriously, even among preschool and school age children".

Incidence and Prevalence

Published studies which specifically report prevalence or incidence of children and adolescents who sexually abuse others are rare. Some information on the extent of the problem can be obtained from official statistics or from studies describing the incidence or prevalence of victimization in child sexual abuse. But the interpretation of this material is complicated by the fact that (as we have noted) definitions of sexual offending or unacceptable sexualized behaviour are not standard. Official organizations in the UK such as the police, the probation services, and some voluntary agencies specializing in this field, require statistics on juvenile sex offending for different purposes which inevitably influence what it is regarded as important or necessary to record. Research studies on incidence and prevalence of child or adolescent sexual abusing also face further methodological problems: what questions should be asked, and of whom, and how should the answers be validated (Peters, Wyatt & Finkelhor, 1986; Wyatt & Peters, 1986; Finkelhor, 1986a; Vizard, 1989)?

In the UK the main source providing even a crude basis for deducing incidence of sexual offending is the criminal statistics (Home Office, 1992). In 1992, a total of 29,500 sexual offences were recorded by the police for England and Wales and 8,400 sex offenders were cautioned or found guilty. Among these 8,400, 30% were under 21 years; 14% were aged 17–20 years; 12% were aged 14–16 years, and 4% were aged 10–13 years. Of all convicted rape offenders, 20% were under 21 years. Davis and Leitenberg (1987) concluded that, at a conservative estimate, 20% of all sexual offences in the US were committed by adolescents (over 95% of them males). Figures from the first four years of the US victim survey showed that 43% of rapes were committed by assailants under 21 years (quoted in Vinogradov, Dishotsky, Doty & Tinklenberg, 1988).

However, for several reasons the figures are probably an underestimate of the numbers of young people involved in sexual offending. First, many children and some younger adolescents are excluded from UK crime statistics, because children under 10 years are exempt from criminal liability, and for those between 10 and 14 years serious criminal charges are rarely brought because of the difficulty in establishing intent. Second, while formal cautions by the police are entered in UK crime statistics, informal cautions are not, and there is some evidence that the police have been using informal cautions increasingly with children and young adolescents caught in sexually assaultive situations (NCH, 1992). Third, obviously not all such offences are discovered or disclosed by victims. Fourth, even when discovered by third parties (e.g., parents), not all such offences are reported to the authorities. When abusive behaviour does come to light, denial and minimization of the significance of the behaviour is not uncommon among parents, police and professionals. Many sexual behaviours are put down to "adolescent experimentation", which others (including the victim) might describe as abusive (Groth & Loredo, 1981; NCH, 1992). In addition, some professionals and parents may be concerned at the serious consequences of a young person being identified as a sexual abuser (Horne, Glasgow, Cox & Calam, 1991).

Comparison of reported sexual offences with information from victims shows that sex offences are particularly likely to be underreported to official bodies (Home Office, 1992). For example, rape and indecent assault were under-reported by 80%; that is to say only 20% of victims report these crimes. By contrast, under-reporting of car theft was only 0.05%. Further under-reporting of adolescent sexual offences may arise from the fact that, at present, the British Crime Survey figures refer only to victims aged 16 years and over (Mayhew, Elliot & Dowds, 1988). Reporting practices of victims also affect official sexual offence rates, for example, the number of reported rape offences has doubled between 1980 and 1990 (Home Office, 1992) and this is almost certainly attributable to the increased willingness of women and men to report sexual victimization to the police, as well as changes within the UK police forces in recording such cases as offences (Grubin & Gunn, 1990). Even with these changes it is likely that the observed increases are still only a partial reflection of the true amount of sexual violence in the UK (Smith, 1984; Garvey, 1991) or in the USA (e.g., US Department of Justice, 1985).

When the victims are children, figures on the ages of perpetrators are revealing. Horne et al. (1991) carried out a study of child sexual abuse (i.e., victim based) investigations in Liverpool between 1989 and 1990. They found that 36% of the perpetrators offending against children were under 18 years of age; 2% of the offences were carried out by children under the age of 7 years, 13% were by children aged 8–12 years, and 21% by young people aged 13–17 years. Thus, significant numbers of children were engaging in inappropriate and exploitative sexual activity, often prior to sexual maturity. Among these children, it is likely that a high proportion are engaged in sexual activities with siblings. Johnson (1988) noted that 46% of a sample of 47 sexually abusive boys were involved in sibling incest. Relationships between young perpetrators and their victims are not, however, regularly recorded. Among 37 juvenile sex offenders studied by Pierce and Pierce (1987), fifty-nine offences had been committed, of which 40% were against sisters and 20% were against brothers. Both these figures included foster siblings and half the young offenders were in foster care at the time of the offence, which suggests a highly selected sample. Kahn and Lafond (1988), in a study of 350 young sex offenders in a correctional institution, found 95% knew their victims and "common victims were siblings and/or children for whom the offender was babysitting" (p. 137).

In a prevalence study of sexual victimization retrospectively reported by a sample of 16–21-year-old college students, Kelly, Regan and Burton (1991) found that 27% of the incidents had involved perpetrators age 13–17 years of age, and 1% had involved child perpetrators under

12 years. Of the sexual victimization by peers, 15% was by female perpetrators. Fromuth, Burkhart and Jones (1991) carried out a questionnaire investigation of the prevalence of sexual aggression among
582 male USA college students. Sixteen (3%) reported activity which
met the study criteria of child molester. Students were only asked about
activities aged 16 or older, and when there was a minimum 10-year age
gap between victim and abuser. It is therefore probable that a large
number of abusive episodes, some of which would have been defined by
Fromuth et al. as severe, would have been excluded by this restriction of
definition of victim and abuser. Females responsible as adolescents for
child abuse were also excluded.

To set against the likelihood of low reporting rates for adolescent
sexual offending, there is some evidence that, once caught, child and
adolescent perpetrators are much more likely to admit to offences
than adults (Horne et al., 1991; Kaplan, Abel, Cunningham-Rathner &
Mittelman, 1990). Horne et al. (1991) also noted that only 60% of
"deniers" had legal proceedings taken against them, as opposed to 82%
of "admitters". They suggest that children could be regarded as "naive
offenders" who are less likely to appreciate the effectiveness of denial in
preventing action being taken against them, particularly in the absence
of medical evidence.

Offence Characteristics

Retrospective and prospective studies of sexual abuse by adolescents
have shown that their behaviour covers the same range as adult
sexual abusers (e.g., Becker, Cunningham-Rathner & Kaplan, 1986a;
Ageton, 1983). Although Ageton's data were derived from self-report
schedules, some of her conclusions have been supported by other
studies using interviews (e.g., Vinogradov et al., 1988). Kahn and
Lafond (1988) found over half of a large sample of incarcerated young
sex offenders had used some force to subdue or persuade the victim;
female offenders were much more likely to use persuasion than force.
Johnson (1988) found that coercion was extremely commonly
employed (83%) by abusive boys, although most of this was verbal
threats or bribes (60%).

Samples of adolescent incarcerated rapists show that prior drug use,
impulsivity and lack of provocation from the victim are common

(Ageton, 1983; Vinogradov et al., 1998; Epps, 1991). In the study by Vinogradov and colleagues, two thirds of the rapists they did not know the victim.

Very few studies have included female adolescent sexual offenders, or differentiated the characteristics of their offending behaviour (see below). However, studies of adult women who sexually abuse children have shown that they can be involved in almost all sexually abusive acts with children of both sexes (Faller, 1987; Margolin, 1986).

Perpetrator Characteristics

It is self-evident, but nevertheless worth emphasizing, that our knowledge of young sex offenders is confined to those cases that come to light and reach the stage of legal and/or therapeutic intervention at which competent histories are taken. It is possible that, if we could investigate all such offenders, a different picture would emerge. Among known cases, it is important to acknowledge that young sex offenders are not a homogeneous group (Becker, 1988; Kosky, 1989). Sociodemographic data (family, ethnicity and religion) show no significant groupings (Ryan, Metzner & Krugman, 1990). Bremer (1993), describing aberrant sexual behaviour, listed a "continuum" which ranges from "inappropriate" to "hypersexualised" and "orgasm-orientated" to "aggressive".

A high proportion of adolescent sex offenders have been reported as isolated from their peers, with poor relationships with family members (Lewis, Shankok & Pincus, 1979; Deisher, Wenet, Paperny, Clark & Fehrenbach, 1982; Awad, Saunders & Levene, 1984; Fehrenbach, Smith, Monastersky & Deisher, 1986; Saunders, Awad & White, 1986; Awad & Saunders, 1989). Williams and Gilmour (1994) have reviewed the multiplicity of approaches to measuring social isolation in children and young people: this is yet another area in which sweeping statements have crept into the literature on young sex offenders, but for which the empirical evidence is poor or difficult to interpret. Lonczynski (1991) studied nonincarcerated adolescent boys who had committed sexual offences against children, and two comparison groups: one out-patient sample of emotionally disturbed boys, and a volunteer sample drawn from church groups. Overall, social isolation and social competence did not vary between the three groups, but no specific items the young sex offenders showed significantly more isolation. DeNatale (1989) also noted that indicators of shyness, timidity and withdrawal were significantly more frequent in a male adolescent sex offender sample than in delinquents of nonsexual crimes. Adolescent child molesters were compared with delinquent males and nonreferred males ($N = 60$) by Chewning (1991), who found that the child molesters were more likely to have less intimate relationships, fewer friends, and fewer female friends. Katz (1990) also compared adolescent child molesters with non-sex-offending delinquents and normal adolescents using standardized measures of social competence, concluding that molesters' social skills deficits and isolation are risk factors which may predispose to sexual crimes against younger children. Fagan and Wexler (1988) found adolescent sexual offenders to be more socially and sexually isolated than same age chronic violent offenders. Nearly all these studies have adopted a descriptive rather than a multi-variate approach to social isolation issues, usually because sample sizes are small. It is not impossible that links observed between social isolation and sexual offending in adolescence are mediated by prior sexual victimization (Rosenthal, 1988; Williams & Gilmour, 1994).

Family dysfunction has been reported in several descriptive studies of young sex offender samples but is difficult to interpret. Abbott (1991) compared adolescent sex offenders and delinquents matched on race, age and family income, and observed no significant differences in family functioning. The author points out that such negative findings call into question many aetiological theories of juvenile sexual aggression. On the same issue, DeMartino (1989) reported that few male adolescent sex offenders in a sample attending treatment were from intact homes and most had experienced divorce or separation of their parents. But Fagan and Wexler (1988) comparing 34 sex offenders with 242 chronic violent offenders found that the former were more likely to be living with their birth parents. However, dysfunctional features, such as violence between the parents and violence towards the children in the family were more common in the families of the sex offenders.

Kaplan, Becker and Cunningham-Rathner (1988) found that parents of adolescent incest perpetrators had high levels of victimization in their own childhoods. Kaplan, Becker and Martinez (1990) found that 48 mothers of incest perpetrators were significantly more likely than 82 mothers of nonincest perpetrators to report their own early sexual victimization, later sexual dysfunction and experience of psychotherapy.

While the studies cited here sought to measure varieties of family dys-function, other studies have tended to deduce such dysfunction from proxies such as the high levels of sexual and/or physical abuse in family members. The dangers of such tautologies are obvious.

Academic and behavioural problems in school are reportedly common (Fehrenbach et al., 1986; Pierce & Pierce, 1987; Lonczynski, 1991), but here again the temporal relationship between problems in the school and the development of sexually abusive behaviour patterns has not been studied in proper detail, and the arguments put forward by Kelly (1992) for a more systematic look at the nature of the relation-ship between academic failure and victimization apply equally to school failure and sexually aggressive behaviour. Learning difficulties and poor school achievement are commonly noted. For example, Epps (1991) found that 44% (8/18) had learning difficulties, half of them having formerly been to special school, and 27% of the sample having received help for speech delay or language difficulties. This seems to support the notion that certain adolescent sex offenders have significant communi-cation problems which may be contributing to their social isolation (bearing in mind the points we have already made about measuring the latter variable).

Some authors have drawn attention to low self-esteem and depres-sive/anxious symptoms in sexually abusive boys, but the evidence is neither clear nor conclusive. Becker, Kaplan, Tenke & Tartaglini (1991) gave the Beck Depression Inventory to 246 male juvenile sex offenders and found a mean score (14.3) markedly higher than published norms: 42% of subjects reported symptom scores indicating serious depression. Subjects who had themselves been sexually or physically abused gave significantly higher scores than nonabused subjects. DeMartino (1989), however, found no evidence of depressive symptomatology.

Sexual victimization is also commonly reported among young sexual offenders (e.g., Longo, 1982; Ageton, 1983; Fehrenbach, 1983; Knopp, 1985; Risin & Koss, 1987; Ryan, 1986; Brannon, Larson & Doggett, 1989; reviewed by Watkins & Bentovim, 1992), but rates vary from 30% to 70% in different studies. Taken with the frequent reports of high rates of sexual victimization in childhood reported by adult sex offend-ers (Seghorn, Prentky & Boucher, 1987), such findings have led to assumptions about a causal link between early victimization and later abusive behaviour. Whichever way the link is studied between childhood sexual victimization and later abusive behaviour (whether as a percentage of victimized children becoming abusers or a percentage of sexual abusers who were victimized) the discontinuities are striking. Becker (1988) pointed out that "The majority of male children who are sexually assaulted do not become sexual offenders" (p. 195), although we should perhaps add: "so far as we now know". Although high proportions of sex offenders report childhood abuse, this is seldom the majority and some studies have failed to find sexual victimization more frequently in adolescent sex offenders than other delinquents (Benoit & Kennedy, 1992).

Awad and Saunders (1991) have, however, suggested that physical violence is more common in the background of young sex offenders than is sexual victimization. The links between the experience of physical victimization and later sexually abusive behaviour needs further clarification.

Although some early studies (e.g., Markey, 1950; Shoor, Speed & Bartelt, 1965; Lewis et al., 1979) found a high proportion of psychiatric disorder in incarcerated juvenile sexual offenders, this has not always been borne out in later samples. Kavoussi, Kaplan and Becker (1988), for example, found that none of the sexually offending boys met the DSM-III criteria for major affective disorder, although 48% met the full criteria for diagnosis of Conduct Disorder, and 67% met some DSM-III criteria for Conduct Disorder, 34% for Attention Deficit Disorder, and 21% for Adjustment Disorder/depressed mood.

Bagley (1992) reported that sexually assaultative children were significantly more likely to show a wide range of psychosocial problems compared with normal children, indicating poor adjustment on health, academic and family variables. These characteristics may, in turn, make peer group integration difficult, and may encourage the development of interest in less demanding, younger children. It does not, of course, explain why this interest in younger children should lead to sexually assaultative behaviour.

In the present state of knowledge about adolescent sex offenders, their characteristics can contribute very little to the debate about the aetiology of these behaviours. While some characteristics observed at disclosure may represent aetiological factors, others may represent risk factors. Causal connections are particularly difficult to identify. Distorted cognition about the negative effects of the offence, and the lack of empathy with the needs of others, combined with distinctive patterns of making claims on others, suggest that the underlying common behaviour may be the coercive and manipulative approach of the offender. While the behaviour is sexual in expression, sexual offending may have more in common with other coercive behaviours, such as bullying, than with the satisfaction of "normal" sexual needs or curiosity (Metzner, 1987; Ryan et al., 1987; Wolfe, quoted by Edmondson & Fisher, 1992).

Adolescent Female Perpetrators

That children and adolescents sexually abuse other children was initially seen as a problem of male abusers, but it is now recognized that female adolescents and children are also involved in sexually abusive behaviour towards other children (Davis & Leitenberg, 1987; Kahn & Lafond, 1988).

Overall, 1% of sex offences are currently attributed to females. The ratio of female to male abusers recorded in UK official statistics has remained constant at 1 : 100 for both the 14–20 and the over 20-year-old age groups. This compares with an overall ratio of female to male offending of 18 : 100. In a sample of sex offenders who entered treatment programmes Kahn and Chambers (1991) found a ratio of 1 : 20 females to males.

Smith and Israel (1987) studied 25 cases of sibling incest: 20% of the perpetrators were girls. Johnson and Shrier (1987) found that female molesters, some of whom were teenagers, were more often known to the victim and more likely to use persuasion than force. Victims of females were as likely as the victims of males to rate the events as traumatic, but boys molested by females were less likely to rate themselves as homosexual.

Adolescent Perpetrators with Learning Difficulties

It has frequently been recognized that some sex offenders, both adult and adolescent, have learning difficulties or very poor educational attainment (Menolascino, 1974; Vera, Barnard & Holzer, 1979). There is little evidence that developmentally delayed adolescents are over-represented in this group of offenders, but it appears that neither are they under-represented (Murphy, Coleman & Haynes, 1983).

The relationship between sexual offending and low intelligence has variably been reported as the rate of sexual offenders with learning disabilities, or the rate of those with learning disabilities who are sexual offenders. Clearly these may be quite different figures, and should always be differentiated. Murphy, Coleman and Abel (1983) have suggested that between 10 and 15% of the sex offender population have learning disabilities, sometimes defined as an IQ score below 70. Taking an alternative perspective, Swanson and Garwick (1990) reported rates of sexual offending as low as 3% in mentally retarded populations.

However, as Breen and Turk (1993) point out, the literature on sexually offensive behaviour by those with learning difficulties is still bedevilled by problems of defining "inappropriate" sexual behaviour. It is also common to find that definitions of learning difficulties or developmental delay are ambiguous or idiosyncratic. For example, Kahn and Chambers (1991) mention that 39% of their sample of 221 juvenile sex offenders were considered "learning disabled".

It has been suggested that the origins of sexually deviant behaviour in people with learning disabilities follow the same patterns as in those without disabilities (Breen & Turk, 1993; Griffiths, Hingsberger & Christian, 1985). However, it is unclear if the particular disabilities of those with low IQs increase or decrease the likelihood of sexually inappropriate behaviour. For example, it has been argued that some aspects of institutionalization, such as social isolation, may increase susceptibility to distorted behaviour patterns, while other aspects, such as staff supervision, decrease opportunities for assaultative behaviour (Schilling & Schinke, 1988). Tudiver and Griffin (1992) found that mentally retarded sex offenders were similar to sex offenders with normal range intelligence in having poor social skills, poor impulse control and lack of empathy.

To date, only one study has compared mentally retarded with non-mentally retarded adolescent sex offenders (Gilby, Wolf & Goldberg, 1989). The authors classified sexual problems as "consented to" (even though inappropriate by society's standards), "assaultive", and "nuisance", the latter including voyeurism, exhibitionism and verbal sexual aggression. The mentally retarded adolescents showed no more sexual problems than the adolescents of average intelligence, but displayed more "nuisance" and fewer "consented to" problems.

There is some suggestion from the studies by Griffiths, Quinsey and Hingsberger (1989) and Gilby et al. (1989) that the victims of mentally retarded male adolescent sex offenders are more likely to be male, adult, and not known to the perpetrator than the victims of adolescent sex offenders of normal intelligence.

The Origins of Sexually Abusive Behaviour in Childhood and Adolescence

The genesis of deviant sexual behaviour in childhood and adolescence is still obscure despite the wide range of descriptive studies and some treatment outcome studies (see below). Some writers believe that earlier victimization is a powerful factor in the aetiology of abusive behaviour (e.g., Becker, 1988; Ryan et al., 1987; Ryan, 1989), but since only a minority of adolescent abusers have been victims, other explanations must be sought.

There is some support for the view that the sexual behaviours of juvenile sex offenders is qualitatively different from exploratory teenage behaviour (Longo & Groth, 1983; Becker et al., 1986a). But there is also evidence which suggests that sexual attitudes and behaviour do not, in any simple way, distinguish "normal" adolescents from young offenders. For example, a proportion of "normal" young men mirror many of the varieties of sexual misconduct or coercive behaviour which would be called "abusive" if they were discovered or reported by "victims" (Templeman & Stinnet, 1991). In this latter survey of 60 college men in a rural area of the USA, it was found that a high proportion of them experienced sexual arousal to deviant and "criminal" activities, including frottage, paedophilia, and rape. It was also found that a high proportion would seek a variety of sexual experiences, at least some of which would be punishable in law. Briere and Runtz (1989) also reported that 21% of college men admitted being attracted to children, and 7% admitted they would engage in sexual activities with children if they could avoid detection. Nussbaum (1991) found 22% of college males and 2% of females reported sexual offending in some manner, but the definitions of "offending behaviour" were broad.

Studies of adolescent sex offenders find a range of personality types (withdrawn and shy, assertive and socially successful, conduct disordered with poor impulse control). Tentative classificatory systems have run up against the fact that there are few patterns of previous experience or current actions, of victim characteristics, or personal demography which can explain more than a small part of the variance between sex and non-sex offenders or normal adolescents. Almost certainly, sexually abusive behaviour in adolescence will be found to be multi-causal, with risk factors located in the abusers' history and personality and in characteristics of the victim and his or her environment (Araji & Finkelhor, 1986). In the absence of prospective studies it is not even possible to be sure that the mechanisms of creating a life-long abuser of children or adolescents are the same as those associated with being a child or adolescent abuser of other children.

Treatment Outcome

Those responsible within health, education or judicial systems for the disposal of young sex offenders are increasingly seeking for more information to guide their choice of suitable programmes, and therefore need systematic evaluation of treatments.

Unfortunately, although the number of facilities treating juvenile sex offenders has risen sharply in recent years (Knopp, 1982) the number of published studies of treatment effectiveness is still extremely small. Davis and Leitenberg (1987) noted that "controlled comparisons between treatment and no treatment, and between one form of treatment and another . . . do not exist". Even those who publish guidelines for the treatment of adolescents may warn that their efficacy has not been tested (Rowe, 1988). Borduin, Henggeler, Blaske and Stein (1988) noted that the treatment literature only covered descriptions of programmes and uncontrolled evaluations, and the National Adolescent Perpetrator Network has noted the lack of consensus on the basic principles of treatment (National Adolescent Perpetrator Network, 1993).

In addition, despite a decade's experience of developing sophisticated assessment procedures and therapeutic intervention with such juveniles, there appears to be little agreement about measures of the key components of treatment. Many of the targets of sex offender therapy (e.g., accepting appropriately the blame for the abuse, or developing empathy with victims) lack standardized measures, and even when developed they are not widely used or regularly replicated. This is surprising because juveniles entering treatment show a common range of deficits and difficulties, which typically inform the treatment provided (Ryan, Lane, Davis & Isaac, 1987).

One further difficulty may have contributed to the absence of agreement about how to evaluate juvenile sex offender programmes, and that is the need to build in a developmental perspective (Zussman, 1989). As children who are involved in sexually offending and coercive behaviour appear to be discovered at younger and younger ages (Cantwell, 1988; NCH, 1992), so it becomes increasingly difficult to apply standardized descriptions of their psychopathology across the whole childhood/ adolescent age group. There is a considerable need to establish age-appropriate ways of describing the distorted cognitions and attitudes on issues such as empathy for others or self-blame. However, as we have noted, this may be problematic for the investigator in the absence of normative cognitions for different age-groups. Evaluation may also be hindered by the difficulties inherent in the long-term follow-up on juvenile sex offenders, because of the poor response rates once the young people are away from the treatment programmes (Sapp & Vaughn, 1990).

It has been claimed that treating the distinctive features of sex offenders in adolescence will be easier than treating them in adult life (Ryan, 1986; Knopp, 1985). McConaghy, Blaszczynski, Armstrong and Kidson (1989), however, found that adolescents were more likely to be judged as needing further treatment at the end of a specific programme, possibly because their sexual urges are under more direct hormonal control than in adults. Set against this point is the dearth of convincing evidence for a significant hormonal or biological contribution to sex offending (Murphy, Haynes & Worley, 1991). Nevertheless, it would be difficult to argue with the view that "since sex offenders commit multiple offences over the course of a lifetime, intervention at an early age is a logical goal" (Sapp & Vaughn, 1990).

Selecting Outcome Measures and Methodology

Methodology

It may be a function of the relatively low level of interest in outcome studies that methodology has received little attention. In consequence outcome studies have been approached in diverse ways. Furby, Weinrott and Blackshaw (1989) and Quinsey, Harris, Rice and Lalumiere (1993) addressed a number of methodological issues in their important critiques of published studies on assessing treatment efficacy for adult sex offenders. Quinsey et al. (1993) pointed to the wide variation in whether to include or exclude those who refuse or fail to complete treatment, and the effects this may have on estimates of recidivism. They also pointed out that different jurisdictions show wide variations in sex offender legislation and police, prosecutor and victim behaviour, and counselled against combining such data in single studies.

The choice of comparison groups in sex offender studies is not easy. For example, it is not unusual to find comparison groups drawn from delinquents who have not committed sexual offences, but it is not clear that the route to discovery, and subsequently into the judicial systems, is the same for sexual and nonsexual crimes or misdemeanours.

Measures

Not surprisingly, most people would regard the reduction of re-offending as the most important indicator of change in sexual offenders and this is most commonly cited in treatment outcome studies. Unfortunately, even these apparently straightforward measures are, in reality, difficult to interpret. For example, adult studies reveal that official records substantially under-estimate recidivism (Marshall & Barbaree, 1990; Groth, Longo & McFadin, 1982), while Carter and Prentky (1993) refer to six different measures of recidivism using criminal statistics alone. Quinsey et al. (1993) add cogency to this point by drawing attention to the practice of plea bargaining in the United States, under which nonsexual charges may be laid for sexual offences. They argue that actual offence descriptions rather than charges are needed to determine true sexual re-offending. For a variety of reasons this may also be the best method of assessing UK recidivism in this field.

In addition, professionals involved in follow-up and post-intervention studies need to develop other definitions of success, if the effects of treatment programmes are to be properly established. Evaluating outcome requires that choices are made, not just about the targets of treatment, but also about how "success" and "failure" should be judged.

Change can be measured in cognitive, behavioural, and social or interactional fields. Judgement of change can be made by direct observation in laboratory or natural surroundings, by direct measurement of certain physiological characteristics (e.g., arousal), or through standardized interviews or questionnaires administered to the young sex offender, members of the family, or professionals. Outcome may also be judged using the records of other institutions, e.g., schools or criminal justice systems. Faced with the choice of methods of assessing outcome it is clear that some settings lend themselves more easily to using some of these measures; for example, the use of plethysmographs is not possible in certain day-time, community-based treatment programmes. In addition, as we have noted, there may be ethical constraints on the use of certain procedures with young sex offenders which might not apply to adult offenders (e.g., plethysmographs, or sexually explicit video or questionnaire material).

Sapp and Vaughn (1990) surveyed 30 juvenile sex offender treatment programmes in USA state correctional institutions, identifying biological, behavioural and psychological regimens; overall, 338 therapies and techniques were being used. Obviously many would use different measures of success, although there would also be measures which could be applied across all regimens.

Stevenson, Castillo and Sefarbi (1990) and Bengis (1986) noted that "total cure" is not a realistic goal with sex offenders and emphasized that reduction and control of behaviour are better treatment targets. The multiple causes of sex offending indicate that outcome should be measured under several headings, but this is not always achieved. Kahn and Chambers (1991) mention that therapists were "simply asked their clinical opinion about offenders' arousal patterns". "Success" under one heading may not be associated with overall success, or with a reduction in re-offences. For example, Hollins (1990) found that social skills training of delinquents changed some aspects of social behaviour but had little effect on re-offending. Other significant issues in treatment have been identified by Ryan et al. (1987) and others (e.g., Scavo & Buchanan, 1989) as denial and minimization, deviant sexual fantasies and arousal, lack of victim empathy, accurate labelling and validation of the offender's own feelings, distorted cognitions preceding and following the offences, sex education, and improving interpersonal skills.

For the offender to accept the responsibility for the abuse is frequently cited as a key treatment task (e.g., French, 1988; Stevenson et al., 1989; Stevenson & Wimberley, 1990; Kahn & Lafond, 1988). Blaming others or external forces for the abuse is seen as an example of the underlying cognitive distortions which enables the child molester to maintain their pattern of offending (Abel et al., 1985; French, 1988; Mezey, Vizard,

Hawkes & Austin, 1990), but professional assessments in this area are unsystematic and inconsistent (Pollock & Hashmall, 1991). Probably for this reason, among adult perpetrators motivation is regarded as an important determinant of treatment success. In addition to the several goals of treatment for their offending behaviour, it is essential to address the victimization experiences of young sex offenders. Suitable measures can be selected on the long-term sequelae of victimization from victim studies (Gomes-Schwartz, Horowitz & Cardarelli, 1990; Monck et al., in press).

Some authors have defined the juvenile sex offenders problem largely in terms of moral and social deficiencies. Margolin (1983) described treatment which included a component focusing on these needs, but confirmed that the internalization of a new normative structure can take years. It is clear that this would be a particularly difficult characteristic to assess, at least partly because of the cultural and religious variation in defining what is "good" or morally right.

Published Outcome Studies

The outcome studies of treatment programmes for adolescent sex offenders are relatively few. Table 13.1 summarizes the main conclusions. Those that have been published are almost exclusively from the United States, where the selection of samples into treatment is likely to vary widely according to the criminal procedures of each state.

The first attempts to assess outcome were almost exclusively conceived in terms of recidivism (Doshay, 1943; Atcheson & Williams, 1954). In the follow-up study conducted by Smith and Monastersky (1986), clinical judgements of the risk of re-offending sexually were not significantly accurate, mostly because the clinicians were too pessimistic. Juveniles who re-offended sexually were described as less depressed or defensive and less likely to deny naively any sexual behaviour than those re-offending non-sexually. The latter also had more experience of sexual or physical abuse from their families.

Saunders et al. (1986) reported a study of 63 male adolescent sex offenders referred by the courts for psychiatric assessment. The adolescents were placed in three categories according to the nature of the offence and the victim characteristics. Although this paper did not report a post-treatment outcome for the juvenile sex offenders, one finding has a bearing on outcome. Nearly half the juveniles (48%) had committed previous offences and were therefore already recidivists, although only seven of these recidivists had committed sexual offences outside the category of the current offences. Thus one important predictor of the severity or type of future offences or the victims' characteristics appeared to have been the previous patterns of offending. This contrasts with the claim that much juvenile sexual offending escalates over time from relatively "minor" to very serious behaviour.

Becker, Kaplan and Kavoussi (1988) followed the progress of juveniles who had victimized other children, most of whom were under 13 years (see table 13.1). Treatment consisted of a structured cognitive behaviour treatment programme and outcome was measured in laboratory conditions by use of erection response to audiotaped descriptions of deviant sexual behaviour. The results suggested that the treatment was more effective with those young offenders who had been involved with male victims; improvement was shown by the offenders with female victims, but not at statistically significant levels. The authors are at pains to point out that the subjects were from inner-city minority populations, and it would be unwise to generalize the findings to all young male offenders. They also point to a number of problems in the use of erectile responses, including the absence of normative data from nonabusing populations, and the possibility that some adolescents, like some adult males, can control their responses (Murphy et al., 1991).

In a not untypical presentation of a treatment model, Scavo and Buchanan (1989) describe a group programme in some detail and present vignettes of adolescent sex offenders whose behaviour has been radically improved by participation. However, no overall figures of "successful" completion are given, and no indication is given about how "success" is defined. The authors conclude with the claim that "Mandatory group therapy is an effective means of . . . treating the adolescent sex offender": while this may be true, the results of this paper do not prove that this is the case. One point is worth noting: the authors state that it is not unusual for offenders to repeat the 13-week treatment up to three times. Few other authors refer to this issue, but clinical information suggests that this happens in other programmes as well.

In a more ambitious attempt to compare different treatment programmes Borduin et al. (1990) randomly assigned 16 adolescent sex offenders to two programmes: multisystemic therapy (MST) (for between 21 and 49 hours – mean 37 hours) or individual therapy (IT) (for an average of 45 hours). Most had committed multiple sexual offences, and "almost all presented long-term emotional and interpersonal difficulties" (p. 107). Three adolescents from each treatment programme failed to complete treatment, but were included in the results. Despite small numbers the higher sexual offence recidivism in the IT group was significant (see table 13.1). The authors concluded that the results add to the growing understanding that MST is effective in treating serious personal and family dysfunction. They argue that MST is effective because of the emphasis on treating the adolescent in his individual social context, and the focus on any combination of the systems in which the adolescent is embedded, including school and peer groups. This study highlights the relative lack of evaluation in treatment programmes operating from a psychodynamic or analytic basis and may reflect the absence of theoretical consensus amongst psychodynamic practitioners.

Pre- and post-treatment data were compared by Hunter and Santos (1990) for adolescent child molesters. The treatment focused on sexual impulse control and the reduction of deviant arousal. Using plethysmograph readings, they found that the adolescent abusers of both female and male child victims demonstrated significantly reduced deviant arousal to male and female paedophilic cues. By contrast, arousal to descriptions of same-age females remained high, thus creating a greater differential between deviant and nondeviant arousal after treatment. The authors concluded that a cognitive–behavioural treatment can effectively change deviant sexual arousal, but suggest that further investigation is needed to determine how long treatment has to be, and exactly which approach (satiation vs. covert sensitization) is most effective. More recent work from this experienced clinical team (Hunter and Becker, 1994) has addressed some of these problems and describes links between phallometrically measured sexual arousal and clinical characteristics in juvenile sexual offenders receiving treatment.

In a paper dealing largely with the content of treatment, Becker (1990) has presented preliminary data from a one-year follow-up of adolescents who had been included in treatment. Of the first 300 adolescents evaluated for the programme, 205 (68.3%) entered treatment. Typically, not all the young people attended all the available sessions: only 56 (27.3%) attended 70–100% of the sessions, 93 (45.4%)

attended at least half the sessions. The follow-up interviews were completed with only 52 (25.9%) of adolescents who had completed therapy. On the basis of self-report and referrals, five adolescents had re-offended. Data was obtained on penile plethysmographs, but are not presented in this paper.

In a follow-up of 20 sexually assaultative children, and of controls who were seen at three-monthly intervals over two years, seven of the sexually assaultative group, and none of the controls, admitted that they had engaged in sexually assaultative behaviour following discharge from their treatment programmes (Bagley, 1992). Five adolescents had engaged in assaults of a serious nature, involving either rape of adult females (three assaults), or sexual assaults against young boys (five assaults). Bagley concludes that, for a minority of assaultative youth, there is a real danger of an escalation of offending in adult life, if early intervention does not occur.

Three recent studies give moderately encouraging short-term figures for repeat offences (Ryan & Myoshi, 1990; O'Brien, 1990; Bremer, 1990) (see table 13.1).

Kahn and Chambers (1991) focused on the issue of re-offence risk in their retrospective evaluation of 10 specialized treatment programmes delivered in out-patient and institutionalized settings in Washington State (see table 13.1). Treatment was eclectic, although all programmes were specialized sexual deviancy therapy. Less than a quarter of the young offenders were released from treatment because they had satisfactorily improved. Very few variables were associated with sexual re-offending. Those who had blamed their victims and used force were more likely to commit new sexual offences. Although the juveniles in the out-patient programmes were slightly less likely to commit new sexual offences than the incarcerated young offenders, this difference did not reach significance; the authors admit that there may have been some initial differences in the characteristics of these two groups. Therapists accurately identified the low-risk offenders, but only 14% of those who were rated "high risk" went on to commit more sexual offences. Kahn and Chambers point out the difficulties associated with getting accurate sexual re-offending figures, when this type of behaviour is so often covert (and victim reporting is low).

Rubinstein, Yeager, Goodstein and Lewis (1993) recently reported a follow-up of 19 young sexually assaultative males and a comparison group of 58.

Table 13.1 Treatment outcome studies for adolescent sex offenders

Authors	Date	Sample Size	Age (years)	Gender	Other characteristics	Follow-up period	Sexual re-offending	Nonsexual re-offending	(% in category)
Doshay	1943	108	adolescent	male	sex offences only	6 years	2 (2/108)	30%	
Doshay	1943	148	adolescent	male	sex and other offences	6 years	16 (24/148)		
Atcheson & Williams	1954	125	adolescent	male	sex offenders	n/k	3	n/k	
Knopp	1985	80	adolescent		residential sex offender programme	n/k	5	11	
Knopp	1982	28	adolescent	male	discharged sex offenders	n/k	7	n/k	
Smith	1984	223	adolescent	n/k	sex offenders attending several different treatment programmes	n/k	7	30	
Smith & Monastersky	1986	112	10–16 (mean 14.1)	male		min. 17 months mean 29 months	14	35	
Pierce & Pierce	1986	37	(av. 15.3)	male/ female		1 year from treatment	19		24% ran away 73% changed home placement at least once 14% showed sexualized behaviour of concern to parents and professionals

Study	Year	N	Age	Sex	Sample	Follow-up period			Comments
Hains, Herman, Baker & Graber	1986	17	16–18	male	incarcerated (a) treatment group (b) untreated group	not discharged			treatment improved sexual knowledge, attitudes and problem-solving, but did not improve moral judgement
Smets & Cebula	1987	21	13–18	male	sex offenders in rural area	3 years from end of treatment	5 (1 boy)	n/k	
Becker, Kaplan & Kavoussi	1988	24	13–18	male	aggressive sex offenders referred by criminal justice system for treatment inner city minority population sample				erectile responses to audiotaped description of deviant sexual behaviour
Kahn & Lafond	1988	350	14–18	male / female	40% incarcerated sex offenders: sentences of 2 m–4 y 15–25% sex offenders	n/k	9%	8%	
Scavo & Buchanan	1989								
Borduin et al.	1990	16	mean 14	male	arrested for sexual offences predominantly lower SES (a) multisystemic therapy (b) individual therapy	treatment period n/k follow-up 21–49 months (mean 37 months)	therapy (a) 12.5 (b) 75	therapy (a) 25 (b) 50	

Table 13.1 Continued

	Sample					Outcome measures			
Authors	Date	Size	Age (years)	Gender	Other characteristics	Follow-up period	Sexual re-offending	Nonsexual re-offending	(% in category)
Hunter & Santos	1990	28	adolescent	male	child molesters	treatment period			reduced arousal to deviant paedophile cues
Becker	1990	205	adolescent	n/k	in treatment programme	1 year	5		
Bagley	1992	20	adolescent	male	sexually assaultative controls	2 years from after discharge from programme			35% engaged in sexually assaultative behaviour
Ryan & Myoshi	1990	69				12–30 months after ending treatment	9.2 re-arrested or questioned		
O'Brien	1990	200	adolescent		nonresidential treatment programme		6 (3 during treatment) (3 after treatment)		
Bremer	1990	149/2 85	adolescent		residential?	n/k	11 (n = 149)		
Kahn & Chambers	1991	221	8–18 years (median 14.7)	5% female 95% male	ten specialized treatment programmes (outpatient and residential	(mean) 20.4 months	c 7.5	45 (6.6% violent crimes)	

Discussion

This review of the research evidence on the origins of sexual offending by young people, the characteristics of victim, offence and offender and the small amount of information on post-treatment outcome suggests that there is a long way to go before we fully understand or effectively meet the needs of these young people. One urgent reason for improving our capacity to judge the efficacy of treatment programmes for young sex offenders is the fact that a considerable proportion appear to go on to a lifetime of sexual offending and child molesting. There is an ethical responsibility also, both to the offender and the victim, that the efficacy of current sex offender treatment programmes can be defended.

It is noticeable, in reviewing this field, how many studies are dependent on small numbers and how few studies replicate the measures used by others. This suggests that certain key tasks now face those involved in intervention and research. For example, it has become increasingly urgent to sort out which juvenile sexual activities are to be labelled as "sexually aggressive" or "sexually abusive", and which may be seen as (in some sense) acceptable. Bremer's (1993) "Continuum" of sexualized behaviours may provide the basis for further work. There are very few studies of the sexual experiences of "normal" girls and boys, and their attitudes to these experiences (Rosenfeld et al., 1984). Some authors have already set out possible definitions for sexually abusive behaviour among the young (Groth & Loredo, 1981; Becker et al., 1986a): future work should consolidate such leads.

The study of treatment efficacy is hampered by the apparent absence, in many programmes, of systematic assessment of the full range of young offenders' needs at the start and end of treatment, and by the absence of measures of many aspects of treatment. As Smith and Monastersky (1986) have pointed out, so little is known about why juveniles re-offend that therapists may be relying on "irrelevant information" in their predictions of risk. Information about re-offending should always be reported in the context of local standards of law enforcement and jurisdiction (Quinsey et al., 1993).

Our review of the treatment outcome literature has also shown that results need to distinguish more clearly between individuals who have or have not repeated a treatment programme, and those who have completed or failed to complete programmes.

For all these reasons, it is important to establish some long-term prospective studies of sexually abusive children and young people, to identify the factors which increase the risk of re-offending. Important policy initiatives in the UK have been taken in relation to adult sex offenders with the result that structured sex offender treatment programmes with an evaluative component are now available in a limited number of British prisons. Recent clinical initiatives have been taken in the United States and in the UK to set up multi-centre treatment outcome studies (Debelle, Ward, Burnham, Jamieson & Ginty, 1993).

Currently, studies of treatment outcome tend to concentrate on the reduction of offending behaviour or other variables specific to sex offences. There has been remarkably little attempt to quantify the influence of factors in the young person's environment, such as family composition, family attitudes and beliefs, the type of care or educational arrangements. Since the family frequently forms part of the environment in which the young person operates, family members may be expected be have some impact on post-treatment functioning (Stevenson et al., 1989). We know that a proportion of young sex offenders show no marked psychosocial difficulties apart from their offending behaviour: what we do not know is if there are later problems for these apparently "symptom-free" offenders, and if so, in what domain of life they appear (Becker, Kaplan & Kavoussi, 1988).

The search for an over-arching theoretical model of sexual offending will continue as more is learnt about the origins of these behaviours and the responses to treatment. Of course, in any review of treatment of juvenile sex offenders it needs to be borne in mind that only a proportion of young sex offenders come into treatment and the large majority of studies have been of males only. For both these reasons our knowledge of the range of needs presented by young sex offenders may change in coming years, as the treated population changes. The most significant challenge, however, lies in the search for effective treatment, which will only be achieved when evaluation is integrated into all treatment programmes. Until this is achieved, it will be impossible to say with any certainty that sexual offenders who are being released from treatment present a smaller risk to society than when they first offended.

References

Abbott, B. R. (1991). Family dynamics, intergenerational patterns of negative events and trauma, patterns of offending behavior: a comparison of adolescent sex offenders and delinquent adolescents and their parents. Unpublished thesis: California Institute of Integral Studies. *Dissertation Abstracts International*, **51**, 4037.

Abel, G. G., Mittelman, M. S., & Becker, J. V. (1985). Sexual offenders: results of assessment and recommendations for treatment. In M. H. Ben-Aron, S. J. Huckle, & C. D. Webster (eds), *Clinical criminology: the assessment and treatment of criminal behaviour* (pp. 191–205). Toronto: M. and M. Graphics, Ltd.

Ageton, S. S. (1983). *Sexual assault among adolescents*. New York: Lexington Books.

Araji, S., & Finkelhor, D. (1986). Abusers: a review of the research. In D. Finkelhor (ed.), *A sourcebook on child sexual abuse*, Chapter 4 (pp. 89–118). Newbury Park, CA: Sage Publications.

Atcheson, J. D., & Williams, D. C. (1954). A study of juvenile sex offenders. *American Journal of Psychiatry*, **111**, 366–70.

Awad, G., Saunders, E., & Levene, J. (1984). A clinical study of male adolescent sexual offenders. *International Journal of Offender Therapy and Comparative Criminology*, **28**, 105–16.

Awad, G., & Saunders, E. (1989). Adolescent child molesters: clinical observations. *Child Psychiatry and Human Development*, **19**, 195–206.

Awad, G., & Saunders, E. (1991). Male adolescent sexual assaulters: clinical observations. *Journal of Interpersonal Violence*, **6**, 446–60.

Bagley, C. (1992). Characteristics of 60 children and adolescents with a history of sexual assault against others: evidence from a comparative study. *The Journal of Forensic Psychiatry*, **3**, 299–309.

Bancroft, J. (1989). *Human sexuality and its problems*. Churchill: Livingstone.

Becker, J. V. (1988). The effects of child sexual abuse on adolescent sexual offenders. In G. E. Wyatt, & G. J. Powell (eds), *Lasting effects of child sexual abuse* (pp. 193–207). Newbury Park, CA: Sage Publications.

Becker, J. V. (1990). Treating adolescent sex offenders. *Professional Psychology: Research and Practice*, **21**, 362–5.

Becker, J. V., Cunningham-Rathner, J., & Kaplan, M. S. (1986a). Adolescent sexual offenders, demographics, criminal and sexual histories and recommendations for reducing future offences. Special Issue: The prediction and control of violent behaviour: II. *Journal of Interpersonal Violence*, **1**, 431–45.

Becker, J. V., Cunningham-Rathner, J., Kaplan, M. S., & Kavoussi, R. (1986b). Characteristics of adolescent incest sexual perpetrators: preliminary findings. *Journal of Family Violence*, **1**, 85–97.

Becker, J. V., Coleman, E. M. (1988). Incest. In V. B. Hasselt, R. L. Morrison,

A. S. Bellack, & M. Hersen (eds). *Handbook of family violence*. New York: Plenum Press.

Becker, J. V., Kaplan, M. S., & Kavoussi, R. (1988). Measuring the effectiveness of treatment for the aggressive adolescent sexual offender. *Annals of the New York Academy of Sciences*, **528**, 215–22.

Becker, J. V., Kaplan, M. S., Tenke, C. E., & Tartaglini, A. (1991). The incidence of depressive symptomatology in juvenile sex offenders with a history of abuse. *Child Abuse and Neglect*, **15**, 531–6.

Bengis, S. M. (1986). A comprehensive service-delivery system with a continuum of care for adolescent sex offenders. Orwell, VT: Safer Society Program.

Benoit, J. L., & Kennedy, W. A. (1992). The abuse history of male adolescent sex offenders. *Journal of Interpersonal Violence*, **7**, 543–8.

Billy, J. O., Landale, N. S., Grady, W. R., & Zimmerle, D. M. (1988). Effect of sexual activity on adolescent social and psychological development. *Social Psychology Quarterly*, **51**, 190–212.

Borduin, C. M., Henggeler, S. W., Blaske, D. M., & Stein, R. (1990). Multisystemic treatment of adolescent sex offenders. *International Journal of Offender Therapy and Comparative Criminology*, **34**, 105–13.

Brannon, J. M., Larson, B., & Doggett, M. (1989). The extent and origins of sexual molestation and abuse among incarcerated adolescent males. *International Journal of Offender Therapy and Comparative Criminology*, **33**, 161–72.

Breen, T., & Turk, V. (1993). Sexual offending behaviour by people with learning disabilities: prevalence and treatment. (Unpublished paper submitted to *British Journal of Psychiatry*). Kent: University of Canterbury.

Bremer, J. (1990). Quoted in Knopp (1985/91).

Bremer, J. F. (1993). The treatment of children and adolescents with aberrant sexual behaviours. In C. J. Hobbs, & J. M. Wynne (eds), *Bailliere's Clinical Paediatrics: International Practice and Research. Child Abuse*, **1**, 269–82.

Briere, J., & Runtz, M. (1989). University males' sexual interest in children: predicting potential indices of "pedophilia" in a non-forensic sample. *Child Abuse and Neglect*, **13**, 65–75.

Cantwell, H. B. (1988). Child sexual abuse: very young perpetrators. *Child Abuse and Neglect*, **12**, 579–82.

Carter, D. L., & Prentky, R. A. (1993). Overview of the program at the Massachusetts Treatment Center. *International Journal of Law and Psychiatry*, **16**, 117–32.

Check, J. V. P., & Malamuth, N. M. (1983). Sex role stereotyping and reactions to depictions of stranger versus acquaintance rape. *Journal of Personality and Social Psychology*, **45**, 344–56.

Chewning, M. F. (1991). A comparison of adolescent male sex offenders with juvenile delinquents and non-referred adolescents. Unpublished PhD thesis:

Virginia Commonwealth University. *Dissertation Abstracts International*, **51**, (7-B) 3557.

Davis, G., & Leitenberg, H. (1987). Adolescent Sex Offenders. *Psychological Bulletin*, **101**, 417–27.

Debelle, G. D., Ward, M. R., Burnham, J. B., Jamieson, R., & Ginty, M. (1993). Evaluation of intervention programmes for juvenile sex offenders: questions and dilemmas. *Child Abuse Review*, **2**, 75–85.

Deisher, R., Wenet, G., Paperney, D., Clark, T., & Fehrenbach, P. (1982). Adolescent sex offence behaviour: the role of the physician. *Journal of Adolescent Health Care*, **2**, 279–86.

DeMartino, R. A. (1989). School-aged juvenile sex offenders: a descriptive study of self-reported personality characteristics, depression, familial perceptions and social history. Unpublished thesis. State University of New York at Albany, *Dissertations Abstracts International*, **50**, 2188.

DeNatale, R. A. (1989). An investigation of demographic, emotional and attitudinal indicators of male juvenile sex offenders. Unpublished thesis. *Dissertation Abstracts International*, **50**, 1103.

Doshay, L. J. (1943). *The boy sex offender and his later career*. Montclair, NJ: Patterson Smith.

Downs, A. C., & Hillje, L. S. (1993). Historical and theoretical perspectives on adolescent sexuality: an overview. In T. P. Gullotta, G. R. Adams, & R. Montemayor (eds), *Adolescent Sexuality*, Chapter 1 (pp. 1–33). Newbury Park, CA: Sage Publications.

Edmondson, L., & Fisher, D. (1992). Treating child sex offenders: the view from America. *NOTA News* (The National Association for the Development of Work with sex offenders) Issue 1, 8–12, April.

Elliott, D. S., & Morse, B. J. (1989). Delinquency and drug abuse as risk factors in teenage sexual activity. *Youth and Society*, **21**, 32–60.

Epps, K. (1991). The residential treatment of adolescent sex offenders. In *Issues in Criminological and Legal Psychology*, **1**, 58–67.

Fagan, J., & Wexler, S. (1988). Explanations of sexual assault among violent delinquents. *Journal of Adolescent Research*, **3**, 363–85.

Faller, K. (1987). Women who sexually abuse children. *Violence and Victims*, **2**, 263–76.

Fehrenbach, P. (1983). Adolescent sexual offenders. *Audio-Digest Psychiatry*, **12**.

Fehrenbach, P., Smith, W., Monastersky, C., & Deisher, R. (1986). Adolescent sex offenders: offender and offence characteristics. *American Journal of Ortho-Psychiatry*, **56**, 225–33.

Finkelhor, D. (1979). *Sexually victimised children*. New York: The Free Press.

Finkelhor, D. (1984). Boys as victims: a review of the evidence. In D. Finkelhor (ed.), *Child sexual abuse: new theory and research* (pp. 151–70). New York: The Free Press.

Finkelhor, D. (1986a). Designing new studies. In D. Finkelhor (ed.), *A sourcebook on child sexual abuse* Chapter 7 (pp. 199–223). Newbury Park, CA: Sage Publications.

Finkelhor, D. (1986b). Abusers: special topics. In D. Finkelhor (ed.), *A sourcebook on child sexual abuse* Chapter 4 (pp. 119–42). Newbury Park, CA: Sage Publications.

French, D. D. (1988). Distortion and lying as defense processes in the adolescent child molester. *Journal of Offender Counselling Services and Rehabilitation*, **13**, 27–37.

Friedrich, W. N., Grambsch, P., Broughton, D., Kuiper, J., & Beilke, R. L. (1991). Normative sexual behavior in children. *Pediatrics*, **88**, 456–64.

Fromuth, M. E., Burkhart, B. R., & Jones, C. W. (1991). Hidden child molestation: an investigation of adolescent perpetrators in a non-clinical sample. *Journal of Interpersonal Violence*, **6**, 376–84.

Furby, L., Weinrott, M. R., & Blackshaw, L. (1989). Sex offender recidivism: a review. *Psychological Bulletin*, **105**, 3–30.

Garvey, N. (1991). Sexual victimisation prevalence among New Zealand university students. *Journal of Consulting and Clinical Psychology*, **59**, 464–6.

Gilby, R., Wolf, L., & Goldberg, R. (1989). Mentally retarded adolescent sex offenders: a survey and pilot study. *Canadian Journal of Psychiatry*, **34**, 542–8.

Gomes-Schwartz, B., Horowitz, J. P., & Cardarelli, A. P. (1990). *Child sexual abuse: the initial effects.* Newbury Park, CA: Sage Publications.

Goodchilds, J., Zellman, G. L., Johnson, P. B., & Giarusso, R. (1988). Adolescent and their perception of sexual interaction. In A. W. Burgess (ed.). *Rape and sexual assault* Vol. 2. (pp. 245–70). New York: Garland.

Griffiths, D., Hingsburger, D., & Christian, R. (1985). Treating developmentally handicapped sexual offenders: the York behaviour management services treatment programme. *Psychiatric Aspects in Mental Retardation Reviews*, **4**, 49–52.

Griffiths, D., Quinsey, V. L., & Hingsburger, D. (1989). *Changing inappropriate sexual behaviour: a community based approach for persons with developmental disabilities.* Baltimore, MD: P. H. Brookes Publishing Co.

Groth, A. N., Longo, R. E., & McFadin, J. B. (1982). Undetected recidivism among rapists and child molesters. *Crime and Delinquency*, **28**, 450–8.

Groth, A. N., & Loredo, C. M. (1981). Juvenile sex offenders: guidelines for assessment. *International Journal of Offender Therapy and Comparative Criminology*, **25**, 31–9.

Grubin, D., & Gunn, J. (1990). The imprisoned rapist and rape. Report to Home Office, UK.

Gundersen, B. H., Melas, P. S., & Skar, J. E. (1981). Sexual behaviour of pre-school children: teachers' observations. In L. L. Constantine, & F. M. Martinson (eds), *Children and sex: new findings. New perspectives* (pp. 45–61). Boston: Little, Brown & Company.

Hollins, C. (1990). Social skills training with delinquents: a look at the evidence and some recommendations for practice. *British Journal of Social Work*, **20**, 483–93.

Home Office (1992). *Criminal Statistics for England and Wales 1992*. London: HMSO.

Horne, L., Glasgow, D., Cox, A., & Calam, R. (1991). Sexual abuse of children by children. *Journal of Child Law*, **3**, 147–51.

Hunter, J. A., & Santos, D. R. (1990). The use of specialised cognitive–behavioural therapies in the treatment of adolescent sex offenders. *International Journal of Offender Therapy and Comparative Criminology*, **34**, 239–47.

Hunter, J. A., & Becker, J. V. (1994). The relationship between phallometrically measured deviant sexual arousal and clinical characteristics in juvenile sexual offenders. *Behavior Research and Therapy*, **32**, 533–8.

Johnson, R. L., & Shrier, D. (1987). Past sexual victimisation by females of male patients in an adolescent medicine clinic population. *American Journal of Psychiatry*, **144**, 650–2.

Johnson, T. C. (1988). Child perpetrators: children who molest other children: preliminary findings. *Child Abuse & Neglect*, **12**, 219–29.

Kahn, T. J., & Chambers, H. J. (1991). Assessing reoffense risk with juvenile sexual offenders. *Child Welfare*, **70**, 333–45.

Kahn, T. J., & Lafond, M. A. (1988). Treatment of the adolescent sexual offender. *Child and Adolescent Social Work*, **5**, 135–48.

Kaplan, M. S., Abel, G. G., Cunningham-Rathner, J., & Mittleman, M. S. (1990). The impact of parolees' perception of confidentiality of their self-reported sex crimes. *Annals of Sex Research*, **3**, 294–303.

Kaplan, M. S., Becker, J. V., & Cunningham-Rathner, J. (1988). Characteristics of parents of adolescent incest perpetrators: preliminary findings. *Journal of Family Violence*, **3**, 183–91.

Kaplan, M. S., Becker, J. V., & Martinez, D. F. (1990). A comparison of mothers of adolescent incest vs non-incest perpetrators. *Journal of Family Violence*, **5**, 209–14.

Katz, R. (1990). Psychological adjustment in adolescent child molesters. *Child Abuse and Neglect*, **14**, 567–75.

Kavoussi, R., Kaplan, M., & Becker, J. V. (1988). Psychiatric diagnoses in juvenile sex offenders. *Journal of the American Academy of Child and Adolescent Psychiatry*, **27**, 241–3.

Kelly, L. (1992). Connections between disability and child abuse: a review of the research evidence. *Child Abuse Review*, **1**, 157–67.

Kelly, L., Regan, L., & Burton, S. (1991). *An exploratory study of the prevalence of sexual abuse in a sample of 16–21 year olds, Report for ESRC*. Child Abuse Studies Unit: University of North London.

Kempe, R., & Kempe, C. H. (1978). *Child abuse.* London: Fontana, Open Books.

Knopp, F. H. (1982). *Remedial intervention in adolescent sex offences: nine programme descriptions.* Syracuse, NY: Safer Society Press.

Knopp, F. H. (1985/revised 1991). *The youthful sex offender: the rationale and goals of early intervention and treatment.* Syracuse, NY: Safer Society Press.

Korbin, J. E. (1981). Introduction. In J. E. Korbin (ed.), *Child abuse and neglect cross-cultural perspectives* (pp. 1–12). University of California Press.

Kosky, R. J. (1989). Should sex offenders be treated? *Australian and New Zealand Journal of Psychiatry,* **23**, 176–80.

Lewis, D., Shankok, S., & Pincus, J. (1989). Juvenile male sexual assaultors. *American Journal of Psychiatry,* **139**, 1194–6.

Lonczynski, C. M. (1991). Adolescent sexual offenders: social isolation, social competency skills and identified problem behaviors. *Dissertation Abstracts International,* **51**, 5040.

Longo, R. E. (1982). Sexual learning and experience among adolescent sexual offenders. *International Journal of Offender Therapy and Comparative Criminology,* **26**, 235–41.

Longo, R. E., & Groth, A. N. (1983). Juvenile sexual offences in the histories of adult rapists and child molesters. *International Journal of Offender Therapy and Comparative Criminology,* **27**, 151–5.

McConaghy, N., Blaszczynsk, A., Armstrong, M. S., & Kidson, W. (1989). Resistance to treatment of adolescent sexual offenders. *Archives of Sexual Behaviour,* **18**, 97–107.

Maletzky, B. M. (1991). *Treating the sexual offender.* Newbury Park, CA: Sage Publications.

Margolin, L. (1983). A treatment model for the adolescent sex offender. *Journal of Offender Counselling, Services and Rehabilitation,* **8**, 1–12.

Margolin, L. (1986). The effects of mother–son incest. *Lifestyles,* **8**, 104–14.

Markey, O. B. (1950). A study of aggressive sexual misbehavior in adolescents brought to juvenile court. *American Journal of Orthopsychiatry,* **20**, 719–31.

Marshall, W. L., & Barbaree, H. E. (1990). An outpatient treatment program for child molesters. In R. A. Prentky, & V. L. Quinsey (eds), Human Sexual Aggression, Current Perspectives. *Annals of the New York Academy of Sciences,* **528**, 205–14.

Mayhew, P., Elliot, D., & Dowds, L. (1988). *The 1988 British Crime Survey.* London: HMSO.

Menolascino, F. J. (1974). The mentally retarded offender. *Mental Retardation,* **12**(1).

Metzner, J. L. (1987). The adolescent sex offender: an overview. *The Colorado Laywer,* October, 1847–51.

Mezey, G., Vizard, E., Hawkes, C., & Austin, R. (1990). A community treatment programme for convicted child sex offenders: a preliminary report. *The Journal of Forensic Psychiatry*, **1**, 12–25.

Monck, E., Sharland, E., Bentovim, A., Goodall, G., Hyde, C., & Lwin, R. (1995). *Child Sexual Abuse: A Descriptive and Treatment Outcome Study*. London: HMSO.

Money, J., & Ehrhardt, A. (1972). *Man and woman: boy and girl*. Baltimore, MD: Johns Hopkins University Press.

Mrazek, P. B., Lynch, M., & Bentovim, A. (1981a). Recognition of child sexual abuse in the United Kingdom. In P. B. Mrazek, & C. H. Kempe (eds), *Sexually abused children and their families* (pp. 35–50). Oxford: Pergamon Press.

Murphy, W. D., Coleman, E. M., & Abel, G. G. (1983). Human sexuality in the mentally retarded. In J. L. Matson, & F. Andrasik (eds), *Treatment issues and innovations in mental retardation* (pp. 581–643). New York: Plenum Press.

Murphy, W. D., Coleman, E. M., & Haynes, M. R. (1983). Treatment and evaluation issues with the mentally retarded sex offender. In J. D. Greer, & I. R. Stuart (eds), *The sexual aggressor: current perspectives on treatment* (pp. 22–41). Van Nostrand, Reinholt, New York.

Murphy, W. D., Haynes, M. R., & Worley, P. J. (1991). Assessment of adult sexual interest. In C. R. Hollin, & K. Howells (eds), *Clinical approaches to sex offenders and their victims* (pp. 77–92). Chichester: John Wiley & Sons.

National Adolescent Perpetrator Network (NAPN). (1988). Preliminary report from the National Task Force on Juvenile Sexual Offending. *Juvenile and Family Court Journal*, **39**(2).

NCH (National Children's Home). (1992). *Children who abuse other children* (p. 3). London: National Children's Home, 85 Highbury Park, London N5 1UD, UK.

Nussbaum, B. R. (1991). Sexual offending and victimisation: prevalence and reactions of adolescent and adult sex offenders and college students. Unpublished thesis. *Dissertation Abstracts International*, **51**, 5036–7.

O'Brien, M. (1990). Cited in Knopp (1985/91).

Peters, S. D., Wyatt, G. E., & Finkelhor, D. (1986). Prevalence. In D. Finkelhor (ed.), *A sourcebook on child sexual abuse* (pp. 15–59). Newbury Park, CA: Sage Publications.

Pierce, L. H., & Pierce, R. L. (1986). Juvenile sex offenders: a follow-up study. Paper presented at the third National Conference on Family Violence. University of New Hampshire, 1987.

Pierce, L. H., & Pierce, R. L. (1987). Incestuous victimisation by juvenile sex offenders. *Journal of Family Violence*, **2**, 351–64.

Pollock, N. L., & Hashmali, J. M. (1991). The excuses of child molesters. *Behavioural Sciences and the Law*, **9**, 53–9.

Quinsey, V. L., Harris, G. T., Rice, M. E., & Lalumiere, M. L. (1993).

Assessing treatment efficacy in outcome studies of sex offenders. *Journal of Interpersonal Violence*, **8**, 512–23.

Rice, M. E., Quinsey, V. L., & Harris, G. T. (1991). Sexual recidivism among child molesters released from a maximum security psychiatric institution. *Journal of Consulting and Clinical Psychology*, **59**, 381–6.

Risin, L., & Koss, M. (1987). Sexual abuse of boys: prevalence and descriptive characteristics of the childhood victimisations. *Journal of Interpersonal Violence*, **2**, 309–19.

Rosenfeld, A. A., Siegel-Gorelick, B., Haavik, D., Duryea, M., Wenegrat, A., Martin, J., & Bailey, R. (1984). Parental perceptions of children's modesty: a cross sectional survey of ages 2–10 years. *Psychiatry*, **47**, 351–65.

Rosenthal, J. A. (1988). Patterns of reported child abuse and neglect. *Child Abuse and Neglect*, **12**, 263–71.

Rowe, B. (1988). Practical treatment of adolescent sexual offenders. *Journal of Child Care*, **3**, 51–8.

Rubinstein, M., Yeager, C. A., Goodstein, C., & Lewis, D. O. (1993). Sexually assaultive male juveniles: a follow-up. *American Journal of Psychiatry*, **150**, 262–5.

Ryan, G. (1986). Annotated bibliography: adolescent perpetrators of sexual molestation of children. *Child Abuse and Neglect*, **10**, 125–31.

Ryan, G. (1989). Victim to victimiser. *Journal of Interpersonal Violence*, **4**, 325–41.

Ryan, G., Lane, S., Davis, J., & Isaac, C. (1987). Juvenile sex offenders: development and correction. *Child Abuse and Neglect*, **11**, 385–95.

Ryan, G., Metzner, J. & Krugman, R. (1990). When the abuser is a child. In K. R. Oates (ed.), *Understanding and managing child sexual abuse* (pp. 258–73). San Diego, CA: Harcourt Brace Jovanovich.

Ryan, G., & Myoshi, T. (1990). Summary of a pilot follow-up study of adolescent sexual perpetrators after treatment. *Interchange*, January.

Sapp, A. D., & Vaughn, M. S. (1990). Juvenile sex offender treatment at state-operated correctional institutions. *International Journal of Offender Therapy and Comparative Criminology*, **34**, 131–46.

Saunders, E. B., Awad, G. A., & White, G. (1986). Male adolescent sexual offenders: the offender and the offence. *Canadian Journal of Psychiatry*, **31**, 542–9.

Scavo, R., & Buchanan, B. D. (1989). Group therapy for male adolescent sex offenders: model for residential treatment. *Residential Treatment for Children and Youth*, **7**, 59–74.

Schilling, R. F., & Schinke, S. P. (1988). Mentally retarded sex offenders: fact, fiction and treatment. *Journal of Social Work and Human Sexuality*, **7**, 33–48.

Seghorn, T. K., Prentky, R. A., & Boucher, R. J. (1987). Childhood sexual abuse in the lives of sexually aggressive offenders. *Journal of the American Academy of Child and Adolescent Psychiatry*, **26**, 262–7.

Shoor, M., Speed, M. H., & Bartelt, C. (1965). Syndrome of the adolescent child molester. *American Journal of Psychiatry*, **122**, 738–89.

Smets, A., & Cebula, C. A. (1987). A group treatment programme for adolescent sex offenders: five steps towards resolution. *Child Abuse and Neglect*, **11**, 247–54.

Smith, E. A., & Udry, J. R. (1985). Coital and non-coital sexual behaviours of white and black adolescents. *American Journal of Public Health*, **75**, 1200–3.

Smith, H., & Israel, E. (1987). Sibling incest: a study of dynamics of 25 cases. *Child Abuse and Neglect*, **11**, 101–8.

Smith, W. R. (1984). Patterns of re-offending among juvenile sexual offenders. Unpublished manuscript. University of Washington, Juvenile Sex Offender Program, Seattle. Quoted by Davis & Leitenberg (1987).

Smith, W. R., & Monastersky, C. (1986). Assessing juvenile sex offender risk for re-offending. *Criminal Justice and Behaviour*, **13**, 115–40.

Stevenson, H. C., Castillo, E., & Sefarbi, R. (1989). Treatment of denial in adolescent sex offenders and their families. *Journal of Offender Counselling, Services and Rehabilitation*, **14**, 37–50.

Stevenson, H. C., & Wimberley, R. (1990). Assessment of treatment impact of sexually aggressive youth. *The Journal of Offender Counselling, Services and Rehabilitation*, **15**, 55–68.

Swanson, C. K., & Garwick, G. B. (1990). Treatment for low-functioning sex offenders: group therapy and interagency coordination. *Mental Retardation*, **28**, 155–61.

Templeman, T. L., & Stinnett, R. D. (1991). Patterns of sexual arousal and history in a 'normal' sample of young men. *Archives of Sexual Behaviour*, **20**, 137–50.

Tudiver, J. G., & Griffin, J. D. (1992). Treating developmentally disabled adolescents who have committed sexual abuse. *Newsletter of the Sex Information and Education Council of Canada*, **27**, 5–10.

US Department of Justice (1985). The crime of rape. Bureau of Justice Statistics Bulletin. Washington, DC: US Department of Justice.

Vera, H., Barnard, G. W., & Holzer, C. (1979). The intelligence of rapists: new data. *Archives of Sexual Behaviour*, **8**, 375–7.

Vinogradov, S., Dishotsky, N. I., Doty, A. K., & Tinklenberg, J. R. (1988). Patterns of behavior in adolescent rape. *American Journal of Orthopsychiatry*, **58**, 179–87.

Vizard, E. (1989). Incidence and prevalence of child sexual abuse. In J. Ouston (ed.), *The Consequences of Child Sexual Abuse*. Occasional Papers, **3**, 10–20. London: ACPP (Association for Child Psychology and Psychiatry).

Watkins, B., & Bentovim, A. (1992). The sexual abuse of male children and adolescents: a review of current research. *Journal of Child Psychology and Psychiatry*, **33**, 197–248.

Williams, B. T. R., & Gilmour, J. D. (1994). Annotation: sociometry and peer relationships. *Journal of Child Psychology and Psychiatry,* **35**, 997–1014.

Wyatt, G. E., & Peters, S. D. (1986). Issues in the definition of child sexual abuse in prevalence research. *Child Abuse and Neglect,* **10**, 231–40.

Zussman, R. (1989). Forensic evaluation of the adolescent sex offender. *Forensic Reports,* **2**, 25–45.

Index